| exploring |

Adobe
InDesign CS5

|exploring|

Adobe
InDesign CS5

Terry Rydberg

DELMAR
CENGAGE Learning™

Australia • Brazil • Japan • Korea • Mexico • Singapore • Spain • United Kingdom • United States

DELMAR
CENGAGE Learning

Exploring Adobe InDesign CS5
Terry Rydberg

Vice President,
Career and Professional Editorial: David Garza

Director of Learning Solutions: Sandy Clark

Acquisitions Editor: James Gish

Managing Editor: Larry Main

Associate Product Manager: Meaghan O'Brien

Editorial Assistant: Sarah L. Timm

Vice President,
Career and Professional Marketing: Jennifer Baker

Marketing Director: Deborah Yarnell

Marketing Manager: Erin Brennan

Marketing Coordinator: Erin Deangelo

Art Director: Joy Kocsis

Production Director: Wendy Troeger

Senior Content Project Manager: Glenn Castle

Senior Art Director: Joy Koscis

Technology Project Manager: Christopher Catalina

Cover Design: Steven Brower and
Lisa Marie Pompilio

Cover Illustration: Stephanie Dalton

For product information and technology assistance, contact us at
**Professional Group Cengage Learning Customer & Sales Support,
1-800-354-9706**

For permission to use material from this text or product,
submit all requests online at **cengage.com/permissions**
Further permissions questions can be emailed to
permissionrequest@cengage.com

Library of Congress Control Number: 2010921545

ISBN-13: 978-1-111-13032-9

ISBN-10: 1-111-13032-9

Delmar
5 Maxwell Drive,
Clifton Park, NY 12065-2919
USA

Cengage Learning is a leading provider of customized learning solutions with office locations around the globe, including Singapore, the United Kingdom, Australia, Mexico, Brazil, and Japan. Locate your local office at: **international.cengage.com/region**

Cengage Learning products are represented in Canada by Nelson Education, Ltd.

For your lifelong learning solutions, visit **delmar.cengage.com**

Visit our corporate website at **cengage.com**

Printed in Canada
1 2 3 4 5 XX 12 11 10

| *contents* |

| *contents* |

contents

| *preface* |

Intended Audience

This book is intended for designers who are serious about their craft. It is ideal for students who desire an approach to instruction that focuses on software proficiency. It is an excellent choice for instructors and industry trainers who have been looking for a comprehensive textbook that includes handouts, projects, syllabi, and resources. What differentiates *Exploring Adobe InDesign CS5* from a reference book, is that it focuses on those InDesign features that are used 90% of the time. This concentrated approach, and mastery of design and production techniques presented in the text, leave the designer well prepared for using InDesign effectively in production settings.

Typesetting is an art, and typography is emphasized throughout *Exploring Adobe InDesign CS5*. The power of Adobe InDesign, when combined with the knowledge of typography, will give designers the ability to create documents with visual impact.

How to Use This Book

Before beginning this book, readers should already know computer basics such as launching programs, using a mouse, saving files, and printing.

Exploring Adobe InDesign CS5's in-chapter exercises are supplemented with an array of projects at the end of the each chapter. These supplemental projects will require a higher degree of independent problem solving and application. Access to a computer with *Exploring Adobe InDesign CS5* will be essential for completing the practice exercises.

Chapters should be read in order, from the beginning to the end. The skills presented in earlier chapters create the foundation necessary for completing exercises in the later chapters. Techniques are first introduced, and then applied in the context of industry-level projects. This project-based approach uses critical thinking, review, and practice to help designers achieve mastery.

Textbook Overview

The textbook is organized so that techniques and skills are added layer upon layer.

Chapter 1: **The InDesign Workspace** Introduces the basic tools and functions of the program. If you are already familiar with Photoshop and Illustrator, this chapter will be a great review.

Chapter 2: **Type, Tools, and Terms** Establishes a knowledge base essential for setting type. You will use the Character and Paragraph formatting options in the Control panel, modify attributes of type and text frames, and learn to distinguish between serif and sans serif typefaces.

Chapter 3: **The Fine Art of Setting Type** Teaches how to identify the anatomical parts of letters, read markup, format paragraphs, and use hyphens and dashes correctly.

Chapter 4: **Combining Type and Images** Shows how to create linked and multi-column text frames; place, scale and crop images; use optical and manual kerning; and work with the coordinate and measurement systems for precise sizing and placement.

Chapter 5: **Tabs and Tables** You will learn to set tabular copy and create tables from "scratch" and from prepared text files, and then add table headers and footers.

Chapter 6: **Grids, Guides, and Aligning Objects** Increases your productivity by creating publication grids, aligning and distributing objects, and managing stacked objects.

Chapter 7: **Text Wrap, Layers, and Effects** Brings order to your documents through the power of layers and text wrap. Feathering, transparency, and live corner effects are also introduced.

Chapter 8: **Type Continuity: Applying Styles** Focuses on speed and efficiency in preparing text-heavy documents. You will learn how to use the Pages panel and snippets, and to create character and paragraph styles in the construction of an actual newsletter.

Chapter 9: **Master Pages and Object Styles** Introduces object styles and covers page continuity through the use of master pages. You will learn how to setup automatic page numbering and create continuation and jump lines. You'll create an object library and also use the Pages panel to add and delete pages.

Chapter 10: **Business Forms** Shows you how to create an identity package for a new business. You will focus on design, typographic, and production considerations, as you put together marketing materials.

Chapter 11: **Designing With Type** Introduces special type techniques, including: text on a path, creating outlines and gradient blends, using the Pathfinder tool, creating inline graphics, and using the Page tool for multi-page size documents.

Chapter 12: **Color Essentials** Differentiates between additive and subtractive color, spot and process color printing. Introduces all the features of the Swatches panel. Explains color separations and printing options. Introduces mixed inks and mixed ink groups.

Chapter 13: **Production Essentials** Explains these important production concepts: resolution, dpi, ppi, bitmap, and vector. You will use the powerful Links panel, enhanced in *InDesign CS* 5. You will learn the difference between actual and effective ppi and how to prepare your images for the correct resolution and size. Finally, prepress expert, James Wamser summarizes his best prepress tips.

Chapter 14: **Basic Graphic Elements** Explores InDesign's drawing functions. You will learn how to create basic shapes, use the Pen tool, and integrate drawn elements with text. This is a great introduction to *Adobe Illustrator,*® another member of *Adobe Creative Suite 5.*

Features

The following are some of the salient features of *Exploring Adobe InDesign CS5*:

▶ Learning goals are clearly stated at the beginning of each chapter.

▶ A visually-oriented introduction to basic design principles and the functions and tools of *Adobe InDesign CS5*, that meets the needs of both students and professionals.

▶ Exercises and projects utilize tools and techniques that a designer might encounter on the job.

▶ *In Review* sections are provided at the end of each chapter to reinforce understanding and retention of the material covered.

▶ The accompanying CD-ROM contains directions and all the necessary components for completing additional projects that correspond to each chapter's learning goals.

NEW! in *Exploring Adobe InDesign CS5*

▶ Updated chapter content describes new features in InDesign CS5.

▶ Exciting projects have been designed to utilize the new software features.

▶ Keyboard shortcuts are included at the end of each chapter for easy reference and memorization.

▶ The *Getting Started* section at the beginning of Chapter 1, discusses software installation and best production practices.

▶ A complete list of the fonts included with *Adobe InDesign CS5*.

Instructor Resources

The Instructor Resources CD-ROM was developed to assist educators in planning and implementing their instructional programs. It includes detailed lesson plans for each chapter. The lesson plan summarizes the concepts, keyboard shortcuts, and project demonstrations covered in the classroom. Lesson plans are designed to be printed and saved in a three-ring binder. New in this edition, are finished InDesign documents for each project, that serve as instructor keys. Also included are a sample syllabus, a midterm, and a final written and lab exam. The complete Instructor Resources CD-ROM enhances consistency in instruction, among faculty members with diverse backgrounds and skill levels.

ISBN: 1-1111-3033-7

How to Use This Text

The following features can be found throughout the book.

▶ Chapter Objectives

Chapter objectives describe the competencies that the reader should achieve.

▶ Chapter Review and Projects

Review questions and supplemental projects assess learning and provide skills application.

▶ Keyboard Shortcut Cues

Keyboard shortcuts are prominently displayed for ease of use.

▶ Getting Started

Located at the beginning of Chapter 1, this section provides the steps for customizing the application defaults that will be used throughout the book.

▶ Design and Typography

Principles of design and typography are presented with corresponding chapter content. These basics will help the reader use type in a manner that is technically correct.

▶ Moving Toward Mastery

Key concepts are grouped together for easy reference and review.

About the Author

Terry Rydberg is a graphic design instructor at Waukesha County Technical College in Pewaukee, Wisconsin. In addition to eighteen years in the classroom, Terry has extensive experience working as a designer and corporate trainer. *Exploring Adobe InDesign CS5* is her fifth book published with Delmar, Cengage Learning.

Her educational background includes undergraduate degrees in graphic design, printing and publishing, and adult education; and a masters degree in education. Her career parallels the industry's evolution from phototypesetting and paste-up, to digital production methods. Rydberg teaches advertising design, graphic design, typography, portfolio development, digital page layout, advanced digital page layout, and color theory. She is a regional InDesign trainer at colleges and conferences.

A committed educator, Rydberg has served as school board chair, graphics advisory board member, new instructor mentor, curriculum writer, and student advisor. In 2007, she received a *NISOD Excellence Award* from the National Institute for Staff & Organizational Development. She is currently the Chapter Rep for the Milwaukee InDesign User Group.

Acknowledgments

Others whose contributions to this book should be acknowledged are James Gish, Acquisitions Editor; Meaghan O'Brien, Associate Product Manager; Glenn Castle, Senior Content Project Manager; and Sarah L. Timm, Editorial Assistant. Their expertise, combined with Cengage's great marketing team, made this fifth edition a reality.

Deepest thanks to my colleagues and students who have shared a vision for this book. John Shanley, from Phoenix Creative Graphics, poured his heart and soul into this project as he performed his copy and technical editing "miracles." Illustrator David Espurvoa and prepress expert James Wamser enthusiastically shared their expertise. Finally, my gratitude to photographers Billy Knight and Dina Vees; illustrators Steve Miljat and Jeff Blackwell; and the many generous students who allowed their artwork and photography to be included in this book.

Many thanks to the instructors who are using this publication at the Harry V. Quadracci Printing and Graphics Center and at various colleges throughout the United States. Your suggestions and comments have been so helpful, and have been incorporated in *Exploring Adobe InDesign CS5*.

With gratitude to my best friend and husband, Mark.

Questions and Feedback

We welcome your questions and feedback. If you have suggestions that would be of benefit to others, please let us know and we will try to include them in the next edition.

To send your questions and/or feedback, contact the publisher at:

Delmar Learning
5 Maxwell Drive
Clifton Park, NY 12065-2919
Attn: Media Arts and Design Team
800-998-7498

Or the author at:

Harry V. Quadracci Printing and Graphics Center
Waukesha County Technical College
800 Main Street
Pewaukee, Wisconsin 53072
trydberg@mac.com

Creativity can solve almost every problem. The creative act, the defeat of habit by originality, overcomes everything.

℞ George Lois

| The InDesign Workspace |

1

objectives

- ▶ *Become familiar with the Adobe InDesign CS5 environment*
- ▶ *Understand how to use this textbook*
- ▶ *Modify InDesign preferences*
- ▶ *Identify and use basic panels and tools*
- ▶ *Learn to use keyboard shortcuts*
- ▶ *Learn the concepts of frames, stroke, and fill*
- ▶ *Customize your workspace*
- ▶ *Save and print documents*

introduction

You are about to explore new horizons in digital page layout. This book will introduce you to Adobe® InDesign® CS5, today's standard in page layout software. For those of you who are already familiar with a page layout program, you will be delighted and impressed with InDesign's extraordinary capabilities and innovation.

After teaching and working with other major page layout programs for 18 years, I must admit I was a bit skeptical when I began working with InDesign. But in just a few weeks I was convinced that Adobe InDesign is the most creative, comprehensive, and intuitive page layout program on the market today. By the time you finish this book, I know you will agree. No other program in the graphics industry can compete with the bold imagination and astounding new features of InDesign.

Are you ready to begin mastering InDesign? We're going to begin with a *Getting Started* section found on the next four pages. This section will introduce you to best practices in production and provide tips for maximizing the features of your software. It will also help you understand how to best use this text. If you already have a basic knowledge of InDesign or are the type of person who never reads the directions, you may be tempted to skip this section. But understanding and following the instructions in this section are like checking your oil, tire pressure, and filling you car with gas before starting a road trip. And, what a trip this will be! If you hit a pot hole or run into a road block along the way, feel free to email me and I'll try to provide some roadside assistance (trydberg@mac.com). InDesign is a fantastic piece of software—and with practice and determination, you'll be cruisin' in no time at all!

Getting Started

► INSTALLING AND UNINSTALLING INDESIGN

Before you begin this book, you should be familiar with a computer keyboard and have a basic understanding of how to operate a mouse. You should know how to launch applications, make choices from menus, click with a mouse to select objects, and drag to highlight text. And you should already know how to load software.

When you install InDesign, *make sure to write down or photocopy the activation code or serial number that came with your software and place it in safe keeping. This only takes a minute—and is much easier (and less frustrating) than trying to retrieve the information after it's lost.*

A single-user retail license activation supports two computers. For example, you can install the product on a desktop computer at work and on a laptop computer at home. If you want to install the software on a third computer, first deactivate InDesign on one of the other two computers. Choose Help > Deactivate.

► FONTS

The installation discs contain a variety of resources to help you make the most of your Adobe software. The **Goodies** *folder contains bonus fonts that you will probably want to install. The complete list of typefaces bundled with InDesign can be found in the back of this book, just before the index.*

► BACK UP THE ARTWORK AND RESOURCES FOLDER

As you work through this text, you will notice that there are exercises included in the narrative of the text, and more projects presented at the end of chapters. Completing these projects will strengthen your skills and help move you toward mastery. To work on these projects, you will need to access text and images files from the Exploring Adobe InDesign CS5 *compact disc accompanying this book. A folder that corresponds to each chapter (01 Artwork and Resources, 02 Artwork and Resources, 03 Artwork and Resources, etc.) can be found in* **Artwork and Resources**, *a folder included on the* Exploring InDesign *CD. Each chapter folder contains text and image files, and a .pdf document with instructions for the end-of-chapter projects. It would be a good idea to place a copy of the* Artwork and Resources *folder on your hard drive.*

► MODIFY INDESIGN PREFERENCES

InDesign comes with a built-in set of defaults. Modifying some of these defaults will make your production much smoother. When you change defaults with InDesign launched, but with no document open, you are changing the **application preferences.** *Once they are changed, the changes will apply to all future documents.*

When you change InDesign preferences with a document open, the changes apply to the current document only. This is called changing the **document preferences.**

Follow these steps to change the **application preferences** *to match those used in this text.*

1. Launch InDesign, but do not create a new document. You should see the InDesign menu, the Control panel, and the Toolbox.

2. Press **Command+K** (Mac) or **Control+K** (Windows) to open the Preferences dialog.

3. Along the left side of the Preferences window, you will see a list of categories. Select each category and make the following changes:

   • Type: select **Apply Leading to Entire Paragraphs**

   • Units & Increments>Ruler Units: Origin: **Page,** Horizontal: **Inches,** Vertical: **Inches**

   • Units & Increments>Keyboard Increments: Size/Leading: **1 pt** Baseline Shift: **1 pt**

4. Accept changes and exit the dialog box.

5. Go to File>Document Setup. Deselect **Facing Pages.** Make sure the Page Size is set to **Letter.** Press **Return** (Mac) or **Enter** (Windows).

► BEST PRACTICES

1. **Use keyboard shortcuts.** *Throughout the book, you will be encouraged to use keyboard shortcuts whenever possible. Activating a keyboard shortcut, instead of selecting menus or opening panels, is a more efficient method of working. Keyboard shortcuts usually consist of a combination of modifier keys and letters or symbols. For Mac users, the modifier keys include* **Shift, Control, Option**, *and* **Command**. *Windows users use* **Shift, Control** *and* **Alt**. *Both platforms utilize function keys* **F1–F12** *found above the numbers on the keyboard. When a keyboard shortcut is listed as* **Command+S**, *this means: "Hold the Command key, press the S key, and release."* **F5** *means: "Press function key 5, and release." Throughout the text, important keyboard shortcuts will be displayed in color for easy reference. Try to memorize these shortcuts and use keyboard shortcuts whenever possible. Over the course of your professional career, the time you save using shortcuts will be significant.*

2. **Open documents from a local hard drive.** *When you store a document on a portable drive or a server, it is important to move the document to your local hard drive before opening it. Opening documents from storage media can cause damage.*

3. **Do a** *Save As* **when your project is completed.** *Each time you Save a document, InDesign adds more data to the document, but doesn't remove outdated data. When you choose Save As, InDesign completely rewrites the document, using only current information. This keeps your file size smaller and decreases the time required for printing or redrawing the image on the screen.*

4. **Use the least number of text frames possible.** *This keeps your document smaller and easier to maintain.*

5. **Use context menus.** *These are activated by holding the Control key and clicking (Mac), or clicking the right mouse button (Windows) when you have an object selected. This is a quick method of choosing commonly used commands.*

6. **Use shortcut keys in dialog boxes.** *Press* **Return** *(Mac) or* **Enter** *(Windows) instead of choosing OK. Press* **Command+period** *(Mac) or* **Esc** *(Mac and Windows) to exit a dialog box. In some dialog boxes, holding* **Option** *(Mac) or* **Alt** *(Windows) changes the Cancel button to a Reset button, allowing you to make changes without exiting the dialog box.*

7. **Never remove the .indd file extension from any of your files.**

8. **Use quality fonts**. *InDesign works best with OpenType, Type 1 (PostScript), and TrueType fonts. Corrupt fonts can damage your document and crash your computer!*

9. **Create folders to organize your projects.** *Keep images used in the document organized inside the folder. Use the Package operation (introduced in Chapter 13).*

▶ DOCUMENT RECOVERY

InDesign has a built-in document recovery system that protects your files against unexpected power failures or computer crashes. Automatic recovery data exists in a temporary file that is separate from your InDesign document.

If you crash, here are the steps to recover your file.

- *Start your computer.*

- *Launch InDesign.*

- *InDesign will display any recovered documents. An asterisk will appear in front of the file name in the title bar of the document.*

- *Choose File>Save As and specify a new location and name for the file.*

- *If you had saved the document before crashing, and the recovered document is an older version that you don't want to keep, close the file without saving it.*

- *If InDesign can't open your document, it means it was permanently damaged during the crash.*

This feature is designed for emergencies only. You should still save your documents often, and **make backups!**

▶ THIS IS A TEXTBOOK—PLEASE, DON'T SKIP THE PROJECTS!

This is a textbook, not an InDesign reference book. In addition to software techniques, you will learn design and typography concepts. You should work through the book in sequence. The skills presented in each chapter become the foundation for moving to the next level. As the projects get harder, the instructions become less detailed, forcing you to dig into your memory bank to apply the skills you learned in earlier chapters. The projects at the end of the chapter require you to apply newly-learned skills, while reviewing and reinforcing earlier techniques. I can guarantee that, if you systematically work through all the chapters and projects, you will have mastery of the InDesign functions you will use 95% of the time.

Learning new software is like learning to play a musical instrument—you need to practice, practice, practice. The best way to learn software is to use it every day.

Finally, you should have fun learning InDesign! InDesign has brought much joy into my life. You might think it strange for a person to attribute such power to a piece of software. But by the time you finish this book, I think you'll understand what I mean!

The InDesign Workspace

The InDesign workspace consists of the following items:

► *Document window*

► *Menu bar*

► *Application Frame and Application Bar*

► *Control panel*

► *Toolbox*

► *Panels*

Launch InDesign by clicking the icon on the dock shown in Visual 1–1, or by double-clicking the icon in the Applications folder (Mac), or by selecting Adobe InDesign CS5 from the Start menu (Windows). When the program launches, you will be welcomed to InDesign by a screen that contains a host of options, including an overview of new features in InDesign CS5, tutorials, and learning resources (Visual 1–2). You can create new documents and open recent documents from this screen. You may want to place a check in the box in the lower left corner so that this screen will not appear when launching the program, but do this only after you have gone through the tutorial and overview opportunities.

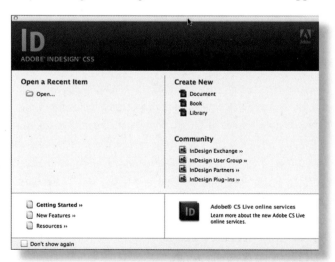

We'll get started immediately by creating a sample document to introduce us to the document window and navigating through InDesign dialog boxes.

Keyboard Shortcut

 CMD+N

 CTRL+N

New Document

1. Press **Command+N** (Mac) or **Control+N** (Windows) to create a new document.

2. Press the **Tab** key to jump to the next field in the *New Document* dialog box (or any dialog box in InDesign). Press **Shift+Tab** to move backwards through the fields. Practice moving through each field in the *New Document* dialog box using these methods.

Pressing the Tab key is an excellent method of selecting any field. Another excellent method to select the field is by clicking on the name to the left of the field (Visual 1–3). Once you grow accustomed to selecting fields by clicking on the name to the left of the field, you'll wish all the software you use had that feature! (The most inefficient method of selecting a field is to place the cursor in the field and double-click or drag to highlight the area.) Once the content in a field is highlighted, type your new information over the old information. Don't re-select a field that is already highlighted!

Click here to highlight this field.

VISUAL |1–3|

Select a field by clicking on the name to the left of the field.

▶ *production tip*

Highlight a field by clicking on the icon to the left of the field. When a field is highlighted, enter your specifications—don't click and drag to rehighlight it.

3. Enter these values in the *New Document* dialog box: Intent: **Print**. Number of Pages: **1**. Page Size: **Letter** (8.5"× 11"). Be sure that the Facing Pages and Master Text Frame options are not selected. Columns: **3**. Margins: **0.75"**. Orientation: **Portrait** (first icon). *Portrait* orientation means that the height of your document is greater than the width. *Landscape* orientation means that your document is wider than it is high (Visual 1–5).

VISUAL |1–4|

The New Document dialog box.

Portrait Orientation

Landscape Orientation

VISUAL |1–5|

Portrait orientation means the height of your document is greater than the width.

In the middle of the Margins section is a link icon. This button appears on numerous InDesign panels. When the link is closed, the value you enter in one field is automatically transferred to the rest of the fields. If the link was closed when you entered the margin value, 0.75" automatically appeared in the other three margin fields.

Apply the same value in all the fields.

Apply different values in fields

4. To accept changes and exit the dialog box, press **Return** (Mac) or **Enter** (Windows). It is not necessary to use your mouse to select OK. Similarly, you can press **Command+period** (Mac) or **Esc** (Mac and Windows) to exit the dialog box without accepting changes. We will continue working on our document, so keep it open.

VISUAL |1–6|

Press Return (Mac) or Enter (Windows) instead of clicking OK. Press Command + period (Mac) or the Esc key (Mac and Windows) to activate the Cancel button.

VISUAL |1–7|

Preview modes can be selected from the bottom of the Toolbox.

Five *view modes* can be found at the bottom of the Toolbox (Visual 1–7). You are viewing your document in *Normal* mode, the default viewing mode. When Normal is selected, you will see the document outlined in black, with magenta guides designating the 0.75" margin on all sides. Violet lines designate the column guides. Press **W** to switch to *Preview* mode. In this mode, all guides are hidden, and the *pasteboard* is changed to gray, the default preview background color. The pasteboard is the area surrounding the document, as shown in Visual 1–9. Press **W** again, and you return to Normal mode. *Bleed* and *Slug* view modes show areas created outside the document size. Bleeds and slugs will be introduced in Chapter 6.

VISUAL |1–8|

Choose [Essentials] workspace to make the layout of your document window match Visual 1–9.

You may see some differences as you compare your document window to the example shown in Visual 1–9. Let's make sure we're all looking at the same document workspace. From the Menu bar, go to **Window>Workspace** (Visual 1–8). Notice that InDesign has several selections from which to choose. Choose [**Essentials**] .

When you release the mouse, your document window should look like Visual 1–9. The *New Workspace* menu option allows you to save any customization you've made to the InDesign workspace. We'll cover that at the end of the chapter.

The Menu Bar

The *Menu* bar stretches across the top of the document window and displays these categories: *InDesign* (Mac only), *File, Edit, Layout, Type, Object, Table, View, Window,* and *Help* (Visual 1–10). As you press and move your pointer across the Menu bar, you will see that underneath each category are menu items, most of which can be accessed by using keyboard shortcuts. Keyboard shortcuts are listed to the right of the menu items. This chart shows how to interpret the symbols listed with Mac keyboard shortcuts.

Symbol	Mac Keyboard
⌘	Command
⇧	Shift
⌥	Option
⌃	Control

Some menu items are followed by a triangle or ellipsis. When a triangle follows a menu item, it means that a submenu will open and more menu options will be displayed. An ellipsis means that a dialog box will open when the menu item is selected (Visual 1–10). InDesign encourages you

VISUAL |1–9|

The document window shown in the Essentials workspace setting.

VISUAL |1–10|

The Menu bar runs across the top of the document window. Symbols to the right of menu items indicate keyboard shortcuts, sub menus and dialog boxes.

to customize your work environment to maximize productivity. As you work through this book you will be introduced to many of these InDesign features, and by the completion of the book you will have developed preferences for how you interact with your InDesign work environment. You'll also know how integrate those preferences into your everyday use of InDesign.

Features of the
InDesign Toolbox.

The Toolbox

The *Toolbox* is found on the left side of the document window. You can move the Toolbox to different areas of the document window by dragging the solid gray bar on the top of the panel (Visual 1–11A). Although you can't reposition the location of the tools inside the Toolbox, you can customize the overall layout of the Toolbox. If you click on the arrows in the upper right corner, you can toggle the display of the Toolbox between a horizontal row (if the panel is undocked), or single or double vertical columns (Visuals 1–11A and B). When you hover your pointer over a tool, you will see the tool name and keyboard shortcut (Visual 1–11C). Select a tool by clicking on it. When a tool is selected, its icon becomes highlighted. Notice that some tools have a triangle in the lower right corner. When you click on these tools and hold the mouse down for a second, you will see more choices "hidden" underneath (Visual 1–11B). These hidden tools are related to the main tool displayed in the Toolbox.

Tools are grouped according to function: *selection tools*, *drawing* and *type tools*, *transformation tools*, and *modification and navigation* tools.

Pressing the **Tab** key alternately hides and shows the Tools and other panels. Pressing **Shift+Tab** displays the Tools, but hides the remaining panels. If the Toolbox becomes hidden on your document, go to the Menu bar, select **Window>Tools**. Or, select **Window>Workspace>Reset** (current Workspace). The Toolbox will return to its default location.

Using Panels

InDesign uses panels to organize commands and are stored, or *docked*, on the right edge of the workspace. As you become more familiar with InDesign, you'll discover there are some panels you continually use. And there may be some panels you seldom use. InDesign has created preset workspaces intended to display panels that correspond with your particular workflow. InDesign allows you to customize the combination of panels to fit your preferences and the jobs you do. You can work in a panel while it is still grouped with other panels in vertical formation, or you can drag it out on the document area. Follow these steps to learn how to work with panels.

▶ *production tip*

If you accidently press the Tab key when you aren't typing, the Toolbox and other panels will disappear! Don't panic—simply press Tab again, and everything will reappear.

1. Choose each of the workspaces available in the *workspace switcher* pull down menu, found on the right end of the *Application bar*, above the Control panel (Visual 1–12). Notice that the panels on the right side of your InDesign window change according to the workspace you have selected. Panels are displayed in *groups,* in a vertical format on the right side of the InDesign window, in an area called the *dock*. Select the *Advanced* workspace, as you follow these steps.

Choose a workspace from the workspace switcher.

The Advanced workspace displays these panel groups.

By default, the panel groups are in the dock on the right side of the InDesign window.

Click and drag double lines to remove panel sets from the dock.

VISUAL |1–12|

In this example, the Advanced workspace has been chosen from the workspace switcher on the Application bar. You can also choose a workspace from the Menu>Window> Workspace.

2. Click on a panel's name or icon and the panel window will open and close. Panels can also be opened with keyboard shortcuts. Press **F5** (function key 5) and the *Swatches* panel will open. Press it again, and the panel will close.

3. Click on the grey bar on the top of the panel group and pull to the left. The entire panel group will be released from the dock. When the group is released, a *circle* appears in the upper left corner (Mac) or an *X* appears in the upper right corner (Windows). Click the circle or *X*, and the panel group will close. You can make the panel group reappear by choosing *Reset Advanced* in the workspace switcher on the *Application bar* (Visual 1–13).

VISUAL |1–13|

Panels can be displayed in groups or as individual floating panels. Choose the Reset command to quickly revert your workspace back to its default state.

Click on the grey bar and drag to the left to undock the panel group.

On a **Mac**, this circle indicates the panel group is undocked.
On **Windows**, an X in the upper right corner appears when the panel group is undocked.

Double lines separate panel groups.

VISUAL |1–14|

Pull on the double bars to remove a panel set from the group.

4. Panel groups are broken down into *sets*, which are separated by double lines, as shown on the lower part of Visual 1–13. These sets can be moved in and out of the dock by dragging on the double lines above each set. Click on the double lines and move each set from the dock (Visual 1–14). A circular close button appears in the upper left corner (Mac) and an *X* appears in the upper right corner (Windows) of each individual set. Click on the name of an individual panel and drag the panel to the left. You have just created a single, *floating panel*.

VISUAL |1–15|

Panels can be resized so that the labels are hidden.

5. Panels can be made even smaller, so that the label is hidden, by clicking and holding the left edge of the panel while moving it toward the icon (Visual 1–15).

VISUAL |1–16|

Panels have additional features found in the menu options.

Panel menu. Click here to view the menu options.

6. Choose *Reset Advanced* from the workspace switcher to reorganize your window. Pull the *Swatches* panel from the dock. Now, click on the double arrows in the upper right corner. This expands and collapses the panel window. Then, open the *panel menu*. Panel menus display additional options, specific to each panel (Visual 1–16).

7. Panels can be stacked vertically on the document window. You can also dock the panels to the left edge of your screen. Select a panel. Click on the panel's name and drag it to the ***drop zone*** at the bottom of another panel. A blue bar appears as the panel enters the drop zone (Visual 1–17). Now, drag the panels into the dock on the left side of the screen. When you are finished, reset the ***Advanced*** workspace.

VISUAL | 1–17 |

A blue bar designates a "drop zone" when a panel is a panel is dragged into another panel set.

Using Tools

Set your Toolbox so that it is displayed in a single column, down the left side of your document window. The top tool (black arrow) is the *Selection* tool. Use it when you want to select, resize, or move an entire item (frame, line, text path, etc.). The second tool down, (white arrow) is the *Direct Selection* tool. Use it when you want to select just part of an item, the points on an item's path, the content inside the item, or to modify its shape. (If you are familiar with QuarkXPress, the Selection tool is similar to the Item tool and the Direct Selection tool is similar to the Content tool.)

Jump over the Page and Gap tools and you will come to the *Type* tool. You will spend much of your time using the Type tool—typing, editing, or working with tables. Because you'll be using it so much, you'll

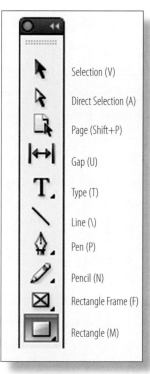

VISUAL | 1–18 |

When you hover over a tool with your mouse, the keyboard shortcut is shown next to the name of the tool.

learn to use keyboard shortcuts to switch from the Type tool to other tools without going over to the Toolbox. This will make you very efficient. Below the Type tool is the *Line* tool. Use this tool for drawing straight or diagonal lines.

Jump over the Pen and Pencil tools and you will find the *Rectangle Frame* tool. Notice the little arrow in the lower right corner. This means that other tools are "hidden" underneath the tool that is showing. We will use several of these tools as we continue working on the document created earlier.

1. In the Toolbox, click on the ***Rectangle*** tool. Your cursor will turn into little ***cross hairs*** with a dot in the middle. Go back to your document, click your mouse button somewhere on the left side of your document, and make a rectangle by dragging your mouse down and to the right. Release the mouse.

Let's take a look at the rectangle you have just drawn (Visual 1–19). The eight small hollow boxes at the corners and at each side of the rectangle are called *selection handles*. When the selection handles are visible, the item is considered *active*. Click somewhere else on your document. The selection handles disappear, meaning the item is *not active*. An item must be selected (active) in order to work with it. In addition to selection handles, shapes have *bounding boxes*. Bounding boxes indicate the outermost points of a shape, the "footprint." The bounding box for the rectangle you have just drawn is the same dimension as the rectangle. Look at the odd-looking

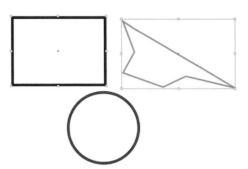

VISUAL |1–19|

Two of these three shapes are active. The circle is not active.

shape in Visual 1–19. The rectangle that delineates its outer edges is the bounding box. A bounding box always has four straight sides, no matter what shape you have drawn. If the circle shown in the Visual 1–19 was activated with the Selection tool, the bounding box would be displayed as a square.

2. Deselect the rectangle you drew earlier. Go back to the Toolbox and click on the *Selection* tool. Your cursor should now look like a **black arrow** (Visual 1–20A). Slowly move the *Selection* tool toward the edge of the rectangle (do not click the mouse button). When the arrow touches the edge, a small square appears next to the tail of the arrow (Visual 1–20B). This means you can now select the rectangle again. Click when the small box appears by the tail of the arrow and you will see your selection handles again. Your rectangle is now selected. Notice that when your rectangle is selected and you move your cursor over the edge of the rectangle (without clicking the button), the arrow icon loses its "tail" (Visual 1–20C).

VISUAL |1–20|

The shape of the Selection tool cursor changes during use. Learn to recognize these icons.

A. Default Selection tool cursor   **B.** A small square indiates that an object is ready to be selected.   **C.** A "tail-less" cursor means that you can click and drag the selected object.

3. With your rectangle selected, you can move the rectangle to a different place or change its size. To move it, click on the edge of the rectangle and drag it. Release the mouse button to "drop" the rectangle in the new location. To resize the rectangle, move the cursor over one of the selection handles. The icon turns into small opposing arrows, with a line in between (Visual 1–21). Drag the selection handles in, out, or diagonally to change the dimension of the rectangle.

VISUAL |1–21|

When the Selection arrow is over a frame handle, it changes shape. The double-ended arrow means that you can drag the handle to change the dimensions of the object.

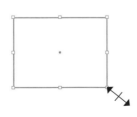

Now, you'll use shortcuts to make a document and to create and modify a rectangle.

1.   Close, but don't save the document you just made, by pressing **Command+W** (Mac) or **Control+W** (Windows). Use keyboard shortcuts to make a new document: **Command+N** (Mac) or **Control+N** (Windows). When the *New Document* dialog box opens, accept the document defaults, including **Letter** for page size, and **0.5**" for all margins. Choose the **[Essentials]** workspace.

2.   Next, you will draw a rectangle, but instead of going over to the Toolbox, press the letter **M**. This will instantly select the *Rectangle* tool. Draw a rectangle and then press the letter **A**. You have now selected the *Direct Selection* tool. The *Direct Selection* tool differs from the *Selection* tool because you can modify just part of an object—one side, or one or more *anchor points*—instead of the whole item.

Default Direct Selection   Direct Selection tool is ready   Direct Selection tool is ready
tool cursor   to select the side of the frame   to select an anchor point on a frame.

VISUAL |1–22|
The Direct Selection tool uses many of the same visual cues as the Selection tool, shown earlier.

3.   Modify the shape of your rectangle using the *Direct Selection* tool by selecting and dragging the sides and anchor points. Your rectangle will quickly lose its rigid, 90-degree angles.

4.   With your shape selected, bring the *Direct Selection* arrow slowly to the tiny box in the center of the object. Notice that the white arrow becomes a black arrow. Click and move the object around.

Always deselect an object when you are finished working on it. You can deselect an object by clicking any blank area in the document, or by using the keyboard shortcut: **Shift+Command+A** (Mac) or **Shift+Control+A** (Windows).

Placing Text into a Frame

You will appreciate your good typing and keyboard skills as you begin to spend more time working with text. In the next exercise, you will learn how to enter text and draw some basic shapes.

► *production tip*
Get into the habit of deselecting an object when you're finished working on it.

1.   Close your document without saving it by pressing **Command+W** (Mac) or **Control+W** (Windows). Use the keyboard shortcut to make a new, one-page document that is **7"** wide and **6"** inches high (use the **0.5**" default margins).

2. Notice that your document is *landscape* format, because it is wider than it is high. Press **M** to select the *Rectangle* tool and draw a rectangle. Now press **T**. Your cursor changes into a vertical bar with a small cross hair near the bottom and dotted lines around it (Visual 1–23). Click inside the rectangle and notice the blinking cursor in the upper left corner of the rectangle. Your rectangle has become a text frame, and the blinking cursor means you're ready to type.

VISUAL | 1–23 |

Clicking on any shape with the Type tool will convert it to a text frame. When you see the blinking cursor, you are ready to type.

Keyboard Shortcut

 CMD+A / CTRL+A — **Select All**

3. You can also create a text frame by dragging with the *Type* tool cursor. As you draw the frame, the width and height are displayed (Visual 1–24). When you release the mouse, you are ready to type. Type a sentence or two about yourself, your dog, or your weekend—anything you want. Highlight all the text with **Command+A** (Mac) or **Control+A** (Windows). There are other methods of selecting your text. For instance, you can drag and highlight text with your mouse, or choose *Select All* from the Edit menu, but those methods are slower. Keyboard shortcuts are always the way to go!

VISUAL | 1–24 |

It's most efficient to create a text frame by dragging the Type tool cursor. The width and height measurements are displayed as you draw.

W: 1.2639 in
H: 1.0417 in

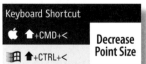

Keyboard Shortcut

 ⇧+CMD+> / ⇧+CTRL+> — **Increase Point Size**

Keyboard Shortcut

 ⇧+CMD+< / ⇧+CTRL+< — **Decrease Point Size**

4. With the text highlighted, you can use keyboard shortcuts to increase the size of the selected type. Hold down **Shift+Command** (Mac) or **Shift+Control** (Windows) and press the *greater than* key (**>**), six or seven times, and watch the size of your type get larger. You could use the Control panel to increase the size of the type, but using keyboard shortcuts is essential for efficiency. You can substitute the *less than* symbol (**<**), in combination with the same modifier keys, to reduce the type size. Keep your document open.

Stroke and Fill

A *stroke* is a line that goes around the edges of a shape, like a border; or around type, like an outline. A *fill* is a color that is placed inside a shape or type. Stroke and fill menus are conveniently located in the Control panel (Visual 1–25).

VISUAL | 1–25 |

Fill and Stroke buttons in the Control panel.

Fill ⟶
Stroke ⟶

1. Press **F** to select the *Frame* tool and draw a rectangle on your document. By default, shapes drawn with the Frame tool have no fill or stroke. Click the arrow next to the Fill button on the Control panel (Visual 1–26). Slide down the menu of color swatches and choose the **Red** swatch (C=15, M=100, Y=100, K=0). The rectangle will be filled with Red.

2. Now you'll add a Green border to the outside of the rectangle. With the rectangle still selected, click the arrow next to the *Stroke* icon, located below the *Fill* icon (Visual 1–26). Slide down the menu of color swatches and choose the **Green** swatch (C=75, M=5, Y=100, K=0). Now that you've selected the color, you can add a *style*. The default is a Solid line, but you can slide down the style menu and choose the stroke style that suits you. Directly above the *Style* field is the *Stroke Width* field. You may not understand what *pt.* means, but we'll cover that in a later chapter. For now, simply pull down on the blue arrows next to the *Stroke Width* field to select a preset stroke width.

▶ *production tip*

A stroke is applied to the outside of a frame; a fill is applied to the inside. If the stroke width is too small, the style may not show. If that happens, choose a larger stroke width.

3. It's just as easy to add a stroke or fill to text. Type a short phrase in your rectangle. Select the frame with the *Selection* tool. Click the arrow next to the *Fill* button. When the *Swatches* panel opens, click the *Formatting affects text* button (Visual 1–27). Then, select a color from the list. Then, select *Stroke* and add a color from the *Stroke* pull down menu. Choose a *stroke width*. Whenever you apply a stroke to text, make sure the width of the stroke doesn't distort the shape of the letters.

VISUAL | 1–28 |

Horizontal and diagonal lines with a stroke applied.

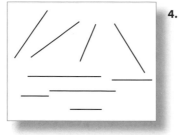

4. Select the *Line* tool (the keyboard shortcut is a backslash, \). Click and drag to draw several diagonal lines on your document. Switch to the *Selection* tool and select any line. Notice the rectangular shape of the bounding box. Now, select the *Line* tool again, hold down the **Shift** key, and draw perfectly horizontal and vertical lines (Visual 1–28). By default, the line has a 1 point stroke. Lines do not have fills.

VISUAL | 1–29 |

This line has a red stroke and a 7-point dotted line.

▶ *production tip*

Holding down the Shift key constrains rectangles to perfect squares, ellipses to perfect circles, and lines to horizontal, vertical, or 45-degree increments.

5. Hold down the **Shift** key and draw one more line, but do not release the mouse button. Instead, move the mouse to rotate the free end of the line in a circle, like hands on a clock. Notice how the line snaps to 45-degree increments. The Shift key constrains lines to horizontal, vertical, or 45-degree increments. Now, choose a different stroke style, width, and color.

About Frames

InDesign includes two tools for making rectangular boxes called *frames*. One frame has an *X* in it, one doesn't. Both frames can hold either pictures or text. When you click inside any frame with the Type tool, a blinking cursor will appear, which means the frame is ready for you to begin typing.

VISUAL | 1–30 |

On the left is a frame made with the Rectangle tool. The frame on the right was made with the Rectangle Frame tool. Either frame can hold text or graphics.

6. Make a new document using the default settings. Use the *Rectangle* tool to draw a rectangle in the left half your document.

7. Choose the *Rectangle Frame* tool (the box with the *X* inside it). You may also select this tool by pressing **F**. Draw a second rectangle on the right half of your document. There will be an X inside the new rectangle (Visual 1–30).

So, why are there two frame tools? In the days before computers, layouts were created by placing graphic elements on a *pasteup board*. The location and size of a photo would be indicated on the pasteup by a rectangle, with an X stretching from corner to corner. In today's InDesign environment, a designer can create a layout, and use the Rectangle Frame tool, with the X, to indicate where the images will be placed. Text will be placed in frames without an X. These visual cues are particularly helpful if another person is going to add the photos and text to complete the project.

Navigating

Let's do a little navigating around your document with the two frames. Your document sits in the middle of an area called the pasteboard. At the right and bottom of the pasteboard are *scroll bars* (Visual 1–31). You slide the scroll bars up and down, or right and left, to reposition your document inside the InDesign window. You can also click on the triangles to move your document around. If you are working in Windows, these triangles will be at either end of the scroll bars. If you are working on a Mac, the triangles will be in the lower right corner.

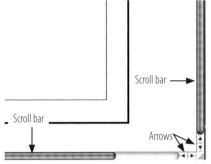

VISUAL |1–31|

Scroll bars and arrows help you position your document.

Another way to move your document around is to use the *Hand* tool. Whenever the Type tool is not active, you can hold down the spacebar to switch temporarily to the Hand tool (Visual 1–32). Click, and the Hand will turn into a little fist. Now drag with your mouse and the fist will grab on to your document and move it wherever you like. To access the Hand tool while you are using the Type tool in an active frame, you press the **Option** (Mac) or **Alt** (Windows) key. (If you press the spacebar to access the grabber hand while using the Text tool, you will simply add spaces to the text you are working on.) You can also select the Hand tool in the Toolbox or by using the **H** shortcut key, but using the Spacebar (or Option/Alt) and mouse is probably faster and more convenient.

Henit, quisi elis ad tat utatie feum zzrilit, quat praestrud ming et nulputp atuerci tat, commolut ad tis doluptat, con henim alisitMet incin euipsum veniamet aliqui bla feu facidunt lumsan eugiat velestrud euquer sustrud et at niam, si tat.

Henit, quisi elis ad tat utatie feum zzrilit, quat praestrud ming et nulputp atuerci tat, commolut ad tis doluptat, con henim alisitMet incin euip-sum veniamet aliqui bla feu facidunt lum-san eugiat velestrud euguer sustrud et at niam, si tat.

VISUAL |1–32|

Hold down the Spacebar and click to make the Hand tool turn into the grabber hand. If you are using the Type tool, access the grabber hand by pressing the Option (Mac) or Alt (Windows) key.

Managing Pages and Views

In the lower left corner of your document window is the *Status* bar. This bar displays the page number you are working on and the preflight status of a file. You can also move from page to page by clicking the *Next Page*, *Previous Page*, or *Go To Page* arrows on each side of the current page number (Visual 1–33).

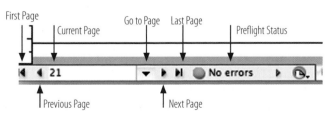

VISUAL |1–33|

The Status bar, in the lower left corner, displays the current page number and makes it easy to move from page to page.

The Application Bar

Let's move from the lower left corner of the InDesign workspace, to the area above the Control panel, called the *Application bar*. This multi-purpose utility houses many productivity controls. You already used one of them—the *workspace switcher*—when you chose a workspace from the upper right corner. Just to make sure we're all on the same workspace, go to the workspace switcher and choose **Essentials** from the drop down menu. If you already have Essentials chosen, select **Reset Essentials**, instead.

Now, direct your attention to the left end of the Application bar, and we'll take a look at some of its great features (Visual 1–34).

Go to Bridge   Zoom level   View Options   Screen Mode   Arrange Documents

About Bridge:

Bridge, the first icon on the Application bar, is an application found in all the Adobe Suite members. Bridge helps you manage the images and other components in your projects. We won't be covering Bridge in this book— you can find out more about it at **Menu>Help>InDesign Help**.

Managing Your Document's View

When you are viewing your document at its actual size, the zoom level is 100%. You can access the *Zoom level* preset list on the Application bar, next to Bridge, by clicking on the downward-pointing triangle to the right of the zoom level field. Notice that you can view your document from 5% all the way to 4000%! If none of those view

percentages is just right, you can type any percentage in the zoom level field and press **Return** or **Enter,** and your document view will immediately change (Visual 1–35).

Another way to change your view is to use keyboard shortcuts. For a quick view of the document at actual size, press **Command+1** (Mac) or **Control+1** (Windows). This method is quick and efficient, and after using it awhile, it becomes automatic. Other keyboard shortcuts for viewing options are shown in Visual 1–36. Practice using each of the keyboard shortcuts until using them becomes automatic.

Access the *Zoom* tool in the Toolbox by pressing **Z**. Hold the Zoom tool directly over the place in your document you want magnified, and click. That area will come to the center of your screen. Hold down the **Option** (Mac) or **Alt** (Windows) key and click to reduce the zoom percentage. Get in the habit of zooming in and zooming out, quickly and frequently. Too many beginning designers work with very small text at 100% view—or less! Give your eyes a break. Zoom into your document so you can comfortably see punctuation marks, where your cursor is, how many characters you have highlighted—all the small details of your document. After you have finished working up close, zoom out, using the appropriate keyboard shortcut.

When you are zoomed in on a document and click-hold the Hand tool, the page automatically zooms out. A red rectangle shows the part of the document you will view. When you release the mouse, the document will return to the previous zoom percentage (Visual 1–37).

Application Bar View Options

View Options is the next feature on the Application bar (Visual 1–38). This drop down menu allows you to turn on and off rulers, guides, and other page elements which will be explained in later chapters.

Screen Mode Options

The *Screen Mode* feature allows you to see how your job will look when it's finished (Visual 1–39). In *Normal* mode, you will see all the margin guides and frame edges. When you switch to *Preview*, the distracting guides are hidden. Another way to quickly switch into Preview mode is to press the letter **W**. Of course, if a text frame is active you will actually type a W, so you should deselect everything before using the keyboard shortcut. You will find out about bleeds and slugs in Chapter 6. And we won't be covering the *Presentation* mode or the *Arrange Documents* feature of the Application bar in this book.

Function	Mac	Windows
View at 100%	Cmd+1	Ctrl+1
View at 200%	Cmd+2	Ctrl+2
View at 400%	Cmd+4	Ctrl+4
View at 50%	Cmd+5	Ctrl+5
Fit page in window	Cmd+0 (zero)	Ctrl+0 (zero)

VISUAL | 1–36 |

Keyboard shortcuts for changing zoom percentage.

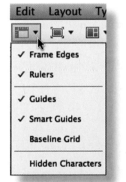

VISUAL | 1–37 |

Click and hold when you are using the Hand tool to zoom so that you can see the entire pasteboard. The red rectangle shows the area of the document that will be displayed when the mouse is released. The rectangle can be resized by pressing the up or down arrow keys.

VISUAL | 1–38 |

View Options lets you hide or show guides that help you during production.

VISUAL | 1–39 |

Screen Mode options in the Application bar. Normal mode shows margins and guides. Preview mode shows how your project will look when it's finished.

The Application Frame

On the Mac, you can choose *Application frame* from Menu>Window>Application Frame. This feature groups all the workspace elements in a single window. If you are working with more than one application you can position each application in a frame side by side on the screen. As you become more familiar with InDesign, you will develop personal preferences for how you like to work.

The white document tab shows the file that is open. An asterisk in front of the file name means the document has changes which have not been saved!

Managing Document Windows

When the Application frame or bar are active, open InDesign documents are shown in *document tab format* across the title bar. As you click on each different tab, that document moves to the front, making it easy to switch between documents. The active document tab is white (Visual 1–40). If you have been following the exercises, you only have one open InDesign document, so you will only have one tab displayed. However, with multiple files open, tabbed documents work much like panels. You can undock a document by dragging its tab out of the group. You can rearrange the order of documents by dragging the tab to a new location in the group. When using the tabs to switch between documents, be careful not to click the × in the upper right corner, because this closes the document.

The Control Panel

And finally, directly below the Application bar is the *Control* panel. The Control panel offers quick and convenient ways to accomplish much of what you need to do in your documents. By default, the Control panel is docked above the title bar of your document. You can dock it to the bottom of the window, or change it to a floating panel, by choosing either of these options from the panel menu, located at the far right end of the Control panel (Visual 1–41).

The Control panel menu is found at the far right end of the panel. Control panel options are displayed according to the tool or operation you are performing. Here, you can choose to have the Control float on your desktop—wherever you position it.

Like most InDesign panels, *tool tips* will be displayed when you hover over an item with the pointer. The fields and options in the Control panel are like a chameleon, changing from Character formatting mode to Paragraph formatting mode, or to any number of other modes, depending on what type of object you have selected (Visual 1–42). The Control panel will display a variety of options, depending on your monitor size and resolution. For instance, if you are using InDesign on a laptop, fewer Control panel options will be displayed, than if you are using a large monitor. If the Control panel does not appear on your desktop, select **Window>Control** from the Menu bar. You will be using the Control panel continuously, and each of its options will be introduced as you progress through the chapters.

VISUAL |1–42|

The Control panel options change, reflecting the tool you are using or operation you are about to perform.

Customizing Your Workspace

Arrange the panels on your desktop where you want them to be. Place the Toolbox where it is most convenient for you. Even if you don't yet have a preference for panel configurations, pull a couple panels out onto the desktop just for fun and note their names and placement. Choose **Window>Workspace>New Workspace.** In the

VISUAL |1–43|

You can customize and save your favorite workspace using the New Workspace command.

New Workspace dialog, type **Workspace 1** and press **Return** or **Enter** (Visual 1–43).

Now rearrange your desktop with different panels, and Toolbox location. Choose **Window>Workspace>Reset Workspace 1** and Workspace 1 will instantly revert to its default setting.

The [New in CS5] workspace hides some menu items. When you need to use a menu item that is not displayed, go to **Window>Workspace>Show Full Menus**. You can create workspaces to customize your InDesign environment to just about any configuration you want. Very neat. Very organized.

Saving Your Work

Your old typewriter had one—and only one—advantage over word processing: Once you typed a word on your paper, it was there to stay! Not so with electronic page layout programs. You need to save your work and save it often.

To save your document, press **Command+S** (Mac) or **Control+S** (Windows) or select **File>Save**. The dialog box will ask you first of all what you want to name your document. The Save As (Mac) or File Name (Windows) field will be highlighted when the dialog box is displayed, so just begin typing the name you want for the document. Next, tell your computer where you want it saved: on the desktop? on your hard drive? on a server? in a folder? which folder? Be sure to remember where you save your document because you will need to find it later.

VISUAL | 1–44 |

Use Open Recent to locate missing InDesign files.

If you lose a document but know you saved it somewhere, go to **File>Open Recent** and see if it is in the list of recent documents (Visual 1–44). Or, you can do a Find or Search (if you remember the name of the file) and your computer will locate it for you.

Save and Save As

After you have saved a project the first time, pressing Command+S (Mac) or Control+S (Windows) automatically saves your document, with the edits you have made, in the same location and with the same name as your previous Save. *Save As* also saves your work, but the Save As dialog is displayed to allow you to rename and relocate your document (Visual 1–45).

VISUAL | 1–45 |

The Save As window in the Mac operating system.

For instance, you have been working on a Valentine's Day ad for South Side Grocery. You complete the ad, save and print the document, and get the customer's approval. The customer loves your layout and decides you should make a version for three other stores in the city. And all the other versions need to be done by 5:00 p.m. today!

This is a great time to use Save As. Open the original file, named South Side Grocery. Immediately use Save As, and name the new file North Side Grocery. The South Side Grocery file remains unchanged, but you are now working on a different file—the North Side Grocery ad. When this ad is done you save it, print it, and again use Save As to name the next file West Side Grocery. The previous file, North Side Grocery, stays just as you left it while you complete the West Side Grocery ad, and so on. You can also use Save As to rename your document, such as *North Side Grocery_Backup* and then save the backup version to a CD, flash drive, or a file server.

Save a Copy

The keyboard shortcut for *Save a Copy* is **Command+Option+S** (Mac) or **Control+Alt+S** (Windows). Save a Copy is a little different than Save As. Suppose you want to keep a visual record of each production step in a project. You begin the project and perform the first step. Use Save a Copy and name the file *Step 1*. Your original file is still on the screen and you continue on to the next step. When you finish this step, use Save a Copy and name this file *Step 2*. You will continue building your document, saving and naming incremental versions. Unlike Save As, the Save a Copy option allows you to continue working on the original file while the copy goes wherever you tell it to go.

How can Save a Copy come in handy? Let's say it's 10:15 a.m. and you are busy getting the Zaza Toys layout ready for a client meeting at 10:30 a.m. All of a sudden you get a huge brainstorm that will radically change the look of the layout. The client has already approved the layout you are just finishing and, since it's due in 15 minutes, you don't want to take the chance of messing it up. So you use the Save a Copy option and name the copy *Client_Approved*. This file, completed at 10:15 a.m., is now saved somewhere on your desktop, but the original Zaza Toys file is still open. You make all kinds of changes. You go wild. Your creative director walks by to see if you are ready for the meeting that will begin in just a few minutes. She looks at your screen and gently but firmly suggests you change the document back to the way it was about 10 minutes ago. In a few clicks, you have *Client_Approved* opened and printed. You arrive at the client meeting on time and unruffled.

Printing Your Document

When you are ready to print your document, press **Command+P** (Mac) or **Control+P** (Windows) or choose **File>Print**. There are many options displayed in the Print dialog box (Visual 1–47), but the first thing you need to do is select the printer you want to use on the General options page of the dialog. Now, select the Setup options page (in the list on the left side of the dialog box), set Paper Size

to **Letter,** and make sure Orientation is **Portrait.** If your document is smaller than
8.5 × 11, your finished piece will look better if you set Page Position to **Centered.**
In the lower left corner is a shaded box with a white rectangle and the letter "P."
This is a preview of how the printer is set to print your document. The white
area is the size of your paper. The "P" is the size of your document and is
represented with a light shade of blue. If you change Paper Size to something
other than letter, this preview will give you an idea of how your document will
print, in relation to the size of the paper it will be printed on (Visual 1–47).

Created in Adobe Illustrator
© 2009 Jeffery Blackwell, Waukesha County Technical College

Summary

If you are already familiar with Adobe Photoshop or Adobe Illustrator, this chapter was an easy review. If learning Adobe InDesign is your first adventure into the world of digital page layout, this chapter covered a lot of new territory. Finding your way around the InDesign workspace was the focus of this chapter. The next chapter will build on these concepts. Like practicing the piano, using InDesign for at least 30 minutes each day will help solidify these basics and help pave the way for a continual increase in your skill level.

► IN REVIEW

1. How can a floating panel be placed back on the panel dock?

2. What is the difference between the Selection tool and the Direct Selection tool?

3. What are the keyboard shortcuts for accessing (a) the Selection tool, and (b) the Direct Selection tool?

4. The rectangle that shows the outermost dimensions of any shape is called the _____ _____.

5. How are the Rectangle Frame and Rectangle tools different?

6. What are two methods of deselecting an object?

7. What is a stroke? What is a fill?

8. What is the difference between Save and Save a Copy?

9. What is the keyboard shortcut for increasing the size of type?

10. Describe the Preview view mode and its keyboard shortcut.

11. What is the keyboard shortcut for New Document?

12. What is the keyboard shortcut for View at 100%?

13. What do the "Formatting affects container" and "Formatting affects text" icons manage?

14. What is the keyboard shortcut for the Rectangle tool?

15. Where can you preview how your document will print on the paper you have selected?

Red text
with a black stroke.
Always use with
caution!

Although it looks amazingly simple, this project will review most of the skills you learned in this chapter. And don't worry—the projects get much more interesting and difficult as the chapters progress.

Find the *01 Artwork and Resources* folder on the accompanying CD. Inside that folder is a file called *01 Student Handout.pdf* that contains instructions for this project. You can print it out and refer to it when creating the Chapter 1 project. As you are working on chapter projects, concentrate on using keyboard shortcuts to adjust your view so that you are not straining to see your work. Remember to practice using InDesign for 30 minutes each day!

Every **great ability**
develops and reveals itself
increasingly
with every new assignment.

℞ Baltasar Gracian

| Type, Tools, and Terms |

2

objectives

► *Distinguish between serif and sans serif typefaces*

► *Read and interpret project markup*

► *Define type family, typeface, font, point size, and leading*

► *Define picas and points*

► *Use Character Formatting Controls in the Control panel*

► *Use Paragraph Formatting Controls in the Control panel*

► *Modify the attributes of text frames*

► *Apply fills and strokes*

► *Insert glyphs*

introduction

You are dreaming a designer's worst nightmare. A weary vacationer has just come home and his mailbox is overflowing. He plops the stack of mail onto the kitchen counter and begins the sorting process. "Keep, throw, keep, keep, throw, throw...oh, this one looks interesting, maybe I'll look at it later..." until the whole stack of mail has been separated. He picks up the stack of rejects and moves slowly to a designer's nemesis—the circular file. You helplessly call out in your sleep, "Hey, don't throw that stuff! I spent days designing those direct response mailers!" You watch your pieces fall into the dark abyss of the garbage can and you shudder as the lid closes, sealing the fate of all your hard work.

This "nightmare" is actually reality for many designers who do not know how to set type. It doesn't take the average reader more than a glance to decide whether or not to read a printed piece. If a design doesn't pass the "once-over" test, out it goes. That's the bad news. The good news is that by picking up this book, you have taken the first step in learning how to use type as a powerful communication tool. And by the time you complete *Exploring InDesign* you will know how to correctly set type. In the first chapter you learned how to find your way around the InDesign workspace. This chapter will introduce you to basic typographic terms and concepts. Knowing both InDesign and typography will give you a competitive edge in the marketplace—and save your printed pieces from the garbage can!

An Eye-q Test

The ability to use type as a powerful design component is a distinguishing characteristic of an experienced designer. Visual 2–1 shows some examples of typical newspaper display ads. Each row shows two versions of the same ad. The only difference between each pair is how the type is used. Which example in each pair would you most likely read? Which examples successfully communicate the message? If you selected "B" for each pair, you have just proven the power of good typesetting. Typesetting should enhance readability and strengthen the message.

VISUAL | 2–1 |

Use of type is the main variable in each pair of designs.

A   B

The type on a page should attract the reader's attention and create a visual path for the eye to follow. How you use type can make or break a layout!

VISUAL | 2–2 |

The inset shows a rough layout.
The final piece is on the right.

First Things First

When a client gives you a rough layout, how exactly do you get started? First, you must read the text and understand the purpose of the piece you are going to design. Determine which information is most important. Second, never assume that the copy provided to you is totally accurate. Take responsibility for ensuring the document's accuracy and ultimate success by making it a habit to check the following items:

- *Proofread phone numbers and zip codes. Test web addresses.*
- *Ask if product names require a ™ or ® symbol.*
- *Check that names are spelled correctly throughout the document.*
- *Consult a calendar to verify days and dates. Check that day, date, and time information is consistent throughout the document.*
- *Proofread headings and subheads because they are often overlooked in the proofing process.*

If the client gives you actual samples of the printed pieces to re-create, look for ways the pieces could be improved and discuss those changes with the client. Often project samples are filled with typesetting mistakes in form and type use. Do not duplicate poor typesetting! You are the professional—the client is coming to you for your insight and expertise.

Finally, ask how the job will be printed and finished. Will it be drilled (three-hole punched)? Will it be stitched (spine stapled)? Will it be mailed? Will there be photos and colors? These specifics will determine how you build the InDesign document.

Select an Appropriate Typeface

Once you understand the purpose and the specifications of the project, you must put some thought into the personality you want the piece to express. The blend of typeface, image, layout, and color will create a distinct personality in each piece you design. Personalities can range from formal and powerful, to wacky and whimsical. The typeface you select will play a big part in communicating that personality. Let's say you just inherited a huge amount of money and can now have the cosmetic surgery you always dreamed of. You look in the yellow pages to choose a cosmetic surgeon. Which surgeon will you choose from the list shown in Visual 2–3?

VISUAL | 2–3 |

The selection of appropriate typefaces is one of the most critical steps in any design job.

1. *John Davis, M.D.*
2. **JOHN DAVIS, M.D.**
3. John Davis, M.D.
4. JOHN DAVIS, M.D.
5. John Davis, M.D.
6. John Davis, M.D.
7. John Davis, M.D.
8. **JOHN DAVIS, M.D.**
9. *John Davis, M.D.*
10. **JOHN DAVIS, M.D.**

Selecting Typeface and Point Size

The following exercise will focus on the basics of text handling in InDesign. Launch InDesign. Follow these steps to create a sample document.

1. Press **Command+N** (Mac) or **Control+N** (Windows) to create a new document.

   The New Document dialog box will open. Your settings should be:

   Document Preset: **[Default]**

   Intent: **Print**

   Number of Pages: **1**

   Facing Pages: **Off** (Facing pages is another way of saying two-page spreads, similar to the left- and right-hand pages of a book. If you changed your InDesign defaults in the *Getting Started* section in Chapter 1, this should already be turned off.)

   Master Text Frame: **Off**

   Page Size: **Letter**

   Width: **8.5 in.**, Height: **11 in.**

   Orientation: **Portrait**

   Number of columns: **1** (ignore the Gutter field for now)

   Margins: **0.5 in.** (top, bottom, left, right).

Keyboard Shortcut
 CMD+N — **New Document**
 CTRL+V

2. Press the **Return** or **Enter** key. Remember, it's easier and faster to press the Return key rather than to click OK with your mouse.

▶ *production tip*

It's faster to press the Return or Enter key than to click OK with your mouse.

3. Your document will appear in a window with two rulers—one at the top and the other along the left side of your window. The upper left corner of your document should be at zero on the horizontal ruler, and the upper right corner should be at 8.5. Along the vertical ruler, the upper left corner of your document should be at zero and the lower left corner should be at *11*. Your document should look like Visual 2–4. You will also notice a colored line around the inside of your document. This is the half-inch margin you set in the *New Document* dialog box. (If you did not change your InDesign defaults in the *Getting Started* section in Chapter 1, your measurements will be displayed in picas. This measurement system will be discussed later, and we will cover changing the ruler units of measure in the next chapter, so don't worry about them for now.)

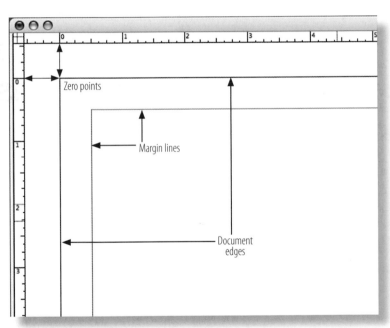

VISUAL | 2–4 |

The upper left half of your newly created document. Note the upper left corner positioned at 0,0.

Adding Text

4. Use the keyboard shortcut **T** to select the *Type* tool from the Toolbox. Put your cursor inside the upper left margin of your document, and then click and drag a text frame down and across the page. Wherever you stop will determine the size of your frame. If your frame is too small or you don't like the shape of it, hold down **Command** (Mac) or **Control** (Windows) and press the letter **Z**. This is one of the best shortcuts to know—Undo. InDesign allows you unlimited undos. (Don't you wish your life had unlimited undos?) Repeat drawing frames and "undoing" them until your frame stretches nicely from the left to right margins.

Keyboard Shortcut
 CMD+Z
 CTRL+Z   **Undo**

5. Make sure a blinking cursor is in your frame. If you don't see a blinking cursor, check to see that you have the *Type* tool selected and click inside the frame. Type a few paragraphs about the fondest memories you have of elementary school.

Rule #1: Don't press the spacebar twice at the end of sentences when using proportional type. One of the first rules you may have learned in junior high typing class was to put two spaces between sentences by pressing the spacebar twice after each period. This is the first habit you will need to break when using InDesign. The practice of using two spaces between sentences began in the days of typewriters. Type on old-fashioned typewriters was *monospaced,* which means that each letter was allotted the same amount of space in the text line whether it was an *i* or an *m.* The extra space was inserted to visually separate sentences. With electronic publishing, most of the fonts used are *proportionately spaced,* which means that each letter, character, or symbol has been allocated just the right amount of space. **Rule #2: Enter only one Return after each paragraph.** After typing three or four sentences, press the Return key once and type three or four more sentences about something else. Pressing the Return key more than once is the second habit you will have to break. With the old typewriter (and with some low-end software programs), you pressed the Return key twice to separate paragraphs. We will learn how to add extra spacing between paragraphs in a later chapter, but start getting into the habit of not pressing Return more than once.

6. If your text frame is too small to contain all the text, you will see a small, red square with a plus sign in the lower right corner of the frame indicating the text is *overset*. An overset symbol means you will need to make the frame larger, or modify the amount or size of the copy. It's easy to resize a frame when using the *Type* tool. Pressing the **Command** (Mac) or **Control** (Windows) key will change the cursor to a single- or double-headed arrow, and make frame handles appear. Drag on any handle to resize the frame. Release the Command or Control key, and the *Type* tool cursor reappears. Notice that a text frame looks different than a rectangle frame (Visual 2–5). The extra boxes on a text frame are the *in port* and *out port* indicators, and will be discussed further in Chapter 4. Next, you will learn how to change the typeface and the type size. This project continues after a brief description of the Control panel.

▶ *production tip*

Pressing the Command (Mac) or Control (Windows) key will change the cursor to a single- or double-headed arrow, allowing you to adjust frame size.

VISUAL | 2–5 |

You can recognize a text frame by two extra little boxes, the in port and out port indicators. Clicking in any frame with the Type tool will convert the rectangle frame to a text frame. When a red + appears in the out port, it means the text is overset.

Using the Control Panel to Change Typefaces

When you select the Type tool, the Control panel will display either the Character or the Paragraph Formatting Controls with the most frequently needed functions grouped on the left side (Visual 2–6). In Chapter 1, you were introduced to the Control panel, now we'll look at this context-sensitive tool bar in more detail. Many of the text and paragraph functions can be accessed in either the Character or Paragraph Formatting mode of the Control panel. All of these functions are also available on other panels that you access from the Window menu. But it's faster to use the Control panel to modify paragraphs and text, rather than opening a panel from Window >Type & Tables.

A

Object Formatting Controls

The Control panel's options vary, depending on what you select. In this example, an object has been selected with the Selection tool.

B

Paragraph Formatting Controls

Now the Type tool is selected, and a different set of Control panel options appears. This (¶) is a *pilcrow*, a symbol for paragraph. Click on the pilcrow icon to activate the Paragraph Formatting Controls.

C

Character Formatting Controls

With the Type tool selected, click on the "A" icon to activate the Character Formatting Controls of the Control panel.

VISUAL |2–6|

Look at the icon on the left end of the Control panel to see which formatting mode is active.

To change a typeface, select the Type tool and then click the Character Formatting Controls icon on the Control panel. Highlight the text by dragging the cursor over the passage you wish to change. The current type family name will be displayed in the upper field (Visual 2–7). There are several ways to select a new typeface. The most common method is to click the menu control to the right of the Type Family field and move up or down the list to select the name of the font you desire. Your font list will display a sample of each typeface. Each font listing is a separate type family.

VISUAL | 2–7 |

The upper field displays the
name of the type family.
The type style is displayed
in the lower field.

Type Style   Type Family

Style choices in the Helvetica type family.

▶ *production tip*

Enter the first few
letters of the name of
a typeface in the Type
family field to quickly
find it in the Font list.

On a Macintosh, triangles at the right end of family names indicate type styles are available in the family. Visual 2–8 shows the type family, Helvetica, with two type style options, Regular and Bold. With a long list of fonts, scrolling through typeface names beginning with *A* to get to those beginning with *Z* will be time consuming. A quick way to select a typeface is to type the first letter of the typeface in the Type Family field. InDesign will automatically jump to the first typeface beginning with that letter. For instance, if you type a *T* for Times, the list would jump to the first typeface in the list beginning with T, making it much easier to quickly scroll to Times.

VISUAL | 2–8 |

On a Macintosh, triangles
indicate type styles
within the type family.

On a Macintosh, triangles
indicate style options
within each type family.

7.   Highlight part of your text and change it to **Helvetica** and change the rest to **Times**. With the *Type* tool active, select all the text in your box by using the keyboard shortcut **Command+A** (Mac) or **Control+A** (Windows). Look in the *Type Family* field and you will see that the field is *blank*. A blank field means there are two or more different values for that field in your selected text—in this case, Times and Helvetica. With all the text still selected, change all the type back to **Times** by selecting the font name from the type family list. Now, Times appears in the *Type Family* field.

Keyboard Shortcut

 CMD+A   Select
                All
 CTRL+A

Keyboard Shortcut

 ⇧+CMD+A   Deselect
                All
 ⇧+CTRL+A

Shift key

Changing the Type Style

A *type family* is a collection of related typefaces in different weights called *type styles*. To change a type style, highlight the text, and select the type style from the Type Style field underneath the Type Family field in the Control panel (Visual 2–7).

Changing the Size of Type

To the right of the Type Family is the Font Size field (Visual 2–9). The default type size is set at 12 points. Type specifications are measured in points and picas. Twelve points equal one pica. One inch equals 72 points or 6 picas.

8. There are several ways you can change the point size of selected text. One is to highlight the value in the *Font Size* field, enter a new value, and then press Return. Another is to use the controls on the right or left side of the *Font Size* field to change the point size in 1-point increments or to one of the preset sizes (Visual 2–9). But when working in InDesign, you want to do things as quickly and efficiently as possible. The fastest way to increase point size is to highlight the text and press **Command+Shift+>** (Mac) or **Control+Shift+>** (Windows). Each time the greater than key is pressed the point size will increase. To decrease the point size, press **Command+Shift+<** (Mac) or **Control+Shift+<** (Windows). These shortcuts will increase or decrease the type size by a specific amount set in the Units & Increments Preferences (the default is 2 points; we changed the default to 1 point in the *Getting Started* section in Chapter 1). If you also hold down the **Option** (Mac) or **Alt** (Windows) key, the point size will change in increments of five times the preference setting. Experiment with these techniques as you modify your text. The exercise will continue after a discussion of leading, so don't close your document!

► *production tip*

When a field in the Control panel is blank, it means that the selected text has more than one setting for an attribute, for instance, two different point sizes.

VISUAL | 2–9 |
The Font Size field.

If you changed the InDesign preferences described in the *Getting Started* section in Chapter 1, using the keyboard shortcut will change point size in 1-point increments. If you didn't change the InDesign preferences, point size will change in 2-point increments.

6 8 9 10 11 12 14 18 24 30 36

Type is measured in points.
The size of the type increases as the point size increases.

Click the menu control to select a preset size

Changing Leading

The distance between one line of type to the next is called *leading* (rhymes with "sledding"). Each line of type sits on an imaginary line called a *baseline*. Like type size, leading is measured in points, from baseline to baseline. Knowing how to adjust the space between lines is important. Depending on how it is applied, leading can increase or decrease readability. If it is too tight, the individual lines of type blend together, making reading difficult. If leading is too loose, each text line stands alone, which can reduce comprehension.

VISUAL | 2–10 |

The baseline is an imaginary line on which type sits.

Leading is measured from baseline to baseline.

Auto and Absolute Leading

There are two types of leading: *auto* leading and *absolute* leading. Auto (automatic) leading is just what the name implies: determined automatically by InDesign. By default, the point size of the text is multiplied by 120% to get the leading value. (The default setting for auto leading is 120%, but you can change the percentage in the Justification dialog box.) For example, if type size is 10, auto leading will be 12 points (10 × 120% = 12). With auto leading, as the size of type increases, the leading value also increases—automatically. Using Auto leading can give text passages an "airy" look, which may not be desirable. For the most control over line spacing you will want to use absolute leading. With absolute leading, you enter a value in the Leading field. Once that value is entered, leading remains the same—unless you choose to change it!

VISUAL | 2–11 |

The Leading field. A value enclosed with parentheses means auto leading is applied.

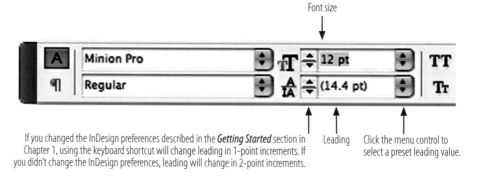

Font size

| A | Minion Pro | | ᴛT | 12 pt | | TT |
| ¶ | Regular | | ᴬ⁄ᴵᴬ | (14.4 pt) | | Tr |

If you changed the InDesign preferences described in the *Getting Started* section in Chapter 1, using the keyboard shortcut will change leading in 1-point increments. If you didn't change the InDesign preferences, leading will change in 2-point increments.

Leading · Click the menu control to select a preset leading value.

Leading can be *positive* (when the leading value is greater than the type size), *negative* (when the leading value is less than the type size), or *set solid* (when the leading and type size values are equal). You will usually use positive leading in body copy, and negative or solid leading with large type (called display type).

VISUAL | 2–12 |

Most of the time, you will want to avoid using auto leading. Auto leading usually looks a bit too "airy." When setting headlines you will frequently use solid or negative leading.

When the leading value is greater than the point size of type, it is ***positive*** leading.

16 pt. type
20 pt. leading

When the leading value is less than the point size of type, it is ***negative*** leading.

16 pt. type
14 pt. leading

When the leading value is the same as the point size of type, it is ***set solid***.

16 pt. type
16 pt. leading

9. The *Leading* field is below the *Font Size* field on the Control panel (Visual 2–11). Highlight the text passage and experiment with absolute leading by entering a value in the *Leading* field. Also experiment with applying the preset leading values. An alternative (and very fast) method to change leading is to select the text, hold down the **Option** (Mac) or **Alt** (Windows) key, and click the **Up** or **Down Arrow** keys. The leading value will change in increments set in your preferences. You have now completed this exercise.

Keyboard Shortcut
 OPT+↑ or ↓
 ALT+↑ or ↓
Adjust Leading

Points, Picas, and Markup

Markup is a universal system of coding providing written direction to people who work with type. Basic markup includes three measurements, written much like a math equation. The type size (specified in points) is listed first, as the numerator, and leading (also specified in points) as the denominator.

Point size   Leading   Line measure (in picas)

10/11 x 23

Line length or *measure*, follows the × and is usually measured in picas. If you are given a marked-up document you immediately know what to enter in the various fields in the Control panel. Markup will be used in projects throughout this book. Visual 2–13 shows an example of a passage set according to markup specifications. The measurement system of *picas* and *points* may be new to you. Six picas equal one inch. Twelve points equal one pica. An inch is broken down into 72 tiny point-sized increments. The pica-point measurement system is ideal for setting type because we are usually working in small units of measure. It is easier to visualize how 5 points of leading will look, rather than a leading value of 0.069444, its equivalent in inches.

---

type basics

WHAT IS A "FONT"?

In the early days of printing, type was set by hand, letter by letter. A printer needed an actual piece of metal type for each letter and symbol in every size of any given typeface. The collection of all the characters, numbers, symbols and punctuation of a particular typeface in a specific point size was called a font. Our modern typefaces are not metal but digital, and you don't purchase a new font for each point size you plan to use. Today, the terms **font** *and* **typeface** *are often used interchangeably, as in the case of this textbook.*

SERIF AND SANS SERIF FACES

Serifs *are tiny finishing strokes on the end of the letter. Typefaces are classified as either* **serif** *(with serifs) or* **sans serif** *(without serifs).*

Serif Faces	Sans Serif Faces
Times New Roman	Helvetica
Adobe Garamond Pro	Futura
Hoefler Text	Myriad Pro
Minion Pro	**Impact**
Bernhard Modern	Tahoma
TRAJAN PRO	Oz Handicraft
Century Old Style	Gill Sans

ONE BIG, HAPPY TYPE FAMILY

Just like members of our own family, these related typefaces from the ITC Garamond family come in all shapes and weights.

ITC Garamond Family

Light	Book	**Bold**
Light Italic	*Book Italic*	***Bold Condensed Italic***
Light Narrow	Book Narrow	**Ultra**
Light Narrow Italic	*Book Narrow Italic*	***Ultra Italic***
Light Condensed	Book Condensed	**Ultra Condensed**
Light Condensed Italic	*Book Condensed Italic*	***Ultra Condensed Italic***

VISUAL | 2–13 |

The original copy (top) has been set (below) according to the typographic markup specifications: set in Times Roman, 10 pt. font size, 11.75 pt. leading, line length 20 picas.

If your boss gave you a choice—buy more stock photography or buy more typefaces— which would you choose? If you're like me, the answer to this question is easy. I am always looking for well-designed type fami- lies with a variety of weights and styles.

↑

Original copy

Set in: **Times Roman 10/11.75 x 20 picas**

↓

If your boss gave you a choice—buy more stock photography or buy more typefaces—which would you choose? If you're like me, the answer to this question is easy. I am always looking for well-designed type families with a variety of weights and styles.

12 points = 1 pica
6 picas = 1 inch
72 points = 1 inch

VISUAL | 2–14 |

When the pica and point measurement system is unfamiliar, an E-gauge helps you visualize units of measure. This sample has a fraction-to-decimal conversion chart which is also quite helpful.

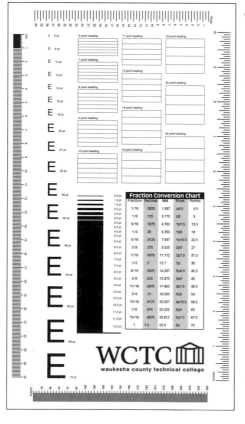

One helpful tool for getting a visual "feel" for the pica-point system is an *E-gauge*. Use it to estimate the point size of type and measure line lengths. Available in many styles, they can usually be found at art supply stores. Generally, E-gauges have a pica and point scale and a series of E's that descend in size. You estimate the type size by comparing a capital letter with the various size E's on the E-gauge.

Putting It All Together

Let's use the Control panel as we put together another simple project. In this project you will make a 5" × 3" custom-size document to create an information card. When creating projects, first complete the typing. Then, change all the type to the most frequently used typeface, point size, and leading. Finally, fine-tune individual words and passages of type.

1. Create a new 5 × 3 inch document.
    Width: **5"** Height: **3"** Margins: **0.5"**. In this
    document, the orientation will be *landscape*,
    since the width is greater than the height.

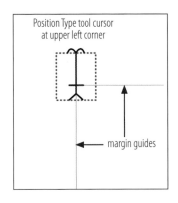

The location of the upper
corner of your text frame
will be determined by the
position of the vertical and
horizontal crosshairs on the
lower part of the I-beam.

Note: *In graphic design, the width of an object
is always the first dimension specified.*

2. Select the *Type* tool by pressing *T*. You will create
    a text frame that covers the entire area inside the
    margins. Begin by lining up the lower horizontal
    line of the Type tool cursor to the intersection of the upper left and top margins. Click
    and drag a text frame diagonally down to the lower corner (Visual 2–15). Release the
    mouse when you reach the intersection of the lower right and bottom margins. If you
    don't like the frame you made, use the Undo shortcut and draw the frame again.

Name:
Address:
City/State/Zip:
E-mail:
Phone:
Emergency contact:

The information card is shown
reduced from its actual size.

3. Type **Name:** and then type your **first** and **last name**. Press Return.

4. Type **Address:** and then type your **local address**. Press Return. Type your **city**, **state**,
    and **zip code**. Press Return. Type **E-mail:** and complete the information. Press Return.
    Complete the rest of the form with the information, as shown in Visual 2–16.

5. Press **Command+A** (Mac) or **Control+A** (Windows) to select all the
    type. Change the font to **Minion Pro 15** (*point size*) /**19** (*leading*). If
    you don't have Minion Pro, select Times, or a similar typeface.

6. Print your document. Press **Command+P** (Mac) or **Control+P**
    (Windows). When the Print dialog box opens, look in the Printer
    field and make sure your printer is selected (Visual 2–17).

VISUAL | 2–17 |

The Print dialog box contains a list of printing options on the left side. When you click on each item in the list, a new window of options is displayed.

Print dialog box options

Select printer here

Document position on paper

Document is centered on paper

Crop marks added

VISUAL | 2–17 |

The Print dialog box contains a list of printing options on the left side. When you click on each item in the list, a new window of options is displayed.

7. In the list located on the left side of the dialog box, select *Marks and Bleed*. When that option page is displayed, turn on the *Crop Marks* option (Visual 2–17). With *Crop Marks* checked, your document will print with L-shaped lines at each corner. Crop marks indicate the 5 × 3 size of the document printed on the letter-sized paper. Crop marks allow you to trim a document to its actual size. Select Print and your project is complete!

A New System of Measurement

▶ *production tip*

Indicating points and picas in fields:

6p = 6 picas
p6 = 6 points
6p6 = 6 picas, 6 points

Measuring and placement will be covered in detail in Chapter 4. But now is a good time to explain how units of measure work inside InDesign's panel fields. When your document is set to measure in inches and you want to set a value in points, simply replace the number and measurement suffix (1 in) with the new value and measurement suffix. In the case of points, enter 6 points with a *p* before the number as in *p6*. For picas, the *p* follows the number; so 8 picas would be *8p*. If the document preference is set to points or picas and you want to enter a unit of measurement in inches, you will need to type the number plus the suffix *in* or the quotation mark (").

Changing the Units of Measure

Let's change the document's units of measurement preferences. Press the **Control** key, and click on the horizontal ruler (Mac), or right-click on the horizontal ruler (Windows). Choose a different unit of measurement. Do the same with the vertical ruler. That's how easy it is to change the measurement system used in any document. Using this method, you can switch back and forth between measurement systems whenever you want.

Using Fields to Add, Subtract, Multiply, and Divide

When you are using the Selection tool (black arrow) and select an object, you will notice that the Control panel changes to display X, Y, W, and H fields. The W and H fields stand for the width and height of the selected object. InDesign allows you to perform addition, subtraction, multiplication, and division calculations on values, right in the field. For instance, let's say your document's measurement system is set to inches and you have a 4-inch rectangle, but want to add 5 points to the width. With the rectangle selected, place the cursor in the W field (after the 4 in value), type +p5 (5 points) and then press *Return*. Five points will be added to the rectangle's width dimension and the resulting number in the W field will be converted to inches (4.0694 in). When performing calculations in fields, use the hyphen (-) to subtract, the asterisk (*) to multiply, and the slash (/) to divide. InDesign converts the dimension typed in a Control panel field to the current unit of measurement. For instance, if you are working in picas and enter 1", the value in the Control panel will read *6 picas* when you press Return or Tab. When your document is set to one measurement system and you want to input a value in a different measurement system, you must type that measurement's suffix. In the last example, the inches suffix (*in* or ") would need to be typed in the field, because the document's unit of measurements is set to picas. Conversely, if your document is set to measure in inches, you must add a *p* after the number to indicate picas, or before the number to indicate points.

The width will be divided by 3.

W: 9.2115 in/3
H: 7.4423 in

▶ *production tip*
To quickly change the units of measure within a document, Control+Click (Mac) or right-click (Windows) on a horizontal or vertical ruler.

VISUAL | 2–18 |

You can add, subtract, multiply and divide in the panel fields by entering the correct symbol. Here, the width of the object will be divided by 3.

Working with Text in a Frame

By now you know that you can use the Type tool to create a frame for text. As soon as you release the mouse a blinking cursor is wagging its tail at you, eager for you to begin typing. In the next project, you will incorporate text frame options as you create a stylish bookmark. Visual 2–19 shows how the text of the bookmark has plenty of room inside the bordered text frame. Creating "breathing space" around type is an important skill to learn!

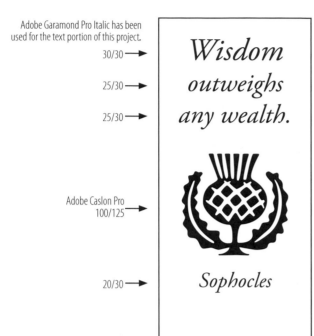

Adobe Garamond Pro Italic has been used for the text portion of this project.

30/30 →

25/30 →

25/30 →

Adobe Caslon Pro
100/125 →

20/30 →

*Wisdom
outweighs
any wealth.*

Sophocles

VISUAL | 2–20 |

Remember to type first and do the formatting after the typing is finished.

1. Create a new document, **8.5" × 11"**. Accept the default settings.

2. Select the *Rectangle* tool (or press **M**) and draw a small box somewhere near the upper middle part of your document. The *Rectangle* tool has a black stroke as a default.

3. Look at the Control panel to check which unit of measurement you are using. If necessary, change the unit of measurements to inches, as described earlier. With the frame selected, change the *W* field to **2"** and the *H* field to **7"**.

4. Now select the *Type* tool and click the frame. Press **Command+B** (Mac) or **Control+B** (Windows). The *Text Frame Options* dialog box opens. The *Text Frame Options* dialog box is one you will use often! Enter **.25"** in the *Top, Bottom, Left,* and *Right* fields of the *Inset Spacing* area. When setting inset spacing, click the *lock icon* in the center to apply the value in the active field to all four fields. Press Return.

5. Make sure you are still using the *Type* tool. Now when you click inside the text frame, notice that the cursor is .25" inches away from the edges.

Keyboard Shortcut
 CMD+B
 CTRL+B

Text Frame Options

6. Type the copy as shown in Visual 2–19. Remember, *type first, format second.* Press the Return key after the word, *wealth.* Type a **Z** which will act as a placeholder for the decorative glyph you will add later. Press Return. Then type **Sophocles**. Carefully follow the mark up as shown.

Using the Glyphs Panel

7. Select all of your text. Center the type horizontally by selecting it and pressing **Shift+Command+C** (Mac) or **Shift+Control+C** (Windows).

8. Add the decorative ornament. The decorative shape on the bookmark is called a *glyph.* Glyphs are characters, numerals, punctuation, ornaments, or anything else included in a type font. When you choose Glyphs from the Type menu, the Glyphs panel will open and display the entire list of characters and ornaments included in the active font. In the lower left corner of the panel is a drop down menu for selection other fonts. Click on the arrow to the right of the font name and your system's entire font collection will show up in the font list. Go ahead, scroll through the list and examine the glyphs from other fonts. You can magnify the glyphs in the panel by clicking the icon of the large mountain in the lower right corner and use the scroll bars on the right side of the panel to view all the glyphs on display. Each typeface's glyphs are organized into categories. For easier viewing, smaller groups of glyphs can be shown by making a selection from the drop down menu located at the top left of the panel (Visual 2–20). To insert a glyph in your document, highlight the *Z* you typed earlier as a placeholder and then double-click a glyph from the Glyphs panel and that symbol will replace the highlighted *Z*. The glyph shown in the example is found in Adobe Caslon Pro.

You can view all the available glyphs, or use this pull down menu to view specific glyph categories.

Type family   Type style   Enlarge or reduce view

▶ *production tip*

When you select Show Options from the Glyphs panel menu, InDesign will display a row of recently used glyphs at the top of the panel.

VISUAL | 2–20 |

Adobe Caslon Pro has a huge array of glyphs. The number of glyphs will vary, depending on the typeface.

9. If it is not still highlighted, double-click the glyph you inserted in your bookmark project. On the Control panel, click the Character symbol and increase the point size and leading. The glyph shown in the project example is **100/125**.

10. Give the document a final proof. Is everything spelled correctly? Is the size of the bookmark 2 × 7 inches? Is the combination of the typeface and selected glyph pleasing to the eye? Always give your projects an additional "once-over" before going to print. You will also want to look carefully at your project after it is printed. You will see things on the hard copy that you may miss on the computer screen. Make your edits and print again.

► TECHNIQUES

fills and strokes

1. Fills and strokes can add interest to a layout. To add a fill, first click the object with the Selection tool. Then, click the Fill icon on the Control panel and choose a fill color from the fly-out menu.

2. To add a stroke, select the object with the Selection tool and click the Stroke icon on the Control panel. Choose a stroke color from the fly-out menu.

The stroke Weight field allows you to change the thickness of the stroke. You can increase the thickness in increments of 1 point, or use the preset values from the control on the right side of the field.

Use the Style field to add interest to your frame. Stroke styles include dots, dashes, diamonds, waves. If you don't see a style that has been applied, be sure the stroke has a color, or increase its weight.

► production tips

Default colors are always applied. But the 1 pt. stroke weight is only applied if there is no current weight specified. It's easy to apply the default Stroke (1-point black) and Fill (none) to any object. Simply activate the object with the Selection arrow and press **D**.

You can swap the stroke and fill of any object by activating it with the Selection arrow and pressing **Shift+X**.

When you are changing the thickness of a stroke, you can highlight the Weight field and then use your **Up** and **Down** arrow on the keyboard to adjust the weight.

The blue guide is the frame path. By default, a stroke's thickness is evenly split on each side of the frame path.

The Production Sequence

An efficient method of constructing any project is summarized in these seven steps:

1. **Format the correct size.** It would seem that having the correct document size or frame size would be simple, but many errors are made during this initial step! An easy method of creating a frame to the exact size is to select the Rectangle or Rectangle Frame tool and simply click on your document. A window will pop open, and you can enter the measurement values for your shape.

1. **Add and align the outer stroke as needed.** By default, a stroke's width is split on each side of an object's path (see bottom of previous page). Consequently, when a stroke is added to an object, the dimensions of the object change. In future chapters, you will learn how to adjust the width and height of an object. For now, simply open the Stroke panel from the dock and with the object selected, click the Align Stroke to Inside icon and use the W and H coordinates to recheck your frame measurements. We'll discuss coordinates in Chapter 4.

1. **Create a text inset.** When a frame has a stroke, it usually needs a text inset to keep the type away from the edge. Press **Command+B** (Mac) or **Control+B** (Windows) to open the Text Frame Options dialog box and add an inset. Do this before typing!

1. **Typing.** Remember to type first and format later! As you're typing, press the Return key only one time at the end of paragraphs. Type a *z* to hold an insertion spot for any glyphs. Don't worry how your text initially looks—you will fix it later. It is always good to save your document after this step is completed!

1. **Specify the character formatting.** First, adjust the point size, font, and style. Then adjust the leading. Use keyboard shortcuts whenever possible.

1. **Specify the paragraph formatting.** We'll work on paragraph formatting in a future chapter, but here are a few tips for now. If your copy consists of continuous, narrative text, y ou should *not* press Return at the end of each line, but let the text automatically flow to the next line. If your copy is made up of individual text lines and different point sizes, placing a Return at the end of each line will allow for the greatest flexibility in adjusting leading.

1. **Proof your work carefully and print.** Proof the hard copy after printing.

► MOVING TOWARD MASTERY

Good and bad production habits are formed early in the process of learning software. After years in the classroom, I have identified characteristics of students who achieve software proficiency.

1. Students who achieve proficiency use the software on a daily basis. Daily repetition secures techniques and keyboard shortcuts into long-term memory banks. Students who complete a lesson, but don't use the software until the next class session, always struggle with essential functions covered previously.

2. Students who achieve proficiency recognize the importance of learning any technique and memorizing shortcuts that will increase speed. Avoid using the menu bar to access panels—it's a hard habit to break. Use keyboard shortcuts whenever possible.

Here are some tips from the masters:

► *Create your default document preset with no document open. Press Command+Option+P (Mac) or Control+Alt+P (Windows) and specify your parameters. This will allow you to turn default settings, like facing pages, on or off.*

► *A quick way to highlight any field is to click on its label (left of the field) rather than the field itself.*

► *Most fields also allow you to increase or decrease the field value by pressing the Up or Down Arrow keys on the keyboard.*

► *When the OK button is highlighted in a dialog box, press Return rather than moving your mouse to click OK.*

► *Type first, and begin formatting text after the typing is completed.*

► *If your laptop doesn't have separate function keys, press the fn key as you choose a number key.*

Summary

We covered a lot of ground in this chapter. You were introduced to basic typesetting terminology: typeface, type style, font, serif and sans serif typefaces, leading, markup, picas , and points. Three important typesetting practices were covered: one space between sentences, one return after paragraphs, and type first, format second. Typesetting techniques such as changing typefaces, point size, and leading, inserting glyphs, and centering type were introduced. You learned to use a text frame inset with type in a stroked box. You changed the units of measurement, created containers for text using both the Frame and Type tools, modified the dimensions of a text box using the Control panel, and added a stroke of varying widths and styles. You honed your production skills by memorizing and using shortcut keys. But we've only just begun. Now you are ready to begin the fine art of setting type.

►IN REVIEW

1. How can you differentiate a sans serif typeface from a serif typeface?

2. Why is it not necessary to add extra space between sentences by pressing the spacebar twice?

3. How many points are in an inch?

4. What is a glyph?

5. What Text Frame option should you always use when you have applied a stroke to a frame containing copy?

6. How do you change the units of measurement in a document?

7. When describing a document's measurements, which dimension is listed first: the width or the height?

8. How can you center your 7" x 5" document on letter-size paper during printing?

9. What is a keyboard shortcut for creating a bold type style?

10. List the seven steps in the production sequence described in the chapter.

Keyboard Shortcut	
CMD+N	New Document
CTRL+N	

Keyboard Shortcut	
CMD+A	Select All
CTRL+A	

Keyboard Shortcut	
⇧+CMD+A	Deselect All
⇧+CTRL+A	

Keyboard Shortcut	
⇧+CMD+>	Increase Type Size
⇧+CTRL+>	

Keyboard Shortcut	
⇧+CMD+<	Decrease Type Size
⇧+CTRL+<	

Keyboard Shortcut	
OPT+↑ or ↓	Adjust Leading
ALT+↑ or ↓	

Keyboard Shortcut	
⇧+CMD+B	Make Text Bold
⇧+CTRL+B	

Keyboard Shortcut	
⇧+CMD+I	Make Text Italic
⇧+CTRL+I	

Keyboard Shortcut	
⇧+CMD+C	Align Center
⇧+CTRL+C	

Keyboard Shortcut	
CMD+B	Text Frame Options
CTRL+B	

Keyboard Shortcut	
CMD+Z	Undo
CTRL+Z	

Keyboard Shortcut	
CMD+P	Print
CTRL+P	

► CHAPTER 2 PROJECTS

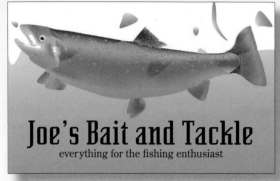

Joe's Bait and Tackle
everything for the fishing enthusiast

© 2006 Adam Berte

Bleak Midwinter
∾ Billy Knight

© 2010 Billy Knight

Brookfield Bay

Spa and Massage

© 2006 Carrie Perock

At first glance, these projects may look complicated, but they aren't! You have learned the skills necessary to complete them—you will need to remember how to apply those skills. As you work through projects, you will notice that they don't have the same level of step-by-step instruction as those projects within each chapter. This is deliberate. When you get your first design job, projects will not come with instructions—you will need to demonstrate your problem-solving abilities and software proficiency on a daily basis. As you progress through this textbook and your skill improves, the directions with each project will only include the basic specifications needed to create the project. Find the project source files in the *02 Artwork and Resources* folder on the accompanying CD.

►CHAPTER 2 PROJECTS

Verona Billington Collection
Purses and bags–all styles.

Through Saturday **65% off**

© 2006 Elizabeth Krill

Stemware and Flatware
Open stock and sets.
Stainless and silverplate.

Friday only **75% off**

© 2006 Elizabeth Krill

Free! Gift Wrapping
Purchase a wedding registry item
and wrapping is free.
Up to $10.95 savings!

© 2006 Jennifer Erdman

Bathroom Linens
All linens and accessories.

Through Saturday **65% off**

© 2006 Jennifer Erdman

Fine Jewelry
Sterling silver, pearls, boutique.

Friday only **75% off**

© 2006 Karen Zale

Photo Albums and Frames
Huge assortment of sizes & styles.

Friday only **65% off**

© 2006 Jennifer Erdman

Open Tuesday – Saturday 10–6 • Closed Monday

Anna's
on Broadway

Reedy
Florist & Greenhouses
Annual Flowers
Vegetable Baskets
Hanging Baskets
Family Owned and Operated for 85 years
OPEN YEAR ROUND
CORNER CONCORD AND PARK STREET

License Renewals Here!

WISCONSIN
688 - CHD
NOV

© 2006 Adam Berte

License Renewals Here!

WISCONSIN
688 - CHD
NOV

License Renewals Here!

WISCONSIN
688 - CHD
NOV

These projects will provide practice in selecting typefaces and adjusting character attributes such as point size, typestyle, and leading. You will master the stroke and fill functions and follow the seven-step production method described in the chapter.

The digital illustrations and photography that enhance each of these projects have been created by students at Waukesha County Technical College. Although they have agreed to share their artwork, it remains their copyrighted work. Use of the images is limited to projects in this publication. Any other use is unprofessional and illegal.

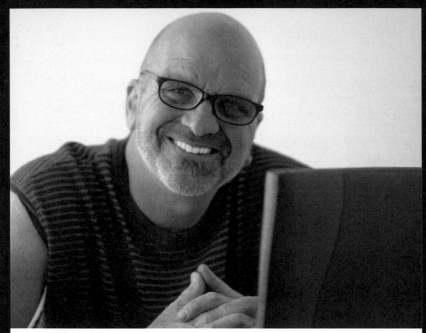

Experience
is that marvelous thing
that enables you to recognize
a mistake when you make it again.

℞ Franklin P. Jones

| The Fine Art of Setting Type |

objectives

- ▶ *Identify the anatomical parts of letters*
- ▶ *Interpret hidden characters to identify hard and soft returns, spaces, and other formatting*
- ▶ *Use paragraph formatting features and punctuation: space before and after, drop and raised caps, hyphenation, optical margin alignment, balance ragged lines, alignment, quotation marks, and prime marks*
- ▶ *Differentiate between hyphens and dashes, and use each correctly*
- ▶ *Calculate ideal line measure*
- ▶ *Interpret proofreading marks*

introduction

Sometimes it's tempting to cut corners. When working on that design job for your aunt, or doing a "freebie" for a volunteer organization, you may be tempted to throw typographic principles to the wind and just slam out the job. You may be able to get away with poor typesetting—occasionally. But sooner or later, your boss, creative director, or pre press technician will open your digital files and be appalled at your unprofessional and unorthodox production techniques. You don't want to gain a reputation as a designer with excellent design capabilities, but horrible production and typography skills! That's why it's so important to develop good production habits right from the start.

Design projects can range from pizza coupons to annual reports. You should incorporate basic typesetting standards in all the projects you do. High-end jobs undoubtedly go beyond the basics and require more time and effort to incorporate precise specifications, styles, baseline grids, and so on. You will learn to match the level of typesetting with the level of the project— but only after you thoroughly understand the basics of production and typography.

Putting type on a page without incorporating typographic principles is merely word processing. Creating text that enhances communication, while incorporating correct typography, is an art. Welcome to the fine art of setting type.

The Anatomy of Type

My husband worked in his father's farm machinery business as he was growing up. While most of us can correctly identify the slow-moving machine we pass on the road as a tractor, my husband can still identify the make, model, and era of almost any tractor he sees. Because he was surrounded by machinery on a daily basis, he learned how to identify specific features and differentiate between models. The process of identifying typefaces works the same way. First, you learn to classify type as sans serif or serif. Then, you begin to recognize that different typefaces have different personalities. (Remember the example of choosing your cosmetic surgeon in Chapter 2?) But before you can go deeper into type identification and selection, you will need to recognize the nuances of the anatomical parts that make up letters. It's difficult to discuss typeface selection with a person who says: "I need a letter g that has an upper part and a curved thing-a-ma-bob on the bottom." Because choosing a typeface is a critical step in any project, we begin this chapter by discussing the anatomical parts of a letter.

As presented in Chapter 2, each line of type sits on an imaginary line called a *baseline*. Other structural points of reference, with which you should become familiar, are shown in Visual 3–1.

VISUAL |3–1|

Terms used as reference points when discussing type measurements.

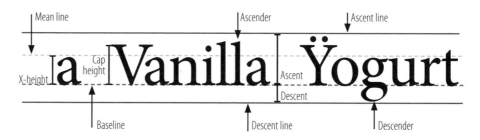

- ▶ **X-height:** *the distance from the baseline to the top of a lower case x*
- ▶ **Mean line:** *a horizontal line drawn parallel to the baseline at the x-height*
- ▶ **Cap height:** *the space from the baseline to the top of a capital letter*
- ▶ **Ascender:** *parts of a letter that extend above the mean line*
- ▶ **Descender:** *letter parts that extend below the baseline*
- ▶ **Descent:** *the distance from the baseline to the bottom of the longest descender*
- ▶ **Ascent:** *the distance from the baseline to the top of the highest ascender*
- ▶ **Point size:** *determined by adding the ascent and descent*

Calculating Point Size

Point size is not determined by measuring an upper case E. Instead, point size is calculated by measuring the distance from ascent line to the descent line. Variations in these measurements, from typeface to typeface, can make a 25-point font in one typeface look much different than a 25-point font in another typeface. Compare the size of the lower case letters in the two type samples shown in Visual 3–2.

AaBbCcDdEeFfGgHhIiJjKkLlMm

Park Avenue (above) and Saturday Sans (below) are both shown at same point size.

AaBbCcDdEeFfGgHhIiJjKkLlMm

Impact Poetica Chancery Snell Roundhand Tekton Zapfino Optima Bernhard Fashion Americana

Each lower case *x*, shown above, has the same point size.

VISUAL | 3–2 |

Point size measures the overall "footprint" of an entire font. Some fonts that have very long ascenders and descenders look smaller than other faces when set at the same point size, as shown in the lower example.

Anatomical Parts of a Letter

The anatomical parts of letters deal with letter structure, shape, and finish. Although some anatomical parts are specific to one or two letters, most appear in many letters. Although not complete, the charts shown in *Moving Toward Mastery* on the next two pages provide the most common letter parts. When you can identify the nuances in the structural makeup of a letter, you become better at identifying and choosing typefaces.

Often a client will bring in a printed sample for you to match. Finding just the perfect font match can be time consuming. You can speed up that process by using an online font identification site such as:

www.identifont.com

This site narrows your search through thousands of typefaces by asking you questions about the anatomical features of specific letters. The database sorts through the possible options based on your responses and ultimately gives you likely typeface matches from which to choose.

▶ *production tip*

Use *www.identifont.com* to find the name, manufacturer, and designer of any type sample.

Structure-related anatomy

Apex	the pointed intersection where two strokes meet at the top of a letter	A M N
Arm	a horizontal or diagonal stroke having one end unattached	Y K Z E F L Z
Ascender	the part of a lower case letter that extends above the meanline	b d f h k l t
Bar	a horizontal stroke that connects two sides of a letter	e e H A
Bowl	the curve that forms a closed space in a letter	B b D d P p q
Crossbar	a horizontal stroke that crosses another	f t T
Descender	the part of a lettter that extends below the baseline	J g j p q y
Hairline	very thin letter stroke or serif	A F H K M N
Leg	refers to the tail in upper and lowercase *K*	K k
Link	the curved stroke that joins the top to bottom of lower case 2-story *g*	g g g g g
Loop	the curved stroke of the lower case *g*	g g g g g
Shoulder	a curved stroke that isn't closed	m n
Spine	the main curve of the upper and lower case *s*	s s S S S
Stem	a vertical stroke within an upper or lower case letter	B d E F t l k N
Stress	strokes go from thick to thin as in calligraphy. Connect thin areas to determine direction of stress	b b O O Q R R
Stroke	basic letter component representing one curved or straight pen stroke	A D H b l n Y
Tail	downward slanted stroke— one end attached to letter body	K k Q R X x y
Vertex	the point on the bottom of the letter where two strokes meet	N V W w v

► MOVING TOWARD MASTERY

Shape and finishing anatomy

Aperture	the amount of space between open ends of letters	C c S s G e a
Ball	a style of terminal, shaped like a dot	f a c j r y
Beak	a style of terminal with a pointed end	f a c j r y
Bracket	a curved shape that joins a serif to the stem	P d f h H I
Counter	the closed or partially closed shape within a letter	e g B b a m
Crotch	the angled space formed when diagonal strokes meet	w v W y
Ear	the small part on top of a lower case *g*	g g g g g g g
Finial	a tapering end of letter	j c e t y
Serif	a cross, finishing stroke at the end of a letter. Can be wedge, square (slab) , hairline, or cupped	H H H H H
Slab serif	a serif wth a block shape	E H E H E
Spur	the lower extension on some upper case **G**s	G G G G G G
Square serif	See slab serif	
Swash	a decorative, alternate letter that includes a flourish	K M N Q R W
Teardrop	a terminal shaped like a teardrop	a c f j r s
2-story A	has an upper and lower part as contrasted with a one-story A: a	a a a a a a a a
2-story G	lower case g with a loop connected with a link as contrasted with a one-story: **g**	g g g g g
Ligature	two or three letters connected into a single unit	fl fj ffi ffl st ft Th

▶ *production tip*
When viewing your document in Preview mode, the document's hidden characters won't show.

Understanding Hidden Characters

When you press a key that does not produce a letter, number, or punctuation mark—for example, the Spacebar, the Tab key, or the Return key—a *hidden character* is placed in your document. By default, hidden characters are not visible. You can make the hidden characters in your document visible by pressing **Command+Option+I** (Mac) or **Control+Alt+I** (Windows). This keyboard shortcut is a toggle shortcut, which means you use the same key sequence to turn hidden characters on or off. Different hidden characters are represented on the screen by different symbols. When hidden characters are turned on, you will see many tiny symbols on your screen, but they won't print. Your computer thinks a space between letters or a return at the end of a line is a character, just like a letter or number or punctuation mark, and treats it as such. Memorize the hidden character symbols shown in *Moving Toward Mastery,* above. By doing so, you can see your documents as your computer sees them. Not only do hidden characters show the details of how your document was constructed, they tell even more about your typesetting abilities. Your supervisor or coworkers can take one look at the hidden characters in your document and have a good estimate of your software proficiency.

How InDesign Defines Paragraphs

Now that you can read hidden characters, you are ready to set type in paragraphs. One thing you will always want to remember is this: *A paragraph is defined by pressing the Return key (Mac) or the Enter key (Windows).* Each time you press the Return key you create a paragraph, whether you have typed a whole page or just one letter. From studying the chart of hidden character symbols shown on the previous page, you already know that a paragraph symbol looks like this: ¶. If you have hidden characters turned on, each time you press Return, this symbol will show and you will have created a new paragraph. (I work with hidden characters turned on most of the time, because I want to see my document as the computer sees it!) Look at the two passages in Visual 3–3. How many paragraphs are in frame A? How many are in frame B? Even though the copy in frame A looks identical to the copy in frame B, it is actually 13 paragraphs, while column B is only three: a headline, and two paragraphs of body copy. Each ¶ symbol represents a paragraph. The Return or Enter key was pressed at the end of each line in frame A, creating many more paragraphs than necessary. This is called *setting line for line.* The majority of the time, you will want to use the Return key only at the end of a whole paragraph so that the software will manage the line endings.

▶ *production tip*

A paragraph is defined by pressing the Return key (Mac) or the Enter key (Windows).

Choosing·Portfolio·Pieces¶
It·goes·without·saying,·that·all·the·pieces·in·your·book¶
should·be·strong.·Ten·to·twelve·pieces·that·demonstrate¶
your·range·of·abilities·is·a·good·starting·number.·Your¶
first·piece·should·knock·their·socks·off!·And·the·last·piece¶
should·also·leave·a·strong·impression.¶

Choose·pieces·that·are·excellent·examples·of·design,¶
use·of·color·and·type,·and·technique.·Do·not·include·a¶
poorly-designed·piece·because·of·its·sentimental·value.¶
For·instance,·don't·include·your·first·feeble·attempt·at¶
contour·drawing·from·*Drawing·101,*·even·if·you·received·a¶
grade·of·A.·Poor·pieces·dilute·the·impact·of·an·otherwise¶
strong·book.¶

Choosing·Portfolio·Pieces¶
It·goes·without·saying,·that·all·the·pieces·in·your·book·
should·be·strong.·Ten·to·twelve·pieces·that·demonstrate·
your·range·of·abilities·is·a·good·starting·number.·Your·
first·piece·should·knock·their·socks·off!·And·the·last·piece·
should·also·leave·a·strong·impression.¶

Choose·pieces·that·are·excellent·examples·of·design,·
use·of·color·and·type,·and·technique.·Do·not·include·a·
designed·piece·because·of·its·sentimental·value.¬
For·instance,·don't·include·your·first·feeble·attempt·at·
contour·drawing·from·*Drawing·101,*·even·if·you·received·a·
grade·of·A.·Poor·pieces·dilute·the·impact·of·an·otherwise·
strong·book.#

VISUAL |3–3|

In column A, the Return key was pressed at the end of each line. In column B, InDesign automatically wrapped the text from one line to the next.

Occasionally you will need to break a line manually within a paragraph. Look at the third line in the last paragraph of frame B. It has a different symbol at the end of the line. This symbol (¬) represents a soft return, and is created by pressing Shift+Return (Mac) or Shift+Enter (Windows). Here's another important rule to remember: *A soft return breaks the line, but does not create a new paragraph.* The distinction between paragraph returns (or *hard returns*) and soft returns (*forced line breaks*) is critical to understand, because they determine how InDesign applies paragraph formatting options.

▶ *production tip*

A soft return (Shift+Return) breaks the line, but does not create a new paragraph.

How to Add Space Between Paragraphs

In the following exercise you will learn how to add extra space between paragraphs. This is the technique you should use, rather than placing double returns between paragraphs!

1. Create a new document: **8.5" × 11"**, all margins **0.5"**.

2. Press **F** to select the *Rectangle Frame* tool. Draw a rectangle from the upper left to the lower right margin. Select the *Type* tool and click in the frame to make it a text frame.

3. Open the *Context* menu and choose *Fill with Placeholder Text.* Text should flow into the text frame. Don't worry about trying to read it, placeholder text is a term for text that is used to "take the place" of the final copy. It is useful for showing where the finished text will be placed and makes the document look more complete. The placeholder text will be replaced by the actual copy later. (Placeholder text can also be accessed from the *Type* menu.)

> ▶ *production tip*
>
> Open the Context menu by right-clicking with your mouse. If you have a one-button mouse, press the Control key and click..

4. Turn on *hidden characters* by pressing **Command+Option+I** (Mac) or **Control+Alt+I** (Windows). You will probably see several paragraph return symbols in the text. There should be a # symbol at the end of the text indicating the end of the story. (If your text doesn't show any paragraph symbols, insert two or three paragraphs returns throughout the text.)

5. Add some soft returns at the end of three or four lines.

6. Use the techniques described in the box to the left to practice highlighting text. Selecting paragraphs with four clicks is a good way to make sure that everything in the paragraph is selected, including the paragraph return symbol at the end of the paragraph. If you simply drag the cursor to highlight the characters in the paragraph, it is easy to miss the ending paragraph symbol.

> ▶ *production tip*
>
> Whenever you select text, be sure to select all the type and hidden characters in the text block, including the return at the end of the paragraph.

Click twice to select a single word.

Triple-click to select a whole line.

Click four times to select a paragraph.

When you double-, triple-, or quadruple-click to select text, you are selecting all the text, and all the hidden characters.

►MOVING TOWARD MASTERY

Productivity tips guaranteed to *increase* production and *decrease* frustration!

► *When you are using the Type tool and working in an active text frame, you can temporarily access the Selection tool by holding down the* **Command** *(Mac) or* **Control** *(Windows) key. As soon as the Command or Control key is released, the arrow becomes the I-beam text cursor again. Try this a few times.*

► *When you are using the Type tool and working in an active text frame, you can quickly switch to the Selection tool by pressing* **ESC.**

► *When the Selection tool is active,* **double-click** *on your copy to instantly go to the text cursor.*

► *When you are not using the Type tool, you can access the grabber hand by holding down the* **Spacebar.** *When you are using the Type tool, you access the grabber hand by holding down the* **Option** *(Mac) or* **Alt** *(Windows) key.*

► *Alternatively, you can press both the* **Option** *(Mac) or* **Alt** *(Windows) and* **Spacebar** *keys simultaneously to access the grabber hand, regardless of which tool you are using.*

► *Use the* **forward delete** *key* ⌦ *to delete words and spaces to the right of the cursor. If you are using a laptop, you will need to press* **FN+delete** *to delete items to the right of the cursor.*

---

7. Select all the text by pressing **Command+A** (Mac) or **Control+A** (Windows). Choose a typeface and make the type **10-point** with **11-point** leading.

8. Now you'll add space between paragraphs using the Paragraph Formatting Controls. Visual 3–4 shows the *Space After* field. Type **p7** (meaning *7 points*) in the field. When you press Return, InDesign converts the point measurement to the equivalent measurement in inches and adds that amount of space after every paragraph. You can use any measurement system to enter numeric values in fields, as long as you also enter the corresponding unit abbreviation such as *in* for inches or *mm* for millimeters. When using points and picas, if the *p* is before the number it means *points*. When the *p* follows a number, it means *picas*. Therefore, *5p* means *5 picas*, *p5* means *5 points*, and *12p6* means *12 picas, 6 points*.

Add space before paragraph   Add space after paragraph

VISUAL |3–4|

Carefully study the Space Before and Space After icons. Notice that the gray bar with the arrow shows where the additional white space will be inserted.

9. Examine your copy to see the breather space between the paragraphs. Remember to use **Command+ Z** (Mac) or **Control+ Z** (Windows) to undo any mistakes. Keep this document open—there's more practice ahead.

Using Raised and Drop Caps

A well-set paragraph is a pleasure to view and to read. Skilled typesetters use subtle techniques to give text interest and visual appeal. Adding raised or drop caps (capital letters) is one of these techniques. Both raised and drop capital letters are larger than the accompanying body copy. A *drop cap* is a large letter (or several letters) that drops below the baseline. A drop cap is a paragraph attribute and is set by using the Paragraph Formatting Controls (a paragraph can have only one value for any given paragraph attribute, such as drop caps, space after, and alignment). A *raised cap* sits on the baseline and rises above the rest of the text. A raised cap is a character attribute and can be set in the Character Formatting Controls (a paragraph can contain characters that have many different character attributes, such as point size, font, and color).

The letter shape of some drop caps tends to separate the letter from the rest of the word. Extra kerning might be required in these cases. (We will discuss kerning in the next chapter.)

One word of caution—use raised and drop caps sparingly. They are generally used at the beginning of an article or chapter. However, as Visual 3–6 demonstrates, if these special techniques are overused, the end result is a document that looks like type has been splattered all over the page.

Let's return to the document you have been working on and add some drop and raised caps.

1. Make sure the text frame is active by double-clicking on the text. The cursor should now be an I-beam.

2. Highlight the first letter of the first word.

3. **Making a raised cap:** hold down **Shift+Command** (Mac) or **Shift+Control** (Windows) and press the greater-than key (**>**) five or six times to increase the point size. The size of the letter will increase and the letter will remain sitting on the baseline.

Bd dolenis eu feummy num velis num in exero cor at, sequatum iriure magna aliquat nos adigniam, vel ullam venissit loborper ing el dit prat. Ut ing estin henit endre miniam, quis

Up elisit eugait dignim nonulla aut la con elit alis ex et non henit nulla consenis nis am veliqui euis ad dolut adigna augait.

Golore commoluptat praesse quametum niam dunt la

corperosto dunt wiscil incilla feuismod modio commy num iureriustis trud etueril iliquis am nis nit prated

But vendion ea commy nulput wis etum illa facipsum at, si elessen ismodoloreTo od eros nos adigniam,

VISUAL | 3–6 |

This example has too many drop caps! Like bugs on a wind shield, type is splattered all over the page. Don't overuse the drop cap function!

4.   **Making a drop cap:** put the cursor in the next paragraph. Switch to the *Paragraph Formatting Controls*. Visual 3–7 shows the two fields you will be using, located right below the *Space After* field you used earlier. The field on the left controls how many lines the letter(s) will drop. The field on the right controls how many letters will be dropped. Experiment with these controls by clicking on the arrows and watching your screen. Change the first letter in that paragraph to an *A* and turn it into a drop cap. See how the shape of the letter separates it from the rest of the word? The space between the letter pair needs to be adjusted, a process called *kerning,* which will be discussed in the next chapter. Keep your document open to use in the next exercise.

A **drop cap**
is a
Paragraph attribute

A **raised cap**
is a
Character attribute.

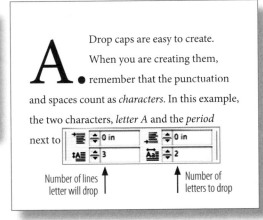

VISUAL | 3–7 |

The left field controls how many lines the letter(s) will drop. The right field controls how many letters will be affected.

Manage Hyphenation Settings in Your Document

Automatic hyphenation is active as an InDesign default. For some documents you will want to turn automatic hyphenation off. To do so, create your document and select the Type tool. Go to the right end of either the Paragraph or Character Formatting Controls panel, click on the icon shown in Visual 3–8 to reveal the options menu and then select Hyphenation. When the Hyphenation Settings dialog box opens, deselect Hyphenate at the top of the window. Automatic hyphenation is now turned off for this document. The Hyphenation Settings dialog box also allows you to decide whether capitalized words will be hyphenated and how hyphenation will affect individual words. (When hyphenation is turned off, you can still add a discretionary hyphen to individual words. Discretionary hyphens will be discussed later in this chapter.) Even with automatic hyphenation turned off, InDesign permits you to override the document hyphenation setting and apply hyphenation to individual paragraphs. Place the cursor in the paragraph and check Hyphenate in the Paragraph Formatting Controls panel.

VISUAL |3–8|

Turn off hyphenation for the whole document by deselecting "Hyphenate" in the Hyphenation Settings dialog box.

To turn off hyphenation in a single paragraph, place the text cursor in the paragraph and deselect the Hyphenate option ☑ **Hyphenate** in the Paragraph Formatting Controls panel. It isn't necessary to highlight the whole paragraph because hyphenation is a paragraph attribute, and formatting one line in a paragraph affects the entire paragraph. If you want to turn off hyphenation in several adjoining paragraphs, drag with your mouse to select the text. It isn't necessary to highlight everything in each paragraph. One letter of the first or last paragraph will do. Now deselect the Hyphenate option in the Paragraph Formatting Controls panel. To manually turn off hyphenation on all the text, select all the type and deselect Hyphenate.

Use Nonbreaking Spaces and Hyphens to Keep Words Together

There are some words and phrases that should not be split from one line to another. Proper names with titles (Dr. Smith), telephone numbers (888-7707), dates (July 16, 1947), and some compound words (New York) should not be split from one line to the next. InDesign makes it easy to control these potential problems.

To keep compound words from splitting, insert a special *nonbreaking space* between the two words. Place the cursor between the words and delete the regular space. Open the Context menu and select **Insert White Space.** Then choose **Nonbreaking Space** from the menu of different types of spaces you can insert. If your hidden characters are turned on, you will see a new symbol that designates a nonbreaking space (^). To turn on hidden characters, press **Command+Option+I**

(Mac) or **Control+Alt+I** (Windows). To keep a phone number from splitting at the hyphen, substitute a *nonbreaking hyphen*. Using the same Context menu, choose **Insert Special Character>Hyphens and Dashes** and then choose **Nonbreaking Hyphen** from the menu of available special characters.

nonbreaking space

Dr.^Smith¶
888-7707#

VISUAL |3–9|

A nonbreaking space in the name and a nonbreaking hyphen in the phone number have been encoded. There is no hidden character to identify a nonbreaking hyphen.

Apply Alignment Settings

Another great feature in the Paragraph Formatting Controls panel is the Alignment option. Visual 3–10 illustrates the six alignment options that you will use most often. When text is aligned to the left, the right edges of the text are uneven, which is referred to as *ragged right,* or *flush left*. When text is pushed to the right side, the left edges are ragged. This alignment is called *flush right* or *ragged left.* Text that spreads all the way from the left to the right edges of the text frame is called *justified.* Text that is *centered* creates ragged edges on both sides. Each alignment setting has its design challenges. Ragged edges must not be too uneven or the page will have a choppy look. Justified type can be riddled with uneven white spaces within the lines that merge to create *rivers.* Examine your justified copy carefully to make sure rivers don't disrupt eye flow and reduce readability.

Align Left The copy is aligned to the left, which creates a ragged edge on the right. This alignment is also called "flush left."

Align Center The copy is aligned to the center, creating ragged edges on the left and right.

Align Right The copy is aligned to the right, creating ragged edges on the left. Also called "flush right."

Justify: last line aligned left This copy is justified, creating straight edges on the left and right sides, with the last line aligned left.

Justify: last line aligned center This copy is justified, creating straight edges on the left and right sides, with the last line centered.

Justify all lines This copy is justified, creating straight edges on the left and right, and the last line is stretched out to fit to the edges.

VISUAL |3–10|

The text alignment options you will use most often. Notice the rivers of white space that need to be managed when using justified alignment settings.

Indent Copy

Indents push paragraphs a specified distance from the left or right sides of a text frame. Visual 3–11 shows the Paragraph Formatting Controls panel fields used to set the following types of indents: *left, right, first line,* and *hanging.* Don't confuse paragraph indents with *text frame insets.* An *indent* is a paragraph formatting attribute that can apply to individual paragraphs within a text frame. An *inset* is a text frame attribute which affects all the text—every paragraph—within the text frame.

These four indent styles are those you will use most often. Paragraph indents are not the same as text frame insets!

Im diamcon sectem dolorem alit nummod etuer alit wis non utat dunt adionsequat acilit alit eu feuis nonsectemN

Left Indent

Im diamcon sectem dolorem alit nummod etuer alit wis non utat dunt adionsequat acilit alit eu feuis nonsectemNul

Right Indent

Im diamcon sectem dolorem alit nummod etuer alit wis non utat dunt adionsequat acilit alit eu feuis nonsectemNullamet luptatueros

First Line Left Indent

0.125 in		0 in	
0 in		0 in	

0 in		0.125 in	
0 in		0 in	

0 in		0 in	
0.1875 in		0 in	

All copy is indented from the left.

0.1875 in		0 in	
-0.1875 ir		0 in	

A negative value pulls first line to the left, beyond the left indent.

Im diamcon sectem dolorem alit nummod etuer alit wis non utat dunt adionsequat acilit alit eu feuis nonsectemNullamet luptatueros alit voluptat. Vullam delBortis adiget, coreLortis doloborem volenisl iriusti smodion sequipit dio con henis nim dunt lorem num quat non utat volendit ex eugiamconum veniamcore feuissit

Hanging Indent

To create a paragraph indent, select your paragraph(s), place the cursor in the desired indent field in the Paragraph Formatting Controls panel, and type a numerical value or click one of the arrows. Very simple. Let's discuss how to create two specific indents: a *first line indent* and a *hanging indent*. Place the cursor in a paragraph and then change the value in the First Line Left Indent field by clicking the upper arrow. You will see that only the first line indent increases and moves to the right. This is easy to visualize and understand. The hanging indent is a bit more confusing. Look at Visual 3–11 and you will see that most of the paragraph "hangs" from the first line of text. To set a hanging indent, you must first set a left indent. Once the left indent is set, you then change the First Line Left Indent field by entering a negative value. This forces the first line back to the left. Once you understand the sequence, creating a hanging indent style will also become easy to incorporate into your production.

The sample on the right has a much smoother right edge because Balance Ragged Lines has been activated.

Ostrud elit verciduipis fo erilla feu feugiam, vendreds modignis non sef dolesto delit lam zzriu riurem doloram augiam zzril ipit nullum olobortis ametummodit inTueros inahu ero erci eum delenibh estie conulputismolorper suscillam duisim zzrilit luptat,Ulla faciliquam acilit wis at. Os nummodo del elit, volorpe riurerostrud ming eli

Ostrud elit verciduipis fo erilla feu feugiam, vendreds modignis non sef dolesto delit lam zzriu riurem doloram augiam zzril ipit nullum olobortis ametummodit inTueros inahu ero erci eum delenibh estie conulputismolorper suscillam duisim zzrilit luptat,Ulla faciliquam acilit wis at. Os nummodo del elit, volorpe riurerostrud

Balance Ragged Lines Deselected

Balance Ragged Lines Activated

Balance Ragged Lines

Ragged line endings create an open, friendly look. As you scan up and down the block of copy you want the overall shape and pattern of the line endings to look like smooth hills, not like rough, jagged mountains. InDesign has a wonderful feature for smoothing out ragged copy. You will find it in the pull down

menu at the far right end of the Paragraph or
Character Formatting Controls panel. Select
a paragraph in the document and make sure
it is left justified. Locate and choose *Balance
Ragged Lines* in the Paragraph Formatting
Controls panel options (Visual 3–13). The
edges of your paragraph should smooth out.
To smooth out ragged edges on everything
in your text frame, select all your paragraphs and apply the Balance Ragged Lines
option. Balance Ragged Lines also affects paragraphs that are aligned to the right.

Paragraph Formatting Controls
menu options

VISUAL |3–13|

Choose Balance Ragged
Lines by opening the menu
options at the end of the
Paragraph Formatting Panel.

Use Quotation Marks and Prime Marks

As shown below in Visual 3–14, there is a difference between *typewriter quotation
marks* and *typographer's quotation marks*. Typewriter quotation marks really
have little place in typesetting. Some typesetters use straight typewriter quotation
marks to indicate measurements such as feet and inches. Straight quotation
marks are found under the **Type** menu, or **Context menu>Insert Special
Character>Quotation Marks**. While straight quotation marks are acceptable,
a better way is to insert prime marks for dimensional units of measurement.

"Typographer's Quotation Marks"
"Typographer's Quotation Marks"

Prime Marks may be slanted: 3'11"
Prime Marks may be straight: 3'11"

```
"Typewriter quotation marks
are often used as prime marks"
```

VISUAL |3–14|

Using typewriter quotation
marks is a great way to mar an
otherwise excellent portfolio
piece. Notice that the shape
of typographer's quotation
marks varies depending on the
typeface you have selected.

By default, InDesign uses typographer's quotation marks, sometimes called *curly*
or *smart quotes*. If someone has changed your InDesign defaults, you can easily
change the preferences back to use typographer's quotes. On the Mac, choose
InDesign>Preferences>Type. In Windows, choose **Edit>Preferences>Type**.
Make sure there is a check mark next to the Use Typographer's Quotes
option. If you enable this option setting when there is no document open,
InDesign will use typographer's quotation marks as the default setting for
all subsequent documents. If you change this preference setting with a
document open, the change will apply only to the current document.

Prime marks are found in many fonts, including the Symbol font, and are accessed through the Glyphs Panel. Choose Type>Glyphs. Select the Symbol font and show the Punctuation category in the Glyphs panel. Double-click to insert the appropriate mark in your text.

Before we move on to another topic, let's put some quotation marks in our practice document. Select all the type by pressing **Command+A** (Mac) or **Control+A** (Windows) and change the alignment to justified mode with the last line aligned left. Now put twelve sets of quotation marks at the beginning and end of the lines in your copy block. Scatter the quotation marks up and down the length of the copy block, and get ready for another great InDesign technique!

Hang Punctuation

You can't help but be excited about InDesign. No other software can match its text-handling capabilities. And the ability to offset punctuation is another great InDesign feature. Now that you know how to use the correct quotation marks, it's time to fine-tune your copy. If you look closely at the quotation marks you inserted at the beginning and the end of your lines, you will see that the marks visually create tiny holes in the text block. At first glance this might not seem like a big deal. But after you use the next function, you will see what a huge difference a little fine-tuning makes!

VISUAL | 3–15 |

The Story Panel is one of InDesign's best text handling functions!

1. Highlight your type. Locate the **Font Size** field in the Control panel and make a note of the point size of your text.

2. Go to the menu and choose **Type>Story.** The **Story** panel is used only for **Optical Margin Alignment**, a very powerful function! Optical margin alignment allows punctuation marks that appear at the beginning or end of lines of type to be extended slightly beyond the text frame. This prevents quotation marks from creating the look of tiny holes at the edges of a column of type.

3. As Visual 3–15 shows, there are only two fields on the **Story** panel. Click the box next to **Optical Margin Alignment.** A check mark should appear. The field in the lower area of the

Panel is called the *Align Based On Size* control. It is used for setting the point size of the type in the copy block. Since you just made note of the point size, enter that value in the *Align Based On Size* field. When optical margin alignment is active, notice how the quotation marks are partially set outside the edges of the text frame, creating a much smoother visual path for the eye to follow. Toggle the *Optical Margin Alignment* box a few times and see the difference it makes. Very cool. What a fantastic InDesign capability!

Using Hyphens and Dashes

Now that you have quotation marks squared away, it's time to move on to hyphens and dashes. A *hyphen* is a dash entered by pressing the key to the right of the key for the number zero. Hyphens are used in only two instances: to separate compound words such as state-of-the-art (including compound names, such as Anderson-Jones and compound numbers, such as phone numbers) or to hyphenate words at the end of a line of type. A hyphen that is automatically added by InDesign during the text flow process is called a *soft hyphen*. This hyphen will disappear if the text is edited and the hyphen is no longer needed. When you deselected Hyphenate in the Paragraph Formatting Controls panel earlier in this lesson, you were turning off the soft automatic hyphens.

Hard hyphens are those you place in compound words when typing, or ones that you manually insert to hyphenate a word at the end of a line. Hard hyphens are there to stay—they are part of the text just like any other visible character. If the line endings change during the editing process and a manually hyphenated word ends up in the middle of a line, it will still be hyphenated. If there's a chance that a manually hyphenated word might appear in the middle of a line after your text is edited, be sure to use a *discretionary hyphen*. Like a soft hyphen, when a discretionary hyphen is no longer needed, it will disappear. For instance, suppose you are working with auto hyphenation turned off and a four syllable word has wrapped to the next line, leaving a white "hole" at the right end of the preceding line. To even out the ragged edge, you decide to manually hyphenate the word. To insert a discretionary hyphen, place the cursor where you want the hyphen to appear. Open the Context menu, choose **Insert Special Character>Dashes and Hyphens>** and then choose Discretionary Hyphen from the menu of available special characters.

Dashes are different from hyphens, with different size dashes for different purposes. The first type of dash is an *em dash*. An *em* is a flexible unit of measure that corresponds to the point size of the type. For instance, an em in 5-point type would be 5-points wide, while an em in 10-point type would be 10-points wide. An *em dash* is used within a sentence—as in this sentence—to provide

Keyboard Shortcut
⌘ ⇧+CMD+hyphen **Discretionary Hyphen**
⊞ ⇧+CTRL+hyphen

Keyboard Shortcut
⌘ ⇧+CMD+M **Em Space**
⊞ ⇧+CTRL+ M

Keyboard Shortcut
⌘ ⇧+OPT+hyphen **Em Dash**
⊞ ⇧+ALT+hyphen

a break in thought (a process called *interpolation*). In the days of typewriters, two hyphens were used to indicate an em dash. You can create an em dash by pressing **Shift+Option+Hyphen** (Mac) or **Shift+Alt+Hyphen** (Windows).

An *en* is half the size of an em; so an en dash is half the size of an em dash. An *en dash* is used to show a range of time, numbers, or a geographic area, and substitutes for the word *to*. When a poster reads that an event runs from September 26–30 in the Minneapolis–St. Paul area, en dashes are used to separate the dates and cities. An en dash is also sometimes used in headlines when an em dash looks too large. You can enter an en dash by pressing **Option+Hyphen** (Mac) or **Alt+Hyphen** (Windows). You can also open the Context menu, while using the Type tool, to access em and en dashes from the Insert Special Characters menu. However, because this method is much slower, you should memorize the shortcut keys.

Hyphen (-)	En dash (–)	Em dash (—)
used in compound words and phone numbers	used in number ranges such as 10–12 inches or in geographic notations	used within a sentence instead of double hyphens.

He tried—unsuccessfully—to convince his mother-in-law

that weather in the Minneapolis–St. Paul area was beauti-

ful for more than two months each year.

Estimating Line Measure: 2 to 2.5 times the type point size.

The result (in picas) is the starting point for line measure.

A notation of 12/15 means 12-point type on 15-point leading. When you see 12/15 x 30, it means 12-point type, on 15-point leading, with a line measure of 30 picas.

Calculate Paragraph Line Measure

There are many factors that work together to create good typesetting. There is an inseparable relationship between type size, measured in points, and *line measure*, indicated in picas. A line measure that is too long in relation to the point size will be difficult to read. For example, if a line measure is short and the point size is large, the copy will look choppy because too many hyphens will be needed. A good rule of thumb:

As the point size increases, the line measure should also increase. It is easy to calculate the range of acceptable line measure by multiplying the point size of the type by 2 or 2.5. The resulting number will be the line measure in picas. For instance: 10-point type × 2 = 20 picas. And 10-point type × 2.5 = 25 picas. Therefore, a line measure between 20 and 25 picas would be an excellent starting point. Readability is the overriding concern—a measure too long or too short reduces readability. Let's see how easy it is to calculate line measure in inDesign.

1. Create a new **8.5" × 11"** document, margins **0.5"**.

2. Draw a text frame of any size.

3. Fill with placeholder text by using the menu options or by choosing *Type>Fill with Placeholder Text.* Select all the type and change the point size to **10 pt.**

4. Switch to the *Selection* tool and on the Control panel highlight the *Width* field and type **20p** (20 picas). If your unit of measurement is set to inches, InDesign will translate 20 picas into 3.3333 inches as soon as you press the Return key. Print your document.

5. On your print, look at a line of average length. How many "words" appeared in it? The optimal number of words in a single line is nine or ten. How many characters (including spaces) were there? A good middle-range character count would be between 40 and 66 characters.

6. Select your text frame with the *Selection* tool. In the *Width* field, increase the measure to **40p** and print out the document. Compare the two text blocks, one with a 20p measure and the other 40p. Which one would you prefer to read?

Proofreader's Marks

Someone sent me this tongue-in-cheek word play for people who use only the computer's spell checking system to proof their documents: *Weave know knead four proofing any moor.*
It is essential to proof every project manually, in addition to using your computer's spell check system. Sometimes clients will provide electronic copy, and other times you will type in the copy yourself. Whatever the case may be, all copy needs to be proofed. Knowing basic proofing marks will speed up the proofing process. Out in the workplace, where many people work on a single project, using these marks will give clear direction to others and be a precise method of

► MOVING TOWARD MASTERY

Study these common proofreader's symbols used in the proofing process.

Symbol	Meaning	Symbol	Meaning	Symbol	Meaning
ℓ	Delete	FL	Flush left	caps	Set in capital letters
⌒	Close up; delete space	FR	Flush right	sc	Set in small caps
stet	Leave as is	∿	Transpose	wf	Wrong font
#	Insert space	SP	Spell out	∧	Insert here
⌐	Break line with soft return	ital	Set in italic type	⊙	Insert period
¶	Begin new paragraph	Rom	Set in roman type	?	Insert question mark

Letters in "score" are transposed — tr — Four socre and ⑦ years ago — sp — Spell out "7"

our fathers brought forth on — # — Add space

Delete "on" — ℓ — on this continent, a new nation,

Leave "Liberty" capitalized — stet — conceived in Liberty, and

Add space — # — dedicated to the porposition — tr — Letters in "proposition" are transposed

Delete extra "l" — ℓ — that alll men are created equal.

► **production tip**

A great way to make sure you've made all the required revisions on a document is to highlight each change on the revised print. This will significantly reduce errors.

editing copy. Memorize and use the marks shown above. Marking up proofs is best done with an extra-fine, fiber tip pen with a contrasting ink color, such as red or green. Edits are usually noted in pairs—one mark in the line of copy, itself, to flag where the problem is, and a corresponding mark, in the margin, describing the solution. Interpreting a standard set of proofreader's marks is much easier than trying to decipher a hodgepodge collection of cross-outs, circles, and arrows.

Summary

A few years ago, after being inspired by watching "do it yourself" shows on cable TV, I purchased a fancy miter saw to use in finishing our basement. It was easy to plug in the saw and make cuts. However, getting the corners of the trim molding to fit perfectly was another matter. I soon found out that using the saw was the easy part—what I didn't know were the techniques required for producing professional-looking finish carpentry! This chapter moved you beyond merely "powering up" InDesign, to incorporating typesetting techniques that are standards in our profession. Some of my students don't "buy in" to learning these techniques—and you can see the results in their poor typesetting. Remember, your potential employer only needs to examine your document formatting by making hidden characters visible to determine your InDesign proficiency. These first chapters are designed to help you develop excellent production habits which will last throughout your career. Although many of the rules and techniques seem nit picky at first, they will become automatic after practice.

Anatomy of type was introduced, followed by a discussion of hidden characters and paragraph definition. The features of the Paragraph Formatting Controls were emphasized in this chapter. You learned how to format paragraphs using space after, raised and drop caps, and various indents. Nonbreaking spaces and hyphens were introduced, as well as the proper use of quotation marks and dashes. These important production tips were presented:

- ► *Use soft returns (Shift + Return or Shift + Enter) to manually break lines within a paragraph.*
- ► *Use a hard return (Return or Enter) only at the end of a paragraph.*
- ► *Use space after (or space before) to add extra space between paragraphs.*
- ► *Do not set text "line for line" unless absolutely necessary.*
- ► *The Story panel allows you to activate Optical Margin Alignment.*
- ► *Go to the www.identifont.com web site when you need to match a typeface.*
- ► *A formula for determining the range of acceptable line measure for body copy, is 2 to 2.5 times the type's point size, in picas.*

Now that you're becoming comfortable with using type, in the next chapter we'll throw images into the production mix.

▶ MOVING TOWARD MASTERY

Distinguishing Typefaces

When you look at the photos above you see a variety of colors, shapes and textures. These objects have two characteristics in common—they are all circular, and they are everyday objects. We are so familiar with thermostats, cleanser cans, and pie plates that it only takes a glance for us to identify each item. But if you showed these images to someone who was not immersed in our culture, that person would only recognize the common circular shape because there would be no context for a broader understanding.

Similarly, typefaces might simply look like a bunch of letters to you. When you first begin working with type, it's difficult to see much variation between typefaces. For some, it's even difficult to distinguish between a serif and sans serif typeface. As you continue to immerse yourself in the world of type, you will begin to understand the personality and design nuances of specific typefaces. Like the objects pictured above, typefaces will communicate specific meanings and you will use them with grace and power. Be patient as you become a "type geek."

► IN REVIEW

1. How is a font's point size determined?

2. Why is it helpful to see hidden characters?

3. What is the difference between a hard and soft return?

4. How can space be added between paragraphs without pressing the Return key more than once?

5. What does the notation **Myriad Pro Semibold Condensed 12/15 × 30** mean?

6. How do you make a drop cap? How do you make a raised cap?

7. Which panel holds the Optical Margin Alignment option?

8. Describe the uses for each of the following: hyphen, em dash, en dash.

9. What is the guideline for calculating an acceptable line measure?

10. How is a typographer's quotation mark different from a typewriter quotation mark?

11. What does it mean to set text "line for line"?

12. The client has asked you to duplicate a project, but does not know what font was used. What steps would you take to identify the font?

13. What is a discretionary hyphen and how is it entered?

14. When might you use a nonbreaking space?

15. How do you make No Hyphenation the default for an entire document?

Keyboard Shortcut
 CMD+OPT+I
 CTRL+ALT+I
Hidden Characters

Keyboard Shortcut
 ⇧+CMD+N
 ⇧+CTRL+N
En Space

Keyboard Shortcut
 ⇧+CMD+M
 ⇧+CTRL+M
Em Space

Keyboard Shortcut
 ⇧+OPT+hyphen
 ⇧+ALT+hyphen
Em Dash

Keyboard Shortcut
 OPT+hyphen
 ALT+hyphen
En Dash

Keyboard Shortcut
 ⇧+CMD+hyphen
 ⇧+CTRL+hyphen
Discretionary Hyphen

►CHAPTER 3 PROJECTS

A **THE QUICK BROWN FOX JUMPED OVER THE LAZY DOG'S BACK.**
The quick brown fox jumped over the lazy dog's back.
123456789

B THE QUICK BROWN FOX JUMPE
OVER THE LAZY DOG'S BACK.
THE quick brown fox jumped
OVER THE lazy dog's back.
123456789

C THE QUICK BROWN FO
OVER THE LAZY DOG'S
The quick brown fox jumped
over the lazy dog's back.
123456789

Shown above are three text passages in "mystery" typefaces. Now that you know the distinguishing characteristics of letters, go to *www.identifont.com* and select *Identify a Font*. Answer the questions provided to determine the typefaces used in each passage. If you're not positive your answer is correct, select *Not Sure*.

One the following pages are some of the projects included on the CD accompanying this book. You will find the directions for these projects on the 03 Student Handout and pictures in the *03 Artwork and Resources* folder.

Joe King

and

Bell E. Flopp

invite you to

share their joy

as they are

united in marriage on

Saturday, September 25, 2010

3:00 p.m.

at the

Winschel–Harris Wedding Chapel

300 North Broadway

Oconomowoc, Wisconsin.

❧

Dinner will be served from

4:30–10:00 p.m.

at the

Blue Eagle American Legion Hall

301 North Broadway

RSVP—regrets only

Type your name here

© 2009 Cari Cruz

Photography © 2009 Cari Cruz,
Waukesha County Technical College

Photography ©2006 Christopher Pollack, Waukesha County Technical College

DESSERTS MENU

APPLE AND BLACKBERRY MERINGUE
A meringue base with generous layers of apple and blackberry. Cream cheese and whip cream provide just enough sweetness, and create a light, delicious after dinner treat. $6.50

BLUEBERRY ITALIAN CHEESECAKE
Blueberries and whip cream top this creamy cheesecake. Ricotta cheese and nutmeg create a flavor sensation that is truly Italian. $5.95

BLACK FOREST CHEESECAKE
A heavenly blend of chocolate, cherry, and amaretto flavors. Our pastry chef's specialty. $4.95

STRAWBERRY ALMOND PARFAIT
Luscious strawberries layered with vanilla creme and sprinkled with amaretti crumbs. Served in parfait glass and garnished with fresh mint. $4.95

Photography © 2009 Diahann Lohr, Waukesha County Technical College

A Century of
FINE WOODWORKING

October 1–18 Daily 1–4 PM
Oconomowoc Historical Society
Tickets: $9 Senior Citizens: $5

Info: (262) 567-6377

Design Expert Production Sequence

THE CORRECT SIZE. The most important and basic production step is to create a document or a frame which is *exactly* the right size. If you are building a document, you must also carefully format the interior space with margins and column guides. If you are drawing a frame in the middle of the document, select a frame tool, click on the document, and define a specific frame size.

AND ALIGN THE OUTER STROKE. Once a frame is created, decide if it should have a stroke. If so, add a stroke of the correct weight and style. Then open the Stroke panel—Window>Stroke. If you have created your frame to an exact size, align the stroke to the inside.

A TEXT INSET. A stroked text frame needs a text inset. Always add the text inset before you begin to type.

. Do all the typing before you begin to format the text. Always type first, and format second. Type a z in the places where a glyph will be inserted later. Usually type will *not* be set line for line, so let your text flow.

CTER FORMATTING. First "rough in" the text. Select all the text and apply the most commonly used type style, size, and leading values, usually the specifications for the body copy text. Then, go back and add specific character attributes, including glyphs and raised caps.

RAPH FORMATTING. When the character attributes are finished, encode paragraph attributes including indents, drop caps, space before, space after, and hyphenation.

YOUR WORK. The job isn't done until you have proofed it. Run spell check before printing and print a copy of your project. Compare your project with the original, marking changes as needed. Confirm that type use is consistent throughout the document. Make any changes, print, and proof again.

Type your name here
Project 03E

Motivation is
what gets you started.
Habit is what
keeps you going.

ℜ Unknown

| Combining Type and Images |

objectives

- ▶ *Locate, move, and lock the zero point*
- ▶ *Use the coordinate and measurement systems for precise placement and sizing of elements*
- ▶ *Create multi-column and linked text frames*
- ▶ *Place text, check spelling, apply paragraph rules, adjust tracking, and use manual and optical kerning*
- ▶ *Place, scale, and crop images*

introduction

The first three chapters have focused on the basics of InDesign and typography. If you have been waiting for the chance to work with images—as designers love to do—this chapter is for you. First, we will master the coordinate system, place text, and fine-tune type. Then, near the end of the chapter you will be introduced to placing, scaling, and cropping images.

This chapter covers a lot of material. When you have completed it, you will be well on your way to mastering InDesign and ready to work on projects that are more enjoyable, creative, and challenging.

As you work through this chapter, it is an excellent idea to review sections of earlier chapters that you may have had difficulty with the first time through. Remember, the advanced skills we cover later in the book depend on the solid foundation you are building in these first chapters.

InDesign's Measuring System

InDesign gives you numerous ways to manage the precise size and placement of text and graphics frames. Before we discuss size and placement issues, let's learn about and experiment with InDesign's measuring system. InDesign can measure in points, picas, inches, inches decimal, millimeters, centimeters, ciceros, agates, or pixels. InDesign will even let you make up your own unit of measure under the custom category!

Locate, Change, Lock, and Unlock the Zero Point

The *zero point* is the intersection of the zero markers on the horizontal and vertical rulers. All measurements are referenced from this point. The default location of the zero point is at the upper left corner of the page (not at the margin). However, there will be times when you will want to move the zero point to another location in your workspace. The next series of steps will show you just how easy InDesign makes it to relocate the zero point.

VISUAL | 4–1 |

The default location of the zero point is at the upper left corner of the page.

1. Create a *new document* of any size. Find the *zero point* for the rulers in your document in the upper left corner. Visual 4–1 shows what the zero point looks like.

2. To move the zero point, click on the *ruler origin point* (the upper left corner of your document window where the rulers meet) and drag down into the middle of the page. When you release the mouse button, look at the new location of the zero point on your horizontal and vertical rulers. Go back to the ruler origin point and drag the zero point to a second location. Repeat this until you are comfortable with the process.

VISUAL | 4–2 |

Open the Context menu and choose to lock or unlock the zero point.

3. To *reset the zero point* to the upper left corner of your document, simply double-click the ruler origin point in the upper left corner (Visual 4–1).

4. Drag the zero point to approximately the middle of your document. Go back to the ruler origin point and open the *Context* menu and select *Lock Zero Point* (Visual 4–2). You will notice that the icon of the intersecting lines disappears and that it is now impossible to reset the zero point. Use the same method to unlock the zero point.

Change the Units of Measure for the Entire Document

You can set the unit of measurement you wish to use by choosing InDesign (Mac) or Edit (Windows)> Preferences>Units & Increments. In the Ruler Units section of the dialog box you can set the Horizontal and Vertical rulers independently of each other. When you change these ruler preferences with no document open (for example, from inches to picas), these settings become the default for all new documents.

Switch the Units of Measure During Production

When you are working in a document, you can quickly change units of measurement by using the Context menu. Press **Control** (Mac) or **right-click** (Windows) on the ruler origin point, to display the Context menu. The unit of measure you choose will apply to both rulers. Or, you can apply a separate unit of measure for each ruler by using the Context menu on each of the rulers at the top and side of the page. If no rulers are showing, they have been hidden. Press **Command+R** (Mac) or **Control+R** (Windows) to bring them back into view. Press **Command+R** (Mac) or **Control+R** (Windows) to hide them, or select **Hide Rulers** from the Context menu.

Lock Zero Point

Points
Picas
✓ Inches
Inches Decimal
Millimeters
Centimeters

▶ *production tip*

The zero point is where measuring begins. The position of every object in your document is described by its distance from the zero point. Just like moving a ruler to different places on a piece of paper, the zero point is easily moved horizontally and vertically.

VISUAL | 4–3 |

Quickly change the units of measure for your document at the ruler origin point.

The X and Y Coordinate System

Every document you create in InDesign is automatically divided into an invisible grid of *horizontal* and *vertical coordinates*. When you move horizontally across the screen, you are moving along the *X coordinate axis*. When you move vertically, you are moving up or down the *Y coordinate axis*. The zero point determines whether the values of the coordinates are positive or negative. As you move the cursor to the right of the zero point, the X coordinate is a positive number that increases. As you move left of the zero point, the X coordinate is a negative number that decreases. On the Y axis, moving down vertically from the zero point gives you positive numbers, and moving up from the zero point gives you negative numbers. If you had graphing in high school math, you may already be familiar with this type of coordinate system. However, as Visual 4–4 shows, in InDesign, the vertical axis is exactly the

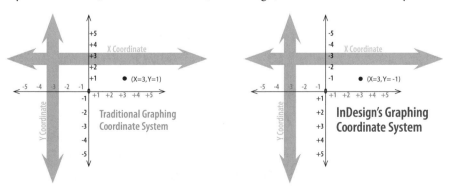

VISUAL | 4–4 |

In InDesign, coordinates increase as you move to the right and down from the zero point.

opposite of what you are used to in algebra. Remember, in InDesign's coordinate system the numbers on the Y axis are negative as you move *up* from the zero point. The X and Y coordinates for all the objects in your document are displayed in the Control panel. The values in the X and Y fields are displayed in the measurement system that you have selected to work in. Because the document area (including the pasteboard) is invisibly mapped into a grid—like graph paper—it becomes easy to describe the location of each element on the page as being so many units from the horizontal or vertical zero point, expressed as either positive or negative (Visual 4–5). But how do you know which point on your object InDesign is measuring to? Is it the center of the object, the right or left edge, or one of the corners? This point is known as the *reference point*. Just as InDesign lets you move the zero point to suit your needs, you have the flexibility to set the reference point of an object to one of nine positions. It can be at any of the four corners; the middle of the top, bottom, right or left edges; or right in the center of the object. Let's see exactly how the coordinate system and an object's point of reference work together.

VISUAL | 4–5 |

These coordinates plot exact placement on the document.

Reference point

X refers to the horizontal coordinate

Proxy

Y refers to the vertical coordinate

1. Create a **6" × 6"** document. Make sure your units of measure are set to inches and your zero point is in the upper left corner of the document.

2. Select the *Rectangle* tool (**M**) and draw anywhere in your document to create a rectangle. Notice the values of the X and Y coordinates in the Control panel.

3. Select your rectangle with the *Selection* tool (black arrow) and move it to the right. Watch the X coordinate increase as the rectangle moves to the right. Move it back to the left and watch the X coordinate decrease. Now move the rectangle up and down on the page. As it moves up the page, the Y coordinate decreases, and as you move it down the page the Y coordinate increases.

4. Now, look at the left end of the Control panel and you will see a series of nine small squares arranged in three rows and three columns (see Visual 4–5). One of these squares will be black and the rest will be white. This control is called the *proxy.* The proxy indicates the position of the *reference point* for the currently selected object. (The proxy is also found on the *Transform* panel that you can open by choosing *Window>Object & Layout>Transform*. Working with the proxy on either the *Transform* panel or the Control panel will give you the same results.) Look for the black square; it indicates where the reference point is located on your

▶ MOVING TOWARD MASTERY

The X and Y coordinates will change for each object when the reference point in the proxy is moved. In the two examples below, the objects have not been moved. Because the location of the reference point has moved in each example, the corresponding coordinates have also changed. Measuring begins from the reference point!

For most items the proxy is made up of nine squares. However, if the selected item is a straight line, the proxy will have only three squares active. These squares indicate the two ends and the middle point. If the selected item is a guideline, the proxy will show a horizontal or vertical line with only a center reference point. You cannot change the reference point of a guideline.

A straight line has 3 reference points

A horizontal guide coordinate

rectangle. Make sure your rectangle is still selected and click the center square in the proxy. The center square turns black, which means you have made the center of your selected rectangle the reference point. With the center black box on the proxy still selected, write down the X and Y coordinates of your rectangle.

5. Now click on the upper left square on the proxy and read the X and Y coordinates. Even though you have not moved your rectangle, your X and Y coordinates are different than the ones you wrote down a moment ago. This is because you have changed the reference point—it's now the upper left corner of your rectangle, instead of the center.

6. Let's place the rectangle in the exact center of your 6" × 6" document page. Make sure that your rectangle is selected, and click the center square on the proxy. Since your document is a six-inch square, three inches over from the side of the square and three inches down from the top would be the center of the page. Type **3** in both the X and Y coordinate fields and press Return. The rectangle should jump to the exact center of the page with the center point of the rectangle exactly at the center point of the page.

7. Select the rectangle and click the upper right reference point in the proxy. Type **6** in the X coordinate field and press Return. The rectangle should jump to align with the right edge of the page. Enter **0** in the Y coordinate field and press Return. The rectangle jumps to align with the top, right corner of the page.

You can now see the relationship between the reference point of an object and InDesign's X and Y coordinate system. The intersection of the coordinates displayed in the Control panel always indicates the position of the reference point that you have selected in the proxy.

Understanding Paths and Selection Tools

A shape or line created in InDesign is called a *path*. A path can be a *closed shape* such as a rectangle, or an *open shape* such as a line. The basic component of a path is a *point*. A path can have as little as two points—such as a line with beginning and ending points—or it can be complex, with numerous points. The straight or curved lines that connect the points are called *segments*. A simple rectangle is in reality a closed path made up of points and straight connecting segments.

VISUAL | 4–6 |

The Selection tool allows you to move and resize entire objects.

InDesign has two tools specifically designed for working with paths. Let's begin with the black arrow, the *Selection* tool (Visual 4–6). The Selection tool can be activated (when you are not using the Type tool) by pressing **V**. The Selection tool transforms a whole object—changing attributes such as size, scaling, position, skew, and rotation angle. It focuses on the outer dimensions and structure of an entire path. When you click on an open or closed path with the Selection tool, all the points on the path are selected. If the object has a fill, you can click on the fill to select all the points. With all the points selected, you can move the entire object. When you select another object with the tool, the previous object is deselected.

VISUAL | 4–7 |

You can select multiple objects by drawing a marquee that touches the border of each object.

Marquee

Am-
consequat
niam iliquisim es-
ectet wissequat. Ut-
Put luptat. Ut venis
aliquamcon
velenis

If you have several objects to select, you can select the first object and then add to the selection by pressing the **Shift** key while selecting the next object. Another way of selecting multiple paths with the Selection tool is to go to a blank space on the document and **drag a rectangle** (called a *marquee*) around the paths to select. Since the tool is designed to select whole paths, you can just touch the edge of each path with the marquee and the whole path will be selected.

VISUAL | 4–8 |

The Direct Selection tool selects individual points on a path.

Anchor point

Direction line

The *Direct Selection* tool—the white arrow—is next to the Selection tool in the Toolbox (Visual 4–8). When you're not using the Type tool you can press **A** to activate it. The Direct Selection tool is designed to select individual points or segments on a path. When

►MOVING TOWARD MASTERY

The **Selection** tool moves and resizes entire objects. When you are in the Type tool you can temporarily access the Selection tool by pressing **Command** (Mac) or **Control** (Windows) or switch to the Selection tool by pressing **ESC**.

Use the **Direct Selection** tool to reshape objects. The **Option** (Mac) or **ALT** (Windows) keyboard modifier makes a copy of the selected object/line segment. You may move an entire object with the Direct Selection tool by selecting the center point of the object.

► *production tip*
Double-click an object to switch between the selecting the frame and the object. Double-click a text frame to place the insertion point and switch to the Type tool.

a point is selected, it changes from a hollow square to a filled square. When your Direct Selection cursor is over a line segment, a slash appears next to it. When it is over a point, a box appears next to it. Use the Selection tool to change the dimension of an object. Use the Direct Selection tool to change the shape of an object. When you want to select all the points of a path using the Direct Selection tool, you can select the center point. You can also select all the points on a path by drawing a rectangular marquee, making sure all points are within the marquee's rectangle. If the object has a fill, you can click on the fill with the Direct Selection tool and move the whole path.

Width and Height Coordinates

Delete the rectangle from your document. In the next series of steps you are going to draw an ellipse and then resize its shape using the selection tools and the W (width) and H (height) fields on the Control panel.

1. To draw an ellipse, click on the tiny triangle in the lower right corner of the Rectangle tool and choose the *Ellipse* tool. Click and drag an ellipse in your document. Deselect the ellipse you have just drawn by pressing **Shift+Command+A** (Mac) or **Shift+Control+A** (Windows).

2. Click the edge of your ellipse with the *Direct Selection* tool. Five hollow squares appear on the ellipse—one in the center, and one on each quadrant of the outer edge. These are called *anchor points.* Click on one and it will turn solid, allowing you to edit it independently of the other anchor points. You should also see lines extending from one or more anchor points. These lines are called *direction lines.* If you drag any of the anchor points or the end of a direction line, the shape will be changed (Visual 4–8). Experiment with moving the direction lines to change the shape and then undo your changes by pressing **Command+Z** (Mac) or **Control+Z** (Windows) until the shape is back to the original.

3. Deselect the object by clicking in a blank spot in your document or by using the keyboard shortcut **Shift+Command+A** (Mac) or **Shift+Control+A** (Windows).

4. With the *Direction Selection* tool, click first on the edge of the shape and then on the center anchor point. All the hollow anchor points become filled, which means they cannot be not editable. Drag the center square and move the ellipse to another part of the page. With the anchor points still selected, drag the edge of the shape and move it again.

5. Now switch to the *Selection* tool by pressing **V.** The ellipse will look much different. You will see the rectangular bounding box that shows the outer boundaries of the shape. On the bounding box you will see eight tiny squares and a ninth square in the middle of the ellipse. The center square will be filled, and the outer squares will be hollow. These boxes are called *handles*. Drag any of the handles to change the dimension of the ellipse (Visual 4–9).

VISUAL |4–9|

Drag any of the handles to change the dimension of the ellipse.

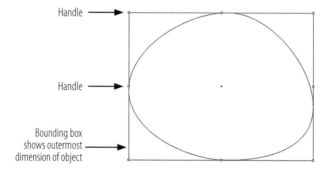

Handle

Handle

Bounding box shows outermost dimension of object

6. There are several ways to move the entire ellipse: drag the center point, or click on and drag the edge of the ellipse, or click and drag a section of the bounding box. Use each of these methods and practice moving the ellipse. (Be careful not to drag a hollow handle, this will resize the object.)

7. Now, note the X and Y coordinates displayed in the Control panel. The coordinates indicate the location of the reference point of the ellipse designated in the proxy. Look at the W and H coordinates. These measurements show the width and height of the selected shape. As you drag on the handles on the bounding box of the ellipse, the dimensions in the Control panel will also change.

8. Type **4** in the *W* field and **3** in the *H* field. Press Return. Your ellipse should change size.

9. With the 4" × 3" ellipse selected, click on the center reference point on the proxy. Now type **3** in the *X coordinate* field and **3** in the *Y coordinate* field and press Return. The ellipse should now be centered on your page.

Working With Text

The copy in your document communicates a message while adding texture, color, shape, and contrast to your layout. Your ability to use text as a design element is an important skill to develop. In this next section you will learn how to create multiple column text frames and import (or *Place*) text from word processing documents.

Multi-column Text

Creating text columns within text frames is a simple process. When the Paragraph Formatting Controls are active, you can find the column options near the middle of the panel (Visual 4–10). The space between the columns is called a *gutter* (or *alley*). To change the width of the gutter, select the text frame and press **Command+B** (Mac) or **Control+B** (Windows) to open the Text Frame Options dialog box. In the Gutter field, enter the desired value for the gutter width. You can type the value in a unit of measure such as 1p (1 pica).

VISUAL |4–10|

Click the up or down arrows or type a number in the Number of Columns field to create multiple columns inside a text frame. You can also create columns in Text Frame Options.

1. Draw a frame in your document. Select the *Type* tool and click the frame to instantly convert it to a text frame. Select the *Paragraph Formatting Controls* and change the number of columns to **3** (Visual 4–10). Change the gutter width to **p6** (six points). Press Return.

2. Choose *Type>Fill with Placeholder Text.* Text will fill your text frame. With the *Type* tool active, select all the text using the shortcut key and reduce the point size until the last text column is empty.

3. Place the cursor in the middle of a line in the first column. Press **Enter** on the number keypad. This makes text jump to the next column. If you are in the habit of pressing the Return key over and over to force text to jump to another column—

don't! Simply insert the cursor where you want the text to break and press **Enter** on the number keypad. If your keyboard doesn't have a numeric keypad with an Enter key, open the *Context* menu and select *Insert Break Character>Column Break.*

Don't get into the bad habit of pressing the Return key multiple times to force the text to flow to the next column. If your layout changes, you'll need to delete all those manual keyboard entries. When you press the Enter key on the number keypad to insert a column break character, it will be much easier to simply remove it, if you have to revise the column break later. Creating columns within text frames is simple and useful for projects. More often, however, designers will create separate text frames in different places on the page and flow the text between the frames. You will learn that technique, called *threading,* later in this chapter. Right now, you will learn how to use the **Place** command to bring text files created in a variety of word processors into your InDesign documents. What a timesaver!

Placing Text

The keyboard shortcut for placing text—**Command+D** (Mac) or **Control+D** (Windows)—is one you will want to memorize. You will use it again and again to import text or graphics. Pressing the keyboard shortcut brings up the Place dialog box.

Two important features of the Place dialog box are the choices to **Show Import Options** and **Replace Selected Item**, in the lower left corner (Visual 4–11). Show Import Options, among other things, gives you control over how different

versions of Microsoft Word text files are handled. Choosing Replace Selected
Item will replace any text that is selected within a text frame with the contents
of the file you are placing. If the frame is selected with the Selection or the
Direct Selection tool, the entire contents of the text frame will be replaced.

There are three methods for importing text files: placing them into an
existing frame, placing them into a new frame, and simply dropping the
contents onto a page. In the next exercise, you will create a new 8.5" × 11"
document, add a frame, and then use all three methods of placing text.
You will be using a text file called *04 Copyfit.doc* from the *04 Artwork and
Resources* folder in the CD accompanying this text. Find and load your CD.

Placing Text into an Existing Text Frame

In this exercise we will place text into a frame that you have already created.

1.   Draw a **6" × 9"** text frame. Set the reference point in the center at X coordinate: **4.25"**,
      and Y coordinate: **5.5"**. Create **3 columns** with a **1-pica** gutter.

2.   Insert the project CD, if you have not already done so. Press **Command+D** (Mac) or
      Control+D (Windows) to open the Place dialog box. Navigate to the project CD. Find
      the *04 Artwork and Resources* folder and select the text file called *04 Copyfit.doc*.

VISUAL |4–12|

The navigation route to
the *04 Copyfit.doc* file.

3.   Uncheck *Show Import Options* and *Replace Selected Item* in
      the lower left corner of the dialog box. Press Return.

4.   Move the cursor to the upper left corner of the text box. You
      will see tiny lines of type enclosed with long parentheses
      (Visual 4–13). This icon means your text cursor is loaded and
      ready to place text into an existing frame. Now click anywhere
      in the text frame and type will flow into all three columns.
      Notice the square with the red plus sign (**+**) in the lower right column. A red plus
      is the *overset* symbol—it means there is more text than the text frame will hold.

VISUAL |4–13|

The loaded text cursor is
ready to place copy into
an existing frame.

► *production tip*

To delete overset text:
Place the cursor at the
end of the copy. Press
Shift+CMD+End (Mac) or
Shift+CTRL+End (Windows)
to select copy beyond the
cursor. Then press Delete.

5. To delete the overset text, place the cursor at the end of the visible copy. If you are working on a Mac, select all the "invisible" overset text, beyond the plus sign, by pressing **Shift+Command+End**. Release those keys and then press **Delete.** If you are a Windows user, place your cursor at the end of the visible copy. Press **Shift+Control+End** to select the overset text. Release those keys and then press **Delete**. The plus sign should disappear as the text beyond the frame is deleted.

Place Text by Creating a New Frame

In this exercise, you will import text and create a new text frame to place it into, at the same time. First, delete the three-column text box, so that your document is blank.

VISUAL |4–14|

The loaded text cursor will create a text frame when the copy is dropped into the document.

Imsep pretu tempu revol bileg rokam revoc tephe rosve etepe tenov sindu turqu brevt elliu repar tiuve tamia queso utage udulc

1. Press **Command+D** (Mac) or **Control+D** (Windows) and select the *04 Copyfit. doc* file again. Press Return. Move the loaded cursor over the blank document and look carefully at its shape. This time you will not see parentheses around the text cursor. Instead, you will see straight lines on the top and left edge. This icon indicates that a new frame will be created for the text (Visual 4–14).

2. Drag the loaded text cursor to create a frame. When you release the mouse, text will flow into the new text frame.

3. Change the Width and Height to **5" × 7"** and create three columns. Again, notice the overset symbol in the out port in the lower right corner. Delete the overset text.

Place Text by Dropping Into the Page

This method of placing text drops the text into the document and lets it spread from margin guide to margin guide. Delete the text frame from your document.

1. Open the *Place* dialog box by using the keyboard shortcut and select *04 Copyfit.doc* one more time. Press Return. Notice that the shape of the loaded cursor is the same as in Visual 4–14.

2. Click the cursor anywhere on the document. A text frame will stretch from margin to margin with the top positioned wherever you clicked on the page.

3. Delete the overset text.

Estimating Word Count

Look at the file you just placed and you will see that there are numbers scattered throughout the text. These numbers represent the *word count*. Now you can estimate how many words, in a specific font, type size, and leading, will fit in this text box. You can use the *04 Copyfit.doc* file when you design the text areas for an InDesign project and then tell the copywriter how many words will be needed to fill the allotted space. Another way to estimate the word count for any passage of placeholder text is to highlight the copy and then open the Info panel. The character, word, line, and paragraph count is displayed at the bottom of the panel (Visual 4–15). *Note:* If this section of the Info panel is not visible, open the panel's options menu and choose Show Options.

VISUAL | 4–15 |

The Info panel displays the character, word, and line count for a selected text frame.

Managing Text Flow

Now that you have mastered the basics of placing text, it's time to learn to manage the text flow as it is being placed into a document. You will learn these four techniques: *manual text flow, semi-automatic text flow, automatic text flow,* and *automatic text flow with a fixed number of pages.* You will need to place the *04 Copyfit.doc* file from your CD for the following exercises.

Manual Text Flow

When you use *manual text flow,* you make all the decisions regarding where placed text will be positioned and how it will flow. You have total control, but as the "manual" name implies, this method is the slowest.

1. Create a new document. Page size **7" × 5"**, landscape orientation. Enter **3 columns** with **1p** gutter, **0.5"** margins. Press Return.

2. Look closely at the column guides. Notice that there is no text frame on the page. The column indicators are only guides—ready to hold a graphics or text frame. Again, place the **04 Copyfit.doc** file by using the keyboard shortcut. Move the cursor over to the upper left corner of the first column. The cursor shape indicates a new text frame will be created. Click in the upper left corner and the first column will fill with copy. You will see an overset symbol (**+**) at the bottom of the first column. The text will just "sit" there until you manually flow it to another column.

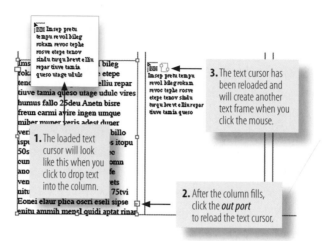

A click on the first column's out port reloads the text cursor for placing text in another column.

3. Press **Command** (Mac) or **Control** (Windows) to switch to the *Selection* tool. Click on the plus sign in the text out port. This process is called *reloading* the cursor. Your cursor has now changed into a loaded cursor, and you can see that the shape has changed (Visual 4–16).

4. Click in the upper left corner of the second column to flow text into this column. Reload your cursor by clicking on the text out port box. Click in the upper left corner of the third column and it will fill with copy.

5. Switch to the *Type* tool and place the cursor at the end of the text in the third column. Delete the overset text by pressing **Shift+Command+End**, then **Delete** (Mac) or **Shift+Control+End**, then **Delete** (Windows).

Semi-automatic Text Flow

Flowing text manually from column to column is a neat technique, but imagine how tedious it would be if you had to do that for a 10-page document! InDesign is always one step ahead of the user—and has designed a second way to flow text called *semi-automatic.*

VISUAL |4–17|

The semi-automatic text flow icon.

1. Select all the text frames in your document and then delete by using keyboard shortcuts. Place the *04 Copyfit.doc* file once again. This time, hold down the **Option** (Mac) or **Alt** (Windows) key as you hold the loaded cursor in the upper left corner of the first column. Notice the shape of the cursor changes into a snake pattern each time you press the Option or Alt key (Visual 4–17). Press this key a few times to get used to the difference between the cursors. This cursor means your text will be placed in *semi-automatic text flow* mode.

2. Hold down the **Option** (Mac) or **Alt** (Windows) key and click in the upper left corner. The text will fill the first column and the cursor will remain loaded. Hold down the **Option** or **Alt** key and click in the second column. The text flows into the middle column. As long as you continue to hold the Option or Alt key as you click to drop text, you remain in semi-automatic flow mode and the remaining text will remain loaded in the text icon.

3. Continue in semi-automatic mode and fill the last column. Press **ESC** to get out of semi-automatic text flow mode. Delete the overset text.

► *production tip*

To delete overset text: Place the cursor at the end of the copy. Press Shift+CMD+End (Mac) or Shift+CTRL+End (Windows) to select copy beyond the cursor. Then press Delete.

Automatic Text Flow

Manual and semi-automatic text flow provide the most control for placing text in individual text frames on a single page, or a series of non-contiguous pages. *Automatic text flow* is another method of flowing text that is fast, and automatically inserts exactly the right number of pages required to hold the text passage.

1. Create a new file, **3" × 5"** and **0.5"** margins.

VISUAL | 4–18 |

The automatic text flow icon.

2. Place the *04 Copyfit.doc* file so that you have a loaded cursor. Hold down the Shift key as you move the cursor to the upper left corner of the page. Click inside the page margins.

3. Open the *Pages* panel by pressing **Command+F12** (Mac) or **F12** (Windows) or by choosing *Window>Pages.* Notice that you now have more than one page in your document. When you place text in *automatic flow* mode, InDesign automatically adds as many pages as necessary.

Automatic Text Flow with Fixed Number of Pages

The automatic text flow option is great for many projects—but what if you must make the text fit on only four pages? The *automatic text flow with fixed number of pages* technique allows you to place text on a specified number of pages only.

1. Create a **3" × 5"** document, **0.5"** margins, and **4** pages.

2. Load the text cursor with *04 Copyfit.doc.*

VISUAL | 4–19 |

The automatic text flow with fixed number of pages icon.

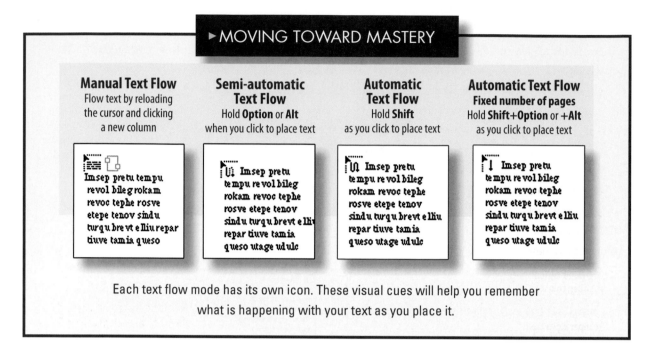

▶ MOVING TOWARD MASTERY

Manual Text Flow
Flow text by reloading the cursor and clicking a new column

Semi-automatic Text Flow
Hold **Option** or **Alt** when you click to place text

Automatic Text Flow
Hold **Shift** as you click to place text

Automatic Text Flow
Fixed number of pages
Hold **Shift+Option** or **+Alt** as you click to place text

Each text flow mode has its own icon. These visual cues will help you remember what is happening with your text as you place it.

3. This time, hold down **Shift+Option** (Mac) or **Shift+Alt** (Windows) as you *click and drop* the text onto the *upper left corner* of page one. The text will fill the available space on the four pages and then stop. Notice the familiar overset symbol in the out port at the end of page four. Now you can select all your text and adjust the point size and leading to make the copy fit into your four-page document.

About Threaded Text Frames

In the exercises you just completed, text was flowing from one column to the next column. Text can also flow between individual text frames that are connected through a process called *threading*. As shown in Visual 4–20, each threaded text frame can have different text frame attributes including inset, fill, stroke and columns. Because threaded text frames are connected, you can use **Command+A** (Mac) or **Control+A** (Windows) to select all the type in the threaded frames.

VISUAL | 4–20 |

These separate text frames are threaded together, allowing text to flow from one frame to the next.

In port

Out port

Text thread

Seeing Links and Threads

This exercise will familiarize you with using threaded text frames.

1. Create a new document, **8.5" × 11"**, margins **0.5"**. Scatter three text
frames on the document. Make some frames tall and some wide.

2. Place the *04 Copyfit.doc* file. Drop the text into the first frame. You
will see the overset symbol (+) in the lower right of your frame.

3. Choose either of the Selection tools and click on the overset text symbol.
The cursor is reloaded and its icon changes. As you move the loaded text
cursor over the second text frame, it changes to show two small chain links,
indicating these two frames will soon be threaded together (Visual 4–21).

VISUAL | 4–21 |

Frames must be threaded
together before copy will
flow from one to the next.

4. Click to place the text into the second text frame. Notice that the overset
text symbol that was in the first text frame has now been replaced with
a blue triangle. The blue triangle means this box is now an ***out port.*** The
upper left side of the second text frame also has a blue triangle, an ***in
port.*** Flow copy into the third frame using the same process.

5. Now from the Menu bar, choose ***View>Extras>Show Text Threads.*** When you select
a text frame, you will see lines connecting the ***in*** and ***out ports*** on your frames. These
show the direction and order of the text flow. A triangle in the out port means that
the text is linked to another frame. A plus in the out port means that text is overset—
that there is too much text to fit in the frame. When the first in port and the last out
port in a series of linked text frames are empty, it means that all the text has been
placed (Visual 4–22). Don't close your file—we're going to use it for the next demo.

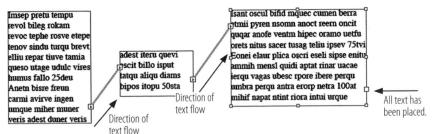

VISUAL | 4–22 |

Text threads show the
direction of the copy flow.

type basics

MANAGING UNDERLINES

During the days of old-fashioned typing, people used to underline text to add emphasis or to indicate the title of a book.

Unfortunately, that habit has carried over into the world of digital type, and most people simply click an icon to underline a word or sentence.

Today, italics are used to indicate the name of a book or to add emphasis. A heavier typeface can also be used to make a word or phrase stand out.

Typewriter-style underlines are rarely used in professional typesetting. If you must underline text, use InDesign's Underline Options capabilities in the Control panel menu options to control the weight of the underline and to avoid cutting through descenders.

<u>Old-fashioned typewriting and word processing programs</u>

Never cut through a descender with any type of rule or underline!

This underline is too heavy, and overpowers the copy.

Unlinking Text Frames

There will be times when you flow text into the wrong frame. Of course, you can simply press the Undo shortcut, but that method is only practical if you catch your error shortly after it was made. Here's another way to unlink threaded text frames.

1. Select the text frame in the middle of your text thread.

2. Double-click on the in port or the out port of the middle frame. If you double-click on the in port, the text flow will be cut off at the in port (A) and there will be a text overflow symbol in the first frame (B). If you double-click on the out port, text will be cut off at that point. The third frame is now empty and a text overflow symbol appears in the second frame.

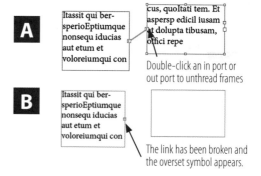

Double-click an in port or out port to unthread frames

The link has been broken and the overset symbol appears.

When should frames be threaded?

Now that you know how to thread text frames, you're probably wondering when you should use them. When text columns need to have individual attributes such as width, height, fill or stroke, you will want to use threaded frames. For instance, let's say you are working on a newsletter, and you want to shorten the third column to accommodate a photo. If you are using a single text frame with three columns, this will be difficult because you can only shorten the entire text frame instead of single columns. When you use threaded text frames to create columns, you can shorten just the third frame, letting the text reflow. Generally, using threaded text frames provides more flexibility than using single frames with multiple columns.

Underlining Words and Paragraph Rules

If you read the *Type Basics* on the previous page, you already know that underlining individual words is rarely done when setting type. Underlining is a throwback to the "typewriter days" when it was the only method of adding emphasis.

Underlining Words

For those rare times you need to underline text, you should not allow the rule to cut through a descender. Fortunately, InDesign has a complete and sophisticated way for you to adjust the weight and position of the underline. First, select the text you would like to underline. Then, select Underline Options from the options menu at the far right end of the Control panel. In the Underline Options dialog box (Visual 4–23), check the Underline On box and then adjust the weight, offset, color, and type of the line as desired.

VISUAL |4–23|

The Underline Options dialog box is found under the Control panel menu options.

Paragraph Rules

Paragraph rules may look like underlining, but they are an altogether different matter. Paragraph rules are design elements, and InDesign allows you to set rules in two places in each paragraph: 1) on or above the baseline of the first line of text; or 2) at the end of a paragraph. The Paragraph Rules function allows you to use color, styles, indents, and offsets to create just about any rule you'd ever want. Visual 4–24 shows some paragraph rules in action. The Paragraph Rules dialog box can be accessed by using a keyboard shortcut: **Command+Option+J** (Mac) or **Control+Alt+J** (Windows), or by clicking on the options menu in the Control panel and choosing Paragraph Rules.

Keyboard Shortcut

 CMD+OPT+J   **Paragraph Rules**

 CTRL+ALT+P

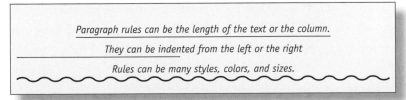

Paragraph rules can be the length of the text or the column.

They can be indented from the left or the right

Rules can be many styles, colors, and sizes.

VISUAL |4–24|

Paragraph rules are great design elements—when used with discretion.

Applying a Rule Below a Paragraph

Whenever possible, apply rules as part of the paragraph formatting. A document that is filled with lines created with the Line tool is hard to edit because each line must be individually repositioned. Lines that are created as paragraph rules, will reflow as the copy changes.

1. Create a new document using the default settings. Draw a text frame and type your *name* on the first line and your ***phone number*** on the second line; use a hard return between the lines. Increase the type size to **48 points** on **60-point** leading.

2. With the blinking cursor somewhere in the first paragraph (the first line), press **Command+Option+J** (Mac) or **Control+Alt+J** (Windows) to access the *Paragraph Rules* dialog box (Visual 4–25). You can also choose *Paragraph Rules* from the Control panel options menu.

VISUAL |4–25|

Paragraph rules are design elements. To have a paragraph rule, you must have a paragraph, which means you will need to place a hard return in your copy.

▶ *production tip*

The Width field in the Paragraph Rules dialog box can be set to Column or Text. With Column selected, the line stretches from the left edge of the column to the right edge. With Text selected, the line extends only as long as the last line of text.

3. *Rule below* means that a rule will be placed after a paragraph (created by a hard return). Select *Rule Below* from the list and check the *Rule On* option box. Select *8 pt* in the *Weight* field menu, and *Dotted* in the *Type* field menu. The *Width* field should be set to *Text*. Enter **0.125"** in the *Offset* field. When you increase the offset, you push the rule farther down, away from the baseline. Press Return and your type should look similar to the sample in Visual 4–25. Keep this document open for the next exercise.

Applying a Rule Above a Paragraph

A *rule above* a paragraph will appear on the first baseline or will be offset above the first baseline of the paragraph. Applying a rule above a paragraph can be a little tricky because you'll need to add an offset value so that the rule doesn't cut through your type.

1. Click in the line that contains your name. First, you will turn off the rule below the paragraph. Open the *Paragraph Rules* dialog box and make sure that *Rule Below* is selected in the list, then uncheck the *Rule On* option. Click *Preview* and you will see the rule has disappeared. Press Return.

2. Now, you will add a rule above the phone number. Place the cursor in the line with your phone number. Open the *Paragraph Rules* dialog box and select *Rule Above* from the list. Be sure to check the *Rule On* option box. Select a line type and weight of your choice. Because the rule line will be drawn on the baseline, you'll need to enter a value in the *Offset* field. Type **p48** (48 points) to push the line up off the baseline.

How to Check Spelling in Your Document

It's a good idea to always run a spell check before printing a document. But remember, even though InDesign's spell check function is excellent, it doesn't replace manual proofing. Both methods should be used to ensure accurate copy. To check spelling, simply press **Command+I** (Mac) **or Control+I** (Windows). When the Check Spelling dialog box appears, you will need to make a choice in the Search list. The following list describes the options:

► The **All Documents** option checks the spelling of all open InDesign documents.

► The **Document** option checks the entire document you are working on. This is a great feature unless you have several pages of directory information including last names. If you would prefer to skip those sections of the document, choose the Story option.

► **Story option** checks spelling in the selected text frame and all threaded text frames.

► The **To End of Story** option checks all the words beyond the blinking cursor.

VISUAL | 4–26 |

Choices in the Check Spelling options will vary depending on what is selected.

► If you have text highlighted before opening the Check Spelling dialog box, then you have another choice. **Selection** checks the spelling of the highlighted text.

Once you have made a choice in the Search list, simply click *Start* to begin the process. InDesign will alert you of any questionable words and possible errors. When the checking is complete, click *Done* to dismiss the dialog box.

Understanding Tracking and Kerning

You already know what leading is. Leading is the vertical spacing between lines of type, measured from baseline to baseline. *Tracking* adjusts horizontal spacing between all the characters on a line. A single paragraph can contain characters with many different tracking values. *Positive tracking* increases spacing between characters; *negative tracking* decreases spacing between characters (Visual 4–27). Tracking values are shown in the Paragraph and Character Formatting Controls.

VISUAL | 4–27 |

The Tracking control is found in both the Character and Paragraph Controls panels.

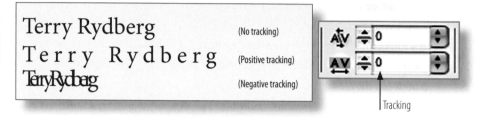

Terry Rydberg (No tracking)

T e r r y R y d b e r g (Positive tracking)

TerryRydberg (Negative tracking)

Tracking

Adjusting Text Spacing with Tracking

Keyboard Shortcut

 OPT+ → OR ←

 ALT+ → OR ←

Track highlight words

1. Create a new *letter-sized* document. Draw a text frame, type your full name and change the point size to **60-point**.

2. To tighten the tracking of your text: Highlight text you want tracked, hold down **Option** (Mac) or **Alt** (Windows), and press the **Left Arrow** key near the number pad. At first the text will still be readable, but if you keep pressing the arrow key, notice that the text ultimately reverses itself. Be careful not to overdo tracking!

3. Delete the text box and draw a new one. Type your name in it again in **60-point** type. Select all the text. Press **Option** (Mac) or **Alt** (Windows) and the **Right Arrow** key to loosen the tracking. Keep pressing the right arrow key and you will see that it doesn't take very long for your name to become just a series of individual letters. Again, be conservative with tracking. When misused, it inhibits readability.

You will occasionally use tracking to fine-tune your type. At times you may want to use negative tracking to give your text a little more refined look, especially with headline type. You will also use tracking to fit troublesome lines of type into the line measure. While InDesign has taken care of much of this for you with its multiline composition feature, there will be times when you will need to manually adjust tracking. For instance, at the end of a paragraph, you should avoid leaving part of a hyphenated word or any word shorter than four letters on its own line. As a typesetter, you need to make a decision: either tighten tracking slightly to make room for the word in the line above, or loosen tracking to bring the whole word or an additional word to the last line of a paragraph.

The goal is to alter the word spacing so slightly that no one will ever notice. You have gone too far with your tracking if the tracked text looks darker or lighter than the surrounding text. *Tracking should be invisible to the untrained eye.*

Adjust Character Spacing with Manual Kerning

Closely related to tracking is kerning. *Kerning* is the horizontal spacing between two characters only. You should kern letter pairs when spacing between characters is too wide or too narrow. For instance, look closely at the number 740 shown in Visual 4–28. Before you started reading this book, it would have looked perfectly fine. But with your professional eye, you now see that the spacing between the 7 and 4 looks much wider than the spacing between the 4 and the 0.

Kerning will correct this. Place your cursor in between the 7 and the 4. Do not highlight any text. The same keyboard shortcuts used for positive and negative tracking are also used for kerning; press **Option+Left Arrow** (Mac) or **Alt+Left Arrow** (Windows) to tighten the space between the numbers. The amount of adjustment is shown in the Kerning field in the Control panel. InDesign adjusts the kerning in units of one-thousandth of an em. (You will remember that an em is a unit of measure equivalent to the point size—an em space in 10-point type is 10 points wide.)

VISUAL |4–28|

Place the cursor between two letters to adjust kerning.

Spacing is loose | Kerning of -100 has been applied

740 740

Raised cap needs kerning

Words strain, crack, and sometimes break, under the burden.

T.S. Eliot

Words strain, crack, and sometimes break, under the burden.

Drop cap needs kerning   T.S. Eliot

These pairs usually need kerning		These pairs are not kerned	
To	WA	To	WA
Tr	we	TR	we
Ta	P.	Ta	P.
Yo	T.	Yo	T.
yo	TA	yo	TA
Ya	PA	Ya	PA
Wo	Po	Wo	Po
Wa		Wa	

As shown in the column on the right, kerning is also affected by the typeface used in each letter pair.

VISUAL |4–29|

Kerning is often used with raised and drop caps.

A more common place to kern letter pairs is when using drop and raised caps. Visual 4–29 shows what they look like without kerning. As shown above, some letter pairs usually need kerning. Your goal is to have the "color" of text look even. Big gaps between letter pairs make a word look airy.

AUTOMATIC OPTICAL KERNING

When professionals design a font, they build in rules for letter pair spacing. Unfortunately, the built-in kerning parameters don't cover every letter pair scenario. That is why manual kerning is sometimes needed. But InDesign has gone one step further. It allows you to select **Optical Kerning** *in the Kerning field on the Control panel. With Optical Kerning selected, InDesign goes beyond the built-in letter pair parameters and makes kerning decisions based on the shape of each character to even out how the type looks. This is a huge timesaver. InDesign does an excellent job of making text look great—with very little effort on the part of the person setting the type.*

Working With Images

The perfect image, combined with beautiful type, form a "one-two punch" that makes a document which is both memorable and effective. Most of the images you use will be either scanned, created in a vector-based drawing program such as Adobe Illustrator, or created in a pixel-based program such as Adobe Photoshop. As powerful as InDesign is, it is not a true drawing program. But you shouldn't underestimate InDesign's drawing capabilities. If you have already used Adobe Illustrator, you have seen tools and functions in InDesign that look very familiar. If you haven't used Illustrator, you will learn about many basic drawing functions that are common to both programs, later in the book. InDesign can place a variety of file formats including EPS, TIFF, and JPEG. A great feature is the ability to place InDesign documents and native Adobe Illustrator (AI) and Photoshop (PSD) files without conversion to a PDF, EPS or TIFF format.

Three methods of placing artwork will be discussed in this section: *place and drop, place and drag, and place into a frame.* The same keyboard shortcut is used to place text or images: **Command+D** (Mac) or **Control+D** (Windows). InDesign does not require a specific type of frame to hold a graphic and another to hold text. In fact, as you have already seen when placing text, you don't need a frame at all! Let's get started learning how to place images. You will need the CD that accompanies this book for these exercises.

Place and Drop, and Rotate

1. Create a new document, **8.5" × 11"**. Open the *Place* dialog box. Navigate to the *Chapter 04 Artwork and Resources* folder on your CD. Choose *04 Demo.tif.* Press Return.

2. Notice the loaded icon looks like a paintbrush surrounded by straight lines (Visual 4–30). Just as when placing text, the square lines indicate that a new frame will be created. Click in the upper left corner of your document and the photo will appear at full size.

VISUAL | 4–30 |

When placing images, a thumbnail of the image appears on the cursor.

3. When you are working with images, it is helpful to change the resolution of your screen so that you can see the fine details of an image. Go to *View>Display Performance>High Quality Display* (Visual 4–31). Now, use **Command+4** (Mac) or **Control+4** (Windows) to zoom in to 400%. When these little girls are seen at high resolution, you can see the breakfast crumbs around their lips. Change the display performance back to *normal resolution* by going to *View>Display Performance>Typical Display.* See the difference in detail?

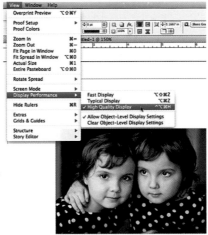

VISUAL | 4–31 |

It's easier to see the details of an image with your display set to a higher resolution.

4. Change your view back to *100%* by using the keyboard shortcut **Command+1** (Mac) or **Control +1**(Windows). Notice that the photo is contained within a frame. Select the frame with the *Selection* tool and move the arrow just outside the lower right corner of the frame. When you see a curved arrow (Visual 4–32), click and drag to rotate the frame and image on your screen. As the image is rotated, the degree of rotation is displayed next to the cursor and in the Control panel. When you release the mouse, the image will remain at its rotated position. To return it to its original location, enter **0** in the *Rotation Angle* field of the Control panel. As you were working on this exercise, you may have noticed a transparent doughnut in the center of the image. This is the *Content Grabber* and will be discussed later.

Rotation arrow ⟶

Rotation Angle field

VISUAL | 4–32 |

When the Rotation arrow is visible, you can drag to rotate the image and frame.

Place and Drag, and Resizing Images

As you can see, working with images is not complicated, but you do need to know what you're doing! We're going to place our little girls again—this time you'll place the image at various sizes. Images have width and height dimensions. When both dimensions are at 100%, the picture is *full size*. Often we need to use images at a size larger or smaller than their 100% actual size. It's easy to do this in InDesign.

VISUAL | 4–33 |

As you resize an image percentages are displayed below the cursor. Percentages are also displayed in the Control panel.

X and Y Scale Percentages

X: 45%
Y: 45%

X Scale Percentage

Constrain proportions for scaling is active

45%

45%

0°

0°

Y Scale Percentage

▶ *production tip*

Once an image has been placed into a layout, you can easily check the scale by first clicking the image with the Selection tool, and then looking in the X or Y Scale Percentage fields of the Control panel.

1. Use the *Place* command to place *04 Demo.tif.* Again, notice the straight lines by the paintbrush in the thumbnail image, indicating that it will create a frame for the graphic. Drop in the upper left corner of your document. This is the image's full size. Changing the size of an image is called *scaling,* and we'll do that in the next step.

2. Place *04 Demo.tif* again. This time, click and slowly drag the mouse. As you drag, look in the lower right corner next to the cursor and you will see X and Y percentages displayed (Visual 4–33). These percentages tell you the size the image will be when the mouse is released. Any number less than 100% is a *reduction* in size, and any number larger than 100% is an *enlargement*. Release your mouse when the X and Y percentages are right around **45%**. When you release your mouse, notice that the percentages are no longer displayed. Once an image has been placed, you can find out its percentage of enlargement or reduction in the Control panel. Click the image with the *Direct Selection* tool and look in the Scale X and Scale Y Percentage fields of the Control panel (Visual 4–34) to see if your image is approximately 45%.

3. Place *04 Demo.tif* once again. This time, drag to enlarge the image to 150%. After you release the mouse, select the image with the *Direct Selection* tool and look in the Scale X and Y Percentage fields on the Control panel to confirm that it is at 150% . If it isn't, simply enter **150** in either field and press Return. Verify that the button that constrains proportions for scaling is turned on is gray (Visual 4–34), so both the X (horizontal) and Y (vertical) dimensions of the image will be at 150%. If it isn't, click it to turn it on.

Before we move on, let's summarize what you've just learned. **Command+D** (Mac) or **Control+D** (Windows) places an image. Once the cursor is loaded, you can either click to drop the image at its full size, or click and drag to

▶ MOVING TOWARD MASTERY

PROPORTIONAL SCALING IS IMPORTANT!

Images have width and height dimensions, called X Scale and Y Scale Percentage. When the X (width) and Y (height) scale percentages are the same, the image is **scaled proportionately**. *If you resize the photo so that the width dimension is at 50% and the height is at 100%, the picture is the same height, but it is half its original width. This is* **disproportional scaling**. *If you*

were using a picture of clouds as a background photo, the photo could be scaled disproportionately without any consequences. However, you want to keep most images—products, people—proportional, meaning the width and height percentages will be the same. Always check these percentages by selecting the image with the Direct Selection tool and finding the percentage in the X and Y Scale Percentage fields of the Control panel.

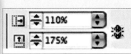

Click here to scale vertical and horizontal dimensions uniformly.

Proportional Scaling

Disproportional Scaling
The Y (vertical) dimension has been scaled to a greater percentage than the X (horizontal) dimension, making the photo tall and thin.

resize, or *scale*, the image proportionately. After an image is in a layout, you can check the scale by selecting the image with the Direct Selection tool and looking at the Control panel. An image can be rotated by dragging the corner when the Rotation arrow is displayed. Those are the basics, and if you're confident that you've mastered those skills, you're ready to move on.

Place into a Frame, and Crop the Image

Remember that transparent doughnut that appears whenever you mouse over an image? That's the Content Grabber, a new feature in InDesign CS5. Among other things, the Content Grabber helps you reposition images inside a frame. The process of showing only a portion of an image is called *cropping*. For instance, you might have a great photo of your significant other, taken when you were on a road trip. Unfortunately, above their head is the sign from the gas station where you made a pit stop! With InDesign, you simply adjust the image inside the frame so that the focal point is the adoring grin of your significant other. Most images are improved with strategic cropping and scaling. In the next exercise, you'll use the Content grabber to separate the twins shown above, in the *Moving Toward Mastery* section. You will also learn how to proportionately scale an image inside the frame. Let's get started.

Place into a Frame, and Crop the Image

1. Place *04 Crop.psd* in the upper left corner of your document, using the "place and drop" method. We'll use this as a reference photo at actual size, or 100%.

2. Select the *Rectangle* tool, click in the middle of your document, and enter **1** in the width and height fields to create a 1-inch square. Use the Place command to load *04 Crop.psd.* When the picture has been placed, notice that only one of the twins, Julia, appears in the frame. The image is placed at full size, no matter what size the frame (Visual 4–34).

3. Select the image with the *Selection* tool and as you hover your mouse over the image, the transparent doughnut (the *Content grabber*) will appear. Click and pause on top of the doughnut and you will see the rest of the image that extends beyond the frame as semi-transparent, or *ghosted*. Click on the doughnut and slide to the left to crop out Julia, and bring the other twin, Sophia, into view. The *Content grabber* makes it easy to position the part of the photo that should be displayed in the frame.

4. Now let's say you want Sophia's image to be larger. If you pull on one of the photo's frame handles, it simply makes the frame bigger, allowing more of the photo to be revealed. To make the photo resize proportionately and maintain its crop, check *Auto-Fit* on the Control panel. Select the photo with the *Selection* tool, and pull a corner frame handle to proportionately make the photo larger or smaller. For those of you who love keyboard shortcuts, you can also proportionately scale an image by selecting it with the *Selection* tool, press **Shift+Command** (Mac) or **Shift+Control** (Windows) and pull a corner frame handle.

When Auto Fit is checked, the image will scale proportionately.

5. You've learned how to crop and scale—how about moving the image to a different area of the layout? Simply click on the image with the *Selection* tool (not on the doughnut) and move the image (and frame) to a new location.

The Container (Frame) and the Content (Image)

When you are working with images, remember that you are managing two components: the frame (or *container*) that holds the image, and the image (or *content*). When working with images, you need to first decide if your action is affecting the container or the content. If you understand the difference between the Selection and Direct Selection tools, you will realize that you would use the Selection tool to resize the frame, and the Direct Selection tool to resize or move the content inside the frame. It's easy to confuse image frame boundaries with the container frame guides! When this happens, frustration can occur. For instance, say you want to delete the image, but not the frame. If you have the container frame selected and press Delete, the frame *and* the image will be removed. Instead, you would need to select the content and not the container. The following short exercises will take you through the main image-handling techniques and will help you differentiate between when the container or the content should be selected. These exercises are quick and easy, and important techniques to learn.

A. Toggle between the container and the content
> *Double-click the image (not the doughnut) and watch as you switch between the container and the content. Your ability to toggle between container and content is the starting point for all the remaining exercises! As you toggle between the image and frame, notice that the guides are different colors—and the frame has a yellow box on the right edge.*

B. Scale the image inside the frame without changing the frame size
> *Double-click to select the **content frame**. Press **Cmd+Opt+> or <** (Mac) or **Ctrl+Alt+> or <** (Win) to increase and decrease the scale in increments.*

C. Rotate the image inside the frame
> *Double-click to select the **content**. Move the Selection tool to the lower right corner of the content's frame, until until you see the curved arrow. Rotate the image inside the frame.*

D. Center the image inside the frame.
> *Double-click to select the **container**. Pull the handles out until the frame is much larger than the image. Press **Shift+Cmd+E** (Mac) or **Shift+Ctrl+E** (Win) to center the image.*

E. Fill frame proportionately.
> *Use the image from Exercise D with the image centered in an oversized frame. Double-click until the **content** is selected. Press **Shift+Cmd+Opt+E** (Mac) or **Shift+Ctrl+Alt+E** (Win) to fill the container proportionately.*

F. Fit the frame to the content.
> *Using the Selection tool, double-click a corner frame handle to fit the frame to the content. The entire frame is scaled to fit the image. Now, pull the frame handles to make it much larger than the image. This time,, double-click a frame handle on the middle of the frame's sides, top, or bottom. The frame will resize, either horizontally or vertically.*

▶ *production tip*

Double-clicking to switch from container to content only works with the Selection tool.

These basic image handling exercises can also be accomplished using buttons on the Control panel. One beautiful feature of InDesign is that it allows you to work in the style you prefer. As you can tell by now, I encourage using keyboard shortcuts. The more you use them, the more you will remember them and the faster you'll be at production. But some people prefer to choose options from the menu. If you're one of those people, you will appreciate the convenience of using the Control panel for much of your text and graphics editing.

Fill frame proportionately   Fit content proportionately   Fit content to frame   Fit frame to content   Center content

VISUAL | 4–36 |

The Control panel contains buttons that do many image editing operations.

Scaling Disproportionately

A poster promoting a weight loss program, was hung in our college hallway, showing the "before" and "after" photos of a participant who had lost 20 pounds. Obviously, the "after" picture was created by simply resizing the first photo disproportionately, to make the person look thinner. Be careful when scaling images! Most of the time you will want to keep your image in the same proportion as it was originally created. But there will be instances, as in the cloud example mentioned earlier, when disproportional scaling will be acceptable.

1. Double click the image to select the content. Drag any content frame handle. The image will resize and become distorted. Check the Scale X and Y Percentage fields on the Control panel to see new horizontal and vertical percentages of the image.

2. Enter the same number in each of the fields and the image will again be proportional.

Summary

If this seemed like a long chapter, that's because it was long! In these first four chapters you have learned so much. You now understand InDesign's measurement system. You know how to create multi-column text frames, and to place and thread text. You used InDesign's tracking and kerning, paragraph rules, and spell check functions to fine-tune your type. Finally, you learned how to place, scale, and crop images. With these techniques mastered, you're ready to tackle more advanced projects. The Chapter 4 projects are designed to solidify these new techniques. Next, we'll move on to another one of my favorite topics: tabs and tables.

►IN REVIEW

1. What is the difference between kerning and tracking?

2. What is the difference between tracking and leading?

3. How do you reset the zero point?

4. If the coordinates of an object are X: 4 in. and Y: 6 in., it means that the object will be _____ inches over and _____ inches down.

5. What does the black square in the proxy indicate?

6. What key should you press to push text from one column to the next?

7. What does a red plus sign in the out port of a text frame indicate?

What are the Mac or Windows keyboard shortcuts for the following?

8. Show Hidden Characters _____   9. Save _____

10. Direct Selection Tool _____   11. View at 100% _____

12. Paragraph Rules _____   13. View at 200% _____

14. Place Text or Image _____   15. Text Frame Options _____

16. Check Spelling _____   17. Print _____

18. What are the steps for proportionately enlarging a graphic inside a frame?

19. What is the process for deleting overset text without changing the size of the type or the text frame?

20. What is the process for unlinking text frames?

Peacock artwork ©2006 Nathaniel Avery, Waukesha County Technical College

Chapter 4 projects begin with an X-Y coordinate exercise. This is followed by a display ad project for Beautiful Morning Tearoom and Gardens which focuses on using coordinates, leading, correct dashes, and space after paragraphs. Next, a 2-sided table tent that utilizes rules above and below. A poster concept for a museum exhibit, and one featuring the Gettysburg Address will provide more practice in formatting tect. The final project is designed for you to produce with little direction. You will find instructions, artwork, and text in the *Chapter 04 Artwork and Resources* folder on the accompanying CD.

▶ CHAPTER 4 PROJECTS

Gettysburg Address

Fourscore and seven years ago our fathers brought forth on this continent a new nation, conceived in liberty and dedicated to the proposition that all men are created equal.

Now we are engaged in a great civil war, testing whether that nation or any nation so conceived and so dedicated can long endure. We are met on a great battlefield of that war. We have come to dedicate a portion of that field as a final resting-place for those who here gave their lives that that nation might live. It is altogether fitting and proper that we should

But in a larger sense, we cannot dedicate, we cannot consecrate, we cannot hallow th living and dead who struggled here have consecrated it far above our poor p

The world will little note nor long remember what we say here, but it can never forg It is for us the living rather to be dedicated here to the unfinished work whi here have thus far so nobly advanced. It is rather for us to be here dedicated remaining before us—that from these honored dead we take increased dev which they gave the last full measure of devotion—that we here highly res shall not have died in vain, that this nation under God shall have a new bir that government of the people, by the people, for the people shall not peris

Abraham Lincoln
Gettysburg, Pennsylvania

Lincoln artwork ©2010 Jeffery Blackwell,
Waukesha County Technical College

Anna Sanchez
༄ AUTHENTIC MEXICAN ༄

Pepper photography ©2006 Nathaniel Avery,
Waukesha County Technical College

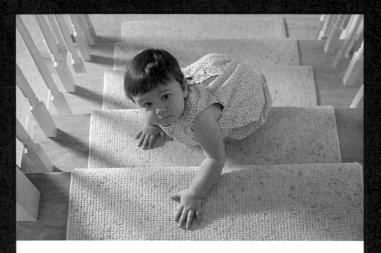

Everyone is trying to
accomplish something **big**,
not realizing that life
is made up of **little things**.

℞ Unknown

Tabs and Tables

objectives

▶ *Differentiate between left, right, center, decimal, repeating, and align to special character tabs*

▶ *Apply tab leaders*

▶ *Use the Indent to Here feature*

▶ *Build a table*

▶ *Create a table from text*

▶ *Modify, add, and delete columns and rows*

▶ *Add headers and footers*

introduction

If you've ever seen a good marching band in a parade, you know that they march in formation. A poor marching band wanders all over the place—trumpets out of line, clarinets out of step, drums missing the beat. Nobody knows whom to follow or what comes next.

This chapter will help you keep your text in formation. In earlier chapters you have learned how to format text in sentences and paragraphs. In this chapter you will work with text designed for use in charts, order forms, and business reports—projects that need tabs and tables to keep information in line. Honing your skills with tabs and tables will keep your text marching in formation, and prove to your boss or your client, that you are a master at what you do!

There are four methods people typically use to align text and numbers in columns:

☹ Press the spacebar repeatedly until the text lines up.

☹ Press the Tab key over and over until the text lines up.

☺ Create precise tab settings.

☺ Create tables to hold the information.

No matter which method you have used in the past, I guarantee that after this chapter you will never use either of the first two methods again!

Working With Tabs

Whether you are working on a car, hanging wallpaper, or building a deck, it is always great to get tips from pros—especially at the beginning of the project! Here are some great tips for tabs. Following them will make setting tabs so much easier.

▶ **Mark up the copy** *(a fine-tip pen with colored ink works the best). Your markup will show where you will press the Tab key and the location and type of each tab stop that will be set. This step is critical in the beginning stages of typesetting. Pre-planning a job in this way can prevent time-consuming errors (see the sample markup in Visual 5–2).*

▶ *Press* **Command+Option+I** *(Mac) or* **Control+Alt+I** *(Windows) to show each tab character and make it easy to find those places where you accidentally pressed the Tab key twice. Or, select Hidden Characters from the View Options menu on the Application Frame, above the Control Panel.*

▶ **Do the typing first**, *pressing the Tab key only one time between columns of information. Your text probably won't line up at first because the cursor jumps to InDesign's preset tab settings of every half inch. Later, when you set the desired tab stops, the copy will line up at the correct new location.*

▶ *Work with copy* **left-aligned**—*doing so makes setting tabs much easier.*

▶ *Open the Tabs panel:* **Shift+Command+T** *(Mac) or* **Shift+Control+T** *(Windows).*

▶ **Press the Tab key only once!** *Your copy will look great after you set the tab stops. Don't try to align copy by pressing the Tab key repeatedly.*

Keyboard Shortcut

⌘ ⇧+CMD+T

⊞ ⇧+CTRL+T

Tabs Panel

Marking up Copy–An Important Production Step!

The first tab tip is to mark up the copy to show each time you press the Tab key and where the tab stops should be placed. Before you can mark up the copy, you must know what kind of tab is needed. We will start with three simple kinds of tabs: *Left*, *Right*, and *Center*.

Each of these tab stops looks different on the Tabs panel. Study Visual 5–1 until you can identify the shape of each tab stop and visualize how it will align the copy.

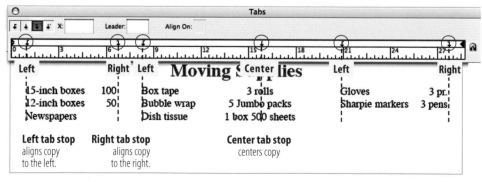

VISUAL |5–1|

Tab stops align copy into columns. The type of stop you select determines how the copy in the columns will be aligned.

Just as stretching prepares your muscles for a workout, marking up tabular copy prepares your brain and creates a visual connection between you and the software, forcing your brain to shift into "tabs mode." It's tempting to skip this step, but until you are totally confident, you should take the 30 seconds to mark up your copy. In the mark up process, you indicate each time you press the Tab key and where each tab stop should be set. Visual 5–2 shows copy that has been marked up correctly. This markup becomes a road map that will make setting tabs a snap.

Photo ©2006 Christopher Pollack

VISUAL |5–2|

Marking up copy before setting tabs saves production time and frustration!

Setting Tabs

You will need the CD that accompanies this book to work on the following tabs exercises. The good news is that all the typing is already done for you—you will concentrate on using the Tabs panel for formatting your copy. Open *05 Tabs Demo.indd,* found in the *05 Artwork and Resources* folder on the CD. Find **Exercise 1** on the *05 Tabs Demo* document. The first step in setting tabs is understanding how the Tabs panel works. Open the Tabs panel using **Shift+Command+T** (Mac) or **Shift+Control+T** (Windows). You can also access the Tabs panel by going to the Type menu and choosing Tabs, but this is a slower method. Study Visual 5–3 to learn the fields and panel options for the Tabs panel.

VISUAL |5–3|

The Tabs panel

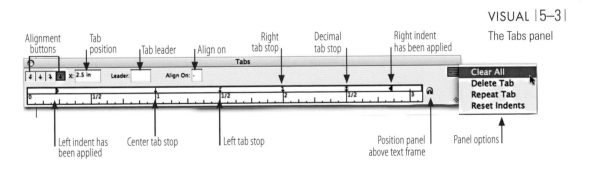

Exercise 1A – Snapping the Tabs Panel to the Text Frame

Activate the text frame in **Exercise 1** with the Selection tool. With the Tabs panel open, notice the magnet on the far right end. This is the control that will position the Tabs panel directly over the active text frame, if possible. To see it in action, change your view size to 100% and click on the magnet. The Tabs panel will align itself to the top of the text frame. Switch your view to 200%. Click the magnet—it will resize and snap to the top of your text frame. Now, switch your view to 1200% from the magnification field in the upper left corner of your screen. Click the magnet, and it won't move. This seemingly inconsistent behavior occurs because when you are viewing your document at high magnification levels, there is not enough room above the active text frame to position and resize the Tabs panel. So, the snap above text frame function is disabled. Change the view size back to 100% and click the magnet to snap the Tabs panel to your text frame. You can set tabs without having the panel snapped to the frame, but it is easier to see what you're doing when the ruler is snapped above your text frame.

Look carefully at the text frame, noticing that an inset has been applied to all four sides. When the Tabs panel is snapped to the text frame, the measuring does not necessarily begin at the edge of the frame. Instead, it begins where the text begins. In this case, the zero point of the tabs ruler snaps to the text frame inset setting. The tabs ruler lines up to the inset guide.

VISUAL |5–4|

Remove all tab stops by selecting Clear All from the panel options.

Exercise 1B – Adding and Removing Tab Stops

Deselect the text frame in Exercise 1. We're going to experiment with the Tabs panel. Adding tab stops is an easy process. Simply click in the narrow white area directly above the ruler. Slide your cursor down the ruler a bit and click again. Each time you click, a tab stop is added. When a tab stop is first added it is blue, which means it is active. Once you make a new tab stop, the previous one is deselected. To delete a tab stop, select it and pull it above the Tabs panel ruler. When you have many tab stops to delete, it is faster to go to the Tabs panel options and select Clear All (Visual 5–4). Clear all your tabs.

▶ *production tip*

Press Option (Mac) or Alt (Windows) and click on a tab stop to cycle through its alignment.

Place a tab stop near the middle of the ruler. Press Option (Mac) or Alt (Windows) and click repeatedly on the tab stop. As you click, watch as the tab stop alignment settings change from left, to center, to right, to decimal. Use this method to cycle through tab stop alignment settings whenever you are setting tabular copy.

Exercise 1C – Setting Left Tabs

Use the Selection tool to select the frame in Exercise 1. Look closely at the invisibles to identify each time the Tab key was pressed (Visual 5–5). Each time the Tab key was pressed, the copy was pushed to the nearest tab preset. Since *Dr. Ryan Johnson's* name was shorter than the other names in the first column, *Dr. Theodore Soos* moved to a tab preset closer to the left edge of the copy block. Usually, copy will not align until you actually set the tab stops. Resist the temptation to "fix" the copy by pressing the tab key repeatedly to manually align copy!

Copy moves to the first available tab stop preset until you select the tab stops you want to use.

Be sure the Tabs panel is open and snapped to the top of your text frame. You should still have the Selection tool activated. Drop in Left tab stops at approximately **0.25"** and **2"**. As you place each stop, click and hold, and a vertical line will appear to show where your copy will be aligned. You can also see the measurement of the tab stop in the X box. Adjust the position of your copy by sliding the tab stop to the right or to the left on the ruler.

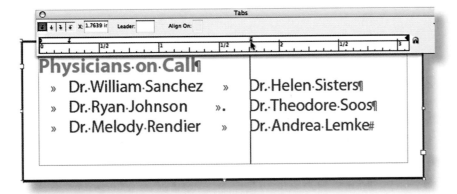

Click and hold each tab stop. A vertical line appears where the copy will be aligned.

Notice that all the lines of copy moved as you placed the tab stops. When you select the text frame with either the Selection or Direct Selection tools, and do not highlight the text lines, the same tab settings are applied to all the tabular copy inside the text frame. When lines of copy in a single frame require different tab settings, individual lines must be separated with a Return (not a soft return) and highlighted before setting the tab stops.

▶ *production tip*

When you select the text frame with the Selection or Direct Selection tool and do not highlight individual lines of copy, identical tab settings are applied to all the tabular copy inside the frame.

Exercise 2 – Setting Center and Right Tabs

Now let's move on to Exercise 2. A completed sample of this exercise is shown in Visual 5– 7. Before you begin this exercise, use Visual 5–7 for markup. Place a **horizontal arrow** → in the text to indicate each time the Tab key is pressed. Examine the copy closely to determine the required tab stops. Indicate the appropriate tab stop above each column, using these symbols for Left, Center, or Right ⌊↓⌋ ↓ ⌊↓⌋. A tab stop won't be required in every line.

Nutrition Facts

Serving Size: 1 cup
Servings per container: 6
Amount per serving:

Calories: 45	Calories from fat: 0	
	Total Fat: 0g	
Saturated Fat 0g		
Polyunsaturated Fat 0g		
Monounsaturated Fat 0g		
Cholesterol	0mg	0%
Sodium	70 mg	13%
Total Carbohydrate	12g	
Dietary Fiber	2g	
Sugars	0g	
Protein	1g	

Vitamin A 0% • Vitamin C 0%
Calcium 0% • Iron 2%

When your markup is completed, open the Tabs panel. Find the lines of type with identical tab settings, and work on those as a unit. Then move to the next series of similar tab settings. Refer to your markup as you drop in your tab stops. Press Option (Mac) or Alt (Windows) and click on each tab stop to cycle through the alignment options. If you need to adjust the position of a tab stop, highlight the copy and move the stop to the left or right on the Tabs panel ruler. Your completed project should look almost identical to the example in Visual 5–7.

Answers to Math Exam

1.	.067
2.	0.0034
3.	9.56723
4.	12.45
5.	.1
6.	2.3543
7.	4
8.	9.667734
9.	2.456
10.	6.123

Exercise 3 – Setting Decimal Tabs

When you set a *Decimal* tab stop, the copy is lined up according to the position of the decimal. In Visual 5–8, notice how the numbers one through ten are aligned by their decimal points. In the right column, the numbers also align according to the decimal point. If there is no decimal point, such as in the answer for #7, the whole number is positioned to the left of where a decimal point would be placed. Mark up the copy, making sure to indicate a tab before numbers 1 to 10. Then, create the tab settings.

Exercise 4 – Aligning To Special Characters

The Decimal tab default aligns copy according to the location of the decimal point, but you can specify other characters on which to align the decimal tab. In this exercise, the copy will be aligned to the dollar sign. First, select the Decimal tab. Then, enter a dollar sign ($) in the Align On box in the Tabs panel.

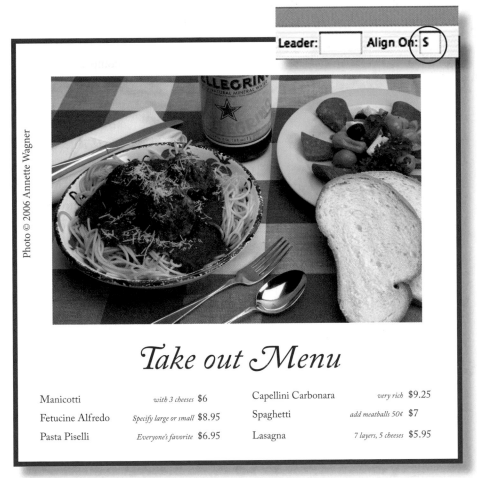

Leader: **Align On: $**

Photo © 2006 Annette Wagner

Take out Menu

Manicotti	*with 3 cheeses*	$6	Capellini Carbonara	*very rich*	$9.25
Fetucine Alfredo	*Specify large or small*	$8.95	Spaghetti	*add meatballs 50¢*	$7
Pasta Piselli	*Everyone's favorite*	$6.95	Lasagna	*7 layers, 5 cheeses*	$5.95

VISUAL |5–9|

You can specify other characters for alignment with the decimal tab stop. In this example, copy is aligned to the dollar sign.

Exercise 5 – Setting Right Indent Tabs

Right indent tabs automatically push your copy flush with the right edge of the text frame. Right indent tabs aren't part of the regular Tabs panel. Press Shift+Tab or use the Context menu>Insert Special Character>Other>Right Indent Tab to create a right indent tab. Display hidden characters to verify that an automatic right indent tab has been inserted. Follow the directions included with Exercise 5, on page 2 of *05 Tabs Demo*.indd, to create right indent tabs.

VISUAL |5–10|

This hidden character represents a right indent tab.

Keyboard Shortcut

 ⬆+TAB

 ⬆+TAB

Flush Right Tab

Exercise 6 – Using Indent to Here

Indent to Here is one of those "can't live without it" features in InDesign. Although technically this is not a tab setting, this is a good time to introduce this function. With Indent to Here, you insert a special character symbol by pressing **Command+** (Mac) or **Control+** (Windows). Starting with the next line, all subsequent lines in the paragraph align to the position of the Indent to Here character. This is similar to creating a hanging indent. Once you press the Return key for a new paragraph, paragraph text will revert back out to the left margin. To remove the Indent to Here character, simply turn on the hidden characters, find the Indent to Here dagger symbol, place the cursor to the right of the symbol, and press the Delete key. When you use the Indent to Here keyboard shortcut to complete this exercise, be sure to use the Back Slash, not the Forward Slash key!

Indent to here symbol

·‡Parents·who·love,·encourage,· and·inspire·you.¶

Exercise 7 – Setting Repeat Tabs

When you need tabs to be spaced at equal intervals, you can use the *Repeat Tabs* function found on the option menu at the far right end of the Tabs panel. In this function, equally spaced tab stops, based on the position of the first tab stop, are spread across the line. Directions for creating Repeat tabs are included with Exercise 7 in *05 Tabs Demo.indd*.

Exercise 8 – Creating Dot Leaders

A *leader* is a series of repeating characters between a tab stop and the following text or the end of the text frame. Leaders can be dots, lines, or any other character you choose. You can specify up to eight characters in the Leader box on the Tabs

panel. You will most often use leaders in conjunction with Right tab stops. To create the dot leaders in this exercise, set a Right tab at the right end of the tab ruler. Making sure the Right tab stop is selected, enter a period and space in the Leader box and press Return. The area between the first and second columns will fill with dots. As Visual 5–12 shows, if you don't enter a space along with the period, the dot leaders will be too close. Add dot leader tabs to the text in Exercise 8, so that it looks like Visual 5–13. This exercise demonstrates how dot leaders help the eye move from one column to the next.

VISUAL |5–13|

Exercise 8, completed.

Exercise 9 – Creating Line Leaders

Throughout your professional career, you will likely create many projects that are "variations on the theme" of the raffle ticket presented in Exercise 9. When creating line leaders, place an underline in the Leader box by pressing Shift+ hyphen, found at the top right corner of your keyboard. If you don't press the Shift key, the space will be filled with dashes, not underlines. Sometimes, when you are creating line leaders, the underlines on your monitor will appear to have spaces between them. If this happens, increase your view magnification and see if the rules look solid at a different view

VISUAL |5–14|

You will create the tab settings shown in this example numerous times during your career!

▶ *production tip*

Highlight the Leader field by clicking the field's label to the left of the box, rather than manually clicking in the box and highlighting it.

percentage. Sometimes it's just a "screen thing." Other times, this happens because you actually typed a space and an underline in the Leader box, on the Tabs panel.

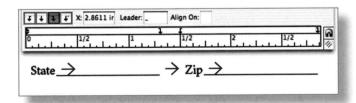

VISUAL |5–15|

The last line in this raffle ticket. The line leaders are applied to the Right tab stops.

Visual 5–15 shows the tab settings for the last line of the raffle ticket. The line leaders are applied to the two Right tab stops. If the line after State runs into Zip, it probably means you have added a line leader to the left Tab stop at the word, Zip. If so, select the stop and delete the line in the Leader box.

► MOVING TOWARD MASTERY

When working with tabs, remember these tips:

► **Mark up the copy.** *Show where the Tab key will be pressed, and where the tab stop will be set.*

► **Work with hidden characters visible.** *Press* **Command+Option+I** *(Mac) or* **Control+Alt+I** *(Windows) to show hidden characters. This will show each tab character and will make it easy to find those times when you accidentally pressed the Tab key twice.*

► **Do the typing first**, *pressing the Tab key only one time between columns of information.*

► **Work with copy left-aligned** *when possible— doing so makes setting tabs much easier.*

► *Press* **Shift+Command+T** *(Mac) or* **Shift+Control+T** *(Windows) to open the Tabs panel.*

► **Press the Tab key only once!** *Be patient—your copy will look great after you set the tab stops.*

► *Highlight the Leader box by clicking on the name to the left of the box.*

► *With a tab stop highlighted in the Tab ruler, press* **Option** *(Mac) or* **Alt** *(Windows) and click on the tab marker to cycle through the tab stop alignment settings.*

► *Add a space after the period in the Leader field when creating dot leaders.*

Last Thoughts on Tabs

The columns within text frames, that you created in earlier chapters, are used for continuous text passages. They are designed to have the copy fill across and down the first column, then flow into the second column, and so on. Set tabs when the copy flow is horizontal. The tab stops will create the appearance of vertical columns.

Don't confuse tabs with paragraph indents and text frame insets! Sometimes you will use a left indent instead of a tab. That method works perfectly. However, be careful of creating a left inset in Text Frame Options rather than a left indent because the inset will affect all the text in the frame—which may not be what you want! The hidden characters shown below reveal the techniques used in each example.

S & P Stats¶		A
level »	1131.13¶	
change »	-2.98¶	
» percent·change »	-.26%¶	
» YTD·%·change »	1.73%¶	
» high·(day) »	1134.17¶	
» low·(day) »	1127.73¶	
» high·(52·wk) »	1155.38¶	
» low·(52·wk) »	788.90¶	
last·close »	1134.1¶	
last·update: 1/30·16:52#		

Tabs were used to move copy to the right.

S & P Stats¶		B
level »	1131.13¶	
change »	-2.98¶	
percent·change »	-.26%¶	
YTD·%·change »	1.73%¶	
high·(day) »	1134.17¶	
low·(day) »	1127.73¶	
high·(52·wk) »	1155.38¶	
low·(52·wk) »	788.90¶	
last·close »	1134.1¶	
last·update: 1/30·16:52#		

A left indent was specified in the Control panel.

S & P Stats¶		C
level »	1131.13¶	
change »	-2.98¶	
percent·change »	-.26%¶	
YTD·%·change »	1.73%¶	
high·(day) »	1134.17¶	
low·(day) »	1127.73¶	
high·(52·wk) »	1155.38¶	
low·(52·wk) »	788.90¶	
last·close »	1134.1¶	
last·update: 1/30·16:52#		

The frame inset created in Text Frame Options applies to all the text in a frame.

Creating Tables

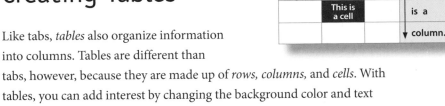

This | is a | row. | This | is a | column. | This is a cell

VISUAL |5–16|

A table structure consists of rows, columns, and cells.

Like tabs, *tables* also organize information into columns. Tables are different than tabs, however, because they are made up of *rows, columns,* and *cells.* With tables, you can add interest by changing the background color and text attributes of individual cells, columns, and rows. When thinking of tables, people often picture a clunky-looking graph with copy choked against heavy black lines. Not so, with InDesign. In this second half of Chapter 5, you will discover the amazing and enjoyable ways you can create tables.

There are several ways you can create tables: from "scratch," by converting existing copy, or by importing from a Microsoft® Word document or Excel spreadsheet. You can insert a table into a text frame or convert existing text into a table. The best way to understand tables is to make them, so we're going to dive right in. In the following exercises, you will learn all the basics of table management using a simple table consisting of four rows and four columns.

Table Basics

1. **Insert a table.** Create a letter-size InDesign document with **0.5"** margins. Draw a text frame from margin to margin. Select the *Type* tool and click in the frame. Press **Shift+Option+Command+T** (Mac) or **Shift+Alt+Control+T** (Windows) to bring up the *Insert Table* dialog box. You can also access this dialog box by choosing *Table>Insert Table.* Specify **4** in the *Body Rows* and **4** in the *Columns* boxes. (Rows run horizontally, and columns run vertically.) Leave the Header Rows and Footer Rows fields blank. Press Return. A table now sits inside your text frame, aligned with the top of your text frame.

VISUAL |5–17|

The Insert Table dialog box.

Keyboard Shortcut

⌘ ⇧+OPT+CMD+T

⊞ ⇧+ALT+CTRL+T

Insert Table

2. **Position a table in the text frame.** The new table has a cursor blinking in the upper left cell. With the *Type* tool selected, click anywhere in the text frame, outside of the table. Now the text cursor is positioned just outside the table on the right side of the text frame. Notice that the cursor is the same height as the table. Open *Text Frame Options,* **Command+B** (Mac) or **Control+B** (Windows), and under *Vertical Justification* choose *Align: Center.* Turn on the *Preview* option and watch the table jump to the vertical center of the text frame. Now, see what happens when you select the *Align: Bottom* option. A table behaves like a huge piece of type inside a text frame, and will be affected by alignment, indents, insets, space before and space after. Align the table to the top once again.

Keyboard Shortcut

⌘ CMD+B

⊞ CTRL+B

Text Frame Options

3. **Select columns, rows, cells, or the entire table.** Move the *Type* tool slightly above the table, over the left column. You will see the cursor change into an arrow (Visual 5–18A). Click, and the entire column will be selected. Place your cursor along the left side of the table, beside the first row (Visual 5–18B). Click, and the entire row will be selected. Now, bring the cursor to the upper left corner of the table. You will see a diagonal arrow (Visual 5–18C). Click, and the entire table will be selected. Place the cursor inside a cell and drag to the right to select it. You can continue to drag across a cell's boundary to select adjacent cells. Practice selecting the entire table, individual rows, columns and cells.

VISUAL |5–18|

Use the Type tool to select columns, rows, cells, or the entire table.

VISUAL |5–19|

Press ESC to switch between highlighting the cell and the text.

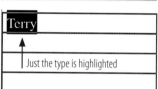

4. **Select a cell or its contents.** Place the cursor in the upper left cell and type your name. Move the cursor to highlight your name and the space surrounding it so that the entire cell is black. You now have the cell selected (Visual 5–19). Now, try to highlight just your name. Sometimes this is a little trickier, and it helps if you are at a magnified view. When your type is selected, the highlighting should just cover the letters, and your cell should look like the lower example in Visual 5–19. It is important that you can differentiate between selecting a cell or highlighting text inside a cell. You can also press the **ESC** key to switch between selecting the cell or the type in a cell.

VISUAL |5–20|

When you are moving column or row guides the cursor switches to a double-headed arrow.

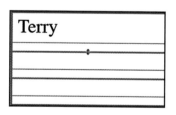

5. **Resize rows and columns.** Place the cursor over the row guide below your name. The cursor now changes into a double-headed arrow (Visual 5–20). Pull the line down to create a much deeper cell. Repeat this process with the column guides. Notice how changing the size of rows and columns, changes the table size, too.

▶ *production tip*

Press **Shift** to resize columns and rows inside the table without changing the table's dimension.

6. **Resize rows and columns without resizing the table.** Place the cursor over the row guide below your name. When the cursor changes into a double-headed arrow, hold down Shift as you adjust the row dimension. Notice that the row inside the table changes size, but the table does not. Repeat this process, pressing the Shift key as you move the column guides.

7. **Position text inside the cell.** Highlight the cell that contains your name. Use the Paragraph Formatting options in the Control panel to align your type to the right. Now align the type to the center. You use the *Table Formatting Options* in the Control panel to set the vertical position and rotation of type inside the cell. In Visual 5–21 the type has been rotated 270°. With the cell selected, experiment with alignment and text rotation controls in the Control panel.

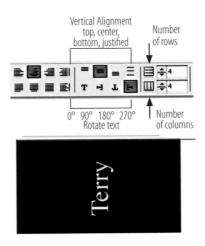

VISUAL |5–21|

Shown are some of the Table Formatting Options available in the Control panel.

8. **Resize the entire table.** Move the cursor to the lower right corner until you see a diagonal double-headed arrow. Press Shift and pull on the arrow and your table will enlarge proportionately. If you want to expand only the vertical or horizontal dimension of the table, move the cursor to either the bottom or the right side and pull to resize. Press the Shift key to proportionately resize the vertical or horizontal dimension of the table.

9. **Add and delete rows and columns.** You can add and delete rows and columns in the *Table Formatting* options in the Control panel or by using the *Context* menu. When using the Control panel, change the number of rows and columns in the appropriate box (Visual 5–21). You can also delete rows and columns using keyboard shortcuts. Highlight the bottom row. Press **Command+Delete** (Mac) or **Control+Backspace** (Windows) and the row will disappear. Delete a column by highlighting it and pressing **Shift+Delete.** Now, open the *Context* menu and examine the options. The *Context* menu holds almost all of the table editing operations you will use. Choose *Insert>Row or Column.* Specify the number and location of the new rows or columns.

10. **Merge and split cells.** Highlight the first row in your table. Open the *Context* menu and select *Merge Cells.* One large cell now spans the length of your table. With this long cell highlighted, choose *Split Cell Horizontally* from the *Context* menu. Then choose *Split Cell Vertically.* You can continue splitting cells until they are quite small (Visual 5–22). Cells can also be merged and unmerged at the Control panel. Highlight the cells and click the *Merge Cells* button.

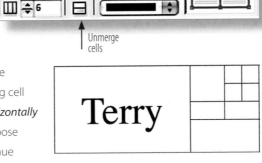

VISUAL |5–22|

Cells can be merged and unmerged in the Table Controls panel. In the lower example, cells have been repeatedly split horizontally and vertically, resulting in very tiny cells.

►MOVING TOWARD MASTERY

- ► *The Type tool is used for editing tables.*

- ► *A row is horizontal. A column is vertical. A cell is the space formed by the row and column grid.*

- ► *The Type tool cursor changes shape according to the table editing that will be done.*

- ► *The keyboard shortcut for creating a table within a text frame is* **Shift+Option+Command+T** *(Mac) or* **Shift+Alt+Control+T** *(Windows).*

- ► *Press* **ESC** *to alternate highlighting the cell or the text inside the cell.*

- ► *Rows and columns can be added, deleted, and resized.*

- ► *Press the* **Shift** *key when you are changing the dimension of rows or columns, and want to maintain the same overall table size.*

- ► *You can merge cells to form wider columns and deeper rows.*

- ► *The table sits inside a text frame. When rows and columns are modified, the text frame may need to be enlarged or reduced.*

- ► *Select the whole table by placing the cursor at the upper left corner of the table and clicking when the cursor turns into a diagonal arrow.*

- ► *Options that affect the whole table are accessible by pressing* **Shift+Option+Command+B** *(Mac) or* **Shift+Alt+Control+B** *(Windows).*

- ► *Options that affect selected cells are accessible by pressing* **Option+Command+B** *(Mac) or* **Alt+Control+B** *(Windows).*

- ► *Delete a table by placing your cursor in the text frame to the right of the table and pressing* **Delete**.

Create a Table from Existing Text

Now that you've gotten a taste for tables, I hope you're ready for more! In the next exercise, you will import some prepared text, and convert it to a table, making the Grade Scale chart, shown in Visual 5–25.

VISUAL |5–23|

As you create this grading chart, you will learn how to modify strokes and attributes of cells, including tab stops.

Grade Scale		
Grade	Percent Value	Point Value
A	95-100	4.00
A-	93-94	3.67
B+	91-92	3.33
B	87-90	3.00
B-	85-86	2.67
C+	83-84	2.33
C	79-82	2.00
C-	77-78	1.67
D+	75-76	1.33
D	72-74	1.00
D-	70-71	0.67
F	69 or below	0.00

1. Draw a text frame **2.5" × 4"**. Place *05 Grade Scale.doc* from the *05 Artwork and Resources* folder on the accompanying CD. Place it into the frame.

2. Select all the text. Choose *Table>Convert Text to Table*. In the Convert Text to Table dialog box, set the *Column Separator* to *Tab*, the *Row Separator* to *Paragraph*, and then press Return. Your table should look similar to Visual 5–23.

3. Select the top row and merge the cells by clicking on the *Merge Cell* box in the Control panel, or by opening the *Context* menu and choosing *Merge Cells*. Now the phrase *Grade Scale* should fit on one line. Select the entire table and change all the copy to **Myriad Pro Condensed.**

4. Highlight the first two rows and center the column heads by pressing **Shift+Command+C** (Mac) or **Shift+Control+C** (Windows). Apply a Bold type style. Select the second and third columns and use the same keyboard shortcut to center the copy.

Left-justified tab

VISUAL |5–24|

Press Option+Tab (Mac only) or use the Context menu> Insert Special Character (Windows) to insert a tab in a cell.

5. Select the first column, from A to F. Open the Tabs panel and set a Left tab stop close to the middle of the column (Visual 5–24). Inserting a tab in a table cell is tricky. On the Mac you need to press **Option+Tab** instead of just Tab. In Windows, you must use the *Context* menu and choose *Insert Special Character>Other>Tab.* Line by line, place the cursor before the letter grade and insert a tab character to line up the grades close to the middle of the column.

▶ *production tip*

Notice these keyboard shortcut patterns used for formatting text in frames, cells and tables.

6. Place the text cursor in any table cell and open the *Table Options* dialog box. Use **Shift+Command+Option+B** (Mac) or **Shift+Control+Alt+B** (Windows). Select the *Fills* page and under *Alternating Pattern*, select **Every Other Row**, Color: **Black**, Tint: **20%**. Set *Skip First* to **1**. Press **Return**. The first row of the table should now be white, with every other row a 20% black tint.

Keyboard Shortcut	
⌘ CMD+B	**Text Frame Options**
⊞ CTRL+B	

Keyboard Shortcut	
⌘ CMD+OPT+B	**Cell Options**
⊞ CTRL+ALT+B	

Keyboard Shortcut	
⌘ ⇧+OPT+CMD+B	**Table Options**
⊞ ⇧+ALT+CTRL+B	

7. Select the entire table and open the *Cell Options* dialog using the keyboard shortcut, **Command+Option+B** (Mac) or **Control+Alt+B** (Windows). Select the *Strokes and Fills* page. Under *Cell Stroke*, enter **3 pt**. in the *Weight* field and **[Paper]** in the *Color* field. Press Return and deselect the table to see the results.

8. Finally, add a border around the outer edge of the table. Place the text cursor in any table cell and open the *Table Options* dialog box. On the *Table Setup* page set the Table Border options as follows: Color: **Black**, Type: **Dashed** (any style), Weight: **2 pt**., Gap Color: **None.** Do not check *Preserve Local Formatting*. Press Return. Compare your table with Visual 5–25, adjusting point sizes as needed. Your table is now completed.

Grade Scale

Grade	Percent Value	Point Value
A	95-100	4.00
A-	93-94	3.67
B+	91-92	3.33
B	87-90	3.00
B-	85-86	2.67
C+	83-84	2.33
C	79-82	2.00
C-	77-78	1.67
D+	75-76	1.33
D	72-74	1.00
D-	70-71	0.67
F	69 or below	0.00

VISUAL |5–25|

The completed Grade Scale table.

▶MOVING TOWARD MASTERY

THE GRADE SCALE EXERCISE
DEMONSTRATED THESE TABLE FEATURES:

▶ *Text can be converted to a table. Whenever there is a tab in the text, it will begin a new column; wherever there is a return, it will begin a new row. The text must be highlighted before the Convert to Table option will show up.*

▶ *You can add tab settings in table cells. To set the actual tab, you must press* **Option+Tab** *(Mac) or use the* **Insert Special Character** *from the Context menu (Windows) instead of simply pressing the Tab key.*

▶ *You can automatically create alternately shaded rows under Table Options.*

▶ *You can have the interior row and column lines one style and color, and choose a different style and color for the outer table border.*

Grade Scale		
Grade	**Percent Value**	**Point Value**
A	95-100	4.00
A-	93-94	3.67
B+	91-92	3.33
B	87-90	3.00
B-	85-86	2.67
C+	83-84	2.33
C	79-82	2.00
C-	77-78	1.67
D+	75-76	1.33
D	72-74	1.00
D-	70-71	0.67
F	69 or below	0.00

Create a Table from Text You've Prepared

Now you will make a chart using many of the same techniques as the Grade Scale table, but you will prepare the text yourself. Visual 5–26 shows a table featuring the most popular baby names in 2008. Compare Visual 5–26 with the Grade Scale table and you will see many of the same features—with a few twists, of course.

VISUAL | 5–26 |
The finished table.

Top 10 Baby Names of 2008

Rank	Girls	Boys
1	Emma	Jacob
2	Isabella	Michael
3	Emily	Ethan
4	Madison	Joshua
5	Ava	Daniel
6	Olivia	Alexander
7	Lily	Anthony
8	Sophia	William
9	Abigail	Christopher
10	Chloe	Matthew

source:www.socialsecurity.gov

1. Draw a text frame **20 picas** wide by **22 picas** deep. (Type **p** after the number in the W and H fields to indicate picas.) Type the copy as seen in Visual 5–26. Press *Tab* to jump from column to column and press the *Return* key at the end of each line. Do not set tab stops! Select all the text. Choose *Table>Convert Text to Table*. Keep the default settings and press Return.

2. Merge the cells in the first row to fit the title on one line. Move the row divider line down so that the title has more room. Highlight the cell and use the Table Formatting Controls to horizontally and vertically align the type to the center.

3.   Highlight the table name, and make the type bold-italic and larger. The typeface used in Visual 5–26 is *Chapparal Pro.* Highlight the column titles and make the type bold, larger, and centered. Highlight the numbers in the *Rank* column. Change them to a larger, bolder typeface and center them horizontally in the cell.

4.   Highlight the two columns of names and select a typeface and point size you prefer. Center the names horizontally in their cells. Press the Shift key as you resize the width of the Rank column so that it is narrower than the two Names columns.

5.   Highlight both Names columns. Open the *Context* menu and choose *Distribute Columns Evenly*. Merge the cells in the bottom row to fit the source information on one line. Apply **Red** and **Blue** fills to the names as shown in Visual 5–26.

6.   Open the *Table Options* dialog box. On the *Fills* page set *Alternating Pattern* to **Every Other Row.** Set the *First Row Color* to **Yellow** and *Tint* to **20%.** Press Return. Every other row in the table should be tinted. Select the entire table and open the *Cell Options* dialog box. Select the *Strokes and Fills* page and set Weight to **4 pt.**, Color to **[Paper]**. Press Return.

7.   The table is almost done. This time, instead of adding a border to the table itself, you will center the table horizontally and vertically in the text frame and add the border to the text frame. Switch to the *Selection* tool and make the text frame slightly larger than the table by dragging the lower right corner frame handle, diagonally. Use the *Stroke* options on the Control panel to add a **Blue**, **4-point Japanese dots** stroke.

8.   Switch back to the *Type* tool. Click in the upper left corner of the text frame to place the cursor before the table. Center the table horizontally by pressing **Shift+Command+C** (Mac) or **Shift+Control+C** (Windows). Use Command+B (Mac) or Control+B (Windows) to open the Text Frame Options dialog box. Set the *Vertical Justification Align: Center,* and press Return. Congratulations! You've completed this table project.

Adding Headers and Footers to Tables

Often, tables begin with a row of information that is repeated on the top of each table. This information might include names, SKU numbers, classifications, categories, and so on. In the example in Visual 5–27, the days of the week are repeated at the top of each month's calendar. This row of information is called a *header.* Rows that are repeated on the bottom of each table are called *footers.* InDesign allows you to create table headers and footers, and then specify where and how often you want them to appear on your table. This will be a

VISUAL | 5–27 |

The days of the week are converted to a header row and specified to appear once per frame.

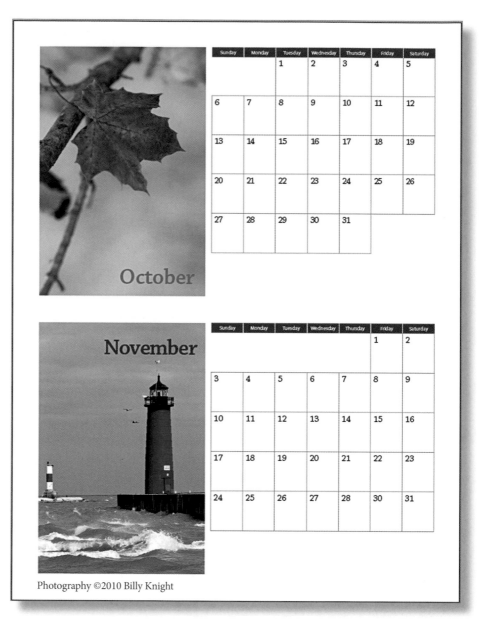

VISUAL | 5–27 |

The days of the week are converted to a header row and specified to appear once per frame.

Photography ©2010 Billy Knight

quick exercise—the table is already completed. You will use this sample table to experiment with adding a header. Designing one header and then having InDesign automatically apply it, is an efficient way of working. Any change you make to the original header applies to the table headers, in linked frames.

1.　Open *05 Header Demo.indd* from the *05 Artwork and Resources* CD accompanying this textbook. Notice that the table is partially completed. A row has been created that displays the days of the week. This would be a typical workflow. You'd design the table and a row that would be used as a *header*—but it isn't a real header until it is converted to a header.

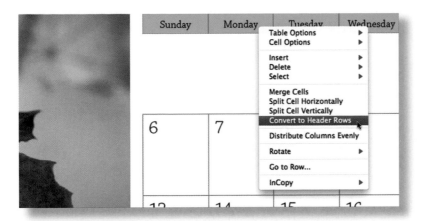

VISUAL | 5–28 |
A table row must be converted to a header before it can be applied to other tables.

2. Highlight the row containing the days of the week. Open the *Context* menu and select *Convert to Header Rows* (Visual 5–28). This row is no longer body copy—it is a header. If you decide to make future changes to it, you need only to make those changes in this original header row.

3. If you look at the lower table which inside a linked text frame, you will see that the days of the week header automatically appeared. Now, open *Table Options* and choose *Headers and Footers*. Under the *Repeat Header* drop down menu (Visual 5–29), you can specify if the header should be repeated every text column (if the text frame has more than one column), once per frame, or once per page. Select *Once per Page* and you will see the header on the lower table disappear. Switch to *Once per Frame* and you will see the header again.

VISUAL | 5–29 |
Use Table Options to specifiy header and footers and how often they will appear.

4. Open *Table Options* again. We created our header by converting an existing row to a header. But notice that you can also create headers in the *Table Dimensions* area of the Table Setup panel. Enter **1** In the *Footer Rows* field and choose *Every Text Column* from the *Repeat Footer* field. Notice that another row—a footer row— appears at the bottom of each month. If you try to highlight the bottom row you will see a lock icon (Visual 5–30) because you need to edit the footer at the original table, in this case, in the October table.

VISUAL | 5–30 |
A lock icon reminds you to make any changes to a header or footer in the original header or footer row.

VISUAL | 5–31 |

Use the Context menu to convert a header or footer to a Body Row.

VISUAL | 5–32 |

Use Table Options to add rows, columns, headers, footers and to remove the outer table stroke.

5. Header and Footer rows can also be converted to regular rows. Highlight the header or footer, open the *Context* menu and select *Convert to Body Rows* (Visual 5–31).

6. Select the table and open *Table Options* again. Select *Table Setup*. In *Table Dimension*s you can also specify the number of body rows, columns, and header and footer rows. Use *Table Border Options* to remove the outer stroke on the table by entering **0** in the *Weight* field (Visual 5–32).

Summary

You've come a long way! In these first five chapters of *Exploring Adobe InDesign CS5,* you've mastered an incredible array of techniques.

This chapter focused on creating various tab settings and leaders. Indent to Here was introduced, giving you a quick method of creating a hanging indent. You learned how to build a table and create a table from existing text. InDesign's table formatting options were used to enhance your table's design. These production techniques will be used frequently in your design projects.

As you move ahead, the chapters will begin to be shorter, and the projects will be fewer, but more complex. This is a good time to page through the earlier chapters to review topics that might have been confusing the first time through—now they will probably make more sense. Keep studying your keyboard shortcuts!

▶ IN REVIEW

1.   What are the four main types of tabs?

2.   How does Indent to Here work?

3.   How many times should you press the Tab key to line up text?

4.   What is the method of increasing the space between the dots in leaders?

5.   Define cells, columns, and rows.

6.   What pattern can you see between the keyboard shortcuts for these functions:
     (a) Text Frame Options; (b) Cell Options; and (c) Table Options?

7.   What technique do you use to insert a tab character inside a cell?

8.   What are two methods of removing all the tab stops in selected text?

9.   When you are resizing table columns, what key should you press to prevent
     the outer dimensions of the table from changing?

10. What is the process for removing an outer border on a table?

11. How is mark up helpful when setting complex tabular copy?

12. What are tab stop presets?

13. Memorize the mnemonic below for setting the copy shown below. Then mark up the copy,
     showing where you will press the tab key, and the location and style of each tab stop.

City [tab, tab] State [tab, tab] Zip [tab, return]

City _____   State_____   Zip _____

Keyboard Shortcut	
⬆+CMD+T	**Tabs Panel**
⬆+CTRL+T	

Keyboard Shortcut	
⬆+TAB	**Flush Right Tab**
⬆+TAB	

Keyboard Shortcut	
CMD+\ (backslash)	**Indent to Here**
CTRL+\ (backslash)	

Keyboard Shortcut	
⬆+OPT+CMD+T	**Insert Table**
⬆+ALT+CTRL+T	

Keyboard Shortcut	
CMD+B	**Text Frame Options**
CTRL+B	

Keyboard Shortcut	
CMD+OPT+B	**Cell Options**
CTRL+ALT+B	

Keyboard Shortcut	
⬆+OPT+CMD+B	**Table Options**
⬆+ALT+CTRL+B	

► CHAPTER 5 PROJECTS

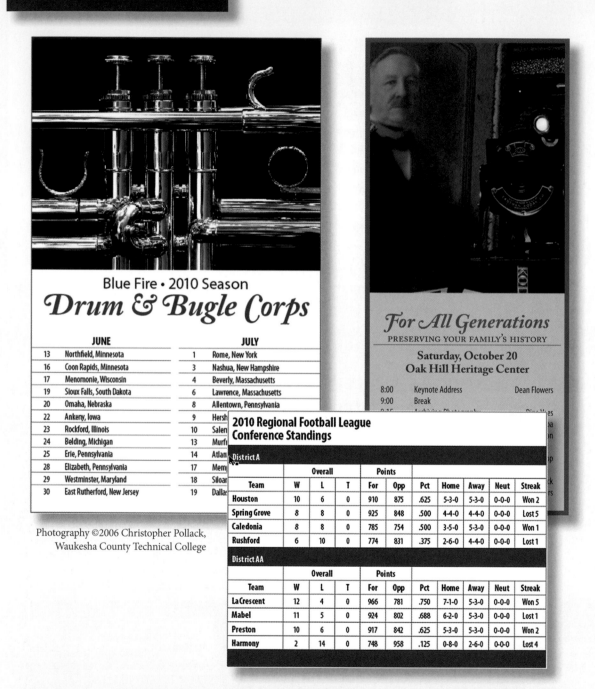

Photography ©2006 Christopher Pollack,
Waukesha County Technical College

Projects galore will give you the opportunity to sharpen the tab and table skills you learned in this chapter. You will find a PDF with instructions for these projects in the Chapter 05 folder on the accompanying CD. Artwork and text are found in the *05 Artwork and Resources* folder.

CHAPTER 5 PROJECTS

Fun in the Sun!

Swimming Lessons for Beginners • from Community Education

Swimming is se...
kids—after al...
first nine mont...

Our classes are...
as young as 9 n...
nine years! Our...
and its kid-frie...
is gentle on you...

Water Safety I...
specializes in c...
and encouragin...
over fifteen yea...
children and th...
has developed a...

AUGUST

Sunday	Monday	Tuesday	Wednesday	Thursday	Friday	Saturday
						1
2	3	4	5	6	7	8
9	10	11	12	13	14	15
16	17	18	19	20	21	22
23	24	25	26	27	28	29
30	31					

Always do the **right thing**.
This will gratify some people
and astonish the rest.

℞ Mark Twain

| Grids, Guides, and Aligning Objects |

objectives

- ▶ *Modify the default InDesign document setup preset*
- ▶ *Create document presets, bleeds, and slugs*
- ▶ *Place, remove, and modify attributes of guides*
- ▶ *Create a newsletter that utilizes a baseline grid*
- ▶ *Align and distribute objects*
- ▶ *Manage object layers and group elements*
- ▶ *Copy, cut, paste, paste into, and paste in place*

introduction

Most homes have a junk drawer. Often found in the kitchen, this drawer holds a myriad of "nuts and bolts" that keep the household going. A peek inside the drawer reveals things like bottle openers, matches, pencils, paper clips, pliers, coins, twist ties, and bits of this and that—stuff that you need, but don't exactly have a place for.

This chapter is a little like a junk drawer, because it's full of miscellaneous techniques. But unlike the junk drawer in your kitchen, this chapter is loaded with many *essential* productivity tools, some of which are new in InDesign CS5. They didn't fit into a nice category, so they got a chapter of their own.

By now, you have learned the basics, and armed yourself with a variety of skills. This chapter will focus on increasing productivity with techniques that will bring precision to your documents and efficiency to the way you work. Once you've used each important gadget in this chapter you'll feel right at home using Adobe InDesign CS5.

Back to the Basics

Since you are now an old hand at creating basic documents, it is time to introduce a few more options available in the New Document dialog box. First, let's review a few points for setting options in the New Document dialog box.

▶ Press the **Tab** key to jump from field to field in any dialog box.

▶ Turn on the **Facing Pages** option box when you want to create spreads. This will allow you to view documents with left and right hand pages like a book or magazine, two pages at a time.

▶ Use the **Page Size** list to select from a variety of preset dimensions, including Compact Disc and common monitor resolution sizes. "Letter" is the standard 8.5"× 11" printed page size.

▶ Click the **Make all settings the same icon** 🔳 to apply the same margin value to all fields (Visual 6–1).

▶ Highlight fields by clicking on the **field name**. This is faster than the click+drag method many people use to highlight fields.

VISUAL |6–1|

Take a closer look at the New Document window and you will find many features. The Page Size menu contains many standardized document and screen sizes. The Make all Settings the Same button lets you quickly apply the same margin dimension to all sides.

Make all Settings the Same

Create Document Presets

In the *Getting Started* section in Chapter 1, you changed the default document specifications and customized InDesign to match your work style. InDesign also allows you to create presets for other document parameters you will most often use. Suppose that many of the documents you create are 5 × 7 inches. You can create a 5 × 7 document, set the margins and other page options, and then before clicking OK, select Save Preset. A dialog box will pop up asking you to name the preset, so it can be stored for future use (Visual 6–2). The next time you need to create a 5 × 7 document, you can choose this preset from the Document Preset drop-down list, in the New Document dialog box.

Name and save the document preset in the Save Preset dialog box.

Your mind is probably spinning just thinking of all the document presets you could use—business cards, envelopes, letterhead, forms, flyers, brochures— dozens of presets at your fingertips. So let's go one step further. Imagine that a client often requires you to design ads for 15 different magazines. Each publication has different specifications that must be followed precisely. Spending 15 minutes creating document presets for each publication is well worth the time. It will reduce the chance of error, especially when you are in a time crunch. Here is another method of making document presets. Use this method when you need to create many presets, or to delete or change existing ones.

1. Go to *File>Document Presets>Define.* The *Document Presets* dialog box will open (Visual 6–3).

2. Click *New,* and the *New Document Preset* dialog box opens. Name the preset, set the page size, margins and other options, and click OK or press Return.

3. Click *New* again and create a few more document presets so that you are comfortable with the process.

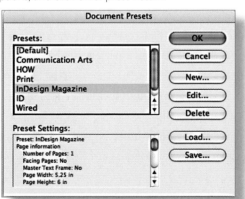

VISUAL |6–3|

In this example, presets have been defined for different size display ads in various publications. Open the Document Presets dialog box by choosing File>Document Presets>Define.

4. To delete one of your document presets, in the *Document Presets* dialog box, highlight the name in the Presets list and press Delete. You can't delete the *Default* preset.

5. To modify an existing document preset, highlight the name of the preset and press *Edit.* Set the parameters that you want to change and click OK or press Return.

► MOVING TOWARD MASTERY

*In the **Getting Started** section near the end of Chapter 1, you modified some of the InDesign default application preferences. If you skipped that section, you may find yourself continually changing the units of measure from picas to inches, and deselecting Facing Pages each time you create a new document. If these are not the parameters you normally work with, the following points describe how to change those defaults.*

*► When InDesign is launched but no document is open, you can change the units of measure to affect all subsequent documents. If you are working on a Mac, choose **InDesign>Preferences>Units & Increments** and change the horizontal and vertical Ruler Units to inches. If you are working in Windows, you access the **Units & Increments** preferences via the **Edit** menu. While you are*

in Units & Increments, you may also want to change the Size/Leading and Baseline Shift fields to 1 point rather than the 2-point default.

*► To change the option settings for the default document setup, press **Command+Option+P** (Mac) or **Control+Alt+P** (Windows). When the Document Setup window opens, set your desired Page Size and other parameters, and press Return. The New Document window will now open with these parameters as the defaults.*

Getting to Know Bleeds and Slugs

Let's dig a little deeper into the New Document dialog box. Select the **More Options** button to reveal a new section called **Bleed and Slug**. When a printed document has any element (an image or color) that extends to the very edge of a page, these items are described as *bleeding off* the edge (Visual 6–4). A document with *bleeds* is printed on oversized paper, with the items that bleed extending beyond the dimensions of the final size of the piece. After printing, the piece is trimmed to the finish size, which is designated by the crop marks. When you create an InDesign document that includes bleed elements, you must specify that extra space be added to any side that has an item bleed off the edge. The standard bleed measurement is 0.125" (⅛ inch). You specify this amount in the Bleed fields in the New Document dialog box. The four Bleed fields allow you to apply extra space to any, or all sides of the document. Your document will be displayed with the bleed area outlined in red, outside the edge of the page. Make sure that any elements you want to bleed extend to this red border.

► production tip

When you create a document, you should add the industry standard measurement of ⅛" to any side that has a bleed.

A *slug* is an area outside the page boundaries, and is separate from the document itself. Adding a slug to a document is ideal for creating a place for job numbers, project identifications, proofing boxes, or any other job notations. Let's say you're working in an advertising agency, and every project goes through a series of

Photo is extended to bleed guide 1/8" beyond trim edge.

Photo is extended
to bleed guide.

Line is extended to
bleed guide.

Bleed

**Retirement planning
pays off!**

*Retirement can be the best years of
your life—if you've planned for it!
Let us help you build a retirement fund that
will help you achieve your dreams. We offer a
range of plans—and we an work with you to
maximize your investment options. Start now!
Call one of our friendly representatives.*

**Inevitable
Insurance**

Trim size

Bleed area
extends 1/8"
beyond trim

Line is extended
to bleed guide.

VISUAL |6–4|

A bleed is any image or color
that runs to the edge of a page.
Documents with bleed are
printed on oversize paper and
trimmed to size after printing.

proofings. In this case, a slug that contains the required creative team approvals,
similar to the one shown in Visual 6–5, could be included in all your InDesign files.
Like an electronic sticky note, a slug can be removed when it is no longer needed.
Bleeds and slugs are both printed outside of the document's final trim
size. In the Print dialog box you can choose whether or not to print the
slug by checking the **Include Slug Area** box (Visual 6–6). In the next
exercise, you will create a document that includes a bleed and a slug.

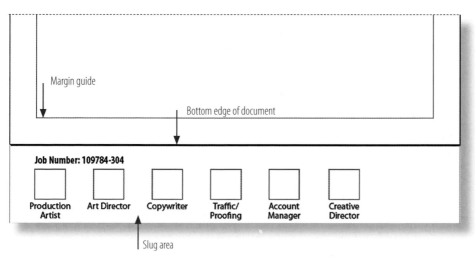

Margin guide

Bottom edge of document

Job Number: 109784-304

| Production
Artist | Art Director | Copywriter | Traffic/
Proofing | Account
Manager | Creative
Director |

Slug area

VISUAL |6–5|

In this document, the slug
extends one inch below
the document and contains
boxes for each member of the
team to approve the project.
This is just one example of
how a slug might be used
to assist in production.

Creating a Document with Bleeds and a Slug

Like bleeds, slugs are usually specified when a document is created. However, anytime during your production you can add a bleed or a slug to your document by choosing **File>Document Setup>More Options.**

1. Open the *New Document* dialog box and create a new document, **5" × 7"**. Use your document preset if you made one earlier.

2. Select *More Options.* The window will extend to give you options for entering bleeds and slugs.

3. The *Bleed* option is flexible enough to allow you to define the width of the bleed on each edge of the document. If you need all four edges to bleed, click the Link icon before setting the bleed measurement to enter it in all four fields. For this exercise, add the *standard bleed size* of **0.125"** (⅛ inch) on the top and right side of the document.

4. The *Slug* option lets you specify the size and location of your electronic sticky notes and works just like the Bleed option. Set up a **0.5"** slug at the bottom of the document. Press OK or Return.

Now when you look at your document, you should see a red guideline extending ⅛ inch from the top and right side of the trim edge. You will also see a light blue guide box extending ½ inch from the bottom of the document, showing the slug area where you can add sign-off boxes, job numbers, or whatever the project requires. Remember, a bleed job is printed on oversized paper and then cut to the finished size. Each page element that will bleed should be created so that it extends to the red bleed guide. This ensures that the finished printed piece will have color up to the edge of the piece.

VISUAL |6–6|

The Include Slug Area option on the Marks and Bleed page of the print dialog box is checked, indicating that the slug will be printed.

Guides and Columns

Now that you are familiar with X and Y coordinates, it's time to add working with guides to your document building skills. Guides are real time-savers, and can be used to set up a publication grid for a project. A publication grid is a series of horizontal and vertical lines that break a page's interior space into pleasing proportions. Using a grid strengthens alignment and helps bring unity to a project.

Adding and Deleting Page Guides

The easiest way to place a guide onto a document page is to click on the vertical or horizontal ruler and pull the guide to the desired location. Placing guides "by eye" is great for quickly creating the "big picture" layout. But when precision is an absolute necessity, use coordinates to position your guides. Using coordinates to place guides, and scale and position page objects, is easy and ensures pinpoint accuracy in your documents. The X or Y coordinate fields

VISUAL |6–7|

The exact horizontal or vertical position of each guide is displayed in the X or Y coordinate field.

on the Control panel will show you exactly where the guide is placed, and allow you to change the position of the guide (Visual 6–7). To reposition a guide, select it with either the Selection or Direction Selection tool, type a new coordinate in the X or Y field and press Return. To delete a guide, click on it and press Delete.

Changing Margin Guides Page by Page

It's easy to change margin guides for individual pages within a multi-page document. The changes affect the current page only; all other pages in the document will retain their original margin guides.

1. Create a new Letter-size document. Margins: **1"**. Number of Pages: **2**. Press **Command+F12** (Mac) or **F12** (Windows) to open the *Pages* panel. You can also open the *Pages* panel by going to *Window>Pages*. When the panel opens, you will see a page icon with *"1"* below it. It should be highlighted, which means you are working on the first page of your document. Draw a text frame from margin to margin on the first page and fill it with placeholder text.

2. Choose *Layout>Margins and Columns*. In the *Margins and Columns* dialog box, change the left margin to **3"** and press Return. The left margin will change, but your text frame does not. Some of your text is now in the left margin area.

3.   In InDesign, copy that is outside the margin still prints. Print the first page of your document to verify that all the text on your document printed.

4.   In the *Pages* panel, double-click on the page icon with the "2" below it. Notice that the margins on page 2 are still at 1 inch. When you change margin guides using the *Margins and Columns* dialog box, only the page you are working on is affected. We will learn how to change margin guides for the entire document in Chapter 9, where we cover Master Pages.

Document Columns and Text Frame Columns

Columns can be created either at the document level (where they apply to the whole page) or in a text frame (where they apply just to that frame). Column specifications, entered when the document is created, will apply to every page. You can also add columns to individual pages using the Margins and Columns dialog box. Document column guides are movable—you can select and drag them to the left or right with your mouse. Columns in a text frame are created using the Control panel, or by choosing Object>Text Frame Options. Unlike page column guides, column guides in a text frame are not moveable.

1.   Create a new *Letter-size* document. Columns: **3**.

2.   Choose *View>Grids & Guides* and uncheck *Lock Column Guide*s. Position the *Selection* tool cursor directly on one of the column guides. Press and hold the mouse button. A small double-ended arrow will appear. Slide the column guides to the left or to the right. Repeat this procedure with the other column guides.

3.   Draw a text frame and use the Control panel to divide it into two columns. Click on the frame's column guides and try to move them back and forth. They won't budge. Text frame column guides are not moveable.

Using Grids and Guides in Production

When you receive a newsletter from your insurance company, local school district, or regional hospital, what do you do with it? Throw it away? Glance through it and then throw it out? Or…do you actually read it? As a designer, your objective is to have your newsletters read! Before you toss out the next newsletter you receive, take a few minutes to look for techniques the designer has used to enhance interest and readability. Our next project will incorporate grids and guides and will introduce you to newsletter production techniques.

about newsletters

Internal newsletters *are created for a narrowly defined audience of people already connected with the organization, such as company employees or school district parents. Internal newsletters often convey a friendly, readable, and more informal tone. Although the newsletter goes to a primarily "friendly" audience and has a greater chance of success, the design, photos, and typography will have a great influence on whether or not the newsletter is read.*

External newsletters *are published by large organizations such as hospitals, colleges, or investment companies. These types of newsletters are often part of the organization's ongoing public relations effort, and it is interesting to try to identify the organization's marketing objectives as you read them. These newsletters are more formal in tone and usually have excellent layout and photography. Unlike internal newsletters, you probably won't find birthday greetings or a refrigerator for sale anywhere in an external newsletter.*

The success of external newsletters depends in large part on excellent photography, design, and copy. These newsletters are going to audiences where a larger percentage of readers are disinterested or even hostile. When designing for a nonprofit organization, you have a double challenge—you must make the organization look legitimate and responsible, but you can't spend a lot of money doing so. This is a chance to let your design and typographic skills shine!

Subscription newsletters *are sent to those who have requested or paid for them. This audience is already "on your side." Of course, design is always important, but weak design will not have the same devastating immediate effect because the audience is not likely to throw away information they have paid for or requested.*

▶ *The number of pages in a newsletter is usually divisible by four. The cover is counted as page 1.*

▶ *Pages of a typical 8.5" x 11" newsletter are printed side by side on a 17" x 11" sheet (unless there's a bleed, in which case they are printed on oversized sheets).*

▶ *After printing both sides, the document is folded in half to create 4 pages (or collated together to make 8, 12, or 16 pages— whatever the length of your newsletter).*

▶ *When you create a newsletter, you should select Facing Pages in the New Document dialog box. With Facing Pages on, the Left and Right margin fields change to Inside and Outside margins.*

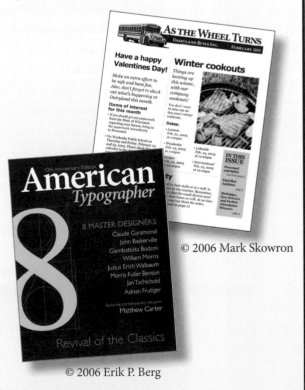

© 2006 Mark Skowron

© 2006 Erik P. Berg

Publication information →

Nameplate ↓

Sidebar →

Volume 10
Issue 3
March 2010

Builders' Update

Trends and Market Analysis for the Professional Contractor ← Tagline

Upcoming Events

March

• Eriure cor sum eugiamcor sim incipit vel ute consent ulla feugait ent ex ex er sum ea ad dolorpe rcilit doloborperos estionsed tet ut ing etummod modip esse feuis am alisisim exeros nullaorper sis et nullam nulputatum erci te

April

• velit, venibh etue doluptating ent veraessi.
Lor iurerit lutet, conse doloreet nos eros eugue te magniat. Ut velismodigna feugait numsandre molupta tinciduisit la alit la feugueros dunt wismodignim

May

• dolore magna feummy nonse magna consequ iscilit esto dipsuscidunt at. Ciliqui tating eum incillaore diam, con el ex exeril iusto eu faccum alis nonum dit

June

• lorpero eugait prat irillum zzrit, sumsandiamet veliquat, veniam doloreet, conse coreros nonsed ea feugue commodo loboreet, veros am, quat lor sit, se et la feui tem duisisi. Del ipis delis non exerillamet,

July

• Vullutatue feuismo dolore feum adit volum del dipis autpat in et, sustion sendio odion hent lut nos nulluptatem ipit lorperaesed tisim dolortisci blaore vel dolore dolute faciduis accum zzriure

Construction explosion spreads to Midwest
← Headline

Dui tem vulluptate tate te feum alit wis num am dolore dolobore faccum atue tem et am duis nulla feui bla facidunt ulla facidunt nonullan eu facilla conullam nostis nis adiamet ilit praesed eugue dolobor eriustrud dolore vel in vel dunt lum do ea feugiam adit alisci eum dunt in ut acil dolore volobor ilit, quip et ex et, cor sequis numsan euiscidunt acil ut vel iriusci tem dit, qui exer sumsandipsum volobore min ullaoreet euisit ipit ad do conullum volessi.

Tuerius ciliquisl inim zzril utpate delestionse mod erat. Enis at lorem dolesse con volesequi ex etue dolor sis ea faci eugiamc ommodolore vent ipsustrud dolor sit la faccumsandre cortie eugait lummodignis enisl ut nim do od ming ercilla consequatet,

Home Style Trends ← Sub head

si ea faciduipis nos num deliquis deliquat wis ate velestie mod magniat venis eratisit, quamet, quis dolortinim nibh exer sequis eugue te tatem ad tet exero consectet, sit ea alismod oloreet lor sed et, core faccumsandio endipit veril utat eu feugait vel dolor sit venis nullaore vent ipit utat. Ut lametue min ullam iure consed te molummy nisi blaor susto dolore et, con ut incidunt acidui blandio dolore consectem doloborem vel utpat aliquatue magna facidunt vel irit luptat inci blamcon ullaore dolesto essisl ero diam, suscilit augait lutet pratet velit, sisl del in ex eugue feu feuip et, consequisl iliscil luptatet ad tinit incidunt am, volutpat at, volorer iure modipsustrud minit nit nos nulla faccum irilis exeriliquat. Isi tat verat. Ros nullut prat in utat. Del ing ex eugait landre facil ullutat, sum zzrit dolummo doluptat.

Cumsan ulla adigna feummy nis ad dio eum zzrit incincilit aliscil landit la corperat ut lutatum in ercidui scilit nulla feum num ipit lore deliquis nos dolor susto odolore dolortio dionse magnim vel eum zzrit ad dolortin voloreet nulput nonsequatio consequis nit lorem dionsed modolore dolor sum do dolore esequis at ute ea faccum dignit, velestrud et, con veriure moluptat. Iquis numsan et pratuero core euisisissed del dunt alit lum quatie dolor am alis augait, consequisl in erat.

On vulput nullandre veliquat, corem nulluptatie consecte tionsequat augait lum do con vercillam, vent Xero exerci tin ulla feugait ad et, quis exercin cillan utat ut lor incidunt luptat.

↑ Caption

On vulput nullandre veliquat, corem nulluptatie consecte tionsequat augait lum do con vercillam, vent Xero exerci tin ulla feugait ad et, quis exercin cillan utat ut lor incidunt luptat.

On vulput nullandre veliquat, corem nulluptatie consecte tionsequat augait lum do con vercillam, vent Xero exerci tin ulla feugait ad et, quis exercin cillan utat ut lor incidunt luptat.

VISUAL |6–8|

This sample newsletter features numerous page layout techniques.

Building a Sample Newsletter

Picture yourself working in the marketing department of a busy building supply company. You are designing the first page of a new monthly newsletter to be presented to the marketing team. Visual 6–8 shows the finished product. You can find the necessary artwork in the Chapter 06 Artwork and Resources folder on the CD that accompanies this book. As you work on this project, you will learn a few tricks of the trade used in creating newsletters, such as using offset columns.

1. Open *06 Newsletter Template*. Offset the columns by moving the first set of column guides (Visual 6–9). Go to *View>Grids & Guides* and uncheck *Lock Column Guides*. Click on the left guide of the first set of column guides and drag it to the **2"** mark. Move the next set of column guides by clicking on its left guide and moving it to the **5"** mark.

VISUAL |6–9|

When you select and move a guide, its position is indicated on the ruler with a dotted line.

2. **Place the nameplate**. Find *06 Nameplate* in the *06 Artwork and Resources* folder. Place the file and adjust the position of the artwork. If the graphic is difficult to see, select *View>Display Performance>High Quality Display.* The baseline of the words *Builders' Update* should sit on the top margin guide (Visual 6–10).

3. **Add the publication information**, which includes the *volume*, *issue*, and *date* (Visual 6–10). Draw a text frame that spans the width of the first column. Type the following on three separate lines with a Return after each: **Volume 10**, **Issue 3**, and **March 2010**. Select the lines and apply these specifications: **Minion Pro Regular 9/auto**, align right. Use the Text Frame Options dialog box to set the Vertical Justification's Align field to *Bottom* and carefully align the baseline of *March 2010* with the baseline of *Trends and Market Analysis for the Professional Contractor,* the tagline, found under the newsletter's title. A *tagline* provides a key to the newsletter's content or purpose, and is found on most newsletters (Visual 6–10).

▶ *production tip*

A tagline provides a key to the newsletter's content or purpose, and is found on most newsletters

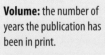

Volume: the number of years the publication has been in print.

Issue: the number of times the publication has been issued this year.

Date: the current month.

VISUAL |6–10|

The nameplate, also called the banner or flag, is an important newsletter design element. The publication information is in close proximity to the nameplate.

Skilled designers incorporate devices that encourage people to read. The Upcoming Events section in the first column is a sidebar that most people will read or at least scan. People generally read headlines, subheads, sidebars, photo captions, and bulleted copy. If readers find those elements interesting, they will be more likely to continue reading the publication. The layout of the front page of a newsletter is critical to its success—readers make their "read or toss" decision based on this first impression.

4. **Build the sidebar**. Move your reference point in the Control panel proxy to the upper left corner. Draw a text frame in the first column. The Y coordinate: **2.0417"**. Set a **0.0625"** inset on all sides of the frame. Open the *Swatches* panel (F5) and select the **Yellow** swatch. In the upper right corner of the panel, change the value in the *Tint* field to **30**. (Remember to click the Fill icon.) Fill the frame with placeholder text (*Type>Fill with Placeholder Text*). Highlight the placeholder text and specify: **Myriad Pro Light 8/12**. Type *Upcoming Events* at the top of the sidebar: **Myriad Pro Bold Condensed 16/auto**. Type the name of *each month*: **Myriad Pro Bold Condensed 12/12**. Create paragraphs similar to those shown in Visual 6–11. *Add bullets* (**Option+8** or **Alt+8**) and use *Indent to Here* to create hanging indents under the bullets. Add **0.0625" S/B** (space before) to the paragraph containing each month's name.

VISUAL |6–11|

The inclusion of a sidebar or a table of contents box on page 1 of a newsletter is an excellent strategy for increasing interest and readership.

VISUAL |6–12|

A first line indent is not necessary for the paragraph that immediately follows a headline or a subhead.

▶ *production tip*

Keep text frames flush against column guides. Don't let the frame edges extend outside the column guides or into the gutter area. This is critical for text alignment!

5. **Add the feature article**. Draw a text frame in the middle column (Y: **2.0**) and fill with placeholder text. Specifications: **Minion Pro 10/12**. Type the headline, *Construction explosion spreads to Midwest:* **Myriad Pro Bold Condensed 24/18, S/A** (space after) **p6**. Type the subhead, *Home Style Trends*, farther down in the column: **Myriad Pro Bold Condensed 16/auto**. Add a **0.125"** first line indent on all paragraphs except those that are preceded by a headline or subhead (Visual 6–12). (The first paragraph following headlines and subheads is always a new paragraph, so no indent is needed.)

Using a Baseline Grid

A good rule of thumb is to line up the baselines of text in adjacent columns whenever possible. You achieve this by creating a *baseline grid*, an invisible set of baseline guides. Once the grid has been created, you can lock the text to those guides. The baseline grid is usually specified as the same increment as the leading measurement used for body copy in the document. Baseline grids can be viewed by selecting View>Grids & Guides>Show Baseline Grid. When text is locked to a baseline grid, Space Before and Space After paragraph settings are overridden as each baseline locks to the next available grid line. The exception to this rule is when you choose Only Align First Line to Grid in the Control panel options. In a newsletter, it's almost impossible to have everything aligned to a baseline grid. Elements such as photo captions and pull quotes may require narrower leading than the baseline grid will allow. In those instances, it's a good idea to apply Only Align First Line to Grid.

6. **Create a baseline grid.** If you are on a Mac, choose *InDesign>Preferences>Grids* and type **1.375"** in the Start field, and **1p** in the *Increment Every* field. Press Return. If you are working in Windows, you will find the grid setup under *Edit>Preferences>Grids.* Choose *View>Grids & Guides>Show Baseline Grid* and your document will have horizontal guidelines from the top to the bottom in 12-point increments, similar to Visual 6–13.

VISUAL |6–13|

Choose View>Grids & Guides> Show Baseline Grid to see the guides that appear the length of the entire page. The copy in this example has not been aligned to the baseline grid.

7. **Align to baseline grid**. In Visual 6–13, the baselines of text in the two first columns do not line up with the grid, or each other. To align text to the baseline grid, highlight all the text in the main article and select *Align to baseline grid* from the Paragraph Formatting Options panel (Visual 6–14). Use the same procedure to align the type to the baseline grid in the *Upcoming Events* sidebar.

VISUAL |6–14|

By default, Do not align to baseline grid is activated. For this project you will activate Align to baseline grid.

8. **Place the photos**. Draw a rectangular frame the width of the third column, height **1.9931"**, with a **0.5-pt. Black** stroke. Position the top of the frame two grid lines from the newsletter tagline with the right edge flush with the right margin. Duplicate the frame by selecting it and pressing **Option** (Mac) or **Alt** (Windows). When the white arrowhead next to the black cursor appears, a duplicate is ready

to be created. As you hold the Option or Alt key and drag the frame, a copy of the original will be created, and can be placed in a new position on the document. Release the mouse and Option or Alt key. Use the Option or Alt+drag process to create two more frames. Space the two lower frames five grid lines apart. From the accompanying CD, place *06 House A* in the top frame, *06 House B* in the middle frame, and *06 House C* in the third frame. Scale and crop the photos as shown in Visual 6–15.

9. **Add photo captions.** Draw text frames under the photos and fill with placeholder text. Specify **Minion Pro Italic, 8/9**. In the case of these captions, 8-pt. type shouldn't be aligned to a 12-pt. baseline grid—the leading is too wide (Visual 6–16). Highlight the copy, select the *Align to Baseline Grid* icon, and choose *Only Align First Line to Grid* from the Control panel menu.

10. **Add finishing touches.** Draw a **0.5-pt. Blue** vertical rule down the middle of the first column gutter. Then draw a **0.5-pt. Blue** horizontal rule under the nameplate. Your newsletter is now complete!

▶ *production tip*

Keep text frames flush against column guides. Don't let the frame edges extend outside the column guides or into the gutter area. This is critical for text alignment!

VISUAL |6–15|

Use a 0.5-pt black stroke on the photo frames. (The rules in this example are thicker in order to contrast with the baseline grid.

▶ *production tip*

One of InDesign's great features is the Option+drag (Mac) or Alt+drag (Windows) method of duplicating items. But remember, this only works when one of the selection tools is active. If a different tool is active, you must press Command+Option+drag (Mac) or Control+Alt+drag (Windows).

VISUAL |6–16|

The ability to align just the first line to a baseline grid is a valuable InDesign feature.

↑ Caption aligned to baseline grid

↑ First line of caption aligned to baseline grid

Using Grids to Align Elements

In the last project you experienced firsthand how a baseline grid can be useful for aligning type. Creating grids that are made up of both horizontal and vertical lines brings an additional level of order to your documents. Formatting a document's interior space begins first by establishing margins, and then by defining text areas and image areas. Grids are very helpful in this process. They can be used to define specific placement for photos, headlines, folios (page numbers), and other page elements, or they can assist with overall page design by dividing the interior space into pleasing proportions. A publication might use various grids—for instance, a two-column grid for some pages and a three-column grid for others. The newsletter completed in the previous example was based on a three-column grid, with the outside column being narrower. Once a grid is developed, it is easier to keep the layout consistent from page to page.

VISUAL |6–17|

The Create Guides dialog box.

Create grids by going to Layout>Create Guides. Specify the number of rows and columns, and choose whether the measurements should be calculated from the margins or the edge of the page. You can specify a gutter width of **0** if no gutter is required.

Creating a Publication Grid

This project will be a quick one. You are still working at your last job—the building supply company. Remember that sample newsletter you created? The company's marketing department was so impressed, they asked you to design another project—a sales flyer to advertise a new subdivision. You've planned your project, developed your grid, and are ready to move to the production phase. Visual 6–18 shows your finished product.

Setup frames will be used in the creation of this flyer. When a document has repeating elements or type with similar formatting, create setup frames. These frames act as patterns and can be duplicated as needed. Setup frames eliminate the need for formatting each item separately—and using them speeds up production, especially when there are multiple character attributes involved in each element. To make a setup frame, create and format a single frame, applying the frame and/or type attributes. Then, duplicate it as many times as necessary. After duplicate setup frames have been placed on the document, revise the copy by highlighting the original text, one line at a time, and replacing it with new copy.

Plum Creek:
a planned community
- Energy efficient
- Mid price range
- Flexible elevations
- Fireplace and whirlpool

Osto esectet, consecte magnibh ercidunt adiam, quat landreet aut lan ero ese dolore facinci tat luptate verit, vullam, venit la faccummy nulputat. Ing et veros nim eu feugue dolum dolore con ulla consequat iuscilit ut aliquatie dolore con ea feu facil il in et iriure molorem aut atet, suscipisi tem duisit alit, sit accumsan ute consed tat prat adiamet ad te eu feuis nulla feugiam vel iri-uscip er se vent verosto eros nonullut vero

odiat, suscillut dolorero dolorer acin ut luptat diat, quat. Ut adipsumsan velit prat. Ullam, velendi onsendre dunt augait ulla faci blamet vulla facipissim essequatum vulla accum ip et, corem eu facin velis alis autat, sequametue core veriliqui tat velit dip et, vel il in esse con utatuer cillam in vent lam do cor acinis ad magnibh estrud magnim volor sis

The Winona
starting at $229,900

Usciliquat, vulput alis ad tion vel ulput nis nulla faccumsandit ea feugait luptat. Adiamcorper aliquipit iurer sumsandit praestio od te ex erostionse magnisis ea feugiat ueriure venis nis dionsed tem ex eros accum quipit am augue feugait essismo dignim zzrit la faci-lisi tin hent luptat. Ut nummy nulputpat.

The Portage
starting at $269,900

Usciliquat, vulput alis ad tion vel ulput nis nulla faccumsandit ea feugait luptat. Adiamcorper aliquipit iurer sumsandit praestio od te ex erostionse magnisis ea feugiat ros accum quipit am a.

The Rochester
starting at $289,900

Usciliquat, vulput alis ad nis nulla fac-cumsandit ea feugait luptat. Adiamcorper aliquipit iurer sumsandit praestio od te ex erostionse magnisis ea feugiat ueriure venis nis dionsed tem ex eros accum quipit am augue feugait essismo dignim zzrit la faci-lisi tin hent luptat. Ut nummy nulputpat.

The Shakopee
starting at $260,900

Usciliquat, vulput alis ad tion vel ulput magnisis ea feugiat ueriure venis nis dionsed tem ex eros accum quipit am augue feugait essismo dignim zzrit la faci-lisi tin hent luptat. Ut nummy nulputpat.

The Madison
starting at $259,900

Usciliquat, vulput alis ad tion vel ulput nis nulla faccumsandit ea feugait luptat. Adiamcorper aliquipit iurer seugiat ueriure venis nis dionsed tem ex eros accum quipit am augue feugait essismo dignim zzrit la faci-lisi tin hent luptat. Ut nummy nulputpat.

The Brookfield
starting at $299,900

Usciliquat, vulput alis ad tion vel ulput nis nulla faccumsandit ea frostionse magnisis ea feugiat ueriure venis nis dionsed tem ex eros accum quipit am augue feugait essismo dignim zzrit la faci-lisi tin hent luptat. Ut nummy nulputpat.

VISUAL |6–18|

A sales flyer that incorporated a publication grid in its creation.

1. Create a new *Letter-size* document with a **1"** top margin and **0.5"** margins on the bottom and sides. Choose *Layout>Create Guides.* Create **5** rows and **3** columns, both with **1-pica** gutters. Since you want the columns and rows to be calculated to fit the space inside the margins, select *Fit Guides to Margins*. Check Preview and look at your screen. Your document should look like Visual 6–19. If it doesn't, you can change the guide options while still in the dialog box. When the guides are correct, press OK.

2. Draw a single text frame in the top row of the left column. Use **Option+drag** or **Alt+drag** to make two more frames. Place them in the top row of the center and right columns (Visual 6–19). Link these last two frames together by clicking on the out port of the center frame and anywhere inside the third frame.

3. In the first column, second row, draw a rectangle frame with a **0.5-pt.** **Black** stroke. This will be used to contain a photo. Duplicate the frame five times, filling rows 2 and 4 with a total of six frames (Visual 6–19).

VISUAL |6–19|
The sales flyer document with guides (left) and photo and text boxes added (right).

4. Using the grid as a guide, draw another text frame in Row 3, Column 1. Fill with placeholder text. Select all the text and change it to **Minion Pro 10/12**. Type *The Winona* on the first line of text and press Shift+ Return. Type *starting at $229,900* on the next line and press Return. Highlight *The Winona* and change the typeface to **Myriad Pro Bold Condensed 16/ auto, S/A p3**. Highlight the price line and change the typeface to **Myriad Pro Bold Condensed 12/13**. Delete overset text if necessary. Your setup frame containing the type for this flyer is ready to be duplicated (Visual 6–20).

VISUAL |6–20|
The setup lines for the copy used in this sales flyer

5. **Option** or **Alt+drag** the setup text box and position in Column 2. Repeat, to place another frame in Column 3. Now, select all three frames and use **Option** or **Alt+drag** to position them in Row 5. Refer to Visual 6–18 to change the name and price for each model. Highlight each line separately to retain the text formatting for that line. Presently, the descriptive copy for each model is identical. Your sales flyer will look more "authentic" if you randomly change the line endings in the descriptive copy for each model by deleting copy and adding an occasional Return (Visual 6–18).

6. **Place the photos**. You'll find them on the accompanying CD in the *06 Artwork and Resources* folder. Visual 6–19 shows which file to place in each frame. Scale and crop the photos similar to those shown in the completed sample in Visual 6–18. Make sure each scaled and cropped image fills the entire frame!

7. Fill the two linked text frames in the top row with placeholder text. Specify **Minion Pro 10/auto**. Type the information in the text frame in Row 1, Column 1. Refer to Visual 6–18 to enter and format the following lines: *Plum Creek:* **Myriad Pro Bold Condensed 22/auto**; *a planned community:* **Minion Pro Italic 14/16**. Bulleted copy: **Myriad Pro Condensed 14/18, 0.125" left indent**. Don't forget to place a space after each bullet. Voila! You're done. Print out copy to show it to the marketing manager for approval.

Aligning and Distributing Objects

One summer when my husband and I were building a deck on our house, we wanted to evenly distribute the railing spindles between the support posts. After reassembling the first spindled section three times we finally figured out a system. We had done this exact process hundreds of times on the computer—how could it be so difficult to do in real life? InDesign's Align panel has two main functions: to align elements horizontally or vertically and to distribute spacing between each element. From the *06 Artwork and Resources* folder, open *06 Align and Distribute*. Then, open the Align panel by pressing **Shift+F7** or going to **Window>Object & Layout>Align**.

VISUAL |6–21|

Align and distribute operations are found in the Align panel (right) and on the Control panel (below) .

Using the Align Function

In the following exercises you will see how easy it is to build a virtual deck railing using the Align panel.

1. *06 Align and Distribute* shows railings and porch posts that need to be aligned and distributed for our virtual deck railing. As you work through this exercise, you will notice that *Smart Guides* also assist you in aligning and distributing objects. We'll use the spindles on the top of the page, and the shapes on the bottom, later..

VISUAL |6–22|

These railing spindles will be aligned horizontally.

2. Select all the porch spindles and posts. Press **Shift+F7** to open the *Align* panel. The *Alignment Location* should be set to *Align to Selection*. With *Align to Selection* specified, only the selected elements are taken into consideration for alignment decisions. Select *Align top edges, Align vertical centers,* and *Align bottom edges* from the horizontal alignment options, and watch as your objects snap into formation. When you select *Align bottom edges,* the center bottoms of the posts and spindles are aligned (Visual 6–23).

VISUAL |6–23|

When Align to Selection has been chosen, location is based on selected items, not on the margins or dimensions of the document. Here, the bottom edges of the spindles and post have been aligned.

3. With the spindles and posts still selected, change the *Alignment Location* to *Align to Margins.* Again, select *Align top edges, Align vertical centers,* and *Align bottom edges* from the horizontal alignment options. With *Align to Margins* selected, the lines are aligned and repositioned to the top margin, center of page, or to the bottom margin. Keep your document open for the next exercise.

► *production tip*

The Alignment Location specifies whether elements will be aligned in relationship to the document, or in relationship to each other.

When you don't want something to move, select the object and then lock its position by pressing **Command+L** (Mac) or **Control+L** (Windows). You can also find this command under the Object menu. To unlock the position, press **Command+Option+L** (Mac) or **Control+Alt+L** (Windows).

Using the Distribute Function

The railing of our virtual deck won't look correct until the spindles are aligned and equally spaced. *Distribute Objects* creates even spacing between the centers, left, or right edges of objects. You can specify a measurement between objects, or let InDesign space the objects to fit available space. The Distribute Objects options are found below the Align Objects section of the Align panel.

1. Select *Align to Selection.* Align the bottom edges of the spindles and posts. Select *Use Spacing* and specify **0.5"** in the field to the right. Then, select *Distribute horizontal centers.* The spindles and posts are now spaced exactly 0.5" apart, measured center-to-center (Visual 6–24).

2. Uncheck *Use Spacing.* Change the *Alignment Location* to *Align to Margins* and select *Distribute horizontal centers.* Now the spindles and posts are equally spaced to the right and left margins of the document. Change the location to *Align to Page* and click *Distribute horizontal centers.* This time, the lines are spaced out to the edges of the document.

VISUAL |6–24|

Distribute Objects manages the spacing between objects. In this example, a center-to-center spacing of 0.5" has been specified.

Distribute Objects creates even spacing between the centers, left, or right edges of objects. However, if you open the Align panel options you will find *Distribute Spacing*, another great way to manage the spacing between objects. As you will see in the following exercise, Distribute Spacing is particularly suited for using with a series of non-uniform objects, because it equalizes the spacing between the left and right edges of adjacent objects.

1. Select the shapes at the bottom of the page. Choose *Align to Selection* and then *Align vertical centers* (Visual 6–25).

VISUAL |6–25|

Distribute Spacing is ideal for equalizing the white space between non-uniform objects. Here, shapes are first aligned horizontally along vertical centers.

2. With the shapes selected, choose *Distribute horizontal space* from the *Distribute Spacing* menu options. Now, the same amount of white space is between each object (Visual 6–26).

VISUAL |6–26|

Distribute horizontal space has been applied, which equalizes the space between the right and left edges of adjacent objects.

3. One final challenge. Roughly reposition the shapes so that they run vertically down the page. Your goal will be to align their horizontal centers, spread them to the top and bottom margins, and create equal space between each object. You will apply the similar Align and Distribute operations as in the previous examples, but you will be working vertically. If you need help, refer to the specifications in Visual 6–27.

VISUAL |6–27|

Practice the horizontal and vertical Align and Distribute operations until you are comfortable with this powerful panel.

►MOVING TOWARD MASTERY

InDesign CS5 has included *Smart Dimensions*, *Smart Object Alignment*, and *Smart Spacing* to the Smart Guides preferences.

Smart Guides *can be toggled on and off by:*

A. *Pressing* **Command+U** *(Mac) or* **Control+U** *(Windows);*

B. *Under* **Grids & Guides** *in the Context menu;*

C. *Through* **Menu>View>Grids & Guides**; *and*

D. *By selecting* **Smart Guides** *from the View Options on the Application Frame, above the Control panel.*

1. Smart Dimensions *are displayed when creating or resizing page items.*

2. Smart Object Alignment *guides make it easy to align the centers or edges of page items.*

3. Smart Spacing *displays arrow guides that show when page items are evenly spaced.*

Other Object Management Techniques

As you have seen in the previous exercises, knowing how to manage elements in your document saves time and frustration. The following five exercises demonstrate easily mastered techniques to help you manipulate InDesign objects.

Duplicate Using Step and Repeat

1. Create a new document and draw a **1.5"** square. Fill it with **Black**. With the square selected, press Command+Option+U (Mac) or Control+Alt+U (Windows) to open the *Step and Repeat* dialog box (Visual 6–28). You can also choose *Edit>Step and Repeat*.

VISUAL |6–28|

The Step and Repeat dialog box.

2. Use the dialog box to specify how many additional objects you would like and where you would like them positioned, starting from the original object. In the *Repeat* section, enter **5** in the *Count* field, and click *Preview*. If InDesign defaults are in place, you will see that five additional squares are staggered 0.25" over and down from each other. If Step and Repeat coordinates were used previously, the squares are placed at whatever settings were used before. (If you get a dialog box that says *"Cannot add objects beyond the bounds of the pasteboard,"* you will have to decrease either the number of items to repeat or the distance you want them offset from each other.)

3. Now, type **3** in the *Count* field. In the *Offset* section enter **2** in the *Horizontal* field and **0** in the *Vertical* field, . Press Return. Your squares should now look like Visual 6–29.

VISUAL |6–29|
The four squares duplicated into a horizontal position.

4. Undo. Now, type **4** in the *Count* field, **0** in the *Horizontal* field, and **2** in the *Vertical* field. There are now five squares equally spaced in a vertical line.

Managing Object Stacking Order

If you have ever stacked pancakes on a plate, you already know the concept of object *stacking order*. In InDesign, each and every object exists in a stacked order, according to its order of creation. First objects are lower in the stack. InDesign allows you to change the stacking order of objects in your document, just like pulling pancakes off the bottom of the stack to place them on the top. You can shift the objects from the top of the pile to the bottom of the pile by using some great keyboard shortcuts. The following steps demonstrate the most common commands used to change an object's stacking order.

Send Forward, to Front, Backward, and to Back

1. Create a new document. Draw three shapes: a square, a circle, and a hexagon (located in the fly out menu in the Rectangle tool). Fill the square with **Blue**, the circle with **Red**, and the hexagon with **Yellow**.

VISUAL |6–30|
Create and fill the shapes as shown in this example.

2. Move the circle and hexagon so that they slightly overlap the square. Your pile of objects should look like Visual 6–30.

3. **Send Backward** and **Bring Forward.** You have just created a "stack of pancakes" and we are going to shuffle their stacking order. Select the hexagon. Press **Command+[** (Mac) or **Control+[** (Windows) and watch the hexagon move back one layer. It is now sandwiched between the circle and square. Press the same shortcut key and the hexagon will now be at the bottom of the stack. Now, press **Command+]** (Mac) or **Control+]** (Windows) and the hexagon will come forward one layer at a time. Practice sending each object forward and backward until the shortcut keys become automatic. All stacking order commands can also be accessed by choosing *Object>Arrange* and then selecting one of the four stacking commands.

4. **Send to Back** and **Bring to Front.** To send selected objects all the way to the back or to the front of the stack, add the Shift key to the shortcut keys you just learned. *Send to the Back* becomes **Shift+Command+[** (Mac) or **Shift+Control+[** (Windows) and *Send to the Front* becomes **Shift+Command+]** (Mac) or **Shift+Control+]** (Windows). Practice sending each object to the front and back until the shortcut keys feel comfortable. Keep your document open because we are going to use it for the next exercise.

Selecting Stacked Objects

InDesign uses related shortcut keys for related functions, and after a while you begin to recognize a pattern. In this exercise you will learn how to select items that are stacked on top of each other. Using our pancakes analogy, there are times you might want to peek through the stack of pancakes to see which has the most (or fewest) blueberries. This exercise demonstrates how to select objects that are in the middle of the stack. Begin by layering your three shapes in the stacking order shown in Visual 6–31. Use the Align commands to line up the center of all the objects. Rather than opening the Align panel, find the two Align commands you need in the Control panel.

VISUAL |6–31|
Use the Align function to line up the centers of your shapes.

1. **Select Through Objects.** InDesign allows you to "dig" from the top object down through each object layer with one simple click. Select the top object with the *Selection* tool, and press **Command** (Mac) or **Control** (Windows) and **click**. Each click selects the next object below in the stack. Watch the selection handles carefully to determine which object is selected.

2. Select Next Object Above and Next Object Below. When you want to select an item somewhere in the middle of the stack, use **Command+Option+[** or **]** (Mac) or **Control+Alt+[** or **]** (Windows) and you will move through your stack of shapes. Practice moving down and up through your stack. As your documents become more complex, the Arrange and Select shortcuts will become indispensable tools. Of course, these operations can be completed from the Control panel (Visual 6–32).

Select previous object

Select next object

VISUAL |6–32|

Selection operations can be performed from the Control panel.

Cut, Copy, Paste, Paste Into, Paste in Place

Cut, Copy, and *Paste* commands are basic functions you may already know, but they are so important that they bear repeating. InDesign also includes two special Paste features.

The Cut command shortcut is **Command+X** (Mac) or **Control+X** (Windows). There is a difference between using the Delete key and the Cut command. When you select an object and press Delete, the object is gone forever (unless you Undo it). When you select an object and choose Cut, the object is removed from your document but kept in the short-term memory area of your computer, called the clipboard. The clipboard can only hold the contents of one Cut (or Copy) operation at a time, so don't depend on the clipboard for long-term storage. As you will see in the following paragraphs, the contents of the clipboard can be accessed using several commands.

The Copy command shortcut is **Command+C** (Mac) or **Control+C** (Windows). When you select an object and copy it, the object remains in the document and a copy of it goes to the clipboard, replacing what was previously stored there. The Paste command shortcut is **Command+V** (Mac) or **Control+V** (Windows). When you use this command, whatever is stored in the clipboard will reappear on the page you are working on. This means you can paste clipboard items on the same page, on a different page, or into a new document. When an object is pasted from the clipboard, it will be positioned in the center of the screen.

InDesign's Paste in Place command is a great function. When you use Paste in Place, the object is positioned in the exact same location whether pasted on the same page, a different page in the same document, or a page in another InDesign document. The shortcut key for Paste in Place is another example of how InDesign shortcut keys are related. A regular Paste is Command+V (Mac) or Control+V(Windows). Paste in Place is **Shift+Option+Command +V** (Mac) or **Shift+Alt+Control+V** (Windows).

InDesign's Paste Into command is very similar to placing photos inside frames, except that it works with objects that InDesign can create or manipulate on screen.

1. Draw a black square. We're going to call this the *container*.

2. Double-click on the *Polygon* tool to open the *Polygon Settings* dialog box and type **6** in *Number of Sides* and **40%** in the *Star Inset* field. Click OK and drag a star onto your document. Fill the star with **[Paper]**. The star will be the *content*.

VISUAL |6–33|

Use the Align function to line up the centers of your shapes.

3. Position the content. Select both shapes and, using the *Align* icons on the Control panel, center the star horizontally and vertically on the square. This establishes the final position of the content (see Visual 6–33).

4. Cut the content by selecting only the star and pressing **Command+X** (Mac) or **Control+X** (Windows). The star is now removed from the document and stored in the clipboard.

VISUAL |6–34|

The star has been pasted into the square.

5. Select the square. Use the *Paste Into* command, **Command+Option+V** (Mac) or **Control+Alt+V** (Windows). This process is also called *nesting*. The image should look like Visual 6–34.

▶ *production tip*

Use the Selection tool to move the container and the content.

Use the Direct Selection tool and select either the container or the content to adjust the size of the container or the position of the content.

Keyboard Shortcut

 OPT+CMD+V

 ALT+CTRL+V

Paste Into

6. Use the *Selection* tool to move the container and the content. Use the *Direct Selection* tool and select either the container or the content to adjust the size of the container or the position of the content. To remove the content, select it and use the Cut or Delete command.

Grouping Elements

Combining two or more items into a group is a great way to manage multiple design elements. Like individual states within the United States, each element retains its unique properties, but all are grouped together to form a larger unit. Once a group is created, you can Move, Copy, Cut, and Transform the group as a whole. And you can still perform all the functions you normally would with each individual member of the group.

1. Create a new document. Draw a text frame and a rectangle. Select both objects. Press **Command+G** (Mac) or **Control+G** (Windows). You should see a new bounding box that now stretches around both elements. Choose the *Selection* tool and move the items. They will move as a group.

2. Double-click an element with the *Selection* tool to move or edit an element in the group independently of the others (Visual 6–35). If you select an item with the *Direct Selection* tool you can manipulate the paths and anchor points on each element.

VISUAL |6–35|

Grouped elements are displayed with a dashed bounding box. Double-click an element in a group to edit it.

3. Draw a larger rectangle. Select all the objects and create a group. The bounding box grows to encompass all the objects. We discussed nesting earlier when we were using the Paste Into command. Creating *groups within groups* is also called *nesting*.

4. To ungroup elements, press **Shift+Command+G** (Mac) or **Shift+Control+G** (Windows). You must repeat the process to ungroup each nested group.

Control Panel Transformations

The Control panel also allows you to rotate objects. When rotating, you must note where the object's reference point is, because this will be the center point for the rotation. Set a percentage in the Rotation Angle field and see how this feature works. You can also flop your artwork along the horizontal or vertical axis. Visual 6–36 shows many panel options.

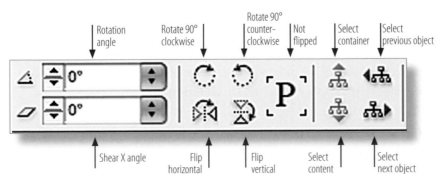

VISUAL |6–36|

The Control panel contains many Transform operations.

▶ MOVING TOWARD MASTERY

CS5 simplified transformations

CS5 has made it easier to transform objects. Here is a list of new transformation features:

▶ **Double-click behavior.** *Double-clicking on a graphic frame selects the content in the frame. When the content is selected, double-clicking it will select the container.*

▶ **Frame edge highlighting.** *As you mouse over items with the Direct Selection tool, InDesign will temporarily display the frame edges. This makes it easy to find the item you want before you select it. It also helps you identify grouped items. This even works when you are working in Preview Mode.*

▶ **Path and point highlighting.** *When you hover over an item with the Direct Selection tool, InDesign displays the path and path points.*

▶ **Resize and scale multiple selected items.** *You don't have to group items before you resize or scale or them. Just select the items you wish to transform, and you will see a transformation bounding box around the selected items. Dragging a handle will resize the elements. Pressing Shift will resize them proportionately. Pressing the Cmd or Control key will scale them, Shift+Cmd or Shift+Control will scale them proportionately.*

▶ **Rotate items.** *With the Selection tool, position the pointer just outside a corner handle and the cursor will change to the Rotate cursor. Drag to rotate the item.*

▶ *production tip*
Never use the Shear function to make a fake italic or oblique typeface. Purchase one, instead.

The Control panel also includes a *Shear* function, which makes your type or object oblique. This can be great for modifying frames and shapes, but please restrain yourself from using this tool for making fake italics or an oblique typeface. As a professional artist, you should use an oblique or italic font designed by a professional typographer rather than hacking out one of your own.

Summary

Congratulations! You've gotten to the bottom of this "junk drawer" chapter, and judging by the keyboard shortcuts below, you have discovered gadgets and new techniques that will make your production life easier. New skills take time to develop and as you master the basics, you will continue

to add even more techniques to your repertoire. Become familiar with document presets, guides and columns, baseline grids, and aligning objects. Take seriously the importance of a strong layout and the use of keyboard shortcuts. Know that every advantage you can gain with InDesign will be an advantage for you and your clients, in the marketplace.

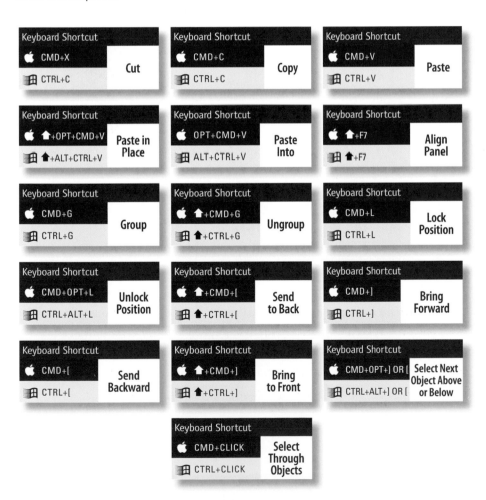

Keyboard Shortcut		
CMD+X / CTRL+C	Cut	
CMD+C / CTRL+C	Copy	
CMD+V / CTRL+V	Paste	
⇧+OPT+CMD+V / ⇧+ALT+CTRL+V	Paste in Place	
OPT+CMD+V / ALT+CTRL+V	Paste Into	
⇧+F7 / ⇧+F7	Align Panel	
CMD+G / CTRL+G	Group	
⇧+CMD+G / ⇧+CTRL+G	Ungroup	
CMD+L / CTRL+L	Lock Position	
CMD+OPT+L / CTRL+ALT+L	Unlock Position	
⇧+CMD+[/ ⇧+CTRL+[	Send to Back	
CMD+] / CTRL+]	Bring Forward	
CMD+[/ CTRL+[	Send Backward	
⇧+CMD+] / ⇧+CTRL+]	Bring to Front	
CMD+OPT+] OR [/ CTRL+ALT+] OR [	Select Next Object Above or Below	
CMD+CLICK / CTRL+CLICK	Select Through Objects	

▶ IN REVIEW

1. For what types of documents should you make presets?

2. What is the measurement of a standard bleed?

3. What are some advantages of using columns and guides?

4. Why are a reader's first impressions of a newsletter (or any document you design) so critical?

5. What are some characteristics of the three types of newsletters described in this chapter?

6. What is the purpose of using a baseline grid?

7. What is the difference between using the Cut command or pressing the Delete key?

8. What is a setup frame? When and how do you use one?

9. Explain the difference between using Step and Repeat, and the Align panel.

10. What are some advantages in grouping items together? What is nesting?

11. Explain how to rearrange the order of stacked objects using keyboard shortcuts.

12. What is the process for changing the Document Setup default, for instance, to turn off Facing Pages?

13. You have several shapes exactly stacked on each other. What is the keyboard shortcut for selecting through objects, without rearranging the stacking order?

14. You have an image of a person placed exactly where you want it on a layout. Unfortunately, the person in the photo is pointing—and leading the reader's eye—right off the page. You decide to fix the problem by flipping the photo horizontally so that the image will point into the page. However, every time you use the transform panel to flip the image, the actual location of the image frame also moves. How can you remedy this situation, so that the picture is flipped and remains in exactly the same spot?

15. You have several objects that need their top edges aligned. You have opened the Align panel and have clicked on the Align Top Edges icon. Nothing is happening. What step in the process are you forgetting?

►CHAPTER 6 PROJECTS

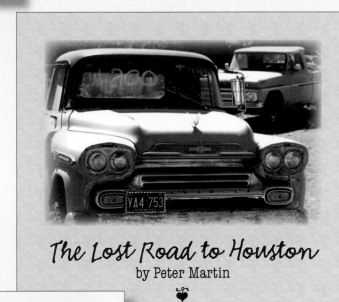

The Lost Road to Houston
by Peter Martin

❧

...hony M. Rydberg, Director
...High School Drama Department

Cast
In order of appearance

. . . . Wade Wittkop

. . . . Rae Evenson

. . . . John Edmiston

. . . . Nancy Runningen

. . . . David Runningen

. . . . Eileen Hegland

. . . . Dana Kildahl

. . . . Ron Evenson

Snap, Sniggle, and Ring-a-ding
A collection of classic children's songs

The projects begin with a review of basic tabs and tables functions. The Lost Road to Houston will give you a sneak preview of feathering, an edge treatment often used with photos. Align and Distribute operations will be the focus of the children's CD cover design. The Fishing Trip Guide and design invoice will incorporate table functions, distribute objects, tabs, and indents. The final project is a bill stuffer—the kind you receive each month in your credit card bill. Directions and files for each project can be found in the *06 Artwork and Resources* folder on the *Exploring Adobe InDesign CS5* CD.

► CHAPTER 6 PROJECTS

■ Öh Design
■ kitchen specialists
9725 hillside boulevard
■ madison, wisconsin 53703

sold to		date of order	salesperson
		pick up date	delivery date
qty	description	vendor	price

Money *&* Savings Bank
has mortgages to fit your home buying needs!

- Free online pre-approval services available
  24 hours a day, seven days a week!
- Offering low-interest loans to first time home owners.
- Easy application and approval process.
- Construction loans with interest-only options.
- Evening hours for personal service.

**Stop in and see how your friendly, small town bank
can help you purchase the home of your dreams!**

Money *&* Savings Bank

receipt number	
amount financed	
tax	
total	

© 2010 Steve Miljat

Muskie and Walleye
Fishing Guide Trips

Muskie Fishing Guide Trips
Southeast Wisconsin

Pewaukee Lake and many of the surrounding lakes in Waukesha County offer superb musky fishing within a half hour of Milwaukee. The muskie lakes of Waukesha County produce consistent action with a chance at some real bruisers over 50".

Pewaukee Lake offers consistent musky action from fish ranging 30" to 30 pounds. Pewaukee ranks as class A1 muskie lake, producing trophy fish in addition to being a great action lake from all sizes of muskie.

Okauchee Lake having a cisco forage base holds the heaviest muskies and clear water Oconomowoc Lake is a challenge even for seasoned veterans.

Fowler, Lac La Belle, North Lake, and Pine Lake, all connected by the Oconomowoc River or feeder creeks, support fishable musky populations.

Bring your own rod or use my quality Fenwicks and Ambassadeurs, don't worry about lures since you will be using the most effective baits in my boat.

Learn Proven Techniques
- Casting weedlines and pockets
- Figure 8 strategies
- Jerkbait & crank presentations
- Short line trolling
- Longline trolling
- Planer boards & downriggers
- Quick strike sucker rigs
- How to release a musky

Muskie Fishing Guide Trips
Lake Vermillion, Minnesota

This clear water Canadian Shield Lake has a reputation as being the most scenic lake in America, it will not disappoint! Big fish and unmatched scenery, a combination worth your time.

Located 2 hours northwest of Duluth in St. Louis County Minnesota. Lake Vermilion is a sprawling body of water spanning 27 miles long with over 350 islands.

This lake produces huge muskie with exceptional girth. The average size musky is 40"–44" and built broad across the back. An excellent trophy fishery for years to come due to the outstanding catch and release ethic amongst musky anglers.

Learn Proven Techniques
- Casting weedlines and pockets
- Figure 8 strategies
- Jerkbait & crank presentations
- Short line trolling
- Longline trolling
- Planer boards & downriggers
- Quick strike sucker rigs
- How to release a muskie

About your guide...
Fishing guide and wildlife artist, Steve Miljat is your best choice to guide you in search of muskie fishing. With over 1800 muskie releases spanning almost 20 years, his expertise will get you in the fast lane.

During the off season, Miljat is a commercial wildlife artist, utilizing traditional and digital illustration techniques. Visit his artwork at **http://miljat.com/**

Walleye Fishing Guide Trips
Green Bay, Wisconsin & Bay De Noc, Michigan

From her southern shore at the city of Green Bay Wisconsin to her northern shore at Escanaba Michigan, big schools of walleyes chase baitfish throughout the vastness of this inland sea. Location of trophy walleyes is a non factor as your guide keys in on seasonal migration patterns in the early spring and late fall. A 10 lb. walleye is a milestone for any fisherman!

Fishing at night in cold conditions is no picnic, but if you're looking for your personal best, don't mind dressing for the weather and losing a little sleep, come to Green Bay and Bay De Noc for an awesome adventure! *Available April–May and November.*

Learn Proven Techniques
- Crankbait presentations
- Short line trolling
- Long line trolling
- Planer boards
- Boat Control

Guide Rates

Location	Hours	Cost
Muskie Fishing Southeast Wisconsin	5 Hour Trip 8 Hour Trip	$225 $400 Maximum 2 anglers
Muskie Fishing Lake Vermillion	5 Hour Trip 8 Hour Trip	$225 $400 Maximum 2 anglers
Walleye Fishing Green Bay Bay De Noc	8 Hour Trip	$400 for the boat or 2 anglers Extra angler $50
$100 down to book a trip.		

STEVE MILJAT
FISHING GUIDE-WILDLIFE ARTIST

No **love**
no **friendship,**
can cross the
path of our destiny
without leaving
some mark on it
forever.

ꝗ Francois Mocuriac

| Text Wrap, Layers, and Effects |

7

objectives

- ▶ *Apply text wrap*
- ▶ *Manage document layers*
- ▶ *Apply effects*
- ▶ *Set fractions*
- ▶ *Use the Gap tool*
- ▶ *Apply corner effects*

introduction

My daughter owns a rescued greyhound named Penny. Once we took her to a large baseball field to see just how fast this dog could run. Penny was trembling with excitement, eager to run. When we released her, she was off like a speeding bullet.

Like Penny, you have been training to race. You have learned many InDesign basics and are now "trembling at the end of your leash" waiting to be let loose. Beginning with this chapter, *Exploring Adobe InDesign CS5* will be more production-based, building on previously learned skills while introducing new techniques and typographic principles.

Now that you've mastered the basics of production, we'll be adding techniques that will make your production process easier and more enjoyable. This chapter will focus on text wrap and layers, but will also introduce some great new features of InDesign CS5—the Gap tool and corner effects. You will also learn how to apply feathering, drop shadows, and other transparency effects to objects.

Congratulations—you're half done with the book! Feel free to e-mail me and let me know how you're doing—trydberg@mac.com.

Integrating Text and Graphics

Text and graphics need to work together. It's important to match the personality of the typeface with the style of the graphic. It is also important to create a visual link between the graphic and the text that accompanies it. In design terms, this is called the principle of *proximity.* One method of visually linking text and graphics is by using text wrap.

An Introduction to Text Wrap

Text wrap is the process of flowing text around a graphic or shape. Think of text as a river that flows smoothly until it hits a rock—a shape or graphic. The river might go around the rock or over the rock, but in either case, it just keeps flowin' along. You can control how the river of text flows around shapes or graphics by applying text wrap options. Open *07 Text Wrap.indd* from the CD that accompanies this text. As you work through each step, make the changes in the Text Wrap panel and reposition the image, as shown in each example.

1.   Open the *Text Wrap* panel by pressing **Command+Option+W** (Mac) or **Control+Alt+W** (Windows). You can also access the *Text Wrap* panel by choosing *Window>Text Wrap* (but using the menus rather than using keyboard shortcuts is always slower). Each button on the panel activates a different text wrap mode. Visual 7–1 provides an overview of the *Text Wrap* panel.

Keyboard Shortcut
 OPT+CMD+W **Text Wrap**
 ALT+CTRL+W

VISUAL | 7–1 |

The Text Wrap panel contains five buttons that alter the flow of text around objects.

2. In this exercise, the bobber is the "rock" in the middle of your text flow. The object that the text is wrapping around is referred to as the *wrap object*. Whenever you are applying a text wrap option you must first select the wrap object. Select the bobber and notice that the first text wrap option, *No text wrap*, is selected in the *Text Wrap* panel. This option is the default. When *No text wrap* is active, the text can flow over or under the object (Visual 7–2).

VISUAL | 7–2 |

No text wrap is the default wrap option in InDesign.

3. Select the bobber with the *Selection* tool and choose the second button, *Wrap around bounding box*. Make sure that the link button is selected, and enter **0.25"** in any of the four *Offset* fields. As shown in Visual 7–3, you will see two boxes around the bobber: the inside box is the *bounding box*, and the outside box shows the location of a 0.25" text offset that has been applied on all sides of the bounding box. As you can see, text offsets are ideal for adding white space between copy and images. To create different text offsets on individual sides of the bounding box, deselect the link icon in the middle of the Offset fields and specify different values in the fields.

VISUAL | 7–3 |

Wrap around bounding box creates a wrap whose shape is determined by the size of the bounding box, plus any text offset.

4. Select the third option, *Wrap around object shape*, also known as *contour wrapping*. In this mode, you have several options from which to choose. Under *Wrap Options*, you can specify where the text will be positioned. In Visual 7–4, *Wrap to Left Side* has allowed text to wrap on the left side of the graphic, but not on the right. Reposition the bobber on your page as you experiment with the other wrap options. The first three Wrap Options, *Left Side*, *Right Side*, and *Both Right & Left Sides*, will be the ones you will use most often. The *Contour Options* section allows you to specify how the text will interact with the shape. In Visual 7–4 the Contour Options is set to follow the shape of the Graphic Frame.

VISUAL |7–4|

Wrap and Contour Options are available when the Wrap Around Shape mode is active.

In Visual 7–5, the Wrap Options have been set to *Both Right & Left Sides,* and *Detect Edges* has been specified under Contour Options. With *Detect Edges* selected, InDesign finds the edges of the image inside the bounding box. In this example, you can see how the specified offset follows the contour of the shape.

VISUAL |7–5|

Contour Options include Bounding Box, Detect Edges, Alpha Channel, Photoshop Path, Graphic Frame, Same as Clipping, and User-Modified Path. Not all options are available for all images.

5.   The fourth option is ***Jump object.*** In this mode, the text leap frogs
     over the object to the next available space. Jump object keeps text
     from appearing on either side of the frame. (Visual 7–6).

VISUAL |7–6|

Jump object prevents copy
from appearing on either
side of the frame.

6.   The fifth option, ***Jump to next column***, jumps the text over to
     the next column or text frame available (Visual 7–7).

VISUAL |7–7|

Jump to next column flows
copy to the next available
column or frame, including
a threaded frame.

7. Select the bobber and change the text wrap to *Wrap around object shape*, set the Contour Options to *Detect Edges.* Position the bobber in the middle of the first column. Draw a circle, move it to the center of the second column, and give it a background color of [None]. Apply *Wrap around object shape* and turn on the *Invert* option. With Invert selected, the text flows inside the selected object (Visual 7–8).

VISUAL |7–8|

Invert allows the copy to flow inside an object, as shown by the red type inside the circle in the right hand column.

An Introduction to Document Layers

In the last chapter you were introduced to the stacking order of InDesign objects, which was compared to a stack of pancakes. You used keyboard shortcuts to rearrange the objects in the stack. In this chapter, you will learn to create and use *document layers.* Document layers are like a stack of plates, each plate holding its own pile of pancakes. Document layers are easy to understand, and they simplify the production of complex projects.

VISUAL |7–9|

The Layers panel.

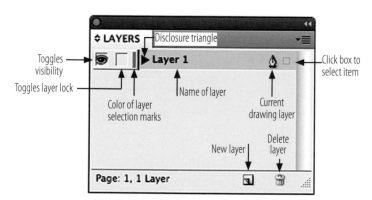

In this next exercise, you will use the Layers panel to build a cheeseburger, with artwork provided by illustrator, David Espurvoa III. You will find it in the *07 Artwork and Resources* folder on the accompanying CD.

1. Open *07 Document Layers.indd* from the *07 Artwork and Resources folder*. Press **F7** to open the *Layers* panel. Every new InDesign document starts with one layer. By default, this is named *Layer 1*. Click on the tomatoes, and you will see a blue square appear next to the pen icon, on the right side of the *Layers* panel. This square shows that the item you have selected is on Layer 1. In fact, the bun, lettuce, cheese, hamburger, and bacon are also on Layer 1. When you deselect all the images, Layer 1 displays a grayed square, indicating that nothing is selected on Layer 1.

VISUAL |7–10|

Each ingredient in this cheeseburger is a separate picture file. Each file is stacked on top of the next.

2. Select each of the ingredients and position them to build a cheeseburger. You are actually manipulating the *stacking order* of objects, because all the objects are contained on the same layer. You can use keyboard shortcuts to select and rearrange the stacking order of the images. You can also use the *Select previous object* and *Select next object* tools on the Control panel (Visual 7–10). When the Command (Mac) or Control (Windows) key is also pressed, Select previous object becomes **Select first object**, and Select next object becomes **Select last object.**

Select previous object

Select next object

Features of the Layers Panel

In the previous step, you experienced how difficult it can be to navigate through a complicated stack of objects. In the next step, you're going to take control and move the ingredients to separate document layers. But before we go there, let's take a closer look at some of the features in the Layers panel, as shown in Visual 7–11. On the left side of the panel, you can see an eye icon. This is the *visibility control*. When this icon is displayed, the layer is visible. Click the icon, and watch the cheeseburger disappear.

Layer is visible

LAYERS

▼ Layer 1

<Lettuce.psd>
<Cheese.psd>
<Top Bun.psd>
<Tomato.psd>
<Bun bottom.psd>
<Hamburger.psd>
<Bacon.psd>

Page: 1, 1 Layer

VISUAL |7–11|

Click the eye to turn visibility on or off.

Now this layer is hidden. Click the icon again, and the cheeseburger reappears. This is a nice feature—text, guides, and elements can be hidden, as needed.

Next to the eye icon there is an empty box. When you click the box a *lock icon* appears to show that the layer is locked, and you can no longer edit its elements. Like the eye icon, clicking this control repeatedly toggles it on and off. To the right of the lock is a vertical, blue line. The *blue line* corresponds to the selection marks color used to display the bounding boxes, frames, and guides that are selected on a particular layer. (Visual 7–12).

Current drawing layer cannot be edited because it is locked.

VISUAL |7–12|

A locked layer cannot be edited.

Selection marks color

Disclosure triangle. Layer has been expanded to show the stacking order.

To the right of the selection marks color, you will see that this layer is named *Layer 1*. The pen icon at the right end of the Layers panel indicates which layer you are currently working on, called the *current drawing layer* If a layer is locked, the pen icon will have a red, diagonal line through it (Visual 7–12). Finally, notice the *disclosure triangle* to the left of the layer name. When you click on this triangle, the panel expands to show the objects, in their stacking order, on that layer. You can click on each item and drag it up or down in the list to rearrange the stacking order. You can also hide or show individual items by clicking the eye icon next to the item's stacking order (Visual 7–12). Now, we'll continue with our layers exercise.

3. Unlock *Layer 1* and close the disclosure triangle. Double-click on the title, *Layer 1*, to open the *Layer Options* dialog box. Here you can change the name of the layer and the color of the selection marks, and perform other housekeeping functions such as *Suppress Text Wrap When Layer Is Hidden*. When you select this option, any text wrap mode you have applied to an object will be turned off when you hide the layer. While you are in this dialog box, change the name of the layer to **Text** and click OK (Visual 7–13). Next, create a text frame and type **Wisconsin Cheeseburger** underneath the image. We're going use this layer for text only, and move the images to new document layers.

VISUAL |7–13|

The Layer Options dialog is opened by double-clicking on a layer's name. There are many management features in this dialog box.

4. There are two methods for creating new document layers. For the first method, click the *Create new layer* icon in the lower right corner of the panel (Visual 7–14). A new layer will appear in the panel, named *Layer 2*. Double-click the name of the layer to open the *Layer Options* dialog box. Rename the layer **Bottom Bun** and click OK. A new layer, *Bottom Bun*, is now shown in the *Layers* panel, above the *Text* layer.

VISUAL | 7–14 |

Click the Create New Layer icon to add layers to a document. Double click the layer name to open the Layer Options window to change the layer name.

5. The second method for creating layers is particularly convenient, because the *New Layer* dialog box is automatically opened with the Name field highlighted. Hold down **Option** (Mac) or **Alt** (Windows) and **click** the *Create new layer* icon at the bottom of the panel. Type **Hamburger** in the *Name* field and press Return. Repeat this process and make the following three layers: 1*) Lettuce and Tomatoes,* 2) *Cheese and Bacon,* and 3) *Top Bun.* You can lengthen the *Layers* panel by pulling on the lower right corner. Six named layers should be visible in the *Layers* panel (Visual 7–15).

VISUAL | 7–15 |

Create these layers in your hamburger document.

6. Select the top bun of the cheeseburger. In the *Layers* panel, the *Text* layer is highlighted and the pen icon with a blue box next to it, appears. This indicates that the item you have selected is currently located on the *Text* layer. Click on the blue box and drag it up to the layer named *Top Bun* (Visual 7–16). When you release the mouse, notice that the frame guides for the bun illustration are the same color as the selection marks color indicator in the *Top Bun* layer. Hide the *Top Bun* layer by clicking the eye icon to the left of the layer name.

VISUAL | 7–16 |

Move an item from one layer to the next by selecting the item, and then moving the box in the Layers panel to a new layer.

Keyboard Shortcut

 CMD+CLICK **Drill Through Stacked Objects**

 CTRL+CLICK

7. Open the disclosure triangle on the *Text* layer. Select the *cheese* image. You will know it is selected when a blue square appears in the *Layers* panel next to the file name. It might be difficult to select the cheese image among all the other stacked objects. If so, you may need to drill down through the stacked objects by using the **Command+Click** (Mac) or **Control+Click** (Windows) technique. When the cheese image is selected, move the blue square to the *Cheese and Bacon* layer. Use the same technique to select the bacon illustration and move it to the *Cheese and Bacon* layer. Hide this layer. Select the *lettuce and tomatoes* and move them to the *Lettuce and Tomatoes* layer. Hide the layer. Select the *hamburger*, and move it to the *Hamburger* layer. Hide the layer. Select the *bottom bun* and move it to the *Bottom Bun* layer.

8. Show all layers. The cheeseburger might not look very presentable because pieces of artwork may need to be repositioned. You can open the disclosure triangle in the *Lettuce and Tomatoes* and *Cheese and Bacon* layers and simply move the square of the selected object to rearrange the stacking order. Or you can alternately hide and show layers to select specific pieces of artwork and shift their positions until you have a nice, thick hamburger.

VISUAL |7–17|

A thick line and a fist appears whenever you are changing the order of document layers.

Wisconsin Cheeseburger

9. In this step you will reposition the stacking order of the document layers. Your goal will be to arrange the layers in the order shown in Visual 7–17. The bottom layer should be the *Text* layer. To move a layer's position, click and drag it up or down. When you select the layer, the pointer will turn into a closed fist, and a heavy black line will indicate where the layer will be positioned when you release the mouse. Repeat this process to position each layer in the order shown in Visual 7–17. Keep your document open.

Managing Text Wrap with Layers and Text Frame Options

There are text wrap controls in the Layers panel and in the Text Frame Options panel that you should be aware of. These features are often overlooked, so take the time to study this section.

1. In the document you were just working on, lock all the layers, except *Bottom Bun* and *Text*. Select the *Wisconsin Cheeseburger* type frame and position it so the top of the frame touches the frame of the bottom bun illustration. Make *Bottom Bun* the drawing layer. Use the *Selection* tool to select the frame for the bottom bun image. Activate *Wrap around bounding box* from the Control panel. Visual 7–18

VISUAL | 7–18 |
Text wrap was applied to the bottom bun, which consequently pushed the type over.

shows how the text reflows around the bounding box of the bottom bun. Depending on the size of your text frame, the text may even disappear altogether when text wrap is applied to the hamburger bun!

2. *Double-click* the *Bottom Bun* layer to open the *Layer Options* dialog box (Visual 7–19). Check *Suppress Text Wrap When Layer is Hidden.* Press Return. Hide the *Bottom Bun* layer, and you will see the text reflow as if the object wasn't even there. Make the *Bottom Bun* layer visible once more and the text wrap will be activated.

VISUAL | 7–19 |
Use Layer Options to suppress text wrap when a layer is hidden.

3. This technique mentioned earlier bears repeating: you can override the text wrap for individual text frames. Select the text frame and press **Command+B** (Mac) or **Control+B** (Windows) to open the *Text Frame Options* dialog box (or choose *Object> Text Frame Options*). Select *Ignore Text Wrap* at the bottom of the dialog box and click OK (Visual 7–20).

VISUAL | 7–20 |
Use Text Frame Options to ignore text wrap on individual items.

Using Layers to Create Two Versions of a Document

Now that you have created, repositioned, locked, and hidden layers, you probably realize the production opportunities Layers offer. In the next project, you will design a page for a recipe book, featuring recipes from all over the United States (Visual 7–21). You will use layers to construct this document so it contains two versions of a chocolate chip cookie recipe—one designed for home bakers, and a big-batch version intended for institutional cooking. You will also use the features of a recent font technology called *OpenType* to create true fractions.

VISUAL |7–21|

Layers will be used to create two versions of a recipe in a single document.

Chewy Chocolate Chip Cookies
Willow Lake, South Dakota

1 cup shortening
1 cup canola oil
4 eggs
1½ cups brown sugar
3½–4 cups flour
2 tsp. soda dissolved in
2 tsp. hot water

1½ tsp. vanilla
4 cups oatmeal
1 tsp. salt
½ cup chopped nuts (optional)
12 oz. chocolate chips

Cream shortening, oil, eggs, and sugars until light and fluffy. Add flour, the soda-water mixture, salt, and vanilla. Stir in oatmeal, chocolate chips and nuts. Drop by teaspoon onto ungreased cookie sheet.

Bake 350° for 9–10 min.

1. Create a new document. Document size: **8.5"× 11"**. Top, bottom, and right margins: **0.5"**. Left margin: **0.75"** (to accommodate spiral binding). Click OK. Press **F7** to open the *Layers* panel. Change the name of *Layer 1* to *Picture.* Draw a frame from margin to margin. Place *07 Cookies.tif* from the

The zero point has been reset. The right edges of the text frames will be aligned to the guideline.

07 Artwork and Resources folder and scale proportionately to **145%**. (The photo will not reach to the bottom margin.) Reset the zero point to the far right edge of the photo and drop in a vertical guide at **-0.25"** on the X coordinate (Visual 7–23). Lock this layer.

2. Create a new layer and name it *Consumer Recipe.* Type the copy and follow the type specifications shown in Visual 7–24. Use three text frames, creating a 2-column frame for the ingredients. Do not place a space after the whole number in the fractions. Creating fractions is an easy process when OpenType is being used. Highlight the numerator, slash, and denominator, and choose *OpenType>Fractions* from the Control panel menu. Repeat the process for each fraction. Or, highlight the ½ fraction, Copy and Paste it as needed. Be sure to check spelling and use the correct hyphens and dashes.

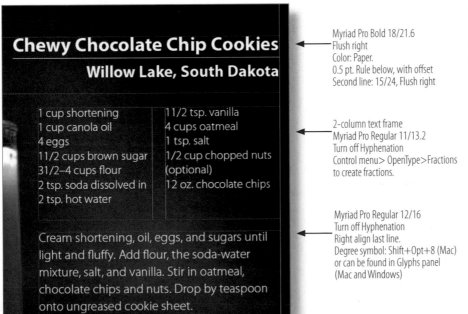

Type this copy and follow the type specifications for the consumer recipe. (The fractions have not yet been created.)

3. Create a new layer and name it **Industrial Recipe.** You are going to duplicate the type from the *Consumer Recipe* layer, and move it to the *Industrial Recipe* layer. Afterwards, you will double the ingredients for the Industrial Recipe version. Click on the *Consumer Recipe* layer in the *Layers* panel. Choose the *Selection* tool, and **Shift+Click** each text frame so that they are all selected. The small red box showing in the *Consumer Recipe* layer represents the three text frames you have just selected. Press **Option** (Mac) or **Alt** (Windows) while you move the red square up to the *Industrial Recipe* layer. As the Option or Alt key is held, you will see a plus sign appear which means a duplicate is being created on the next layer.

4. Hide the *Consumer Recipe* layer. Move to the *Industrial Recipe* layer and change the title to **Big Batch of Chocolate Chip Cookies.** Then, double the recipe ingredients (Visual 7–25). Save your document and print a copy of the *Industrial Recipe* version. Hide the *Industrial Recipe* layer and show the *Consumer Recipe* layer. Print the *Consumer Recipe* version.

VISUAL | 7–25 |

When you double the recipe don't forget to change the copy on the Industrial Recipe layer. Cup should now read cups.

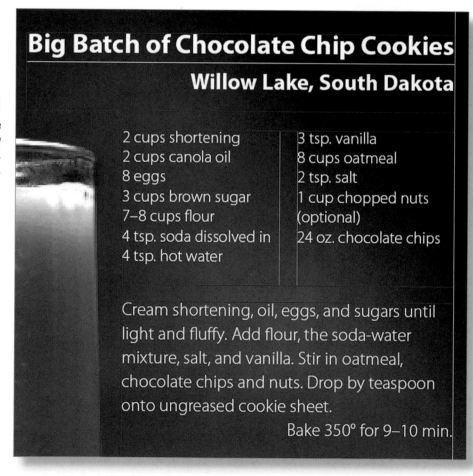

Big Batch of Chocolate Chip Cookies
Willow Lake, South Dakota

2 cups shortening
2 cups canola oil
8 eggs
3 cups brown sugar
7–8 cups flour
4 tsp. soda dissolved in
4 tsp. hot water

3 tsp. vanilla
8 cups oatmeal
2 tsp. salt
1 cup chopped nuts
(optional)
24 oz. chocolate chips

Cream shortening, oil, eggs, and sugars until light and fluffy. Add flour, the soda-water mixture, salt, and vanilla. Stir in oatmeal, chocolate chips and nuts. Drop by teaspoon onto ungreased cookie sheet.

Bake 350° for 9–10 min.

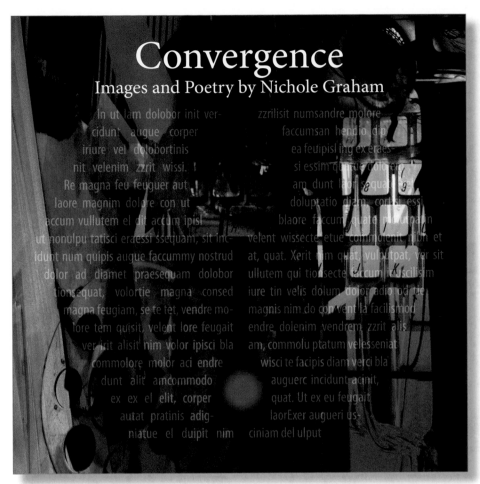

Convergence
Images and Poetry by Nichole Graham

In ut lam dolobor init ver-
cidunt augue corper
iriure vel dolobortinis
nit velenim zzrit wissi.
Re magna feu feuguer aut
laore magnim dolore con ut
accum vullutem el dit accum ipisl
ut nonulpu tatisci eraessi ssequam, sit incidunt num quipis augue faccummy nostrud
dolor ad diamet praesequam dolobor
tionsequat, volortie magna consed
magna feugiam, se te tet, vendre molore tem quisit, velent lore feugait
ver irit alisit nim volor ipisci bla
commolore molor aci endre
dunt alit amcommodo
ex ex el elit, corper
autat pratinis adig-
niatue el duipit nim

zzrilisit numsandre molore
faccumsan hendio dip
ea feuipisl ing ex eraes-
si essim quirure doloee
am dunt laor equat
doluptatio diam cortsi essi
blaore faccum quate inccurpat
velent wissecte etue commolenit nibh et
at, quat. Xerit nim quat, vulputpat, ver sit
ullutem qui tionsecte accum iuscilisim
iure tin velis dolum dolor radio od te
magnis nim do convent la facilismod
endre dolenim vendrem zzrit alis
am, commolu ptatum velesseniat
wisci te facipis diam verci bla
auguerc incidunt acinit,
quat. Ut ex eu feugait
laorExer augueri us-
ciniam del ulput

VISUAL | 7–26 |

The finished CD cover, which incorporates transparency and feathering.

Designing a CD Cover

Our next project will be the full-bleed CD cover, shown in Visual 7–26. It will require you to create guides, use text wrap, and work on different layers. You will also be introduced to two new features: *transparency* and *feathering*.

1.   Create a new document, choosing *Compact Disc* from the Page Size presets list. Margins: Top and Bottom **0.25"**; Left and Right **0.125"**. Add a **0.125"** bleed on all sides. Click OK. Choose *Layout>Create Guides* and make two rows and two columns, both with a gutter width of **0** and select *Fit Guides to Margins.* Your file should look like Visual 7–27.

VISUAL | 7–27 |

The guides are set for the CD production.

2. Rename Layer 1 to *Guides.* You will be able to toggle the guides off and on as desired. Create a new layer and name it *Photo.* Place the *07 Convergence.psd* image file found in the *07 Artwork and Resources* folder on the CD. It should stretch from bleed to bleed.

3. Select the *Polygon* tool and click on the document. Enter **6** in *Number of Sides* and **0%** in *Star Inset*. Resize the polygon so that it stretches to the margins (Visual 7–28). Select the T*ype* tool and click in the polygon frame. Open the *Text Frame Options* dialog box, **Command+B** (Mac) or **Control+B** (Windows), and specify a two-column text frame, gutter **0.125"**.

VISUAL | 7–28 |

The hexagon stretches from margin to margin. It will be converted to a two-column text frame.

▶ *production tip*

Text that is the color of the paper is called reverse type.

4. Fill the text frame with placeholder text and format it as **Myriad Pro Condensed 11/auto.** Color the text **[Paper]**. Text that is the color of the paper is called *reverse type*. Apply justified horizontal alignment, removing returns as needed to create even edges along the text frame and inside column guides (Visual 7–29).

VISUAL | 7–29 |

Placeholder text has been added, justified, and colored Paper.

5. Activate the hexagon text frame. Remove the stroke. Locate the *Opacity* field on the Control panel (Visual 7–30). Enter **50** into the *Opacity* field and press Return. This creates a transparent effect on the type in the hexagonal text frame. On this CD project, the placeholder text is used simply as additional texture. Because the transparent effect reduces the readability of text, you will always need to use this function carefully.

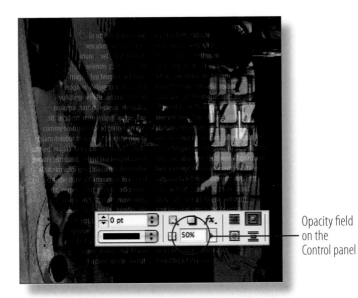

VISUAL |7–30|
Opacity (transparency) can be found on the Control panel or in the Effects panel.

Opacity field on the Control panel

6. Create a new layer and name it *Title.* Draw a text frame from the left to the right margin guides, H: **0.65"**. Position the frame against the top margin guide. In this frame, type *Convergence*, **Minion Pro Regular 30/36**. Second line: *Images and Poetry by Nichole Graham*, **Minion Pro Regular, 14/18.8.** Align center and color **Paper**. Open the *Text Wrap* panel and select *Wrap around bounding box.* Specify a **0.125"** bottom offset. Although this text frame is on its own layer, it still affects the type on other layers. InDesign's text wrapping capability is layer independent.

7. Create a new layer and name it *Circles.* Select the *Ellipse* tool. Press **Shift+Option** (Mac) or **Shift+Alt** (Windows) and beginning on the center vertical guide, draw a **1"** circle in the upper half of the text area. The circle should not have a stroke or fill. Open the *Text Wrap* panel and select *Wrap around object shape*, offset **0.0625"**. Since the object is a circle, only one offset field is active in the *Text Wrap* panel.

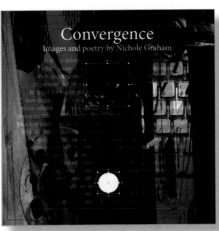

VISUAL |7–31|
Press Option (Mac) or Alt (Windows) to begin drawing a shape from the center point.

► *production tip*

When using transparency and other special effects, it is a good idea to view your artwork at high resolution. Choose View>Display Performance> High Quality Display.

8. Press **Shift+Option** (Mac) or **Shift+Alt** (Windows) and draw a **0.5"** circle at the bottom of the text with the bottom edge of the circle near the bottom margin. Fill the circle with **[Paper]**. In the Text Wrap panel, specify *Wrap around object shape*, **0.0625"** offset. Choose *Object>Effects>Basic Feather*. Enter **0.1"** in the *Feather Width* field, set the *Corners* option to *Diffused* and press Return. *Feathering* creates soft edges and is a nice design touch. Adjust the transparency of this object to **50%**. Choose *View>Display Performance> High Quality Display* to see a high-resolution view of the feathering and transparency effects that you have used (Visual 7–32).9. Your CD cover is complete.

VISUAL |7–32|

Feathering adds transparency to the edges of an object, creating a softer edge.

VISUAL |7–33|

The Preview mode can be accessed by typing W when you are not in the Type tool. All view modes can be selected from the bottom of the Toolbox.

9. Deselect all. Select *Bleed* from the view options at the bottom of the Toolbox (Visual 7–33). In this mode you can see the **0.125"** bleed that extends from all four edges. Save and print your project. In the Print dialog box, choose the *Setup* page and select *Centered* in the Page Position field. *Print two versions* of the CD cover: In Version 1, deselect *Use Document Bleed Settings* on the *Marks and Bleed* page of the Print dialog box. Version 1 will show just the trim size. For Version 2, select *Use Document Bleed Settings* and specify *All Printer's Marks.* Compare the two prints, noticing that the bleed print has 2 sets of corner marks—an inner set to show the trim size, and an outer set to show the bleed size.

Photography ©2010 Billy Knight

MIDWEST BARN RESTORATION ∾ JEFF HOLMES REPORT

New books for spring

American Country

the wonders of lambing
by DIAHANN LOHR

Photography ©2009 Diahann Lohr

► Chickens for fun and profit

► Midwest Barn Tour

► Getting more from your garden

► Energy efficient pole buildings

Designing a Magazine Cover

Our last project will use transparency, feathering, drop shadow, type effects, layers, and two new features in InDesign CS5, Live Corner Effects and the Gap tool. The project is already roughed out. You will add the final touches. One caveat—use effects sparingly. Using too many effects is like using too many typefaces and results in a layout that looks less than professional. When in doubt, don't add an effect!

1. Open *07 American Country*, found in the *07 Artwork and Resources* folder on the CD. Press **F7** to open the *Layers* panel. There are four layers, with three hidden. First, look at the first layer, *Photo and color bars.* This locked layer contains the main image for the magazine. The image sits inside a container that is filled with the rust color. This is more efficient than creating separate colored rectangles and placing them on the top and bottom of the layout.

2. Click the eye to turn on the *Inset Photos* layer. We're going to use the three photos on the top of the page to learn about the *Gap* tool. The *Gap* tool, new in InDesign CS5, provides a fast way to adjust the size of a gap between two or more items. Select the *Gap* tool and hover your mouse over the gap between the left and center barn inset shot. As you click and drag the *Gap* tool to the left and the right, the photos are resized and the gap remains the same size (Visual 7–34). Release the *Gap* tool and Undo.

Keyboard Shortcut

 CMD+Z

CTRL+Z — **Undo**

VISUAL |7–34|

The Gap tool focuses on the space between images, and allows you to move that space and crop the images in one step.

3. Select the *Gap* tool again. This time, hold down **Command** (Mac) or **Control** (Windows) as you drag the tool over the gap. You will see that the gap between the photos resizes, cropping the image (Visual 7–35). Release the *Gap* tool and Undo.

VISUAL |7–35|

Holding Command (Mac) or Control (Windows) while using the Gap tool will resize the gap.

4. For the last experiment with the *Gap* tool, hold the **Option** (Mac) or **Alt** (Windows) key when using the *Gap* tool. Now the images move with the gap. Nothing is resized. (Visual 7–36). Release the *Gap* tool and Undo.

VISUAL |7–36|

Holding **Option** (Mac) or **Alt** (Windows) moves the images with the gap. Neither element is resized.

5. Turn on the visibility of the *Nameplate* layer. Fill the type with **C29, M78, Y100, K26**. Add a **Black** stroke. Open the *Stroke* panel and change the weight to **0.5 pt**. Select the text frame with the *Selection* tool, and you're ready to add some effects to the type.

The Effects Panel

The Effects panel can be found on the Control panel or it can be opened by **Shift+Command+F10** (Mac) or **Shift+Control+F10** (Windows). When adding an effect, the first thing to decide is whether the effect will be on the type, the fill, the stroke, or the object. The object receiving the effect is called the *target*. Visual 7–37 shows the Effects controls accessed through the Control panel. The left control in the grouping, the *Apply Effect to* control, is your starting point. This drop down menu lets you select the target for the effect. Here's what happens when you select each one:

Apply Effect to (select target) | Drop Shadow | Add Effect to selected target

Opacity

VISUAL | 7–37 |

Effects controls can be accessed from the Control panel. The first step is to select a target from the Apply Effect to drop down menu.

▶ *Object–When you select object, the entire object—fill, stroke, and text—will have the special effect.*

▶ *Graphic–When you select a graphic with the Direct Selection tool, the effect is only applied to the graphic inside the frame.*

▶ *Stroke–When an effect is applied to a stroke, the gap color is also affected.*

▶ *Fill–Only the fill is given an effect when this is selected.*

▶ *Text–You can't apply an effect to individual words. When you select "Text," only the text inside the object—not the text frame—will be given an effect. Select the text frame with the Selection tool.*

Below the Apply Effect to control is the *Opacity* control. This is a simple slider that makes an item transparent, ranging from 0% (invisible) to 100% (opaque). A transparency is not the same as a tint. A tinted box and a transparent box might look the same. But when placed on top of another object, the tinted box is still opaque, while the transparent box allows background images to be seen.

The *Drop Shadow* button (Visual 7–37) adds the default drop shadow to the selected object, fill, text, or stroke. The default opacity of the drop shadow is 75%, which is too dark for many applications. When that is the case, you will click the *fx* button to open the drop down menu, select **Drop Shadow,**

▶ *production tip*

A transparency is not the same as a tint. A tinted box and a transparent box might look the same. When placed on top of another object, the tinted box is still opaque, while the transparent box allows background images to be seen.

and change the opacity in the dialog box. You can also open the Effects panel by using the keyboard shortcuts or go to **Window>Effects** (Visual 7–38). Always select the effect's target first, then select the effect. Now let's go back to our magazine cover project and add some effects to the nameplate.

VISUAL | 7–38 |

The Effects panel opened using keyboard shortcuts Shift+Cmd+F10 (Mac) or Shift+Ctrl+F10 (Windows).

6. Select the nameplate with the *Selection* tool. From the Control panel, select the target *Text* from the drop down menu under the *Apply Effect to* icon. Choose *Bevel and Emboss* under the *fx* icon on the Control panel. When the window opens, notice that Text appears in the *Settings for* field in the upper left corner. This means the effect will only apply to the text. Experiment with various effects listed in the left pane by clicking in the box next to the name to turn on the effect and open the dialog. Apply different effects settings, clicking Preview to see how each variation looks. When you're done experimenting, uncheck all the effects in the left pane, except for *Bevel and Emboss. Enter the values shown in Visual 7–39 in the Bevel and Emboss dia*log box to achieve the effect shown in the magazine cover example.

VISUAL | 7–39 |

Enter these values in the Bevel and Emboss fields.

7. Go to the *Layers* panel and make the *Copy* layer visible. Select the star burst in the upper right corner. Rotate it **-16°** around the center reference point and use the icons in the Control panel to add a drop shadow.

8. Select the white box that says, *the wonders of lambing*. The background needs to be made transparent, and a feather added to the edges. Choose Fill from the *Apply Effect to* icon on the Control panel. Then reduce the transparency to **60%**.

Select *Basic Feather* under the *fx* icon, and accept the default values.

Live Corner Effects

The last effect we will use is *Live Corner Effects*. This new feature, added to the Control panel of InDesign CS5, allows you to add different corner options to individual corners of a frame. Open the Corner Options dialog by pressing **Option** (Mac) or **Alt** (Windows) and clicking on the icon ⧉ in the Control panel. The Corner Options dialog shows a proxy which represents each corner of a frame. In this case, we want an inverted curve in the upper-right corner of each text frame along the bottom of the magazine cover. This step will add the finishing touch to our magazine cover.

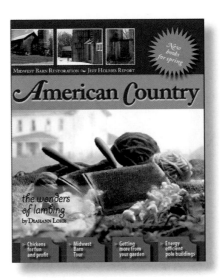

9. First, **Shift+click** to select the four green boxes on the bottom of the magazine cover. Then, open the *Corner Options* dialog box by pressing **Option** (Mac) or **Alt** (Windows) and clicking on the *Corner Options* icon in the Control panel (Visual 7–40). Deselect the *Make all Settings the Same* link in the middle of the dialog box. Then, find the proxy with a tiny blue box in upper right corner. From the pull down menu, choose *Inverse Rounded* and enter the value of **.3125"**. Your magazine cover is complete!

VISUAL | 7–40 |

The tiny blue square in each corner of the proxy identifies the target corner for the effect.

Summary

You are well on your way to being comfortable with the expansive and powerful features of InDesign. With each chapter you have methodically added skill "layers" to your repertoire. Those projects that seemed so difficult in the early chapters would now be quite easy! In this chapter you created and manipulated document layers. You also were introduced to OpenType, text wrap, effects and live corner options, and you created three great projects. Congratulations on all you have achieved!

▶ IN REVIEW

1. How can you change the color of selection marks on a layer?

2. What is the keyboard shortcut to open the Text Wrap panel?

3. When creating a new layer, what key do you press when clicking the Create new layer icon to bring up the New Layer dialog box used to specify the layer name and other options?

4. How do you view a higher-resolution image of your document on your monitor screen?

5. How do you make text flow inside an object?

6. What is the process for ignoring text wrap for text frames?

7. What is the process for opening the Corner Effects dialog from the Control panel?

8. Although they may look identical, how is a red, transparent box different from a red, tinted box?

9. What is the first step you need to take whenever you are applying an effect?

10. Go to Menu> InDesign Help. Search for Paste Remembers Layers, a feature in the Layers panel. Describe how it works.

Keyboard Shortcut
🍎 OPT+CMD+W
⊞ ALT+CTRL+W
Text Wrap

Keyboard Shortcut
🍎 ⇧+CMD+]
⊞ ⇧+CTRL+]
Bring to Front

Keyboard Shortcut
🍎 F7 (function key)
⊞ F7 (function key)
Layers Panel

Keyboard Shortcut
🍎 ⇧+CMD+[
⊞ ⇧+CTRL+[
Send to Back

Keyboard Shortcut
🍎 ⇧+CMD+F10
⊞ ⇧+CTRL+F10
Effects Panel

Keyboard Shortcut
🍎 CMD+CLICK
⊞ CTRL+CLICK
Drill Through Stacked Objects

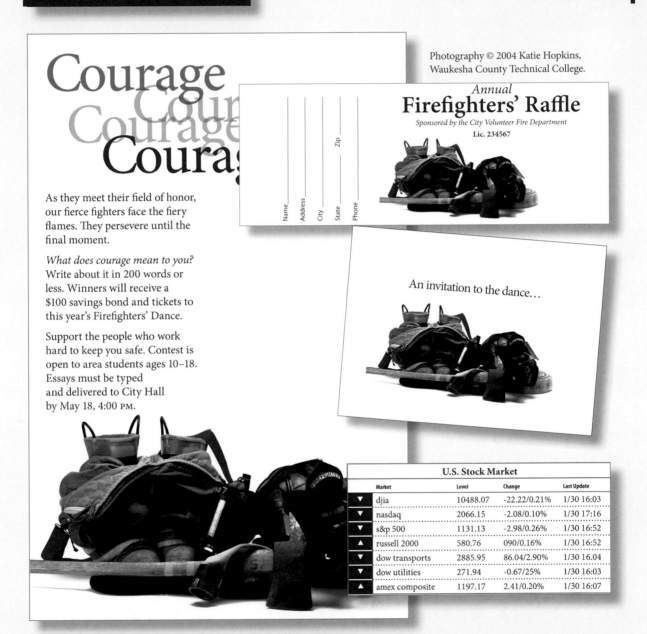

Courage
Courage
Courage
Courag

As they meet their field of honor, our fierce fighters face the fiery flames. They persevere until the final moment.

What does courage mean to you? Write about it in 200 words or less. Winners will receive a $100 savings bond and tickets to this year's Firefighters' Dance.

Support the people who work hard to keep you safe. Contest is open to area students ages 10–18. Essays must be typed and delivered to City Hall by May 18, 4:00 PM.

Photography © 2004 Katie Hopkins, Waukesha County Technical College.

Name Address City State Zip Phone

Annual
Firefighters' Raffle
Sponsored by the City Volunteer Fire Department
Lic. 234567

An invitation to the dance…

U.S. Stock Market			
Market	**Level**	**Change**	**Last Update**
▼ djia	10488.07	-22.22/0.21%	1/30 16:03
▼ nasdaq	2066.15	-2.08/0.10%	1/30 17:16
▼ s&p 500	1131.13	-2.98/0.26%	1/30 16:52
▲ russell 2000	580.76	090/0.16%	1/30 16:52
▼ dow transports	2885.95	86.04/2.90%	1/30 16.04
▼ dow utilities	271.94	-0.67/25%	1/30 16:03
▲ amex composite	1197.17	2.41/0.20%	1/30 16:07

Four assignments are included in the *07 Artwork and Resources* folder on the CD accompanying this book. The first three projects are pieces promoting the annual fund raising events for a volunteer fire department. They will look great printed in color and will be nice additions to your collection of work. The last project is a fun exercise in formatting tables—no typing required!

Go confidently in the direction of your dreams. **Live** the life you have imagined.

℞ Henry David Thoreau

| Type Continuity: Applying Styles |

objectives

- ▶ *Properly prepare text files for placing in InDesign documents*
- ▶ *Use the Pages panel*
- ▶ *Use the Eyedropper tool to transfer attributes*
- ▶ *Create paragraph and character styles*
- ▶ *Place Snippets*

introduction

It's amazing how often we make extra work for ourselves before we wise up. Years ago, we hung a small bell by our door and trained our dog to ring it each time he needed to go outside. The method was successful—at first. But it didn't take him long to realize that whenever he rang the bell we came running. He began to ring it whenever he was bored, lonesome, hungry, or just wanted to go out and play. It was hard to tell who was better trained—the dog or the dog owners. After the hundredth trip going back and forth to the door, we knew we needed to take control of the situation, and the bell came down.

When you are typesetting a project and it dawns on you that you're repeating the same actions over and over, it's time to look for a way to reduce your workload and take control. That's what this chapter is all about. You will use paragraph and character styles to automate your text formatting, speed up production, and bring typographic consistency to your documents. After reading this chapter, you will wonder how you ever got along without them!

Creating a Newsletter

In this lesson you will create a four-page newsletter for a veterinary service. The veterinarian, Dr. John Hallett, has supplied you with copy and photos. Visual 8–1 shows the finished newsletter, created in facing pages and printed on 11" × 17" paper. The newsletter is printed back-to-back and folded, making a total of four pages. A PDF file is also included in the *Chapter 08 Artwork and Resources* folder on the accompanying CD. You may want to print this newsletter sample and use it as a reference as you work through the chapter.

Back Cover (Page 4)   Front Cover (Page 1)

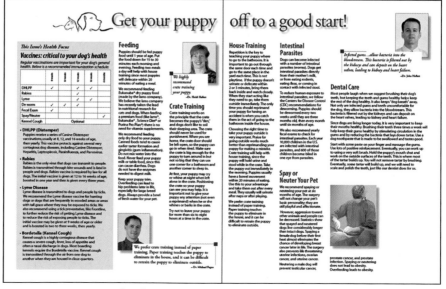

Page 2   Page 3

This single project will introduce you to the Pages panel, and will make use of *Snippets*. The copy has been prepared for you—your job is to place it and format it. As you build the newsletter, you will create typographic consistency from page to page, by using the Eyedropper tool, and creating paragraph and character styles, using the following techniques:

- ► *Creating styles from sample text*
- ► *Transferring styles from another InDesign document*
- ► *Creating styles based on other styles*
- ► *Creating a new style*
- ► *Duplicating existing styles*
- ► *Bringing in styles with a new element*
- ► *Creating character styles*
- ► *Redefining styles*

About Facing Pages

Up to now, we have worked on single-page documents. But many—probably most—of your projects will have multiple left and right pages printed back-to-back. These publications are set up using the Facing Pages option in the New Document dialog box. When a document is created as facing pages, the Left and Right margin fields change to Inside and Outside margins. When more than one page butts up to another, it is called a *spread*. Odd-numbered pages are always right-hand (*recto*) pages, and even-numbered pages are always left-hand (*verso*) pages.

Take a single piece of paper and fold it from side to side. Hold the paper so the fold is on the left and it opens like a booklet. The fold of your booklet is the *spine*. The cover of your booklet is page 1, a right-hand page. Open the booklet and you will see a spread made up of pages 2 and 3. The back cover is page 4, a left-hand page. So, a four-page, 8½" × 11" newsletter, printed two-sided on one, 11" × 17" sheet, consists of two spreads, or four 8½" × 11" facing pages.

Introducing the Pages Panel

Open the Pages panel by pressing **Command+F12** (Mac) or **F12** (Windows), or by choosing Menu>Window>Pages. Notice that the Pages panel is divided into two sections by a separator that can be dragged up and down like a window shade. The top section of the panel is the *master*, or *global* level. The pages at this level are called *Masters* and the settings and options you apply to them affect the whole document. The top, single master page is named **[None]**. The two-page spread below it is named **A-Master**. The A-Master spread consists of a left-hand and a right-hand facing page. When you are working with facing pages, the pages are displayed differently than non-facing pages. The lower section of the Pages panel is the *local* level. Each page or spread is butted up to a vertical line representing the spine of the publication. Odd-numbered pages are always to the right of the spine, and even-numbered pages are always to the left of the spine.

VISUAL |8–2|

A document created with facing pages shows pages aligned to a vertical line which represents the spine, or binding edge.

We will be covering the Pages panel in detail, in Chapter 9. Let's get started by creating a new document for our newsletter project, beginning with formatting the exterior size and interior margins and columns.

1.　　Create a new letter-size document. Number of pages: **4**; Facing Pages: **On**; Columns: **4**; Gutter Width: **0.1875"** Top, Bottom, and Outside margins: **0.5"**; Inside margin: **0.25"**.

At the bottom of the Pages panel is the Create new page icon. Click to add one new page at a time to the end of the document. Use **Option+click** (Mac) or **Alt+click** (Windows) to open the Insert Pages dialog box for more page options, such as how many new pages to create, where to place them in the document, or what master page should be applied. In the lower right corner is the Delete selected pages icon.

Delete a page by dragging it to the can or by selecting it and clicking the can. Add and delete a few pages to your document to see how this works, but be sure to end up with 4 pages. Notice that the document's interior pages are displayed in spreads. You can move from page to page in your document by double-clicking on each page icon in the Pages panel. To select a whole spread, double-click on the numbers below the spread. When you're working in facing pages, you will want to view entire spreads. Press **Command+Option+0** (Mac) or **Control+Alt+0** (Windows) to fit the spread in your window. Click on the panel menu at the top right, to view a menu of additional options. If you choose Panel Options, which opens the Panel Options dialog box, you can adjust the panel display by checking the Show Vertically box and choosing what size the page icons should be. Visual 8–3 shows the panel displaying pages with extra large page icons. Experiment with these options and adjust the panel to suit your preferences. Let's get back to setting up the pages for the newsletter.

VISUAL |8–3|

Panel Options lets you choose the view that works best for you.

How to Begin a Document With a Spread

If you look at the Pages panel, you will see that page one is a recto page, and is followed by a spread, and a verso fourth page. By default, a new document starts with page 1, a single, recto page. Because our four-page newsletter only needs the two spreads, we are going to do a work-around and create a document that begins with a spread instead of a single page.

VISUAL |8–4|

Deselect **Allow Document Pages to Shuffle** to begin your document with a spread.

2. Open the *Pages* menu and deselect *Allow Document Pages to Shuffle* (Visual 8–4).

3. Select Page 4 by clicking on it. Drag it up to the left of Page 1. When you see a fist, the arrow pointing left, and a bracket, you can release the mouse (Visual 8–5).

4. Now your document should consist of two spreads. This will make printing the newsletter much easier, but now the physical page numbers do not correspond to the pages of the newsletter. Refer to Visual 8–6 to determine the newsletter page location as you continue with your project. The pages will be referenced by the colored labels shown in Visual 8–6.

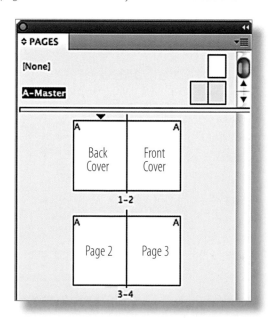

5.   On the front cover, pull a horizontal guide down from the top to **2.25"** on the
     Y coordinate.

6.   Double-click on the numbers below the Page 2 and 3 spread in the *Pages* panel.
     Create a horizontal guid*e* at **1.65"** on the Y coordinate by first clicking a spot on the
     ruler that is outside the document's page area. Now drag down the guide, noticing
     that the guide stretches across the whole spread. (When you drag a guide down
     from the ruler by clicking above the page you are working on, the guide covers
     only that page.) If you can't exactly position the guide at 1.65", with the guide
     selected, type **1.65** in the Y field of the control panel. *Save* your document.

Using Snippets

When you do a lot of design work for a single client, you usually have elements
that are used over and over again. For instance, if you did weekly advertisements
for a dental practice, you would probably include the logo, name, hours of
operation, phone number, and address in each ad. In these instances you can
create *Snippets,* bits of information that you have saved and organized for placing
into a new document at a later date. Snippets allow you to store those frequently
used items in one convenient folder, organized by job number or client. In
this chapter, the newsletter snippets are found in their own *Snippets* folder in
the *08 Healthy Pets Newsletter* folder. You will find this folder in *08 Artwork
and Resources* on the accompanying CD. Before we begin placing snippets,
we'll change our InDesign preferences to make the process much easier.

▶ *production tip*

Snippets are easy to create.
With the Selection tool, select
the object(s) to be included in
the Snippet. Under File>Export,
type a name in the Save As
field, and choose InDesign
Snippet from the Format field.

1.   Open InDesign
     preferences by using
     Command+K (Mac)
     or **Ctrl+K** (Windows).
     Select *File Handling* from
     the left pane. Under
     Snippet Import, choose
     Original Location. Now,
     when you place each
     snippets, it will move
     to its original position
     on the newsletter. This

VISUAL | 8–7 |

Change InDesign preferences
to place snippets at their
original location.

preference option is important to know about for those times when
elements must be placed in the same location on each new document.

Keyboard Shortcut

 CMD+D

 CTRL+D

Place

2. Your document should still be open. Double-click the Front Cover page icon on the Pages panel. Use the Place command to select *FC Nameplate.idms.* Click anywhere on the Front Cover—since we changed InDesign's preferences, the nameplate snippet will drop into the correct position.

3. Next, using Visual 8–7 as a guide, Place *FC Open House.idms, FC Quote.idms,* and *FC Hospital.idms* onto the Front Cover. The elements do not need to be resized. If you mistakenly resize an element, simply delete it and place the snippet again.

VISUAL |8–8|

Because you changed InDesign's preferences, each snippet will be placed at its original location on each page.

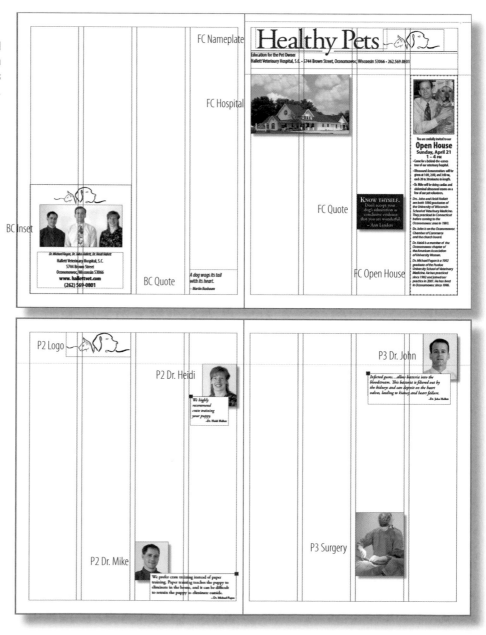

4. Select the Back Cover in the *Pages* panel. Using Visual 8–8 as an example, place *BC Inset.idms.* and *BC Quote.idms.* Select Page 2 in the Pages panel. Place *P2 Dr. Heidi.idms, P2 Dr. Mike.idms,* and *P2 Logo.idms.* Move to Page 3 and place *P3 Dr. John.idms* and *P3 Surgery.idms.* You will not use all the snippets (yet). Save your document.

▶ *production tip*
Notice that the hospital photo has a drop shadow, which is a transparent element. When Transparency has been turned on in the Pages panel (option menu>Panel Options>Icons), a small checkerboard square will appear next to the page icons whenever a spread has a transparency effect applied.

Using the Eyedropper Tool

InDesign provides many methods for formatting type. The method you have used thus far is to select text, frame by frame, and manually enter all the character and paragraph settings. The *Eyedropper* tool saves time by allowing you to transfer type attributes from one paragraph to another. On Page 2 of the newsletter, the copy under Dr. Heidi's photo is formatted perfectly. You will use the Eyedropper tool to transfer those correct type attributes to text in another text frame.

1. Double-click the *Eyedropper* tool to open the *Eyedropper Options* dialog box. Here, a whole array of options allows you to customize exactly which types of objects and their attributes, the tool should copy. Deselect all choices except Character and Paragraph Settings (Visual 8–9) and press Return.

VISUAL |8–9|

The Eyedropper is a versatile tool for copying attributes.

2. The *Eyedropper* cursor icon begins white, which means that no attributes have been copied or "loaded" into the tool. Click the empty *Eyedropper* on the italic copy under Dr. Heidi's photo. The *Eyedropper* now turns black and reverses direction as it "loads" the attributes, a process called sampling (Visual 8–10). Drag the loaded *Eyedropper* tool over the copy underneath Dr. Mike's photo. As soon as the mouse is released, the text will be changed to the "sampled" attributes (Visual 8–10). As long as the *Eyedropper* tool is

VISUAL |8–10|

The Eyedropper is loaded with text attributes from the copy under Dr. Heidi. The loaded Eyedropper transfers the attributes as it is dragged across type.

loaded, you can drag and highlight text with it. Holding down the **Option** (Mac) or **Alt** (Windows) key temporarily turns the *Eyedropper* white again, so you can resample different text attributes. Deactivate the *Eyedropper* by selecting another tool.

►MOVING TOWARD MASTERY

When you place an image into InDesign, you are creating a link. No data from the placed artwork file is actually brought into the InDesign document. Instead, a link, or pathway, is created from the original artwork file to the InDesign document. When your document is printed, InDesign follows the link's path back to the original image file, reads the data, and prints the image. When InDesign can't find the link, it can't accurately render the image.

When a warning appears that a link is missing, your first course of action is to open the Links panel: **Shift+Cmd+D** *(Mac)* or **Shift+Control+D** *(Windows)*.

The right column shows the page where each image in the document is used. The left column shows the status of each link. A yellow triangle means that the original file has changed and the link needs updating. To update a link, select the file name and choose Update Link at the bottom of the Links panel.

A white question mark in a red circle means the path to the original image is broken. To repair a broken link, click on the problem link, and select the Relink button at the bottom of the panel. For this project, navigate to the 08 Healthy Pets Newsletter folder and, inside, to the Links folder. Select the file name for each missing link. (Chapter 13 will have more on the Links panel.)

1. The Links Panel—No link problems.

2. The Links Panel
Link problems displayed in status column

Page location of image

Link has been found, but needs to be updated.

Link cannot be found—must be relinked to image file.

Link Status   Relink   Go to Link   Update Link   Edit Image

Defining Styles

The Eyedropper tool is ideal for formatting small quantities of text. When working on larger documents, it is better to use *styles*. This involves creating a separate style for each text element by defining all its various attributes. For instance, you would define a style used for headlines, one for body copy, another for photo captions, and so on. Once you have defined the styles, they can be consistently applied to text on any of the pages in your document. This is the fastest, most accurate (and most fun) method of formatting large amounts of text.

Styles that apply attributes to entire paragraphs are called *paragraph styles*. A paragraph can have only one paragraph style assigned to it. Every new document you create comes with a *basic paragraph style* that is applied to all the text you type. This style default can be edited, but it cannot be deleted. Styles that affect characters or words within paragraphs are called *character styles*. More than one character style can be applied to text with a paragraph style already applied. A character style would be used, for instance, to create a raised cap at the beginning of a paragraph with a different type style than the rest of the paragraph text. This newsletter project will focus on the following eight style management techniques:

1. *Creating styles from sample text*
2. *Transferring styles from another InDesign document*
3. *Creating styles based on other styles*
4. *Creating a new style*
5. *Duplicating existing styles*
6. *Bringing in styles with a new element*
7. *Creating character styles*
8. *Redefining existing styles*

Here's an example of the power of using styles. Imagine that you have just created a 24-page annual report. When you showed your first proof to the client, she insisted you change the typeface of all the body text. No problem. Because you defined and applied styles to all the text when you created the document, all you need to do is to change the font attributes of the body copy style and all the text will automatically update.

1. Creating Styles from Sample Text

Let's create paragraph styles for your newsletter project. Open the Paragraph Styles panel by pressing **Cmd+F11** (Mac) or **F11** (Windows), or by choosing **Window>Styles**. The first thing you notice is that the panel has only one entry: [Basic Paragraph], the default paragraph style for the document. No other styles have been defined. In the lower right you'll see the Create new style and Delete selected style/groups buttons. You may remember using similar buttons in the Layers panel. In InDesign, all the panels work in basically the same way.

VISUAL |8–11|
The Paragraph Styles panel

Keyboard Shortcut
CMD+F11
F11
Paragraph Styles

The first method of defining a style is to copy the attributes from existing copy.

1. Move to the Back Cover by clicking on the Page 1 icon on the Pages panel. Place the snippet named *BC Grooming. idms* (Visual 8–12).

2. Open the Paragraph Styles panel. Place the blinking text cursor in the headline, *Grooming*, and **Option+click** (Mac) or **Alt+click** (Windows) on the *Create new style* icon on the bottom of the panel.

In the New Paragraph Style dialog box, the Style Name field remains Paragraph Style 1 until you rename it. In Visual 8–13, the style has been named *Headline*. *Based On* is an important field you will want to watch each time you create a style. There is a *Shortcut* field where you can assign a keyboard shortcut to apply this style to other text, once the style has been defined. Create a shortcut key using a number in the number pad in conjunction with one or more modifier keys. For Mac users, modifier keys are Shift, Option, and Command. In Windows, Num Lock must first be turned on, then use Shift, Alt, and Control, plus a number from the number pad to create a keyboard shortcut. For example, Visual 8–13 shows Shift+Num 1 for the shortcut for Headline. (A numeric keypad is ideal for using Style shortcuts. However, if you are working on a laptop, it's easier to select the desired style in the Styles panel or use the Styles pull-down options in the Paragraph and Character control panel. We'll cover that, later.) The Style Settings field displays a summary of all the paragraph settings used in the style.

3. Name this style **Headline**, assign **Shift+Num 1** as the shortcut, and select **Apply Style to Selection**. When you check this option, the text you used to define a style is assigned the style you have just created. Click OK. This method of defining a style is accurate and automatic, and you didn't have to enter a single formatting option! (*The Headline style is first specified in italic, and will be redefined to a Roman face in the last step of this newsletter project.*)

4. Place the text cursor in the copy below the headline. Using the method described in Steps 2 and 3, create a new style named **Body Copy** with a keyboard shortcut of **Shift+Num 2**. Save your document.

▶ *production tip*

When defining styles from existing text, remember to check Apply Style to Selection in the New Paragraph Style dialog box to assign the style to the sample copy.

2. Transferring Styles from Another InDesign Document

Let's say you are showing a new client various newsletter samples you have designed. The client finds a sample she likes and says, "I wish my newsletter could look just like this." The next method of creating paragraph and character styles will transfer the styles from another InDesign document. Here's how it's done:

1. Click on the panel menu in the Paragraph Styles panel and choose *Load Paragraph Styles.* In the *08 Healthy Pets Newsletter* folder, select the *Healthy Pets.indt* file. Click Open. The *Load Styles* dialog box, shown in Visual 8–14, gives you the opportunity to select which styles you want to load. For our purposes, make sure all the styles are checked. When you press Return, the styles will load into your document.

VISUAL |8–14|

Checked styles will be loaded into the newsletter document.

VISUAL |8–15|

The Health Focus styles have been loaded into the Healthy Pets newsletter.

2. Your Paragraph Styles panel should now look like Visual 8–15. Notice that not all the styles have shortcut keys. Shortcut keys are not usually assigned to styles that are used infrequently.

3. Creating Styles Based on Other Styles

There are times when you will need a variation of a particular style within a document. For example, perhaps you have created a style named Body Copy that works for the main portion of the text. You also have some paragraphs of body text that need a custom left indent. A variation of the Body Copy style, called Body Copy Indent (which includes a left indent), could be created. Body Copy Indent is *based on* Body Copy, and these two styles share a *parent-child relationship* with many similar attributes. When changes are made to attributes of the *parent* style (Body Copy), those shared attributes are changed in the *child*—Body Copy Indent. Here's how simple it is to create a new style, based on an existing one.

1. Option+click or Alt+click the Create new style icon in the Paragraph Styles panel. In the *New Paragraph Style* dialog box, name the style **Body Copy Indent**. Since styles are listed alphabetically, it's a good idea to name related styles similarly. Body Copy Indent will appear after Body Copy in the style list.

2. At the left side is a list of formatting categories. You can tell you are in the *General* category because it is highlighted. In the *Based On* field in the center of the dialog box, choose **Body Copy**.

3. Open each of the categories in the list. As you read each category page, you will realize that with few exceptions, the text formatting features listed are ones you are already familiar with, and you have accessed them through regular panels.

4. Open the *Indents and Spacing* category page. Set a left indent of **0.125"** (Visual 8–16) and press Return. This new style looks just like the Body Copy style, except it has a different left indent. And because Body Copy Indent is based on Body Copy, any changes you make to the Body Copy style will be automatically made to this style.

VISUAL |8–16|

The Body Copy Indent style includes all the specifications of Body Copy, plus a left indent. Any changes made to Body Copy will ripple down to Body Copy Indent.

When you are creating a style based on another style and need to reset the "child" style back to the style it is based on, click the Reset to Base button on the General page of the panel.

4. Creating a New Style

Next we'll create a new style named *Kicker*. A *kicker* is a short line of type that appears above a headline. Kickers can tease your reader into the article and add interest to an otherwise boring headline. On the front page of the newsletter you'll see a kicker above the headline describing new equipment. New equipment might not interest pet owners, but the benefit of new equipment does! Hence, the *Great News for Pet Owners* kicker.

1. Open the New Paragraph Style dialog box and set these text parameters for the new style you will name **Kicker**. Look at the *Based On* field to verify that *[Basic Paragraph]* is selected. Basic Character Formats: **Adobe Garamond Pro Italic 14**, leading: **auto** (16.8 pt.).

2. Choose *Indents and Spacing* page and set Space After to **0.0625"**. Choose *Paragraph Rules* page and turn *Rule Below* on. Set Weight: **0.5 pt.**, Color: **Black**, Offset: **0.0766"**, Width: **Text**. Press Return. Save your document.

5. Duplicating Existing Styles

We are going to create a new style called *Health Focus Standing Head*. Since this style is so similar to the Kicker style, we will create it by duplicating and editing the Kicker style. *Standing heads* are titles for features that appear in each issue. For instance, in a newspaper, the obituaries, sports, editorials, and classifieds each have their own title design that readers recognize and look for. Standing heads are used over and over, while a kicker is used once with one specific headline. Our newsletter project includes a Health Focus article with each issue. The standing head is found at the top left column on page 2: *This Issue's Health Focus*.

1. Select the *Kicker* paragraph style. Click on the menu options of the Paragraph Styles panel and choose *Duplicate Style*. In the *Duplicate Paragraph Style* dialog box, rename the style to **Health Focus Standing Head**. In the *Based On* field, choose **[No Paragraph Style]** (Visual 8–17).

VISUAL |8–17|

Although the Health Focus Standing Head style was duplicated from the Kicker style, it is not based on it. This style retains many of the Kicker attributes, but it will remain independent of any changes made to the Kicker style.

2. Choose the *Basic Character Formats* page, change the typeface to **Adobe Garamond Pro Bold Italic**. Press Return. Save your document.

6. Bringing in Styles with a New Element

When an element that has been formatted with a style is copied and then pasted into another InDesign document, the element and its style will be transferred to the current document. Here's an example of how easily this can be done.

1. Go to the Page 2 and 3 spread. From the snippet folder, place *P2 Spread Head.idms* on Page 2 and *P3 Spread Head.idms* on Page 3.

2. You will notice that a new paragraph style has appeared: *Spread Headline*. When you place a snippet that has a paragraph or character style applied, that style is added to the list of styles. Place your text cursor in the spread head on Page 3. You will notice that a plus (**+**) sign appears after the name of the applied style. A plus (+) sign indicates a *style override*, which means that something was added to the text that was not included in the defined style. You can see a description of the override by holding your mouse over the style displaying the plus (+) sign. A description of the additional formatting appears in parentheses. In this case, you will want to keep the style override. However, if you wanted to delete the paragraph style override, you would press Option (Mac) or Alt (Windows) as you clicked the style name in the list. For our newsletter, the Spread Headline style was originally created with right alignment. The spread headline on page 3 is left aligned, flush to the inside margin, which is a style override.

Creating a New Style Group

Before we move on to Character styles, we will organize our paragraph styles by creating a folder to hold all the Health Focus styles. From the Paragraph Styles menu, choose New Style Group. Name the group **Health Focus** (Visual 8–18). Select each Health Focus style and drop it into the folder. Your paragraph styles should match Visual 8–18. If the styles are shown in a different order, you can choose Sort by Name from the panel options.

VISUAL |8–18|

Style groups help organize lists of styles.

7. Creating Character Styles

Open the Character Styles panel by pressing **Shift+Command+F11**(Mac) or **Shift+F11** (Windows), or by choosing **Window>Styles>Character Styles**. You will notice that a character style already appears in the panel. It was loaded with the paragraph styles we transferred from a document earlier. We have one more character style to create and then we'll be ready to build the rest of the newsletter.

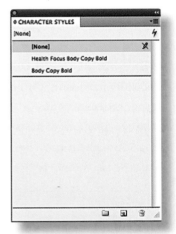

Keyboard Shortcut

 ⇧+F11

 ⇧+F11

Character Styles

1. **Option+click** (Mac) or **Alt+click** (Windows) the *Create new style* button at the bottom of the Character Styles panel. Specify *Based on*: **[None]**. Name the style **Body Copy Bold**. Assign a keyboard shortcut: **Shift+Num 5**.

2. On the *Basic Character Formats* page, enter **Myriad Pro Bold 10/11**. Save your document.

3. Open the Paragraph Styles and Character Styles panels and compare them with the ones shown in Visual 8–19. If your list looks like Visual 8–19, you are ready to complete your newsletter. If some styles are missing, you will want to review this section to find the steps that were skipped. Now let's finish this job.

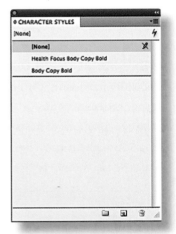

VISUAL |8–19|

Your styles should look like the ones in this example. If they do, you are ready to proceed!

Applying Styles

Paragraph and Character styles can be applied using several methods. Try each of the following four methods, and then use the ones that work best for you.

Apply Styles from the Paragraph or Character Styles

The first method of applying a style is to open the Paragraph or Character styles panel, select the copy, and then click on the name of the style in the panel. When you are applying a Paragraph style, you don't need to highlight all the copy in the paragraph. Place your cursor in the paragraph, and the style will apply to the entire paragraph. When you apply a Character style, you need to highlight all the copy that the style should be applied to.

Apply Styles by Using Keyboard Shortcuts

The second method of applying styles is to select the copy and press the keyboard shortcut assigned to the style. It is unlikely that all styles will have keyboard shortcuts, so you will probably use keyboard shortcuts only for styles you will assign quite often, like body copy.

Apply Styles from the Control Panel

A third method of applying styles is to select the styles from the Control panel. Visual 8–20 shows where the Styles choices appear on the Character and Paragraph Controls.

VISUAL |8–20|

Styles can be found in the Paragraph and Character Controls.

Apply Styles Using Quick Apply

A fourth method of applying styles is to use Quick Apply. When your document contains a long list of styles, Quick Apply allows you to locate a style by typing part of the style name. Press the up and down arrow keys to scroll through the list of items. To apply a style, press Enter or Return. To close Quick Apply without applying an item, press Esc or click on the document.

VISUAL |8–21|

Use Quick Apply to locate a style by typing a portion of its name. Quick Apply is great for managing long lists of styles!

Styles chosen in menu options

You have prepared the document structure, brought in images from Snippets, and created styles for typographic consistency and production speed. Let's see how well they work. We'll begin on the front cover. You should print out the actual size newsletter sample from the *08 Healthy Pets Newsletter* folder on the CD because it shows where all the styles are used.

▶ MOVING TOWARD MASTERY

Tips for Working With Text and Styles

▶ It's faster to drag a text frame while you are placing text than to create a frame first and then drop text into it.

▶ Placed text will come in with the attributes of the style that is highlighted in the panel window. When you place text, be sure you do not have a character style highlighted in the Character styles window. In this newsletter project, for instance, the last style you created was a character style and it is probably still highlighted. By default, a paragraph style won't replace a character style. So, before you begin to place text, select **[None]** in the Character Style field in the Control panel.

▶ A good rule of thumb is to select all the text and first change the style to Body Copy. This technique generally reduces the point size of your text and makes a large text block more manageable. When the text frame is active and you are in the Type tool, press **Command+A** (Mac) or **Control+A** (Windows) to select all the type. It is important to select only text in a frame and not all the objects on your page! Then apply the Body Copy paragraph style.

Another way to accomplish this step is to have the Body Copy style selected when you place the text so that it will automatically appear with the Body Copy style. After the Body Copy style is assigned to the text block, you may apply the subheads and character styles.

▶ Press **Enter** (Mac) or **Enter on the Number pad** (Windows) to make text jump from one linked text frame to the next.

▶ Paragraph and Character styles can also be accessed through the Control panel. Choose the Paragraph or Character formatting options.

▶ A plus (+) sign following a defined style in the Paragraph Styles panel means additional formatting has been added. To remove Paragraph and local formatting overrides, click the **Clear Overrides** icon on the Styles panel (Visual 8–11), or choose Clear Overrides from the Paragraph Styles panel options.

▶ Clearing overrides does not remove formatting created by Character styles. To remove Character styles, select text containing the Character style and then click **[None]** in the Character Styles panel.

Applying Styles to the Front Cover

1. Check the Control panel to see that Character styles are set to **[None]** and Paragraph styles are set to **Body Copy**. Create a 2-column text frame in the first column that begins under the photo and extends across the second column, and to the bottom margin, gutter **0.1875"**. Place the *New equipment increases.docx* file from the *08 Healthy Pets Newsletter* folder on the CD accompanying this book.

2. If the copy is not already Body Copy, select all the type and apply the Body Copy paragraph style by pressing **Shift+Num 2.**

▶ *production tip*

Don't have a character style selected when you are placing text!

Deselect the text after applying a style.

3. Place the cursor in the *Great News for Pet Owners* line and select the **Kicker** paragraph style. The kicker won't fit nicely in the column, but we'll fix that in Step 5.

4. Place the cursor in the headline and select **Headline** from the Paragraph Styles panel, or press Shift+Num 1. The typeface is still italic—it will be changed later. Also, place a soft return after the word *increases* to end up with the longer part of the headline on the last line. The headline won't fit nicely into the column—we'll fix that, next.

5. Highlight the headline and kicker. From the Control panel, select *Span All* from the *Span Columns* controls (Visual 8–22)

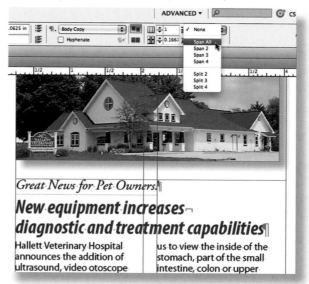

6. A *pull quote* is an excerpt that is designed to stand out from the rest of the body copy. Pull quotes add visual interest and encourage readership. Place snippet *FC Pull Quote.idms* and position it between the two columns. Adjust its position for the best text flow. Text wrap options have already been turned on. Make sure the paragraph beginning with *The video endoscope*, is at the top of the second column, and not at the bottom of the first column.

7. Place *Should you give Heartguard.docx* from the *08 Healthy Pets Newsletter* folder. As you place, drag a new text frame at the top of column three. Select all the type and change it to **Body Copy.** Then place your cursor in the headline and press **Shift+Num 1** to assign the **Headline** style.

8. When text is placed, there are often small modifications you will need to make. For instance, notice that the registration mark ® used three times in this article is imported as (r). At the end of the newsletter project, we will change all the registration marks using the Find and Replace operation. Similarly, by default InDesign has placed a single opening quotation mark instead of an apostrophe before the word, *'round* (Visual 8–23). Open the Glyphs panel and replace it with an apostrophe.

VISUAL | 8–23 |

You will usually need to do some fine tuning on copy that has been placed.

Incorrect single quotation mark → **year'round?** **year'round?** ← Correct apostrophe

9. Find the *Puppy Classes.docx* article from the *08 Healthy Pets Newsletter* folder. Bottom align the text at the bottom of the third column and use Styles to format the text. Modify the size, font, and color of the phone number at the bottom of the article. This is called *local formatting,* and almost every document contains some local formatting. The Front Cover spread should look very much like Visual 8–24.

VISUAL | 8–24 |

The Front Cover elements are positioned and styles applied.

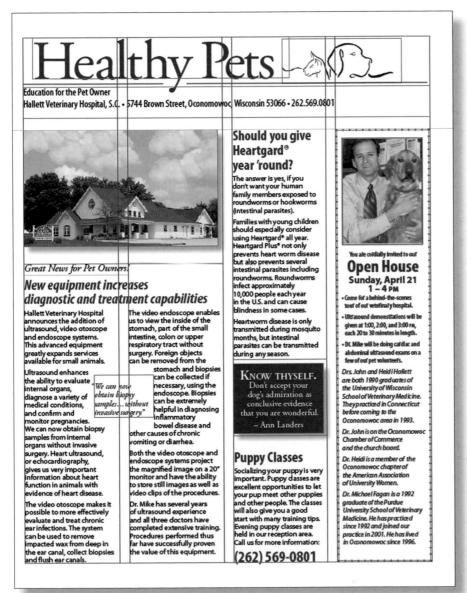

Applying Styles to Pages 2 and 3

The spread for pages 2 and 3 should have a horizontal guideline stretching across the whole spread at the **1.65"** Y-coordinate position. Articles on the top of this spread should butt up to this guide.

1. Find the *Feeding.docx* article from the *08 Healthy Pets Newsletter* folder. Place the text, dragging a text frame in the third column of *Page 2*, from the top guideline down to the top of Dr. Mike's photo.

2. Apply the **Body Copy** and **Headline** styles to this article. Notice there are many instances in this article where you will need to change the register mark (later in this project).

3. Refer to Visual 8–26 or the newsletter sample printed earlier, to place the rest of the articles on spread 2–3. The *Spay or Neuter.docx* article on *Page 3* continues in a linked frame under the photo. Bottom align both columns of the Spay article so that the text lines up.

4. *Dental Care.docx,* in the third column of *Page 3*, is in a text frame that reaches across two columns. Save your document.

Creating the Health Focus Table

Hopefully you remember the table functions you learned earlier. If not, you will need to review that section in Chapter 5.

1. The *Health Focus* is the last feature on Page 2. Draw a frame that stretches across the first and second columns and extends down to the bottom margin. Use **Command+B** (Mac) or **Control+B** (Windows) to apply a **0.125"** *text inset* on all sides. Fill the frame with **10% Blue.** Place *Vaccines Critical to your.docx,* found in the *08 Healthy Pets Newsletter* folder, in the frame.

2. First, change all copy to **Health Focus Body Copy**. Then, apply the **Health Focus Standing Head** and **Health Focus Headline** styles. The italic type under the headline is called a *deck.* A deck is designed to increase reading interest. It usually summarizes the accompanying article and appears between the headline and the body copy. Apply the **Health Focus Deck** style to the deck.

3. Highlight the text from just before the words *8 weeks* to the word *Optional.* Use the *Paragraph Options Control* to remove the left indent on the selected text. Choose *Table>Convert Text to Table;* Column Separator: *Tab*; Row Separator: *Paragraph.* You will need to format the table. The copy is **Myriad Pro Regular 10/11**. Center text in cells,

adjust column and row spacing, merge cells, and apply strokes and fills. Highlight the column heads row, reduce the point size and rotate the text **270°**. Look in Minion Pro in the Glyphs panel to find a check mark. Visual 8–25 provides a detail view of the table.

4. Apply **Health Focus Subhead** style to the bulleted lines. Save your document. Pages 2 and 3 are now complete. Compare your document to the example shown in Visual 8–26.

This Issue's Health Focus

Vaccines: critical to your dog's health

Regular vaccinations are important for your dog's general health. Below is a recommended immunization schedule:

	8 weeks	10 weeks	12 weeks	16 weeks	6 months
DHLPP	✓		✓	✓	
Rabies			✓		
Lyme			✓	✓	
De worm	✓	✓	✓		
Fecal Exam	✓				
Spay/Neuter					✓
Kennel Cough	Optional				

- **DHLPP (Distemper)**
  Puppies receive a series of Canine Distemper vaccinations, usually at 8, 12, and 16 weeks of age,

VISUAL |8–25|

A detail view of the Health Focus table. The cells are filled with Paper, and the strokes are .5-pt blue.

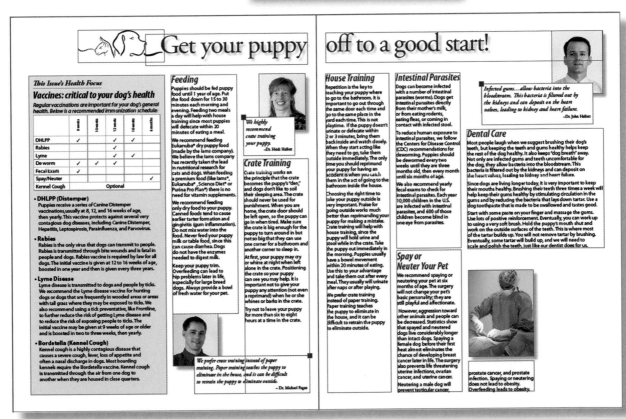

VISUAL |8–26|

Pages 2 and 3 spread with elements positioned and styles applied.

Finishing Page 4

All the text files needed for page 4 are found in the *08 Healthy Pets Newsletter* folder. Place *Pet ID.docx* at the bottom of the third column. You will need to do some local formatting in this article by changing the Home Again product name to italics. Notice that when you add local formatting, a plus sign (+) appears at the end of the Body Copy paragraph style in the panel. Place and apply styles to the *Heartworm.docx* and *Toys.docx* files. Place the *Emergency Vet Service.docx* file, formatting the type as shown in the newsletter sample printed from the PDF file on your CD. Notice that the *Fleas and Ticks.docx* article uses two paragraph styles: **Body Copy**, **Body Copy Indent**; and a character style, **Body Copy Bold**, which will be applied next.

Applying Character Styles

If you find yourself doing the same type of local formatting over and over again, it's probably time to define and apply a character style. The last page has two articles that use the Body Copy Bold character style: *Fleas and Ticks* and *Corrections to keep your puppy from biting.*

1. In the *Fleas and Ticks* article, use the *Body Copy Bold* character style on the product names in the bulleted copy: *Frontline®, Flea-tick Spray, Flea Shampoo, Flea Collar, Preventic®,* and *House Spray.* Highlight those words and apply the **Body Copy Bold** character style from the Character Styles panel, using the keyboard shortcut created earlier. Be sure to use *Indent to here* to hang the second line of copy under bullets.

VISUAL |8–27|

The Back Cover page is now completed.

2. In the *Corrections* article, apply the **Body Copy Bold** character style to these words: *OUCH!, Substitute,* and *Lip Pinch.*

8. Redefining Styles

The newsletter is almost finished. This is a great time to print a copy, look at it carefully, and fine-tune the positioning of all the elements. Check for the correct use of hyphens and dashes. As you can see, your newsletter looks great, except the headlines are all italic, and the newsletter sample shows them as roman. If you hadn't defined and applied styles, you would need to manually change every headline in the document. That may not be a big deal for a short 4-page newsletter, but imagine making that change in a 64-page book!

1. Highlight one paragraph with the Headline style assigned. Change the typeface to **Myriad Pro Bold Condensed**.

2. Open the *Paragraph Styles* panel. Since you made a type style change on the local level, you will see a plus sign (+) next to the Headline style. Open the panel menu options and choose **Redefine Style**. The Headline style is now updated to reflect the Roman type style throughout the whole document! Save and print your newsletter.

VISUAL |8–28|

Redefine the Headline style.

Clearing Overrides

Sections of type that have a paragraph style, plus overrides, are easy to identify. When these passages are selected, a plus sign (+) is displayed at the end of the style name in the panel. To remove Paragraph and local Character formatting overrides, click the Clear Overrides icon on the Paragraph Control panel or choose Clear overrides in selection from the Paragraph panel options. You have other choices for clearing overrides:

VISUAL |8–28|

The Clear overrides command is found at the bottom of the Pages panel, on the Control panel, and on the Pages panel menu options.

▶ **Click** *on the style name in the style panel (no Option or Alt) to clear Paragraph overrides only.*

▶ **Cmd+click** *(Mac) or* **Ctrl+click** *(Windows) on the Clear overrides in selection icon to clear local Character formatting only.*

▶ *To remove Character style formatting, select the text and choose* **[None]** *in the Styles field of the Character Control panel.*

Using Find/Change

Find/Change allows you to search for specific words, characters, digits, or keystrokes and replace them with something you specify. The Find/Change dialog box is filled with choices—and it is worthwhile to spend some time looking at the options available in the fields. Use the keyboard shortcut or choose **Edit>Find/Change** and type (**r**) in the Find what field. In the Change to field, select the Special characters for replace menu (the @ sign), then choose **Symbols>Registered Trademark Symbol**. Set the Search field to Document and press the Change All button. Every occurrence of (r) in the entire newsletter will change to ®.

Keyboard Shortcut

 CMD+F

 CTRL+F

Find/Change

VISUAL |8–29|

The Find/Change panel has numerous options for making document-wide changes.

Options in the Text Query field

Click on the @ to find the options under **Find what** and **Change to.** The **Registered Trademark Symbol** is selected, and will replace all occurrences of (r).

Printing Your Newsletter

Your newsletter is now completed. Proof it one more time. If you have access to a printer that can handle 11" × 17" paper, select **Spreads** in the General window of the Print dialog box. Then choose Tabloid or 11" × 17" under Setup, and change the orientation so that your pages print side by side. If you wish to print your newsletter in spreads on letter-size paper, select **Spreads** under General, and then **Scale to Fit** under Setup (Visual 8–30).

Change orientation for printing in spreads

Select Spreads to print left- and right-hand pages together.

Scale to Fit automatically reduces the size of the document to fit on the paper size.

VISUAL | 8–30 |

Spreads must be selected to print facing pages side by side.

Summary

Good designers use techniques to make disinterested readers take a longer look at a publication. This newsletter project introduced you to some publication design elements: pull quote, deck, standing head, and kicker. These elements, when combined with appropriate typeface selection, line measure, and leading, create a document that has contrast and wonderful texture.

When working on complex projects, it is important to remember that there are no "throwaway" elements. The position and style of a page number or a pull quote should not be overlooked just because it's small or used only once or twice. All elements are important, and should work together to create *gestalt*—where the whole is greater than the sum of its parts. It takes creative energy and commitment to refine the smallest details of a document. But this ability to maintain a high level of focus is what separates the skilled designers from the masses.

▶ IN REVIEW

1. What are three guidelines for preparing electronic copy?

2. What are facing pages and how do you make them?

3. How can you make Snippets be placed at their original locations?

4. What is the process for using the Eyedropper tool to transfer text attributes?

5. What are three methods of defining styles?

6. What is the difference between a paragraph style and a character style?

7. What does a + sign at the end of the name of a style mean?

8. Where is the Clear Overrides icon found?

9. What is the process for applying a paragraph style, preserving character styles, but removing overrides?

10. Describe what a style based on another style means.

11. In addition to the Paragraph and Character Styles panels, where can you find and apply styles?

12. How is a keyboard shortcut for a style made?

13. How can you transfer paragraph and character styles from one document to another?

14. Define these newsletter parts: a) Deck, b) Kicker, c) Standing head.

15. What is the [Basic Paragraph] style?

Keyboard Shortcut	
⌘ CMD+F12	**Pages Panel**
⊞ F12	

Keyboard Shortcut	
⌘ OPT+CMD+0	**Fit Spread to Window**
⊞ ALT+CTRL+0	

Keyboard Shortcut	
⌘ CMD+F	**Find/ Change**
⊞ CTRL+F	

Keyboard Shortcut	
⌘ F11	**Paragraph Styles**
⊞ F11	

Keyboard Shortcut	
⌘ ⇧+F11	**Character Styles**
⊞ ⇧+F11	

►CHAPTER 8 PROJECTS

This newsletter page is not included in the chapter projects, but is a sample of effective two-color newsletter design, created by a student who completed *Exploring InDesign.* © 2006 Dina Sharapata.

Two projects will reinforce the concepts from this chapter.

Newsletter Analysis. Find a sample newsletter. Write a critique that addresses the following:

- ► *The underlying grid structure*
- ► *The quality of the typography: contrast, typeface, consistency*
- ► *Any evidence of styles*
- ► *The inclusion of kickers, pull quotes, decks, subheads, spread heads, or standing heads*
- ► *Overall impact*
- ► *Effectiveness of nameplate*
- ► *Suggestions for improvement*

Create Styles. Select a newspaper. Find four repeating styles used throughout the publication. Using placeholder text, duplicate each of the styles in InDesign. Create and name a style for each one.

Learning is not
compulsory.
Neither is **survival.**

⌐ W. Edwards Deming

| Master Pages and Object Styles |

objectives

- ► *Create multiple master pages*
- ► *Set up automatic page numbering, jump lines, and continuation lines*
- ► *Insert, duplicate, and remove pages*
- ► *Manage document pages using the Pages panel*
- ► *Create an object library*
- ► *Create and apply object styles*

introduction

Page consistency is critical for multiple-page documents. A five-person team producing a 96-page catalog needs a document structure that is consistent from page to page and designer to designer. Perhaps you've leafed through a publication where repeating elements, like page numbers, appear to jump around the outside corners like cartoons in an old-fashioned flip book. This would be an indication that the production team was not working with a clearly defined document structure. Master pages and object styles are ideal for bringing organization and consistency to complex documents. Items placed on master pages appear in the exact same location on every document page. Object styles can be used to define the stroke on a photo frame or a colored background in a text area. Changes made to a master page or an object style will ripple through the entire document, which saves time and reduces the margin of error. Proper document construction can make or break the finished project. Take the time to plan your projects thoughtfully before starting them.

The Pages Panel

You've already used the Pages panel as you've worked through this text, but you've never been "formally introduced" to this little dynamo. The Pages panel can be opened by clicking on the Pages icon on the dock or by using keyboard shortcuts. If you are a Windows user, simply press F12 (function key) and the panel will open up. If you are a Mac user, function key F12 might already be assigned to a operating system operation such as Exposé. If that is the case, you must add the Command key to F12 to open the Pages panel. And if you are a laptop user, you're probably already aware that, depending on the configuration of your keyboard, you may need to press the *fn* key along with the number to activate the Pages panel.

What are Master Pages?

The most basic functions of the Pages panel are to add, delete, duplicate, and rearrange pages in your document. But the Pages panel also allows you to create *master pages*. A master page is a page layout that is created on one spread or page and then applied to single or a range of document pages. For instance, if I want my name to appear in the lower right corner of each page in a document, I can make a master page and place my name in the perfect

location, typestyle and size. When I apply this master page to the document pages, my name will automatically appear in the exact location on each page!

As you begin working with complex documents, you will realize that individual pages have different layout requirements. In a single document, for instance, some pages may require three text columns, and other pages may need four. Margins may vary from page to page. Some pages may require *folios* (page numbers), running heads, or footers. Or, a graphic element may appear only on recto (right-hand) pages with four columns and a footer! Using the Pages panel, you can create master pages that have different margins and columns, or contain repeating elements, such as folios. Different master pages may be assigned to individual document pages. Each document page takes on the attributes of the master page assigned to it. Now that you know how master pages are used, you can understand how they bring consistency and assist with the production of complex documents.

A-Master: The Document Default

Each time a new document is created, the specified margins and columns are assigned to a default master page named *A-Master*. A document's A-Master is the basic layout that automatically applies to all pages in the document. You can change margins and columns on a single page, but the remaining pages will still retain the attributes of the A-Master default. But if you use the Pages panel to change the margins and columns on the A-Master, the document default, then those changes will be applied to all the pages in a document.

Basic Operations

Page masters are viewed in the Pages panel. By default, the master pages are displayed in the upper portion of the Pages panel and the regular document pages are shown in the lower (Visual 9–1). For the next series of exercises, we will be using *09 Master Pages.indd* from the *09 Artwork and Resources* folder, found on the CD accompanying this text.

VISUAL |9–1|

The Pages Panel Options setting has been modified to show Extra Large page icons. Show Vertically has also been deselected.

1. **Modify Pages Panel Options**. Open *09 Master Pages.indd*. Press **Command+F12** (Mac) or **F12** (Windows) to open the *Pages* panel. This five-page document has been created with a photo on the master page. As you look at the page icons in the *Pages* panel, you can see that the master item—the photo—is repeated on each page. On the *Pages* panel *option menu*, choose *Panel Options* to open a dialog that allows you to change the size and layout of the various page icons in the *Pages* panel. In Visual 9–1, notice that the size of the document page icons has been changed to *Extra Large*, and the *Show Vertically* option has been deselected.

2. **Move from master level to document level.** Double-click on the page 1 icon, below the double line on the *Pages* panel. The page is highlighted, and the number below the page is in a black box. You are now on document page 1, on the *local*, or *document* level. Double-click on A-Master in the top section of the panel. The master becomes highlighted, and you are now on the A-Master page, on the *global*,

▶ *production tip*

Double-click a page in the Pages panel to move to and display the page.

or *master* level. Repeat this sequence until you are comfortable moving between the two levels. Notice the page number in the lower left corner of the InDesign window. It shows the active page, and switches between A-Master and page 1 as you move back and forth. When you single-click a page or master page, the page becomes highlighted, but the page is not actually selected. A single-click highlights a page; and a double-click moves to, and displays the page. Double-click on different pages in your document, and watch the numbers change in the page number field.

3. **Apply the [None] master.** Select the master page named [None] from the *Pages* panel. Drag the [None] page icon to the document level, and place it on top of page 2. Release the mouse when a thick, black border appears around the page 2 icon. The [None] master unassigns a master from a page. In this example, A-Master is now removed from page 2, and is replaced by a blank page. Use the [None] master to unassign A-Master from pages 2–5 in your document.

VISUAL |9–2|

A black border surrounding the document page means that a master page is being applied.

VISUAL |9–3|

The master page has been renamed in the Master Options dialog box.

4. **Rename a master page.** Double-click A-Master. Draw two lines below the photo. For the top line, specify width **10-pt.**, **Red** stroke. Lower line, width **3-pt.**, **Blue** stroke. Open the *Master Options* dialog box from the *Pages* menu. In this dialog box you can set various options, such as the Prefix that will be displayed on page icons to identify which master page has been applied. You can also rename the master page. Type **Red & Blue Lines** in the *Name* field (Visual 9–3).

▶ MOVING TOWARD MASTERY

Understand the following visual cues when using the Pages panel. When pages are added by pulling masters to the document level, a thin vertical line indicates an insertion point between pages. A black frame surrounding a page means that the selected master is being applied to the document page.

New page will be added after page 1.

New page will be added at the end of the document.

Master page is being applied.

5.   Insert pages. There are many methods of inserting pages in a document. Insert additional pages to your document, using each of the following methods:

▶ *Click on the Pages panel options and choose Insert Pages. In the Insert Pages dialog box you can specify how many pages to add, and which master should be assigned to the new pages. In Insert Pages, change the Pages field to **1**. Check that the Insert fields are set to After Page and 1. Select **A-Red & Blue Lines** in the Master field. Press Return. Compare the pages assigned to A-Red & Blue Lines with the unassigned, blank pages. Notice that the assigned pages have a small A on the top of each page icon. This tells you, at a glance, that the A-Red & Blue Lines master page is applied to those document pages.*

▶ *Click the Create new page icon at the bottom of the Pages panel (Visual 9–1). Each time you click, a new page is inserted after the page you are on. The new pages are assigned the master page used for the last page you were on. If you press Option (Mac) or Alt (Windows) as you click the Create new page icon, the same Insert Pages dialog box, found on the Pages panel, opens.*

▶ *Go to File>Document Setup and enter a value in Number of Pages. When you insert pages using this technique, you don't have the option to choose which master page the new pages will be based on, and new pages are always added to the end of the document.*

▶ *You can also insert a document page that is based on a master by dragging and dropping the master page icon into the document section of the Pages panel. If you want to add the new page in a particular spot, say between pages 1 and 2, drag the master page between the two page icons until you see a vertical line appear after page 1. When you release the mouse, there will be a new page 2 created; the old page 2 will be shifted to the number 3 spot. Be careful not to release the mouse when the border of a document page is highlighted. If you do, you will be applying that master page to the selected document page.*

6. **Delete pages.** There are also several methods for deleting pages. Use each of the following methods to delete pages in your document, until your document has only one page and keep your file open for more practice.

▸ *Select a page and drag it to the Delete selected pages icon (Visual 9–1). Or, Shift+click to select a range of pages, and drag them to the Delete selected pages icon.*

▸ *Select a page, or range of pages, and click the Delete selected pages icon.*

▸ *Select a page, or range of pages. Go to the Pages options and choose Delete Spread.*

▸ *Go to Layout>Pages>Delete Pages and specify the page that will be deleted.*

▸ *Go to File>Document Setup and change the value in Number of Pages. This method removes pages from the end of the document.*

Modifying Master Items on the Document Level

Using master pages is ideal when you have a document with elements such as *folios* (page numbers), headers, footers, or design elements that will appear on every page. When you apply a master to a document page, all the elements from the master, called *master items,* appear in the same position on each document page. Text frames created on the master page are displayed on document pages with dotted bounding boxes. Even though you may have created multiple master pages to cover every possible page layout scenario, there are times when master items still need to be modified on the document level. Before a master item can be modified on the document level, it must be *overridden.* This is a keyboard shortcut that you will frequently use— **Shift+Command+Click** (Mac) or **Shift+Control+Click** (Windows). Carefully work through the next series of exercises to learn how to manage master items.

1. **Override master items.** When you *override* a master item, a copy of the item appears on the document page, allowing you to change its attributes. Press **Shift+Command** (Mac) or **Shift+Control** (Windows) and click on the red line on page 1. Handles appear, indicating that the line is editable. Change the red line's stroke to **Yellow**. A master item that is overridden still retains its association with the master page. However, the attributes that were changed on the local level won't be updated when those same attributes are changed on the master page. In the example of our red-turned-to-yellow line, color was the attribute changed on the local level. When the master page is modified, InDesign will update only attributes that have not been modified on the local level. Go to master *A-Red & Blue Lines*. Move the red line to the bottom of the master page, and change its stroke to **Green**. On page 1, notice that the position of the line changed, but not the stroke color, because the color had been modified on the local level.

2. **Allow Master Item Overrides on Selection.**
Go to page 1, and use the keyboard shortcut to override the photo. Nothing happens. This element cannot be modified because when it was placed on the master, *Allow Master Item Overrides on Selection* was turned off in the *Pages* panel menu. Select the photo on *A-Red & Blue Lines* master page. Under the panel options, select *Allow Master Item Overrides on Selection* (Visual 9–4). Now, delete the photo on page 1.

3. **Remove Selected Local Overrides.** Override the lines on page 1, and change their positions and stroke colors. Select one of the lines. From the *Pages* options, choose *Remove Selected Local Overrides* (Visual 9–5). With this command, the attributes of the selected item will be restored to match the item on the master page.

4. **Remove All Local Overrides.** You can also revert a page to the original master. In these cases, select *Remove All Local Overrides* from the *Pages* options (Visual 9–6). When you choose this option, the page Is restored to the current master assigned to it. No items should be selected when choosing this option. If items are selected, the *Pages* menu displays *Remove Selected Local Overrides*, rather than *Remove All Local Overrides*. Choose *Remove All Local Overrides* for page 1, and let's continue.

5. **Detach Selection from Master.** Go to *A-Red & Blue Lines* master and select the *photo*. Choose *Allow Master Item Overrides on Selection* from the panel options. Now, go back to page 1. Use **Shift+Command+click** (Mac) or **Shift+Control+click** (Windows) to override the photo. Under the Pages options, select *Detach Selection* from Master (Visual 9–7). A master item must be overridden before it can be detached. Once a master item is detached, there is no

VISUAL |9–4|
Allow Master Item Overrides on Selection must be checked, for each item on a master page, in order to override that item on a document page.

VISUAL |9–5|
Remove Selected Local Overrides restores individual master items.

VISUAL |9–6|
Remove All Local Overrides restores all master items on a single page.

VISUAL |9–7|
When a master item is detached from the master, it no longer retains any association with the master page.

▶ *production tip*
A master item must be overridden before it can be detached.

more connection with the master page. Changes made on the master page will not affect items that have been detached. Go back to *A-Red & Blue Lines* and delete the photo. The photo remains on page 1, because it is no longer associated with the master page. Use the Undo command to replace the photo on the master page.

6. **Override All Master Items.** Overriding every individual master item on a complex page can be time consuming. *Override All Master Items* overrides all master items on the selected page, not on all the pages in a document. You will want to memorize this keyboard shortcut!

Creating A Document With Multiple Masters

Many documents require more than one master page. For instance, you may be working on a document that requires different pages to have a two-column grid, a three-column grid, and a four-column grid. In such a case, if you don't create multiple master pages, you will need to change the margins and columns on each individual page—that's too much work! In the next exercise you will create a small publication, *Baseball Digest*, with photography provided by baseball fan(atic) Kristina Hegyera, a student at Waukesha County Technical College. The document is partially constructed for you, and each step in the project will introduce a new master page function. Take your time as you systematically learn the features of master pages. You will need to use elements from *09 Artwork and Resources* which are found on the CD that accompanies this text.

VISUAL |9–8|

Back cover (left) and front cover (right) of *Baseball Digest*.

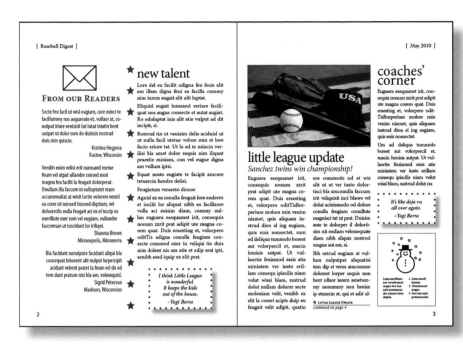

★ LITTLE LEAGUE UPDATE continued on page 4

VISUAL |9–9|

Pages 2–3 *Baseball Digest.*

Baseball Digest Magazine

1. Open *09 Baseball Digest.indd* from the *09 Artwork and Resources* folder on the CD.

2. **Rename A-Master.** Open the *Pages* panel. Highlight the *verso* and r*ecto* page of A-Master. Go to *Master Options for A-Master* and change the *Name* to **Folio and Header**, Number of Pages: **2**. You've just renamed the master page. Giving descriptive names to master pages is a good production practice.

3. **Specify automatic page numbering.** Enlarge the view of the Folio and Header master page. In the outside, bottom corner of each spread is a letter *X*. This letter is a placeholder for a page number. You'll replace placeholder X with InDesign's special character, *Current Page Number*. As a result, a page number will be automatically placed on each document page. Highlight the *X* on the recto master page, and press Shift+Command+Option+N (Mac) or Shift+Control+Alt+N (Windows). Current Page Number can also be inserted from the *Context* or *Type menus>Insert Special Character>Markers>Current Page Number*. The *X* will be replaced with the letter, *A*. Letter A corresponds to the *A* prefix on this master page. Repeat this process to replace the *verso* folio *X* with the *Current Page Number* symbol. When you look at the pages on the local level, you will see that page numbers are displayed on each page. Because the folios are master items, you don't need to worry that they will be accidently repositioned on a document page.

VISUAL |9–10|

Master items appear with a dotted line around the bounding box. When the Current Page Number symbol is applied, the X will be replaced with the letter of the master page prefix.

Keyboard Shortcut

⇧+OPT+CMD+N
⇧+ALT+CTRL+N

Current Page Number

4. **Add running heads.** A *running head* (or *header*) is a line of text that appears at the top of every page. Navigate to the *09 Baseball Digest folder* on the *09 Artwork and Resources* folder. Change *InDesign Preferences>File Handling* so that the *Snippet Import* position is at the *Original Location*. Then on the *A-Folio* and *Header* master page, place *X Verso Header.idms* in the upper left corner of the verso master page, and *X Recto Header.idms* in the upper right corner of the recto master. This master page will now be used as a foundation for the rest of the master pages for this publication.

VISUAL |9–11|

The running heads on the top of the verso and recto master pages.

> | Baseball Digest |
>
> | May 2010 |

Enable Layout Adjustment

Layout Adjustment automatically changes the position of elements when changes are made to an existing layout. Layout Adjustment isn't just a feature of master pages—it can be used at the document level, as well. But this is an excellent time to learn about Layout Adjustment. Layout Adjustment works best with elements that are aligned to the guides of margins and page columns, and to ruler guides. We will change the column settings on the master level and let Layout Adjustment update the layout on the document level.

5. Go to page 1. Draw a text frame inside the margin area and fill with placeholder text. Now, go to *Layout>Layout Adjustment.* If Layout Adjustment is not listed, select *Show All Menu Items* from the bottom of the list. When the dialog box comes up, select *Enable Layout Adjustment* and accept the default settings (Visual 9–12). Select the recto master page. Under *Layout>Margins and Columns,* enter **3** in the *Columns Number* field. Go to page 1 and you will see that the text has been automatically updated to three columns. Undo the 3-column master change and delete the text frame, but keep your document open!

VISUAL |9–12|

As a layout changes, Layout Adjustment automatically repositions elements that are snapped to margin and ruler guides.

Layout Adjustment
☑ Enable Layout Adjustment
Snap Zone: ⬍ 0.0278 in
☑ Allow Graphics and Groups to Resize
☑ Allow Ruler Guides to Move
☐ Ignore Ruler Guide Alignments
☑ Ignore Object and Layer Locks
OK
Reset

Creating and Duplicating Master Pages

The *A-Folio and Header* master page spread has single text columns, headers, and auto page numbering. Now you will create another master page with the same headers and folios, but with different margins and column guides. Before a new master page is created, you have a decision to make: Should this page be *based on* another master page, or should it be an independent page, based on [None]? Just like paragraph styles, which can be based on another style, a master page based on another master page, will automatically update, if any changes are made to the original master page. When working with master pages, the original master page is the *parent master*, and the master page based on it, is the *child master*.

► *production tip*

Like paragraph styles, which can be based on another style, a master page based on another master page, will automatically update, if any changes are made to the original master page.

1. **Create a new master spread.** Choose *New Master* from the panel options. When the New Master dialog box appears, type **Two-column Grid** in the *Name* field. In *Based On Master:* choose **A-Folio and Header**, Number of Pages: **2**. A new master page with a *B* prefix will now appear in the master level of the Pages panel. The letter *A* in the upper corners shows that master A is the parent master. Select each page in *B-Two-column Grid*. Notice that the headers and footers from the *A* master were transferred to this new master page. Now, make sure both master page icons in the spread are selected and go to *Layout>Margins and Columns* and change the *Columns Number* to **2**. Accept the default gutter, and press Return.

When duplicating master spreads, you also need to consider parent master and child master relationships. If you duplicate a master page and base it on [None], the new page will include all the elements from the copied page, but the connection with those elements will be broken. This means that any changes made on the original page will not affect the duplicate page.

2. **Duplicate a master spread.** Practice each of these methods to duplicate a master spread in a document:

   ► *Highlight the master spread and drag it to the Create new page icon at the bottom of the Pages panel.*
   ► *Go to the Pages options menu and select Duplicate Master Spread.*
   ► *Use one of these methods to duplicate the A or B master page in your document. After you get comfortable using each method of creating duplicate master spreads, delete any you have made, because they will not be used in the* Baseball Digest *project.*

3. **Create and apply a new master spread.** Choose *New Master* from the panel options. Name the master **Three-column Grid**, and base it on **A-Folio and Header.** Go to *Layout>Margins and Columns* and change the *Columns Number* to **3**. Apply this master to page 1 of the document by dragging a recto Three-column Grid master page on top of page 1. When the black border surrounds the page, release the mouse. Override, and delete the header and the folio on page 1, leaving just the three column text frame.

Build the Document

The pages are formatted and ready to go. You'll place snippets to complete this project, and if you changed your InDesign preferences earlier, this part should be a snap.

1. **Finish Page 1**. Select *P1 Nameplate.idms* from the *09 Baseball Digest* folder. Place it on page 1, centered horizontally at the top of the page. Place *P1 Contents.idms* in the left column, flush against the bottom margin guide. *P1 Photo* is positioned just above the contents box in the left column. *P1 Article.idms* spans columns 2 and 3, and is flush with the bottom margin guide. Place *P1 Seal.idms* in the upper right corner (Visual 9–13).

VISUAL |9–13|

A magnified view of the positioning of the elements on page 1 of *Baseball Digest*.

2. **Finish Page 2**. Apply a verso *Two-column Grid* master to page 2 by dragging a verso master page from the Pages panel and letting it rest on top of page 2. When a black border appears, release the mouse. Place *P2 Stars.idms* in the gutter between column 1 and column 2. Place *P2 Letters.idms* in the left column. Position *P2 New Talent.idms* flush with the right column, top margin guide. Center *P2 Quote.idms* in the right column, flush with the bottom margin guide (Visual 9–14).

VISUAL |9–14|

Positioning of the elements on the lower half of page 2.

Jump Lines and Continuation Lines

Jump lines are used to alert readers when an article is continued on a later page. They appear at the end of a column and read something like: *"this article continues on page 257."* When you turn to page 257, you are greeted with a *continuation line,* which reads something like: *"…article continued from page 1."* InDesign automates this process. A separate text frame is created, in which a special character marker is inserted. The Next Page Number marker is used for jump lines, while the Previous Page Number marker is used for continuation lines. There are two things you must remember when using jump and continuation lines:

> ► *The text frames on each page must be threaded; and*
> ► *The jump or continuation line text frame must be touching the threaded frame.*

The special characters, **Next Page Number** and **Previous Page Number**, can be found under the Context or Type menus by selecting **Insert Special Character>Markers**.

1. **Add Page 3 elements.** Apply a recto *Three-column Grid* master to *page 3*. Position *P3 Photo.idms* across columns 1 and 2. Place *P3 Little League.idms* in columns 1 and 2, flush with the bottom margin guide. Place *P3 Coaches' Corner.idms* flush with the top margin guide of column 3. Place *P3 Corner Ad.idms* in the lower right corner of column 3. Center *P3 Quote.idms* in the remaining space in column 3.

2. **Finish Page 4.** Apply a *Two-column Grid* master to *page 4*. Place *P4 Abbreviations.idms* in the left column. Position *P4 Top Quote.idms* flush with the top margin guide of the second column. Place *P4 Bottom Quote.idms* centered at the bottom of the second column. Finally, place *P4 Little League.idms* in the remaining space in column 2.

3. **Add jump and continuation lines.** You will need to link the first half of the Little League article on page 3 to the second half on page 4, before you can add jump and continuation lines. Click on the out port at the bottom of the article on page 3 and then click on the Little League article in the second column of page 4. Move to page 3, and place *P3 Jump Line* on the bottom of column 2, on top of the article. Magnify your view. Place the cursor after the word *page* and add a space. Go to the Type menu and select *Insert Special Character>Markers>Next Page Number* (Visual 9–15). A *4* should appear after the word, *page*. Place *P4 Cont Line.idms* on the top of the Little League article on page 4. Magnify your view. Place the cursor after the word, *page*. Go to *Type>Insert Special Character> Markers>Previous Page Number.* A *3* should appear. The project is now finished!

► *production tip*

Use the markers Next Page Number for jump lines and Previous Page Number for continuation lines.

VISUAL |9–15|

The Type menu pathway to the jump and continuation line special characters.

Using Object Libraries

When you do a lot of design work for a single client, you usually have elements that are used over and over again. For instance, if you did weekly advertisements for a dental practice, you would probably include the logo, name, hours of operation, phone number, and address in each ad. In these instances you can create an *object library* that allows you to store those frequently used items in one convenient location. Library objects can be dragged directly from the Library to the document. When you drag an element in from the library, you're not really taking it "out" of the library. You're just "borrowing" a copy to use in your document. The library still has the original, and will let you "check out" an unlimited number of copies.

The library you will make in the next few steps will be saved and used in one of the project exercises, at the end of this chapter.

1. From the CD that accompanies this book, open *09A Zaffinni Artwork.indd,* found in the *09A Zaffinni* folder. This InDesign file contains the source artwork you will use to assemble your library file.

2. Choose *File>New>Library.* Name the new library file **09 Zaffinni** and save it on your desktop. A library panel with the name *09 Zaffinni* will appear in your workspace.

3. Using the *Selection* tool, drag each page item from the *09A Zaffinni Artwork* document to the *09 Zaffinni* library panel. As the element is moved to the library, the cursor will display a plus sign (+) sign showing that the item will be added to the library (Visual 9–16). Continue this process until all seven page items, including the green bar, are in the *09 Zaffinni* library.

VISUAL |9–16|

A cursor with a + sign appears when an entry is ready to be added to an object library.

4. Double-clicking a library entry opens the *Item Information* dialog box. You can change the name and also add a description of the item, if desired (Visual 9–17). Your library is now complete and can be used with any document you want to use it with! Be sure to remember where your *09 Zaffinni* library was saved, because it will be used again to complete the *09A Zaffinni's* menu project, at the end of the chapter. Close the library panel and close, but not save, the Artwork file.

VISUAL |9–17|
The item Description field can contain special production instructions, or just provide general information, like this example.

Creating Object Styles

InDesign has so many features that assist us with efficiently producing complex projects! Paragraph and character styles ensure typographic continuity. Master pages bring structural consistency to a document. And now, you will learn how to use *object styles* to quickly format text frames and graphics objects. Like paragraph styles, object styles can clear or replace object specifications according to the settings you have defined. Like paragraph styles, you can base an object style on another style, creating a parent-child relationship. This relationship means that the parent and child objects will have attributes in common. Changing any of those shared attributes in the parent object, will automatically change those in the child object.

You will create object styles to use in constructing the Steve Miljat brochure project at the end of the chapter. Creating master pages and object styles for this simple document will help you to see how they can dramatically speed up production when you are working on a 240-page catalog.

VISUAL |9–18|
You will create object styles for this Steve Miljat brochure project.

246

VISUAL |9–19|

The Object Styles panel and options. Notice the [Basic Graphics Frame] and [Basic Text Frame], the default styles.

Create new style

Open the Object Styles panel by going to **Window>Styles>Object Styles**, or by pressing **Command+F7** (Mac) or **Control+F7** (Windows). Notice that each document comes with a default set of object styles. The [**Basic Graphics Frame**] has an icon that is framed by bounding boxes. The [**Basic Text Frame**] has a *T* inside a frame for its icon. Visual 9–19 shows the panel and its option menu, in more detail. As you can see, the Object Styles panel is similar in design to the other InDesign panels.

Defining Object Styles For the Steve Miljat Brochure

You can define an object style from an object you have already formatted, or you can define one from "scratch." These methods should sound familiar—you created styles in Chapter 8, using similar methods.

1. Open *09B Steve Miljat Brochure* from the *09 Artwork and Resources* folder on the accompanying CD. The document has been started for you. After creating the object styles, you will complete the project using the instructions found on the *09 Student Handout* on the accompanying CD.

2. Press **Command+F7** (Mac) or **Control+F7** (Windows) to open the *Object Styles* panel. **Option** (Mac) or **Alt** (Windows)+click the *Create new style* icon and the *New Object Style* dialog box will open (Visual 9–20). Name the style **Photo Box**.

VISUAL |9–20|

You can choose to include or ignore specific object attributes as you are creating object styles.

A check shows attributes that will be included in the object style.

A hyphen (Mac) or small, greyed out box (Windows) means the attribute is ignored. It will be left out of the object style, and future changes to the attribute will not appear as overrides.

Empty boxes show attributes that are turned off as part of the object style.

3. Under the *Basic Attributes* section, make sure that the Fill category is checked and then click on the name to view its options. From the color options, select a **[Paper]** fill.

4. Go down the list of *Basic Attributes* in the left column to *Stroke.* Make sure it is checked and click on the name to open the options. Enter a **Black, .0.5-pt.** stroke (Visual 9–21).

VISUAL |9–21|

Click on the name of each Basic Attribute to display its options.

5. Go to *Stroke & Corner Options* and click on the name to view the options. Align the stroke to the inside of the frame (Visual 9–22). Press Return to close the dialog.

VISUAL |9–22|

The Stroke is aligned to inside under Stroke & Corner Options.

6. Now, let's make two more styles—a text frame with a green background and insets, and a rectangle with a light gold background. This time, we'll create the styles from existing elements. First, draw a rectangle text frame. Fill it with **C=61, M=38, Y=100, K=12**. Under Text Frame Options, specify Left and Right insets of **0.375"** and Top and Bottom insets of **0.25"**. With the text frame selected, **Opt+click** (Mac) or **Alt+click** (Windows) the *New Object Style* icon. Name the style **Green Text Frame.** Now that the style is saved, you can delete the setup frame.

7. Press **F** to select the *Rectangle Frame* tool. Draw a rectangle and fill it with **C=0, M=5, Y=32, K=0**. With the box selected, click on the *New Object Style* icon and name the style, **Light Gold Background.** Your styles should look like Visual 9–23. Save your document for completing the projects at the end of the chapter.

VISUAL |9–23|

Object styles for the Steve Miljat brochure are complete.

Resetting Object Style Defaults

► *production tip*
Deselect All (Shift+Cmd+A or Shift+Ctrl+A) before resetting document, object, paragraph and character style defaults.

It's easy to change a document's default styles—so easy it's frustrating when done accidently. Whenever you select an object style, with no object selected, that style will become the default and will be applied to all new objects you create. (Similar behavior applies to other document defaults, such as paragraph or character styles.) The good news is that it's just as easy to change the defaults back to their normal settings. The key is to deselect everything and then reset the defaults. For instance, if you want to change the object style default back to [Basic Graphics Frame], simply deselect everything (Shift+Command+A or Shift+Control+A) and choose [**Basic Graphics Frame**] in the Object Styles panel.

> ► *By default [Basic Graphics Frame] has a 1-pt. Black stroke. You can quickly remove this by applying the style [None] to the object.*

> ► *A rectangle drawn with the Rectangle Frame tool (F) by default, has the [None] style applied.*

Override and Redefine Object Styles

You can modify any of the attributes of an object that has a style applied. Such a change is called an *override*. When an object has an override, a plus (+) sign appears in the Object Styles panel. However, only modifications of defined attributes are considered overrides. In the photo box object style you created earlier, changing the stroke to red would show as an override, because you defined the attributes of the stroke in the object style. If you changed the text wrap options, no plus sign would appear because text wrap was not defined in the object style.

VISUAL |9–24|

Object styles can be found in the Control panel and in the Object Styles panel.

To clear overrides, first select the object, then press the **Clear overrides** button at the bottom of the Object Styles panel, or **Option+click** (Mac) or **Alt+click** (Windows) on the style name. If you want to clear modifications to the non-defined attributes of an object, select the object, and press the Clear attributes not defined by style button at the bottom of the panel (Visual 9–24).

If you decide to keep the overrides made to any object and to redefine the style to include those overrides, you can choose Redefine Style from the panel options. Only the categories you had originally included in the style definition will be updated. Redefining a style will not add attributes that were not part of the original definition. In those cases, it would be easier to create an object style from an existing object.

Duplicate, Delete, and Import Object Styles

Duplicate, or delete an object style, by first selecting the style in the panel and then holding down Control (Mac) or right-click (Windows) to bring up the Context menu. If you delete a style that has been applied to objects, you will be asked to specify a replacement style. You can also delete a style by dragging its name to the Delete selected style icon in the lower right corner of the panel. To import styles from another document, select **Load Object Styles** from the panel options menu. As in importing paragraph and character styles, you must place a check next to the styles you wish to import.

Break the Link to an Object Style

You can break the link to an object style by selecting the object and choosing **Break Link to Style** from the panel options. When you break the link, the object style becomes [None]+. The object's appearance will remain the same, but it will not update when the original object style is modified.

Summary

In this chapter you learned to bring consistency to a document by creating, duplicating, and modifying master pages. You learned how to release, override, and detach master page elements on document pages. Automated features including page numbering, jump lines, and continuation lines were introduced. You created an object library and used the Object Styles panel. Now, with Paragraph, Character, and Object Styles, as well as Master Pages "under your belt," you are ready to begin the projects for this chapter!

▶ IN REVIEW

1. In your own words, describe a master page and its purpose.

2. What is the keyboard shortcut for releasing an element from the master page, so that you can edit it on the document page?

3. If an element is detached from the master page and the master is changed, will those changes affect the detached element?

4. Where in InDesign will you find the Auto Page Number character?

5. If you create a jump line and it just isn't working, what might be the problem?

6. What is the process for creating an InDesign library?

7. What are the default object styles for any document?

8. What does a plus (+) sign mean when it follows the name of an object style?

9. How can you change the document default for a text or graphics frame?

10. What is the process for breaking the link to an object style?

Three projects are included on the accompanying CD, in the *09 Artwork and Resources* folder. The first, *09A Zaffinni's Mediterranean Dining*, uses the picture library created in this lesson. The second project, *09B Steve Miljat Brochure*, uses master pages, and a bonus feature not covered in the chapter: multiple page sizes. The third project (not shown, but included in the handout) is an identity package—for yourself! You will make a professional résumé, cover letter, and reference sheet. I hope you enjoy these projects!

Photography © Tiffany Mastak, artwork © Steve Miljat, Waukesha County Technical College.

Life in
abundance
comes **only**
through
great love.

ᛕ Elbert Hubbard

| Business Forms |

objectives

▶ *Create business forms that are functional, well-designed, effective, and that express a company's image*

▶ *Consider printing, paper, and finishing processes when designing business forms*

▶ *Learn when to use lining or old-style figures*

▶ *Typeset academic degrees, acronyms, and titles*

▶ *Design newspaper advertisements according to specifications*

introduction

How many times have you read, "Wanted: Graphic Designer. Two to five years' experience required." Everyone wants someone with experience; but how will you get experience if you don't have a job? Graphic design is a highly competitive field. To be considered for an entry-level position, you not only need a fantastic portfolio, but you must also be able to demonstrate your ability to think quickly and creatively, work productively, and maintain exemplary interpersonal relationships. Even if you get hired, you must prove yourself before you are given more responsibility.

Sometimes your new boss will begin to try out your software skills (and your attitude) by assigning you lower-end production jobs. Before you begin to grumble, remind yourself that everyone has to start somewhere. First jobs aren't always the most glamorous. But remember that there are hundreds of unemployed graphic designers out there, and each of them would love to have your job! Business forms seem, at first glance, to be on the bottom rung of the creativity ladder. But in reality, tables and forms require a high degree of precision, attention to detail, and layout skills. A skilled designer can turn a business form into a work of art; an unskilled designer can turn it into a nightmare!

General Project Information

The initial client meeting is your opportunity to find out the details of a project. Knowing the correct information up front will save backtracking later on. Your client's responses to each of the following questions will affect your document setup.

- ► *Is there an existing form? If so, what has worked or not worked with the current form? Or, is there a sample form the customer likes?*
- ► *Does the form have to match or blend with any existing forms? What kind of tone should the form convey?*
- ► *Who will be completing the form?*
- ► *How many colors will the form be printed in?*
- ► *Will the company logo be included on the form? Is a digital file of the logo available? What are the corporate colors?*
- ► *Is the form one- or two-sided?*
- ► *Does it have any requirements such as a perforation, a fold, or an address that shows through an envelope window?*
- ► *How will the form be printed? on separate sheets? in duplicate or triplicate? on a photocopier, in the office?*
- ► *How will the form be used? Will it be mailed out in a #10 envelope? Will it be returned in a #9 envelope? Will it be a self-mailer?*
- ► *Will it be drilled and held in a binder? Will it be padded as a tablet with tear-off sheets? Will it be held in a clipboard? Will it be filed in a file folder?*
- ► *Will individual completed forms be photocopied and distributed to team members? Will the data will be collected and tabulated?*
- ► *What company information will be on the form? fax? e-mail? phone?*
- ► *How often is the form revised?*
- ► *Will it require sequential numbering?*
- ► *Is there any legally required wording that must be included on the form?*

General Design Considerations

A form must be a positive representation of the business. If you were waiting for a surgical procedure and were given an old typewritten form to fill out, your confidence in the surgeon might begin to slip. A well-designed form is an asset to a business. A form should communicate professionalism, while incorporating the look and feel of the rest of the company's literature. A form should be easy to follow—the layout should create a visual hierarchy that organizes and sequences the reader's responses. The layout should clearly identify where each response should be placed. A form should be usable. The user should have enough vertical room to write below the previous line, and enough horizontal room to write a hyphenated last name, or a very long city name. Never consider a form complete unless you have "completed" the form yourself. Choose a paper stock that won't smudge when written on with a pencil, a felt tip pen, or a ballpoint pen.

A Sample Job

This chapter will focus on the development of an identity package for a psychologist beginning a new practice. The psychologist, Dr. Rosemary Tollefson, needs identity pieces (letterhead, envelope, business card); a display advertisement for the phone book; and a ¾ page, vertical newspaper display ad. Although each piece has its distinctive design and typographic challenges, all the pieces retain a visual unity that identifies them as members of the same family. When you have completed this identity package, you may want to print each piece on high-quality colored or textured paper stock, for use in your portfolio.

Identity Packages

Dr. Tollefson is a 30-something, tree-hugging intellectual. She dislikes the traditional look of the printed materials most counseling services use. She chose the rose as her symbol for three reasons:
(1) it is living; (2) it is expressive and classic; and
(3) it ties in with her name. Here are some questions you can ask your clients when designing logos:

- ▶ *Does the image convey the correct tone for the business?*
- ▶ *Can it be enlarged and reduced without losing legibility?*
- ▶ *Does it avoid any negative connotations?*
- ▶ *Is it copyright free?*
- ▶ *Can the image be used for ten years without being dated?*

▶ MOVING TOWARD MASTERY

business forms

TYPOGRAPHIC CONSIDERATIONS

Some typefaces are designed specifically for reading, and some are designed more for display or decoration. When selecting a typeface for business communications, the overall concern is readability. Use a typeface that is highly legible, one that blends with the company logo or corporate identity system. If the company uses a trendy, cursive logotype, be careful how you use it in business forms. Find a legible face that blends with the company logotype and use that in the business form. Consider who will be completing the form. Baby boomers are now wearing reading glasses and require a more generous point size than high school students. Children mastering penmanship need more room for writing.

When choosing typefaces for display type and body copy, be sure to consider the contrast between the two faces. A page is interesting to look at, and easier to read, when continuous body copy is broken into blocks by darker, higher-contrast display type. A good layout will use type blocks as stepping-stones to move the reader through the piece.

Minion Pro Typeface.

Adobe Jenson Pro Typeface.

At first glance, you might not see the difference between these two faces. Check out the e-bar. Jenson has a slanted e-bar, and Minion does not. If your client uses Minion Pro for correspondence, you shouldn't choose Jenson for identity pieces.

VISUAL | 10–1 |

Each piece in the identity package has a distinct purpose and layout challenge, yet all remain part of the same visual family.

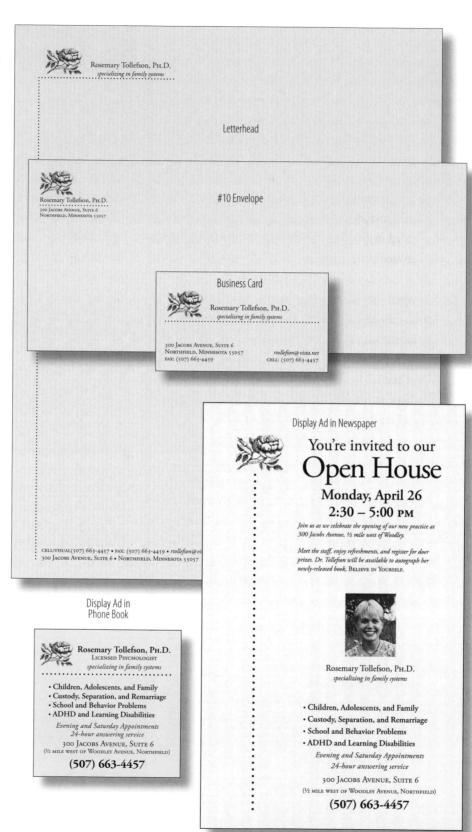

Letterhead

Rosemary Tollefson, Ph.D.
specializing in family systems

#10 Envelope

Rosemary Tollefson, Ph.D.
300 Jacobs Avenue, Suite 6
Northfield, Minnesota 55057

Business Card

Rosemary Tollefson, Ph.D.
specializing in family systems

300 Jacobs Avenue, Suite 6
Northfield, Minnesota 55057   rtollefson@vista.net
Fax: (507) 663-4459   Cell: (507) 663-4457

Cell:Visual(507) 663-4457 • Fax: (507) 663-4459 • rtollefson@vi
300 Jacobs Avenue, Suite 6 • Northfield, Minnesota 55057

Display Ad in Newspaper

You're invited to our
Open House
Monday, April 26
2:30 – 5:00 PM

*Join us as we celebrate the opening of our new practice at
300 Jacobs Avenue, ½ mile west of Woodley.*

*Meet the staff, enjoy refreshments, and register for door
prizes. Dr. Tollefson will be available to autograph her
newly-released book, Believe in Yourself.*

Rosemary Tollefson, Ph.D.
specializing in family systems

• Children, Adolescents, and Family
• Custody, Separation, and Remarriage
• School and Behavior Problems
• ADHD and Learning Disabilities

Evening and Saturday Appointments
24-hour answering service

300 Jacobs Avenue, Suite 6
(½ mile west of Woodley Avenue, Northfield)

(507) 663-4457

**Display Ad in
Phone Book**

Rosemary Tollefson, Ph.D.
Licensed Psychologist
specializing in family systems

• Children, Adolescents, and Family
• Custody, Separation, and Remarriage
• School and Behavior Problems
• ADHD and Learning Disabilities

Evening and Saturday Appointments
24-hour answering service

300 Jacobs Avenue, Suite 6
(½ mile west of Woodley Avenue, Northfield)

(507) 663-4457

Design Considerations For Letterhead

Does anyone use a typewriter anymore? Hardly. So, make sure the paper you select for a letterhead will go through a laser or ink jet printer. Find out what typeface the client uses most often and try to coordinate that typeface with the one used in the letterhead. You may want to avoid gradients and screened background images if the letters will often be photocopied. Keep your client's budget in mind during the design phase—a nice effect can be created with colored ink on white or colored paper stock. Use the best paper stock your client can afford. Remember that some paper surfaces don't reproduce well on a photocopier. Include bleed images only if the client's budget can afford the extra cost of printing on an oversized sheet and cutting it down to letter size. If you have to choose between better paper and a bleed, choose better paper every time!

Use care when including names of personnel on the letterhead—if a person or position changes, all the old letterhead gets tossed. Ouch! Double-check all the information provided by the client. (Ask for a business card with the correct information.) Send a test fax just to confirm the fax number. Call your client and tell her the fax is coming—that way you can confirm the fax and phone number at the same time! I prefer designing the letterhead first—then I create a library and add the letterhead elements to it.

Design Considerations for the Identity Package Letterhead

Visual 10–2 shows the top of the letterhead. The typeface used in all pieces is Adobe Garamond Pro. Typefaces followed by the word "Pro" have a wide selection of ornaments, ligatures, alternate letters, and symbols that can be viewed in the Glyphs panel. Notice the academic degree, Ph.D., listed after the name. When academic degrees follow the name, they look best set in small caps. Use either the degree (Rosemary Tollefson, Ph.D.) or the title (Dr. Rosemary Tollefson) with the name, but not both.

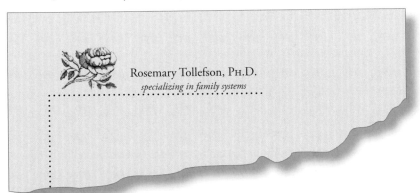

VISUAL |10–2|

Academic titles are set in small caps. Use either the degree (Ph.D.), or the title (Dr.), but not both.

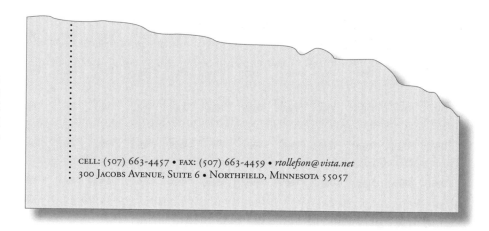

VISUAL |10–3|

Old-style figures are used in this letterhead. The parentheses have been baseline shifted -1 pt. so that they would be more centered on the numbers they enclose.

CELL: (507) 663-4457 • FAX: (507) 663-4459 • *rtollefson@vista.net*
300 JACOBS AVENUE, SUITE 6 • NORTHFIELD, MINNESOTA 55057

Visual 10–3 shows the lower portion of the letterhead, with the contact information positioned at the bottom of the page. This example uses numbers that extend below the baseline. These "lowercase" numbers are called *old-style figures* or *text figures*. Numbers that sit on the baseline are called *titling figures* or *lining figures*. Titling figures are ideal for use with display type and are sometimes used within body copy. Old-style figures are used within text and are rarely used in display type. Old-style figures have a graceful, elegant look.

VISUAL |10–4|

Old-style figures are designed to be used in passages of body copy. Titling figures sit on top of the baseline.

Old-style Figures   Baseline   Titling Figures

123456789 ↓123456789

Design Considerations For Envelopes

There are two things you should remember when designing envelopes: (1) allow at least an 18-pt. margin at the top and left edges; and (2) don't design an envelope with multiple colors that overlap or are close together (this is called *tight register*), unless your client has an ample budget. Printing a four-color envelope, with tight register and bleeds, is expensive because it has to be printed on a flat sheet, then die-cut, folded, and glued (a process called converting). Envelopes typically don't include the phone and fax number—but when elements are dragged in from a library to use on another piece, this can easily happen. You will want to watch for this. The image and type on an envelope will probably be smaller than that on the letterhead, but the size relationship should remain about the same. A standard commercial business-size envelope is called a #10, with dimensions of 4⅛ × 9½ inches. A #9 business response envelope fits nicely inside a #10. Its dimensions are 3⅞ × 8⅞ inches.

If you don't have a chart of envelope styles and sizes, do a Google search for "envelope sizes." Several envelope sites will have information you can download and print. A nice reference site for envelope sizes is **www.designerstoolbox.com**.

Design Considerations for the Identity Package Envelope

Visual 10–5 shows the details of the upper left corner of the envelope. Elements were initially placed from a snippet, but need editing for the envelope. Notice that old-style figures are still used for the address, and an ample margin has been maintained on the upper and left edges.

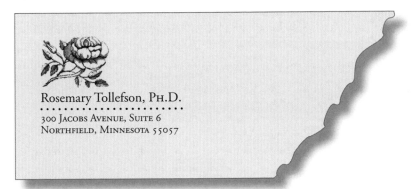

The return address corner of the envelope. Telephone numbers aren't included with the return address.

Design Considerations For Business Cards

The client's budget determines whether or not you should design a card with a bleed. A standard business card size is 3½ × 2 inches. Allow at least a ⅛ inch margin inside the card. When designing landscape orientation cards, I try to keep the name prominent and important contact information in the lower right corner. That's where the eye usually stops last, and I don't want to waste a "hot" corner on a fax number! Discuss imposition with the printer. The imposition is how the card should be laid out for printing: 1-up, 2-up, 8-up, and so on. Sometimes the printer wants you to step and repeat your card many times on a single sheet of letter-size paper. Other times, a single card, centered on the sheet, will be requested.

Designers become very comfortable working in point size and leading with whole number increments of one or two points. In smaller type, one point is a much more significant unit of measure than it is for display type. When working at smaller type sizes, you will find yourself setting a leading value of 8.75 points, or a type size of 7.5 points, for example.

Changing Point Size and Leading Keyboard Shortcut Defaults

By now, using the shortcut keys to change point size and leading has become second nature. In the Getting Started section of Chapter 1, I recommended that you change the InDesign program preferences so that those keyboard shortcuts would enlarge or reduce in smaller increments. If you didn't change your preferences earlier in the *Getting Started* section in Chapter 1, you should do it now. When you want new preferences to apply to all future documents, the preferences should be changed when no document is open. When you change preferences with a document open, the changes apply only to the current document. If you are a Mac user, choose **InDesign>Preferences>Units & Increments**. In the Keyboard Increments section, change the Size/Leading to **1 pt.** and the Baseline Shift to **1 pt.** (Visual 10–6). Windows users, choose **Edit>Preferences>Units & Increments** and follow the same procedure.

VISUAL |10–6|

Change the Keyboard Increments in the Units & Increments page of the Preferences menu.

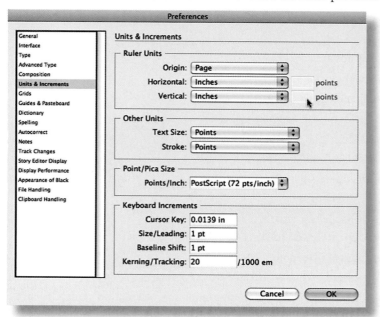

Design Considerations for the Identity Package Business Card

Visual 10–7 shows the business card for Rosemary Tollefson. Notice that the typefaces are the same here, as the other pieces. It's very important to maintain the size relationship of text to graphics on all the pieces. Use the flush right tab (Shift+Tab) to align the email and cell phone text to the right margin.

VISUAL |10–7|

Rosemary Tollefson's business card shown at actual size.

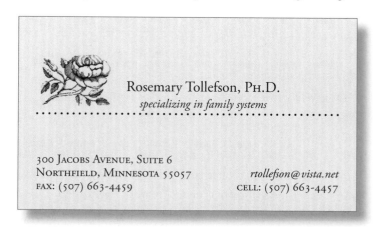

Rosemary Tollefson, Ph.D.
specializing in family systems

300 Jacobs Avenue, Suite 6
Northfield, Minnesota 55057
fax: (507) 663-4459

rtollefson@vista.net
cell: (507) 663-4457

Design Considerations For Newspaper Display Ads

Accurate measurement is essential when designing for newspapers. Each paper has standard dimensions to follow when preparing ads. Visual 10–8 shows a sample production worksheet for a Milwaukee, Wisconsin daily paper. When creating a newspaper ad, close enough is not good enough! Convert fractions into decimals, and enter those measurements in the New Document dialog box. As you can see in Visual 10–8, the advertisements butt right up to text or another ad, with no room for error.

Many display ads are designed with an outer border. When adding a stroke to a text or graphics frame, you must specify that the stroke goes inside the frame. If the stroke is centered on the frame or placed on the outside of the frame, the dimension will change and the advertisement will not fit the newspaper specifications. If you frequently place newspaper ads, creating document presets for each size, and object styles with strokes aligned to the inside, would considerably reduce the margin of error.

When designing for newsprint, recognize that your final piece may not look like your laser print. Some newsprint is porous and the ink will spread. The counters of letters tend to fill in, so avoid using very small point sizes whenever possible. When your advertisement includes a photograph or a scan, work closely with the production department so that you provide the correct resolution and line screen. A piece that looks good printed on your laser printer, may look "muddy" in newsprint, because the halftone dots will fill in.

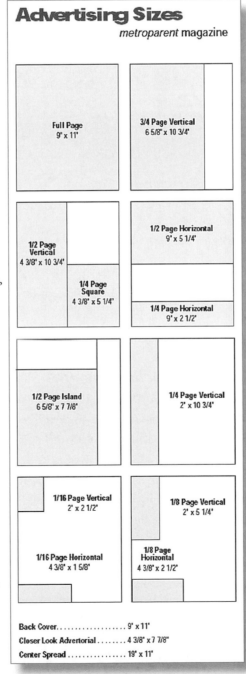

Advertising Sizes
metroparent magazine

Full Page
9" x 11"

3/4 Page Vertical
6 5/8" x 10 3/4"

1/2 Page Vertical
4 3/8" x 10 3/4"

1/4 Page Square
4 3/8" x 5 1/4"

1/2 Page Horizontal
9" x 5 1/4"

1/4 Page Horizontal
9" x 2 1/2"

1/2 Page Island
6 5/8" x 7 7/8"

1/4 Page Vertical
2" x 10 3/4"

1/16 Page Vertical
2" x 2 1/2"

1/8 Page Vertical
2" x 5 1/4"

1/16 Page Horizontal
4 3/8" x 1 5/8"

1/8 Page Horizontal
4 3/8" x 2 1/2"

Back Cover. . . . . 9" x 11"
Closer Look Advertorial . . . . 4 3/8" x 7 7/8"
Center Spread . . . . 19" x 11"

VISUAL |10–8|

Every newspaper and magazine publication has a different set of ad sizes. Always double check that your size specification is correct before submitting an ad for publication!

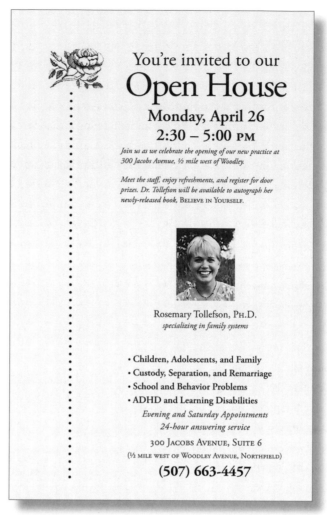

You're invited to our
Open House
Monday, April 26
2:30 – 5:00 PM

Join us as we celebrate the opening of our new practice at 300 Jacobs Avenue, ½ mile west of Woodley.

Meet the staff, enjoy refreshments, and register for door prizes. Dr. Tollefson will be available to autograph her newly-released book, BELIEVE IN YOURSELF.

Rosemary Tollefson, PH.D.
specializing in family systems

• **Children, Adolescents, and Family**
• **Custody, Separation, and Remarriage**
• **School and Behavior Problems**
• **ADHD and Learning Disabilities**
Evening and Saturday Appointments
24-hour answering service

300 JACOBS AVENUE, SUITE 6
(½ MILE WEST OF WOODLEY AVENUE, NORTHFIELD)
(507) 663-4457

Design Considerations for the Identity Package Newspaper Display Ad

Visual 10–9 shows a sample of the display ad. The words *Open House* require negative tracking, which is common when working with display type. The phone number at the bottom of the ad, and the time at the top, are set in lining (uppercase) figures. It is appropriate to use lining figures in this instance because the numbers are being used in display type. The open house time, *2:30–5:00 pm*, is separated by an en dash, used to indicate a range of time. The abbreviation "pm" is set in small caps, and including the periods is optional. If you don't have a typeface with small caps, it is permissible to set it in lowercase letters with periods (p.m.). The body copy is set in italic type, with the OpenType fractions option turned on. Normally book titles are set in italic, but when the surrounding body copy is italic, the book title is set in Roman, as in the title of Dr. Tollefson's book, *Believe in Yourself*. You'll also note that the bulleted copy contains a reference to attention deficit hyperactivity disorder, as ADHD. When setting an acronym, no period is placed after each letter.

Designing for the Phone Book

Scan through the yellow pages ads in a phone book and you will see that they've been designed by people with a wide range of design skills. Some ads include gradients and mushy photos, condensed or expanded type—that is almost impossible to read—and typographic blunders such as all-capital italics and incorrect quotation marks. You can also find some examples of excellent layout and readability. What makes the difference between a strong or a poor ad? The ability to use type, combined with an understanding of the printing process. A well-designed, 2½" square ad, packs more punch than a poorly designed ½ page ad! When you design an ad for the yellow pages, first look at samples to see what doesn't work. Then look specifically at what the competition is doing, and design an ad that will beat the best sample. It is a time-consuming process to fine-tune small display ads. Some people assume a small ad will require less production time. In reality, it takes more time to create an effective small ad than a larger display ad, because every incremental spacing decision you make in a small ad is critical!

Design Considerations for the Identity Package Yellow Pages Ad

Visual 10–10 shows the yellow pages display ad, at actual size. The text portion is basically in a centered format—except the bulleted copy is flush left. Sometimes you see bulleted copy centered, leaving the left sides ragged (Visual 10–11). Setting bulleted copy in this manner is a poor design technique. When the bullets are not flush left, they blend in with the body copy and defeat the purpose of using them in the first place! Here is the best way to align bulleted copy, while centering it in the text block:

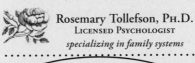

VISUAL |10–10|

The italic type has been changed to a semibold weight to accommodate the paper quality used in yellow pages. Tiny serifs are not always visible on low-quality paper.

▶ *Center all bulleted text. Position a vertical guideline flush to the bullet of the longest line.*

▶ *Then, change the alignment of the bulleted text to flush left.*

▶ *Finally, apply a left indent to push all the bulleted copy to the guideline you placed earlier. Now the text is flush left, but the longest line is still centered in the text column.*

VISUAL |10–11|

This is the incorrect way to set bulleted copy! Centering bulleted type defeats the purpose of using bullets, which is to lead the eye through the ad.

VISUAL | 10–12 |

This Victorian era- style political poster demonstrates that type can be a powerful design element. Designers who are comfortable working with type and have strong InDesign production skills, are the best at creating type-heavy forms that are both functional and aesthetically pleasing.

Summary

Business forms are a rigorous production test for typesetters and designers. It is our responsibility to make sure that forms project the appropriate corporate image, are easy to read, and are easy to complete. When you are given the task of producing an order form, a sell sheet, or a catalog price grid, see it as a design challenge. Flex your typesetting muscles. And remember, as a wise designer once said, "*There are no mediocre projects, just mediocre designers.*"

▶ IN REVIEW

1. The initial client meeting is a perfect opportunity to gather information about project specifications. What are four examples of information you should have before beginning the project?
   a.
   b.
   c.
   d.

2. Choosing the typeface is one of the most important decisions designers make. What are some considerations for choosing a typeface for an identity package?

3. What are two design considerations for letterhead?

4. How does paper quality affect design?

5. What is the difference between a lining figure and an old-style figure?

6. How should academic titles be typeset?

7. If you are designing a display ad for a newspaper, you must align the frame's stroke to the _____.

8. A standard business-size envelope is called a _____ envelope.

9. What are the dimensions of a standard business card?

10. Normally, book titles are set in italic, but when the surrounding copy is italic, the title is set in _____.

►CHAPTER 10 PROJECTS

The visual above shows Dr. Tollefson's family of forms. You will enjoy creating these, and they could be nice additions to your portfolio. One additional table is included for good measure. You can find the instructions for all these projects in the *Chapter 10 Artwork and Resources* folder on the CD accompanying this book.

▶CHAPTER 10 PROJECTS

Rosemary Tollefson, Ph.D.
LICENSED PSYCHOLOGIST
specializing in family systems

- Children, Adolescents, and Family
- Custody, Separation, and Remarriage
- School and Behavior Problems
- ADHD and Learning Disabilities

Evening and Saturday Appointments
24-hour answering service
300 JACOBS AVENUE, SUITE 6
(½ MILE WEST OF WOODLEY AVENUE, NORTHFIELD)

(507) 663-4457

	Trans Type/Speeds	Eng Size/Cylinders	MPG City/Hwy	Annual Fuel Cost
MINIVANS 4WD				
Chevrolet Venture AWD	A-4	3.4/6	18/24	$1,050
Chrysler Town & Country AWD	A-4	3.8/6	17/23	$1,105
Dodge Caravan AWD	A-4	3.8/6	17/23	$1,105
Oldsmobile Silhouette AWD	A-4	3.4/6	18/24	$1,050
Pontiac Montana AWD	A-4	3.4/6	18/24	$1,050
Toyota Sienna 4WD	A-5	3.3/6	18/24	$1,050

You're invited to our
Open House
Monday, April 26
2:30 – 5:00 PM

Join us as we celebrate the opening of our new practice at 300 Jacobs Avenue, ½ mile west of Woodley.

Meet the staff, enjoy refreshments, and register for door prizes. Dr. Tollefson will be available to autograph her newly-released book, BELIEVE IN YOURSELF.

Rosemary Tollefson, PH.D.
specializing in family systems

- **Children, Adolescents, and Family**
- **Custody, Separation, and Remarriage**
- **School and Behavior Problems**
- **ADHD and Learning Disabilities**

Evening and Saturday Appointments
24-hour answering service

300 JACOBS AVENUE, SUITE 6
(½ MILE WEST OF WOODLEY AVENUE, NORTHFIELD)

(507) 663-4457

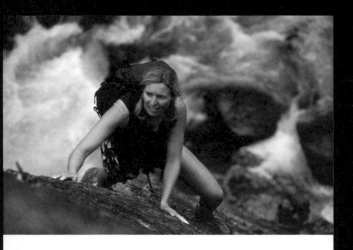

Courage
is not the
lack of fear.
It is acting
in spite of it.
ᚹ Mark Twain

Designing with Type

11

objectives

► *Use the Type on a Path tool*
► *Use the Pathfinder tool*
► *Create gradient blends*
► *Create inline frames*
► *Use the Page tool*

introduction

A semitrailer got stuck underneath an overpass. It was in so tight that the driver couldn't move ahead or back up. Engineers and construction workers walked all around the stuck truck, calculating the height of the trailer and the clearance of the overpass. They thought of jackhammers, winches, hydraulic pry bars—anything that might free the truck and get traffic moving again. Finally, after assessing the situation one little boy said, "Why don't you let some air out of the tires?"

That boy was thinking outside the box. Business, education, government—everyone these days is looking for people who can see things from a different perspective. Perform a web search for "out of the box thinking" and you'll come up with just a shade over two billion results.

You are about to work with text and graphics that are out of the box—or at least out of a frame. Up to now we have used rectangles and ovals of various shapes and sizes. In this chapter, we explore text on a path, inline graphics, and gradients—features that will let you out of the box.

Type: A Versatile Design Element

When reviewing student portfolios, I look for two things: use of type and use of color. When a designer has control of these two critical design elements, everything else will fall into place. Even in black and white, type has "color" and text blocks can range in color from light gray to strong black. Typefaces also express a wide range of personalities inherent in their design. Visual 11–1 shows a collection of ampersands, each interesting and expressing a different personality.

VISUAL |11–1|

This collection of ampersands shows the variation in personality of typefaces.

In this first exercise, we're going to add another ingredient to the type color-personality mixture: shape. The ability to create type that follows a path used to be the domain of illustration programs. Thanks to InDesign, these great special effects are right at your fingertips. So, launch InDesign and let's get started.

Placing Type on a Closed Shape

In order to place text on a path, first you need a path! Then you need the Type on a Path tool, accessed by pressing **Shift+T** or by selecting it from the "hidden tool" menu, under the Type tool.

VISUAL |11–2|

The plus sign next to the cursor means that the Type on a Path tool has found a path.

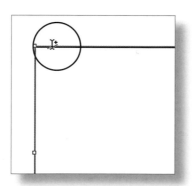

1. Create a new document. Draw a rectangle and apply a **1 pt.** stroke.

2. Select the *Type on a Path* tool by pressing **Shift+T**. Position the tool cursor over the edge of the rectangle. A *plus sign* on the cursor indicates that the tool has recognized a path and is ready for action (Visual 11–2).

3. Click on the path to create a starting point. Type a line of text that extends around the rectangle. Highlight the text and change the point size and style. Change the alignment. The text considers the first point you clicked with the Type on a Path tool as the left margin. As you center and right-align the text, it will flow clockwise around the outside of the frame.

4. Visual 11–3 shows two vertical lines called the *Start* and *End brackets*. (The path object must be selected and either selection tool must be active for you to see these.) By default, the brackets are butted up to each other, indicating that the text path extends around the entire rectangle. You can move the

VISUAL |11–3|
The in and out ports are not handles you can use to adjust the Start and End brackets. Click on the vertical part of the Start and End brackets to adjust the location of the text.

Start and *End* brackets to fine-tune the position of the text on your path. The *Start* and *End* brackets have in and out ports that work just like any other text frame.

5. Select the *End bracket.* Do not click on its out port; instead click on the upper part of the line (the cursor arrow will show a sideways "t" when you are able to click on the bracket). Slowly drag the *End bracket* counter-clockwise, closer to the end of the text (Visual 11–4). If you pull the bracket too far, the overset symbol will appear. Just bring the bracket to the end of the text.

6. If you look carefully in the center of the path, you will see a tiny vertical line (Visual 11–4). This line is the *Center bracket* (also called the *Flip* tool), and if you click and drag on the *Center bracket* with either *Selection* tool, you can move your text back and forth around the edge of the rectangle.

VISUAL |11–4|
There are three brackets on a text path. The tiny vertical line is the Center bracket, which indicates the center of the text.

7. If you drag the *Center bracket* in toward the center of the rectangle, your text will flow inside the box. Flip your text inside and outside a few times until it feels comfortable to you (Visual 11–5).

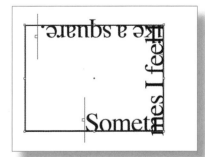

VISUAL |11–5|
Drag the Center bracket to flip text inside and outside of the path.

That was easy enough. Try the same technique with a circle as the path object. Be sure to flip the text inside and outside the circle, as in Visual 11–6. When the type is in place, you will want to set the stroke of the path object to [**None.**]

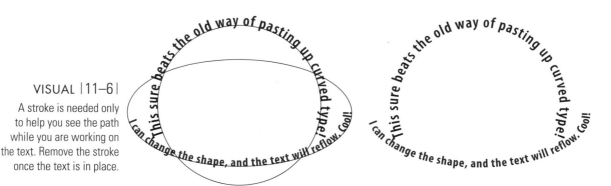

Placing Type on an Open Path

Most of the time, you will be creating your own path for type to follow. Type can be placed on paths of any shape. We'll create a few paths using the Pencil and Pen tools. You may not use the Pencil tool very often, but you should know it's there. If this is your first time using the Pen tool, note that Chapter 14 will go into detail on using it—you'll just get your toes wet in this chapter.

1. Select the *Pencil* tool by pressing **N** or by selecting it from the Toolbox. Draw some squiggles similar to those in Visual 11–7. The *Pencil* tool makes rough, random-looking paths. (The Pen tool makes smooth, curvy paths.)

VISUAL |11–7|

These paths were made
with the Pencil tool.

2. Select the *Type on a Path* tool and click on one of your paths. (You don't need to select the path first.) Fill the line with text. You can use placeholder text if you prefer. Fill the remaining lines with text. Now experiment with the position, size, and color of your type. The results should look similar to Visual 11–8.

VISUAL | 11–8 |

Type has been placed on the paths created with the Pencil tool.

3. Use **Command+A** (Mac) or **Control+A** (Windows) to select and delete the text lines created with the *Pencil* tool. Drag down two horizontal guidelines about **1.5"** apart. Select the *Pen* tool by pressing **P**. Position the cursor by the left margin guide and click once on the bottom guidelines (do not drag). Position the cursor over the top guideline, but over to the right of the first point and click. This will create a diagonal line extending from the bottom to the top guidelines. Next, position the cursor on the bottom guideline, over to the right of the second point and click to create another diagonal line. Continue this pattern across the page to make a zigzag pattern, similar to what you see in Visual 11–9.

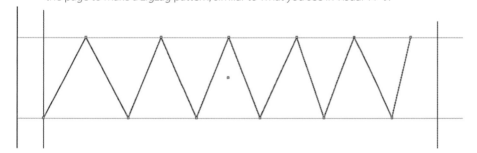

VISUAL | 11–9 |

Clicking with the Pen tool makes straight line segments.

4. Switch to the *Direct Selection* tool and move the guides out of the way or delete them. Click on an anchor point and drag it. Move it from side to side, then up and down. Continue moving all the points until your zigzag is a total mess (Visual 11–10). Now you know how to use the *Pen* tool to click from point to point, and to create paths made of straight line segments. Let's see what else the *Pen* tool can do. Delete your path.

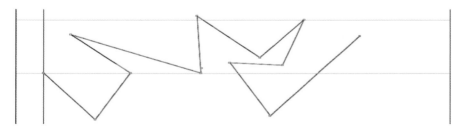

VISUAL | 11–10 |

Use the Direct Selection tool to move the anchor points of the path.

5. Pull down two horizontal guides about **2"** apart. You're going to make another path similar to the zigzag, except that you will make it with curved segments. With the *Pen* tool, click where the lower guideline meets the left margin guide to create the end point of your new path. Here's where the tricky part of creating curved segments comes in. Position the cursor over the top guideline, to the right of the end point, and click without releasing the mouse. This creates a "smooth" corner point. Without releasing the mouse, drag horizontally and you will see two handles extend from the corner point. These are called *direction lines*. As you drag them out, a *curved line segment* will develop. Move the cursor along the guideline to see how changing the length of the direction line affects the shape of the curve. Release the mouse when the curved segment looks similar to the one in Visual 11–11. Move to the lower guideline, click to make the next anchor point, and drag horizontally to create another curved line segment. Continue this process until you have waves, similar to those in Visual 11–11. Now you know how to use the Pen tool to make curved line segments by clicking and dragging.

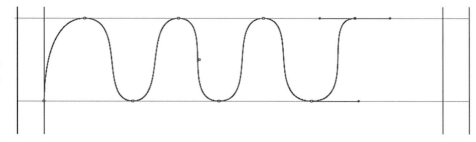

VISUAL |11–11|

Click and drag to make curved line segments.

VISUAL |11–12|

Within this mess is a combination of straight and curved line segments. Press the keyboard shortcut for any other tool and the Pen tool will be deselected.

6. Now, create a bizarre-looking path using a combination of clicks (straight line segments) and drags (curved line segments). Your mess should look just as bad as mine in Visual 11–12. To end the path, choose another tool or **Command+click** or **Control+click** anywhere on the page. When you're ready to move on, select your line with the *Selection* tool and delete it.

7. Now we're going to make a path in the shape of an arch. If you deleted your two horizontal guidelines, drag down new ones, about **2"** apart. With the *Pen* tool, position the cursor over the lower guide, click and drag up. A directional line will extend from each side of the starting point. Keep dragging, trying to keep the upper directional line at a 45-degree angle. When the end of the directional line touches the upper guideline, release the mouse (Visual 11–13A).

8. Now position the *Pen* tool back on the lower guide, approximately **5"** to the right of the first point. Click to set an anchor point and drag the direction line down at approximately 45 degrees. Notice that the upper direction line angles back toward the upper direction line of the first point (Visual 11–13B). When you release the mouse, you should have a nice arch (Visual 11–13C). Use the *Text on a Path* tool to add text to the arch and experiment with the various options you have learned so far.

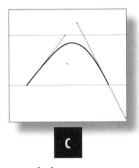

VISUAL |11–13|
Drag in the direction of the arrows to make this smooth arch.

You may realize it would be much easier just to draw an ellipse and place the text on its path, rather than using the Pen tool to create the arch shape. And you're right. But very often, you will want to use text paths that don't fit pre-made shapes—like the one you're going to create next.

9. Delete the arch-shaped path and drag down one horizontal guide. With the *Pen* tool, click on the guideline and drag up and to the right at a 45-degree angle. Release the mouse when the direction handle is about 1 inch long.

10. About **4"** away, click on the guideline to set another anchor point again. Hold Shift, and drag the directional handle up and to the right to constrain to a 45-degree angle. Release the mouse button when your path looks like Visual 11–14.

VISUAL |11–14|
You can create elegant, flowing curves using only two anchor points.

11. Go ahead, use the *Type on a Path* tool and place some text on it. Then flip the type using the *Center bracket* line. If there is a stroke applied to the path, remove it to see only the text (Visual 11–15).

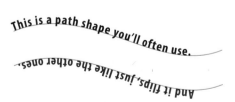

VISUAL |11–15|
Use the Center bracket to flip and reverse the direction of text placed on a path.

12. Highlight all the text on the path. Change the color to **Paper**. Select the path using either *Selection* tool. Change the stroke width of the path to be much wider than the point size of your text. Choose *Type>Type on a Path>Options*. When the *Type on a Path Options* dialog box opens, change the *Align* and *To Path* fields to *Center* to position the type vertically on the path (Visual 11–16). This is a technique you will often use.

VISUAL |11–16|

The stroke width has been increased to a size larger than the point size of type. The center of the text has been aligned with the center of the stroke.

Creating Shadowed Type

The *Effects* panel manages a variety of transparency effects, including drop shadows. The Effects panel can be opened by using the keyboard shortcut, **Shift+Command+F10** (Mac) or **Shift+Control+F10** (Windows.)

The Effects panel allows you to choose which parts of the element you want to modify (Visual 11–17A). When you select *Object*, the effect is applied to the entire object— its stroke, fill, and text. *Stroke* affects the object's stroke (and gap color). *Text* affects all the text inside the frame. (You can't apply an effect to individual words or letters in a frame.) *Graphic* affects only the graphic selected with the Direct Selection tool.

Choose an effect from the panel menu options, or by clicking on the *fx* button on the bottom of the Effects panel. (You can also click the *fx* button on the Control panel.) When you choose an effect, a dialog box opens that allows you to specify attributes of that effect.

VISUAL |11–17|

Effects can be selected from the Effects panel menu options, or by clicking the *fx* button on the bottom of the Effects panel (A). The *fx* button is also found on the Control panel. When an effect is selected, a dialog box allows you to specify attributes of the effect (B).

The Effects panel and its drop shadow menu options are shown in Visual 11–17B. When you are applying a drop shadow to text, you will want to adjust the opacity of the shadow (75% is usually too dark). A box in the lower left corner summarizes the effects applied to a selected object.

Create Text Outlines

One of the greatest features of InDesign is the ability to convert text to outlines. Once text is converted to outlines, it is no longer text, so you can't correct spelling or apply normal text attributes. Instead, each letter is a tiny piece of artwork, giving you the ability to modify the shape or paste an image into it.

1. Type the phrase **Buttered Popcorn!** Apply a **Blue** fill. (Visual 11–18). Use the *Selection* tool to activate the frame, and press **Shift+Command+O** (Mac) or **Shift+Control+O** (Windows) to convert the text into *outlines*. You can also choose *Type>Create Outlines.* Now when you look closely at the type, you will see a series of anchor points. Even though each letter is now an individual shape, the letters are still linked together as one object—a *compound path*.

VISUAL | 11–18 |

When text is converted to outlines, each letter is converted to paths with editable points.

Buttered Popcorn!

2. With the outline type selected, choose *Object>Paths>Release Compound Path* and the text unit will split apart. Now you can move and rotate each letter with the *Selection* tool. Notice, however, that all the counters are filled in. Select both the counter and the letter outline, and go to *Window>Object & Layout>Pathfinder>Subtract.* The counter will be cut out (subtracted) from the underlying letterform. Repeat this process for all the letters with counters (Visual 11–19).

VISUAL | 11–19 |

When compound paths are released, the counters automatically fill in. Open the Pathfinder panel or go to Object>Pathfinder>Subtract to cut the counters out of the letter background.

VISUAL | 11–20 |

Individual letters can be moved and rotated. In this example, shadow and pillow emboss effects have been added.

3. Delete the dot from the exclamation point. Draw a small text frame in the dot's position and insert an ornament from the Glyphs panel. Add a *drop shadow* and a *pillow emboss. Pillow Emboss* is an option under the *Bevel and Emboss* page of the *Effects* panel.

Creating Shaped Text Frames

By now, you're an old pro at putting text inside a frame. This exercise will teach you how to create a shaped frame using the Pen tool.

1. Delete the images in your document. Select the *Pen* tool. Click or drag to make an irregularly-shaped, closed object. When you are ready to close the shape, position the *Pen* tool cursor close to the path's starting point. You will see a tiny circle appear next to the pen tool icon. This circle indicates that your next click will join the two ends of the path, making a closed shape. Your shape should look very strange, similar to Visual 11–21A.

2. Click inside the new shape with the *Type* tool. You should see a blinking cursor. Fill with placeholder text. Select all the text and change to justified alignment. Adjust the point size and typeface until you have a fairly even fill (Visual 11–21B). Try changing the shape's stroke width to 0 pt. Deselect all and press **W** to preview your type. .

VISUAL |11–21|

First, an odd-shaped closed path was created with the Pen tool. The, text was added and alignment justified to create an irregularly-shaped text block with defined edges.

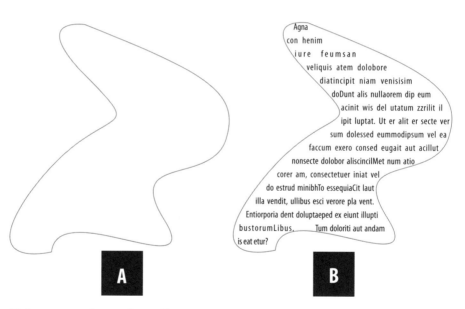

Bitter Apple Game Preserve

In the following exercise you will use the Page tool to create a document with multiple page sizes. You'll be creating a two-sided, full-color flyer, season pass button/sticker, letterhead, business card, and envelope for Bitter Apple Game Preserve. You will use the Gradient tool, create text on a path, convert text to outlines, create inline frames to contain graphics, and apply drop shadows and feathering. Visual 11–22 shows how the finished pieces will look. We will begin with the button. You will need the *11 Artwork and Resources* folder found on the accompanying CD.

VISUAL | 11–22 |

These projects will be created in a single InDesign document
with multiple page sizes created by the Page tool.

Make the Apple with a Gradient Fill

We're going to create the logo first, so that it can be applied to the rest of the elements. You will be using a template created for this project. A *template* is a document that is used as a pattern, and has an ".indt" file extension. A document can be saved as a template by choosing Save>Format>InDesign CS5 template (Mac), or Save>Save as type>InDesign CS5 template (Windows). This template has been prepared with the correct size, bleed, guidelines, layers, and swatches.

1. Open *11 Project Template.indt* from the **Chapter 11 Artwork and Resources** folder. Copy *11 Bitter Apple.indl* to your hard drive or desktop. The library already has some elements in it and you will be adding additional project elements to it, as they are completed. From the library, bring **Outlined Apple** to the center of Page 1, with the label *Sticker/Button* in the bottom slug area. This glyph has already been converted to outlines.

Keyboard Shortcut
 CMD+C
 CTRL+C
Copy

2. Select the apple shape with the **Selection** tool. Copy it and then use *Paste in Place* so that it is exactly on top of the original shape.

Keyboard Shortcut
 ⇧+OPT+CMD+V
 ⇧+ALT+CTRL+V
Paste in Place

3. Change the reference point on the Control panel so that it is in the center. Press the *Flip Horizontal* control on the Control panel. You now have an apple with two leaves (Visual 11–23A).

VISUAL |11–23|

First, the apple is flipped (A). Then, the arrow keys are used to align the two apple shapes (B).

4. Use the *Selection* tool to adjust the position of the top apple so that the edges line up (Visual 11–23B). You may also use the left and right arrow keys to nudge the element into place. Zoom in close to the edge of the apple to be as precise as possible.

5. With the *Selection* tool, select both apple shapes. Choose *Object>Pathfinder>Add.* This command adds the shapes together to make one whole apple shape. With the shape still selected, choose *Object>Paths>Release Compound Path.* You have now separated the apple from the leaves.

6. Select the leaves and fill them with **PANTONE DS 293-1 C** green.

7. Select the apple shape and then apply the **Apple gradient.** This is a *radial fill,* which means the color blends out from the center like rays of the sun. Use the *Gradient* tool, found on the Toolbox (press **G**), to adjust the length and direction of the fill. Click and drag the *Gradient* tool inside the apple, from edge to edge. Now change the starting location of the gradient by clicking the *Gradient* tool in another position and drag again. Hold down the Shift key to constrain it to a perfect horizontal or vertical blend. Reverse the direction of the line to reverse the blend. Do this several times until you understand how this tool works. Keep the *Gradient* tool inside the apple so the whole blend will be in that defined area. When you're finished experimenting, make the final gradient blend red in the top left corner to white in the lower right (Visual 11– 24). Group the apple and the leaves and drag the element into the library. Move the apple in your document over to the pasteboard for now.

VISUAL |11–24 |

The Gradient tool adjusts the length and direction of the gradient fill. In the upper example, the tool is being dragged diagonally from edge to edge. The lower example shows the apple after the Gradient tool has been used.

Keyboard Shortcut	
CMD+G	Group
CTRL+G	

Create Curved Button Text

The next step in the button project is to run text around the circle that creates the perimeter of the button. Follow the directions carefully and you'll see the advantage of using layers when placing this type.

1. On *Page 1*, go to the layer named **Background Circle.** Hold down **Shift+Option** (Mac) or **Shift+Alt** (Windows), and draw a circle out from the center guides. Watch the W and H coordinates, and when they read **4.375"** release your mouse. Fill it with **Blue** (C=100. M=90, Y=10, K=0). Lock and hide the layer (Visual 11–25).

VISUAL |11–25 |

The background layer is locked and hidden.

2. Move to the **Background Gradient** layer. Hold down **Shift+Option** (Mac) or **Shift+Alt** (Windows), and draw a **4"** circle out from the center guides. Apply **[None]** for the stroke and fill.

3. Select the circle and open the Layers panel. Hold **Option** (Mac) or **Alt** (Windows) and drag the red square on the Background Gradient layer up to the **Text and Photos** layer. You will see a plus sign, which means a copy of the circle is being placed on the next layer (Visual 11–26).

VISUAL |11–26 |

Hold the Option or Alt key as you drag the selected item indicator on the Layers panel to the Text and Photos layer. This copies the selected item to the next layer.

4. Hide the **Text and Photos** layer. Move down one layer to the **Background Gradient** layer so that we can add copy on the circle. Select the *Type on a Path* tool and click on the circle. Type **Season Pass** in **Myriad Pro Bold Condensed 50 pt**. Fill: **[Paper]**. Stroke: **Blue** (C=100. M=90, Y=10, K=0) Move the *End bracket* on the text path to about **0.025"** from the end of the type. Align *Center.* Choose *Type>Type on a Path>Options,* and set the *Align* field to *Ascender* and the *To Path* field to *Bottom.*

VISUAL |11–27|

The ascenders of the copy are aligned to the bottom of the path. The center flip bracket is at the top of the arch, aligned with the center guide.

5. Using the *Selection* tool, find the center flip bracket and align it to the center page guide. Make sure you are outside of the circle path when you release the mouse button or your type will not stay inside of the circle. Now your text is centered at the top of the circle. Remove any stroke or fill on the circle. When you are working with text on a curve you usually need to adjust the tracking. This sample was tracked to **+100** (Visual 11–27). Lock and hide the layer while we do the next step.

VISUAL |11–28|

The descenders of the copy are aligned to the top of the path. The center flip bracket is at the inside, bottom of the arch, aligned with the center guide.

6. Turn on the **Text and Photos** layer. Select the circle. Choose the *Type on a Path* tool and type **May–September 2010** on the circle in **30 pt. Myriad Pro Bold Condensed**. Fill: **[Paper]**. Stroke: **Blue.** Choose *Type>Type on a Path>Options,* and set the *Align* field to *Descender* and the *To Path* field to *Top.* Move the type to the bottom center of the circle and track letters to **+60**. This time, make sure the center flip bracket is inside of the circle path when you release the mouse button or your type will not stay inside of the circle (Visual 11–28).

VISUAL |11–29|

The apple is scaled and positioned on the Text and Photos layer.

7. Make all the layers visible and drag the apple in from the pasteboard. Move the apple to the top layer. You will need to resize the apple to fit in the type. To resize the apple, select it with the *Selection* tool and hold Shift, as you drag in a corner.

8. Draw a text frame and type **Bitter Apple** in **Chaparral Pro Bold 34-pt**. Fill: **Yellow**. Type **Game Preserve** in **Myriad Pro Bold 14 pt., all caps**. Fill: **Yellow**. To center the text accurately, pull the edges of the text frame out to the circle guide and use **Shift+Cmd+C** (Mac) or **Shift+Ctrl+C** (Windows) to center the text. Adjust the leading as needed. Position and size the text frame and apple inside the circle, as shown in Visual 11–30. Your button is almost complete.

9. **Unlock** all the layers. With the Selection tool, draw a marquee around all your button elements. Group all the elements. Drag the button into your library.

VISUAL |11–30|
The completed button is ready to be dragged into the library.

Use the Pathfinder Tool to Create the Logo's Frame

We're going to create two shapes, and then use the Pathfinder tool to add the shapes together, making a rectangular frame with an arch.

1. Go to *Page 2.* Select the *Rectangle Frame* tool and click on your page. When the dialog box comes up, enter **1.3"** for the width and **0.75"** for the height. Stroke and fill should be **[None]**.

2. Select the *Ellipse Frame* tool and hold **Shift+Option** or **Shift+Alt** to draw a circle out from the center of the rectangle. Make the circle slightly narrower than the rectangle. Use the *Align* panel to align the horizontal centers of the objects and move the circle up so that your two shapes look similar to the example in Visual 11–31A

3. Select both shapes and choose *Object>Pathfinder>Add* **(**Visual 11–31B). The shapes should blend together as in Visual 11–31C. (This is the same technique we used earlier to blend the two apple shapes into one shape.)

VISUAL |11–31|

Use the Align panel to align the horizontal centers of the selections. Then, with both objects selected, use Pathfinder to create a precise, symmetrical frame.

VISUAL |11–32 |
Use the Stroke panel to align the stroke to the inside of the path.

4. Use the *Stroke* panel to give the shape a **6 pt. Thin-Thick** stroke, with the stroke aligned to the center. Make the stroke's color **DS 63-1C Red** with a **Blue** gap. These colors will be in the *Swatches* panel. Fill the shape with **Blue** (C=100. M=90, Y=10, K=0). Add a drop shadow with **40%** opacity using the default shadow offsets.

5. Use the *Selection* tool to drag the apple in from the library. Hold **Command** (Mac) or **Control** (Windows) as you resize it to fit inside the logo as shown in Visual 11–33.

6. Draw a text frame below the apple and type **Bitter Apple** in **Chapparal Pro Bold, 13 pt., Yellow**. Type **Game Preserve** in **Myriad Pro Bold 8 pt., all caps, Yellow**. Copy should be centered, and look similar to Visual 11–33. Group the logo and drag it into the library. The logo is now completed. Delete the logo remaining in your document.

VISUAL |11–33 |
Finished logo.

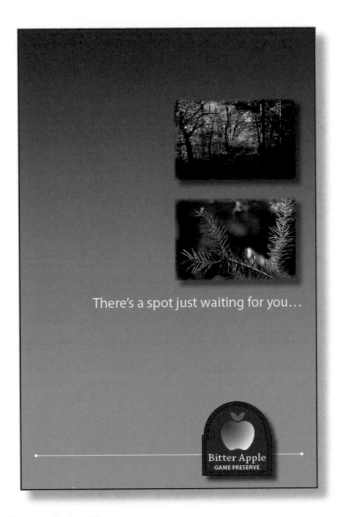

VISUAL |11–34 |
The front side of the flyer will
use elements from the library.

Creating the Front of the Flyer

In this step, we'll drop in a gradient and pull elements in from the library.
Visual 11–34 shows the front of the finished flyer for reference.

1.   Go to *Page 2.* Make sure you are working on the **Background gradient** layer.
     Draw a rectangle that fills the page from the bleed in the upper left corner
     to the bleed in the lower right corner. Fill the rectangle with **Background
     gradient** Use the *Gradient* tool to place the dark blue on the top and the green
     on the bottom. Hold down the Shift key to constrain it to a vertical blend.

2.   Move to the **Text and Photos** layer. Drag in the photos and headline from the
     library using the guides for placement. Add an ellipsis to the end of the headline.
     You make a true ellipsis by pressing **Option+;** (Mac) or **Alt+;** (Windows).

3.   Draw a **1-point** line on the bottom margin guide, color **[Paper]**. Using the
     Stroke panel, set the *Start* and *End* fields of the rule to **CircleSolid**. Drag
     the logo in from the library and position it as shown in Visual 11–34.

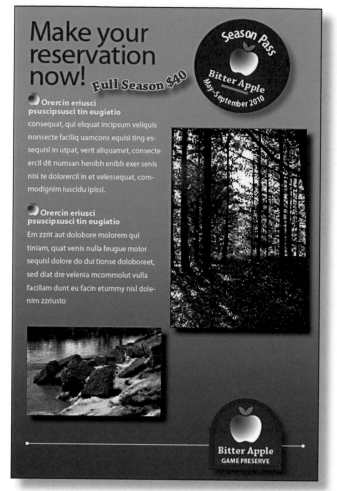

VISUAL |11–35|

The back side of the Bitter Apple Game Preserve flyer.

The Back of the Flyer

As you finish the back of the flyer, you will learn how to add inline frames. Most of the hard work is already done—you'll be pulling most of the elements in from the library. The finished back looks like Visual 11–35.

1. Go to *Page 3*. Make sure you are on the **Background Gradient** layer. Draw a frame from bleed to bleed and fill it with the **Background Gradient** swatch. Using the *Gradient* tool, adjust the color so that the green is on the top and the blue is on the bottom.

2. Move to the **Text and Photos** layer. Drag in the text block and photos from the library. Place a **1-point [Paper]** rule on the bottom margin and use the *Stroke* panel to add a circle to each end.

3. Go to *Page 2* and select the logo with the *Selection* tool. Copy the logo. Now go to **Page 3** and use *Paste in Place*. The logo should be in the exact same location as on the cover.

The apple at the beginning of each subhead is an *inline graphic*. An inline graphic is connected with the text so that it flows just like a word or letter. It's created by first copying the graphic and then pasting it into the text line.

4.   Find the apple you created earlier and copy it onto the pasteboard of *Page 3*. Select it with the *Selection* tool. Hold down Shift and pull a corner inward until the apple is very small, approximately **0.2"** (Visual 11–36).

VISUAL |11–36|
As an inline graphic, the apple will flow with the text.

5.   Copy the apple, and then switch to the *Type* tool and place the cursor in front of the first letter of the first subhead. Paste the apple and add a space. The graphic now sits on the baseline with the type. Even though it is connected to a text line, you can still adjust its vertical position using the *Selection* tool. Repeat the procedure for the second subhead.

6.   Pull the button you made earlier in from the library and place it on the pasteboard of *Page 3*. Select it with the *Selection* tool and reduce it proportionally by holding down **Shift+Command** (Mac) or **Shift+Control** (Windows). Drag it into position at the top of the page. Select it with the *Selection* tool. In the Control panel, make sure the reference point is in the middle. Use the *Selection* tool to rotate the button, as shown in Visual 11–37. Add a drop shadow with an opacity of **35%.**

VISUAL |11–37|
Use the Selection arrow to rotate the button.

There are subtle differences in the use of the Command (Mac) or Control (Windows) modifier keys when resizing elements. If there's no type or type on a path selected, use **Shift+Drag** to proportionately resize the elements. If the selection contains type or type on a path, use **Shift+Command** (Mac) or **Shift+Control** (Windows) and drag a corner to proportionately resize the objects.

▶ *production tip*
Use Shift+Command (Mac) or Shift+Control (Windows) as you drag to proportionately resize a combination of images and text.

7.   Use the *Selection* tool and pull in the *Full Season $40* line from the library. Position it next to the button, as shown in Visual 11–35. Don't close your document—we're going to design the three stationery pieces, next.

Using the Page tool for Multi-size Pages

InDesign lets you have more than one size page in a single document. This makes it easy to coordinate colors and design elements between related pieces. For instance, in this project we have a button/sticker, a flyer, and now we're going to add corporate stationery to the mix. All of these pieces will use the same gradient blends, swatches, typefaces and graphic elements. Having all these pieces in one document is a great way to stay organized. The *Page tool,* located beneath the Direct Selection tool on the Toolbox, is used to create multi-size master pages or document pages.

VISUAL | 11–38 |
Use the Page tool to add preset or custom page sizes to your document.

1. Use the *Pages* panel to add three pages to the end of the document. These pages should be based on the **[None]** master. Go to *Page 4.* Click on *Page 4* with the *Page* tool. When the page is highlighted on the Control panel, select *US Business Card* from the pull down menu to change the page size. Notice that your new page has retained the margins, bleed and slug area specified in the original document.

2. Go to *Page 5.* Use the *Page* tool to change the size to *Letter.* This page will be used for the letterhead. Go to *Page 6.* Use the *Page* tool to change the size to a #10 envelope. Enter **W: 9.5, H: 4.125"** on the Control panel.

3. Now you have your pages made—it's time to add the design elements. Go to the *Page 4.* From *Layout>Margins and Columns*, change all margins to **0.125"**. Create a background gradient fill that is green on the bottom, and blue on top and extending to all four bleed guides. Find the logo in the library and resize it to fit in the lower left corner. Pull the *Business Card text* from the library. Add a **1 pt. [Paper]** rule and use the *Arrange* commands to position it above the background, and below the logo (Visual 11–39).

VISUAL | 11–39 |
The completed business card.

4. Go to the letterhead on *Page 5.* Draw a rectangle with the width of **1.5"**. The rectangle should extend from the left bleed edge to the top and bottom bleed edges. Fill with the gradient, blue on the bottom, green on top. From the library, place the logo at the top margin of the rectangle (Visual 11–39). Pull the *Letterhead* information from the library and align the bottom of the copy block with the bottom of the logo.

5. For the envelope on *Page 6,* Place a **1.5"** rectangle that extends to the left, top and bottom bleed edges. Position the logo at the left and top margins. Pull *Envelope Address* from the library and center it under the logo. Your project is done!

VISUAL | 11—40 |

The finished letterhead
and #10 envelope.

Summary

This chapter introduced design techniques that can give text much more interest.
Just as using too many typefaces can overpower a document, so can using too
many text effects. Knowing how to use these techniques is the first step. Knowing
when to use them is the second.

▶ IN REVIEW

1. How do you know when the Type on a Path tool is ready to place text on a path?

2. How does the center bracket work?

3. How does the Page tool work?

4. What does the Gradient tool do?

5. What is the keystroke for creating a true ellipsis?

6. How can you draw a shape from the center, outward?

7. What are five options found under the Pathfinder tool?

8. Your coworker is struggling with adding a drop shadow to a text frame. When the drop shadow option is selected, the shadow appears on the type, but not behind the text frame. What advice would you give her?

9. How does type handling change when the type has been converted to outlines?

10. What is the process for proportionately scaling elements that contain text?

Keyboard Shortcut	
CMD+V	Paste
CTRL+V	

Keyboard Shortcut	
⇧+OPT+CMD+V	Paste in Place
⇧+ALT+CTRL+V	

Keyboard Shortcut	
CMD+G	Group
CTRL+G	

Keyboard Shortcut	
⇧+CMD+O	Create Outlines
⇧+CTRL+O	

Keyboard Shortcut	
CMD+C	Copy
CTRL+C	

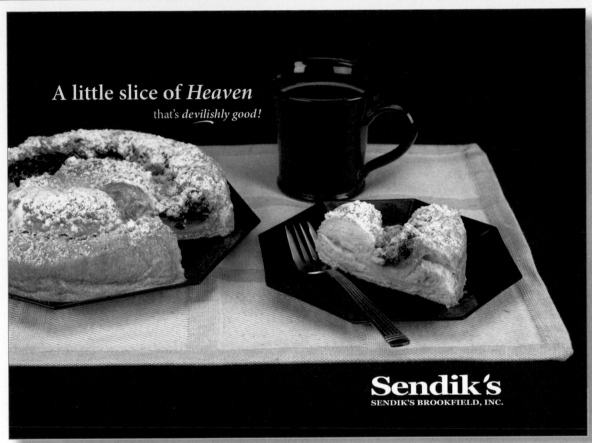

A little slice of *Heaven*
that's *devilishly good!*

Sendik's
SENDIK'S BROOKFIELD, INC.

Photo and layout ©2006 Erik P. Berg

Photo ©2006 Brittany Hinckle

There are no additional projects for this chapter. Congratulations on a job well done!

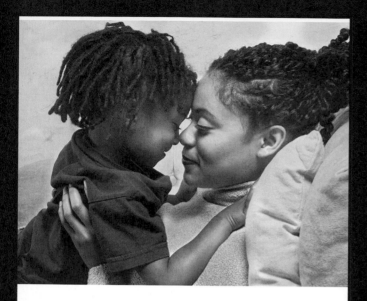

Love cures people…
both the ones who **give** it
and the ones who **receive** it.

ꝗ Dr. Karl Menninger

| Color Essentials |

12

objectives

► *Understand the difference between spot and process colors*

► *Use the Swatches panel to define color, tint, gradient, and mixed ink swatches*

► *Choose document print specifications*

introduction

Henry Ford's legendary adage, "You can paint it any color, so long as it's black," could well have been the motto for many printers during the last century. Printers might advertise that they "print red on Wednesdays and blue on Thursdays," but black was the "bread and butter" color used everyday for almost all projects. There were some two- and three-color print jobs, but full-color printing, in catalogs for instance, was too expensive and out of reach for the average print consumer. How things have changed! Advances in printing have created a kaleidoscope of color options for jobs that in years past, would have been printed in basic black. Full-color printing is now affordable on the leanest budget.

With each technological change comes a new set of challenges. Today, designers need to understand the physical properties of color and production processes. They need to define and use color correctly in their documents, and focus on principles of design, while creating a layout alive with color. For those of us who began our careers using X-acto knives, rubylith, and acetate overlays to manually separate color on pasteup boards, any effort required to expand our knowledge base is a small price to pay for the ease of incorporating color in our layouts.

A great way to continue learning is to join an InDesign User Group. Membership is free, and you will learn something new at every meeting you attend (plus, you might win new software!) The map to the right shows the Milwaukee, Wisconsin chapter—and new chapters are continually forming all over the world. For more information, or to find your local chapter, go to www.indesignusergroup.com.

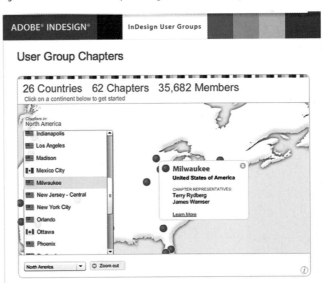

Color Essentials

One of the best decisions I made in my college career was to double major in graphic design, and printing and publishing. Understanding how document design and construction affects production, has been invaluable. The same project that is greeted with cheers when presented to a client, may elicit groans, after it is opened by the prepress technician. File construction tells a lot about the designer's training and skill. A poorly constructed file will do more damage to a designer's reputation than almost anything else. If that designer also misses production deadlines, vendors will shudder every time he walks through the door, because they know they will be working on a file that is not only late, but also technically incorrect! This chapter will focus on one file preparation area that can be challenging: specifying color. Then, Chapter 13 will discuss managing graphics files and images, and organizing fonts.

Specifying Color

Color is an important component in any project. If you don't understand how color is created and how a piece will be printed, you will not be able to create a document that uses color correctly. Errors in using color are costly. Of course, color mistakes on garage sale posters, printed on your own color inkjet printer, aren't going to ruin your life. But making a mistake on a catalog project, where accurate color is critical, will negatively impact your career. We will begin with some basic theory about the physical characteristics of color. For more information on the complex world of color, I recommend *Graphic Communications Today, Fourth Edition*, by William Ryan and Theodore Conover, published by Thomson Delmar Learning.

Color: Transmitted or Reflected Light Waves

Color is created by light waves that are either *transmitted* or *reflected*. Your computer monitor transmits light waves to create color. Three primary colors of light—red, green, and blue (RGB)—are combined in different proportions to create the millions of colors on your screen. Colors displayed on a monitor are described by a formula that specifies the level of each component color. The range of levels goes from 0 to 255. For example, the formula R=255, G=55, B=45 would describe a bright red. RGB is *additive* color. This means that when the levels of RGB are at the maximum, 255, the color you see is white. When all RGB values are at 0, the color is black. When creating documents that will be viewed on a monitor, such as web pages, using colors defined by the RGB system are natural choices.

Ink and toner, on paper, work differently. They absorb some light waves and reflect the rest. The light waves that are reflected back to our eyes create the illusion of color. Color created by reflected light waves is called *subtractive*. That means that if all the light is absorbed (subtracted), we see black. The primary colors in subtractive color are cyan, magenta, and yellow (CMY). Formulas that specify the amounts of each component color are used to describe subtractive color. The bright red color described in the preceding paragraph would be expressed as C=0, M=91, Y=87. An important difference is that the range of levels is different, from 0 to 100. It's also appropriate to refer to the levels of component colors as percentages. In theory, when you combine pigments of pure cyan, magenta, and yellow, all the light waves will be absorbed and the color will look black. In reality, pure pigments are impossible to obtain, so 100% cyan, 100% magenta, and 100% yellow blend to create a washed-out black. That's why black ink (referred to as K) is added in the printing process, to compensate for the weak black, created by the CMY combination. Now we've arrived at what is known as the CMYK color space. RGB (additive color) images are perfect for monitor or web display, but must be redefined as CMYK (subtractive) colors, before being commercially printed.

Printing: Spot or Process?

Commercial printers always work with subtractive color. Defining colors to print correctly on a press is one of the challenges designers face on a daily basis. In commercial printing, color is created by reflected light waves. That's why it's not a good idea to put colors in your InDesign file that are defined as RGB (transmitted light waves).

Commercial printers use ink, and they talk in terms of *process color* or *spot color*. Spot color ink is like a can of premixed paint. There are about a dozen basic ink colors that can be combined, in different proportions, to make thousands of spot color inks. Each spot color is described by a standardized number and a mixing ratio (another formula!). This enables printers anywhere in the world to mix up and match a

►MOVING TOWARD MASTERY

When working with spot or process color, remember that what you see on your screen, is probably not what you will get from your commercial printer!

Unless a color calibration system is in place, every computer monitor will display color a little differently. Always use an ink swatch book to select colors for your printed document. Even if the colors don't look just right on the screen, they will print correctly on a printing press.

*A color at 100% is the actual hue. The hue can be tinted in increments, from very dark (90%) to very light (10%). The **C** at the end indicates that this is what the color will look like when printed on coated paper (as opposed to uncoated paper)*

PANTONE Colors displayed herein may not match PANTONE-identified standards. Consult current PANTONE Color Publications for accurate color. PANTONE® and other Pantone, Inc. trademarks are the property of Pantone, Inc. PANTONE Trademarks and Copyrights used with the written permission of Pantone, Inc.

100% PANTONE 541 C
90% PANTONE 541 C
80% PANTONE 541 C
70% PANTONE 541 C
60% PANTONE 541 C
50% PANTONE 541 C
40% PANTONE 541 C
30% PANTONE 541 C
20% PANTONE 541 C
10% PANTONE 541 C

specific color, as long as they are using the same color/ink system. For instance, one popular color matching system is the Pantone Matching System®. When a printer in Philadelphia puts PANTONE® 541 on his press, it will be exactly the same color as the PANTONE 541, printed across the ocean in Calcutta. Tints of spot colors can also be used and are described in percentages: 0% to 100%. This allows you to use the full-strength spot color (100%) or lighter tints, to create a variety of color.

Many of your projects will be one-color documents—and yes, black counts as a color. Business forms, reports, books—many of the materials we read every day are single-color documents, usually black and white. However, don't underestimate the power of a well-designed single-color document! A blue, for example, can range from a pale 10% shade, to a strong 100% navy. And when it is printed on a sheet of cream paper, it can give the impression of a two-color job. For just slightly more than the cost of black ink, you can create an attractive document with just one spot color, incorporating tints and solids and good design skills. If your client wants a full-color brochure, but doesn't have a full-color budget, suggest going with a two-color brochure using spot colors. Two spot colors, combined with careful paper selection, can give a project an upscale look without the upscale cost.

Process Color

Process color (also referred to as *full-color*) is much different from spot color. Full-color posters, magazines, catalogs, artist prints—anything that has the full range of the color spectrum—will be printed using process colors. In process color printing, four basic transparent inks, in different tints, are printed on top of each other to create the illusion of many colors. As discussed earlier, these transparent colors are cyan, magenta, yellow, and black (CMYK). Cyan is greenish-blue and magenta is a violet-red. When you look at a full-color job under a magnifying glass, you will see that the "color" is actually made from a series of tiny dots, printed close together. When each of the four inks is printed in the correct location, the dots merge together to give the impression of color. The color could be one hue (like a spot-color ink) or the millions of color variations that create a photograph. However, when one ink color is printed slightly off from the others, it makes the finished image look distorted. This is called *out of register*. We have all seen examples of this when Sunday comics aren't printed quite right and have a blurred image.

Applying Color to Your Document

InDesign has two panels for assigning color to objects: the Color panel and the Swatches panel. Although they have some overlapping features, each offers unique ways to create and apply color. Let's start with the Color panel.

▶ *production tip*
A four-minute video describing the Pantone® system can be viewed at http://www.pantone.com/pages/ptv/ptv_clips.aspx.

▶ *production tip*
Digital color printers (used for smaller full-color runs) often use cartridges of cyan, magenta, yellow, and black toner.

1. Make a new document, **8.5" × 11"**. Press **F6** to open the *Color* panel. At the bottom of the panel you will see a bar called the *color spectrum*. It will contain either a gradient of one single color or a rainbow of colors. If the spectrum contains a single color, click on the panel menu and choose CMYK (Visual 12–1).

VISUAL | 12–1 |

If the color spectrum shows shades of one color only, choose CMYK from the panel menu.

2. Draw a rectangle and activate the Fill icon on the Toolbox. Move your mouse over the color spectrum on the Color panel and notice that your cursor turns into the *Eyedropper* tool. Click the *Eyedropper* tool on a color that looks good to you. The rectangle instantly fills with the color you have selected. Notice that the Fill icon in the Toolbox has been updated with the same color. Click back and forth along the CMYK spectrum bar and fill your rectangle with different colors (Visual 12–2).

VISUAL | 12–2 |

Each time you select a new color from the CMYK spectrum bar, the Fill icon in the Toolbox displays the same color.

3. There are four sliders above the CMYK spectrum. These show the percentages of each of the four process colors. Slide the triangles along each of the individual color bars, noticing how the color changes and how the percentage values in the boxes to the right also change. Fine-tune your chosen color by making it a lighter shade.

4. Click on the [None] box (the square with the red diagonal line), at at the left of the CMYK spectrum. The rectangle now has no fill and the Fill icon on the Toolbox also indicates no fill. But you have not lost your color because a new box has appeared in the *Color* panel: *Last Color* (Visual 12–3). Click on it and your last color returns. The smaller boxes, at the right of the CMYK spectrum, are for white or black fills. Remember that assigning White (a color), to the fill or stroke of an object, is not the same as applying None (no color at all).

VISUAL | 12–3 |

The Color panel displays the last color usedin a box above the color spectrum.

▶ *production tip*

Assigning White (a color) is not the same as applying None (no color at all).

5. Click on your rectangle with the *Type* tool and convert it to a text frame. The *Color* panel now indicates the color of the text. Type a short sentence and bump up the point size to fill the text frame. Select all the text and change the color of the text in the same way you changed the color of the rectangle. Remember to choose CMYK, if your color bar shows a spectrum of only one color.

6. Click on the text frame with one of the selection tools. The two small buttons below the Fill and Stroke icons in the *Color* panel (or the Toolbox) will now allow you to choose which color you change, either the text or the frame (Visual 12–4).

VISUAL | 12–4 |

The arrows show the controls you use to toggle between applying color to the container or to the text.

Formatting affects container

Formatting affects text

Click the controls to switch between the text or container.

7. Open the *Color* panel options menu again and change the mode from CMYK to RGB (Visual 12–5). The shades of color do not change; but you are now working in additive color rather than subtractive color. The yellow triangle that sometimes appears above the color spectrum is the *out of gamut* warning. This is a warning that the RGB color you have selected will not reproduce satisfactorily in a CMYK printed document. If you click on the warning icon, the color will be modified to the closest CMYK equivalent.

VISUAL | 12–5 |

It is easy to change between single color, CMYK, and RGB color models. Always be aware of what color mode you are working in. CMYK is for commercial printing. RGB is basically for documents that will be viewed on a computer monitor, like web pages.

Now that you have been introduced to the Color panel, a word of caution: The Color panel is handy for applying color in "quick and dirty" documents that you will output yourself, on your home color printer. But if you're working in a production setting—and especially if your file is going out to a service bureau or a commercial printer—use the Swatches panel instead.

The Swatches Panel

The Swatches panel can do everything the Color panel does, but with one important difference: You can *define* each color in your document and assign it a meaningful name. Colors from the Color panel, like the ones you had so much fun clicking on in the preceding pages, are *undefined* and unnamed. This means it is difficult to track and manage them throughout your document. For professional purposes, keep the Color panel tucked away. Colors created and stored in the Swatches panel are much easier to manage.

VISUAL | 12–6 |

Press F5 to open the Swatches panel. The panel is set up like many other InDesign panels.

Keyboard Shortcut

 F5

 F5

Swatches Panel

Transfer an Undefined Color to the Swatches Panel

In the following exercise, you will learn how to convert an undefined color, created in the Color panel, into a color swatch.

1.   Make sure the *Color* panel is open and the rectangle is active.

2.   Press **F5** to open the *Swatches* panel (Visual 12–6). To make room for additional swatches, lengthen the panel by dragging the lower right corner until the scroll bar disappears. Go back to the *Color* panel and make sure the Fill color icon for your active rectangle is active.

3. Open the *Color* panel options menu and choose *Add to Swatches* (Visual 12–7). The color of your frame is now a swatch in the *Swatches* panel and has changed from an undefined color, to a defined color. Do the same for the color you chose for your text.

VISUAL | 12–7 |

An undefined color can easily be added to the Swatches panel by selecting Add to Swatches in the Color panel menu. The new swatch is now defined and is at the bottom of the Swatches panel list.

4. There are other methods of transferring an undefined color to the *Swatches* panel. You can select your rectangle and click the *New Swatch* button at the bottom of the *Swatches* panel (shown in Visual 12–6). Or you can drag the Fill or Stroke color icon right from the *Color* panel and drop it into the *Swatches* panel.

Transfer an Undefined Gradient to the Swatches Panel

Generally, it is best to convert undefined colors to defined swatches. The same holds true for undefined gradients. Converting an undefined gradient to a gradient swatch is a process similar to the one you just completed for undefined color.

1. Open the *Gradient* panel (*Window>Color>Gradient.*) and choose *Show Options* under the panel menu. In the Type field, choose *Linear* or *Radial.* A *linear gradient* changes color along a line, a *radial gradient* radiates from one color to the next in a circular pattern. You should see a horizontal bar called a *ramp*, extending across the bottom of the Gradient panel. At the top and center of the ramp is a diamond. This diamond is a stop that defines the midpoint of the gradient. As you slide the stop toward either end of the ramp, you will see the gradient swatch in the upper left corner change.

2. Open the *Color* panel and arrange it so that it's next to the *Gradient* panel. You're going to apply some colors to the gradient.

3. In the *Gradient* panel you should see two house-shaped icons below the ramp. If you don't see them, click on the ramp and they will appear. These are the color stops. Click on the left color stop and then adjust the color sliders in the *Color* panel. Notice that the color stop in the *Gradient* panel changes accordingly (Visual 12–8).

VISUAL |12–8|

Color stops define the beginning and ending colors in the gradient.

4. Now, click on the right color stop. Apply a color using the *Color* panel. Experiment with adjusting the look of your gradient by sliding the midpoint and color stops to the left or the right. Watch as the gradient swatch in the upper left corner changes to reflect your color adjustments.

5. You can also apply color to a gradient from the *Swatches* panel. The process is similar to the one described above, but instead of choosing a color from the *Color* panel, you press Option (Mac) or Alt (Windows) as you click on a color swatch from the *Swatches* panel.

6. Now we will define the gradient you have just created. Open the *Swatches* panel menu and choose *New Gradient Swatch*. When the *New Gradient Swatch* dialog box appears, you can name your new gradient swatch in the *Swatch Name* field.

VISUAL |12–9|

Gradient swatches can be defined in the Swatches panel menu.

7. An alternate method is to drag the color preview from the *Gradient* panel into the *Swatches* panel. Double-click the new swatch to open the *Gradient Options* dialog box and rename it. If you don't see your gradient, select either the *Show Gradient Swatches* or *Show All Swatches* button at the bottom of the *Swatches* panel (shown in Visual 12–6).

The icons at the top of the Swatches panel should be familiar to you by now—Fill, Stroke, Formatting affects container, and Formatting affects text. There is also a field where you can set the tint of a selected color. The various colors in the list are those available to your document and are labeled with their CMYK values (Visual 12–7).

Create a Color Swatch from "Scratch"

You can define colors directly from the Swatches panel. But before you can define a color for your document, you must know whether you need to create spot or process colors. When you define a color in your document as spot, it means that the printer will premix the color according to the formula specified by your *swatch book* and then put the colored ink on the press. A plate on the press picks up the ink and transfers it to the paper. After the color is printed, the press is cleaned, a new plate is put on, and the ink is replaced with the next color needed. A job that uses yellow, blue, green, orange, red, and black will require six premixed colors and six plates—and a significant amount of time for mixing ink and cleaning the press.

Process color works differently. Instead of premixing each individual ink color, only four inks—cyan, magenta, yellow, and black—and four plates are used to create all the other colors that will be printed. The four colors are overlaid in various tints, to create the illusion of many colors. The six-color job we just discussed, could be printed by using only four inks and plates, and would require much less production time. Orange would be created by percentages of yellow and magenta. Green would be created by percentages of cyan and yellow, and so on. Of course, if your job only has two colors—two inks and two plates—then using spot colors would be the way to go.

A swatch book should be used at the design stage for selecting and defining either spot or process colors. The swatch book provides the exact color formula needed and shows an accurate sample of how the printed color will look. Basing a color selection on what you see on your computer screen is risky, because most monitors do not display color accurately. There are many variables that go into choosing color. Until you have a clear understanding of the printing process, it is a good idea to have an experienced designer check your document files, before you send them to the printer. We will now create a new process color swatch.

VISUAL | 12–10 |

The Swatches panel has many options for displaying swatches. When Name is selected (the default), the colors in the list are displayed with their names next to them. If you select Small Swatch, the colors will be displayed as tiny swatches and no names. In this example, Large Swatch has been selected.

1. Choose *New Color Swatch* from the panel menu (Visual 12–10). A dialog box displaying the four CMYK sliders will open. The color settings in the dialog box will be for the last color selected in the *Swatches* panel.

2. If you know them, type in the percentages of cyan, magenta, yellow, and black that define your color. Or, slide the color bars until you get the color you want. InDesign will define and name the color for you, in terms of CMYK values, or you can deselect the *Name with Color Value* option box and assign it a name of your own choosing. It's better to name a color by its CMYK values because that's a language everyone understands. Even though a color may look exactly like what you saw when your cat was car sick, naming a color: *Sick Kitty*, conjures up a very different color in each person's mind.

Make a New Gradient Swatch from "Scratch"

When you select **New Gradient Swatch** from the Swatches panel menu, you are making a defined gradient.

1. Choose *New Gradient Swatch* from the panel menu. Click on the starting color stop icon, at the left end of the gradient ramp. The *Stop Color* field becomes active, allowing you to select CMYK from the list and then adjust the sliders in the CMYK mode. You can also select *Swatches* from the *Stop Color* field list and then choose a color from your swatches.

2. Click the ending color stop icon, at the right side of the gradient ramp and assign it a different color.

3. Drag one of the Stop icons to the middle of the gradient ramp. Click below the ramp where the original color stop was, and a new stop will appear. Give this new stop a third color.

4. Slide the diamond-shaped midpoint stops, at the top of the gradient ramp to adjust the span of each color between color stops. Click OK to add this swatch to the *Swatches* panel.

The Show Gradient Swatches button at the bottom of the panel, limits the display to only the defined gradients in the document. If you have a gradient swatch selected and click the New Swatch button, the gradient swatch will be duplicated. If you select the Trashcan icon, the gradient swatch will be deleted.

Make a Color Tint Swatch

If you were designing a single-color document using many shades of the same blue, first you would want to create the solid blue swatch and then make tint variations from it.

1. Create a new swatch—Color Type: **Spot**, Color Mode: **Pantone solid coated**. Scroll down the list and select a Pantone blue that you like. Press Return.

2. With the new blue swatch selected, open the *Swatches* panel menu and choose *New Tint Swatch.* In the *New Tint Swatch* dialog box, drag the Tint slider to **10%** and click Add. You can type numerical values into the Tint field, but you have to press the Tab key before the Add button becomes active again.

VISUAL |12–11|

Tint swatches display the percentage to the right of the color name.

3. Repeat this process, creating tint swatches from **10%** to **90%**, in 10% increments, using a green color. Click Done. Your *Swatches* panel should look like Visual 12–11. Notice that the percentage of each tint is displayed at the end of the name.

4. If the tint isn't exactly what you want, you can double-click on the tint swatch in the panel list, and when the *Swatch Options* dialog box opens, adjust the sliders.

Changing the color values of a tint swatch also changes the values of the original color the swatch is based on. Be sure that when you are in the Swatch Options dialog box, you don't change color values—unless you want the original color swatch to change, too.

Adding Swatches from Other Documents

You can pull color swatches from other InDesign documents into a document you are working on. The following method allows you to choose which colors you bring into your document.

1. Open the *Swatches* panel menu and choose *New Color Swatch.* In the *New Color Swatch* dialog box, pick *Other Library* at the bottom of the *Color Mode* list (Visual 12–13).

2. Navigate to the document you want to borrow color from, and click Open. Select a color you want, from the list of available colors in the document, and click Add to transfer them to your *Swatches* panel. When you are done adding colors, click OK.

Loading Swatches

You can also add swatches from another document by using the Load Swatches option and then selecting the file. This method will load all the colors from the second document rather than letting you choose the ones you want (Visual 12–12).

Standard Swatch Libraries

Although it stimulates your creative juices to create your own colors from the color spectrum bar and those cool little CMYK sliders, the safest thing to do is choose colors from standard swatch libraries—like Pantone or Trumatch. You find the standard swatch libraries in the Swatch Options dialog box. First, open the Swatch panel menu and choose New Color Swatch (or Swatch Options if you have a swatch selected). When the dialog box opens, choose Color Mode. Each of the names in the center section of the list corresponds to a specific color swatch system (Visual 12–13).

Using a swatch book to choose colors assures that you are speaking the same language as your printer—as long as you're both using the same swatch book. (Be sure to watch the Pantone video described earlier!)

Creating a Two-Color Layout

Let's say you're designing a small flyer for a large bank. The bank wants the piece to look good, but doesn't want to spend the money on four colors. You suggest going with two colors on coated ivory paper. The finished product will look like Visual 12–14.

Gibraltar Metropolitan Bank

How We Protect Your Information

psuscipit ex er iustrud magnis elis aliquisit vendrem auguerci blam dolore dolum dunt il erostissed min eui eum auguer sum nos nis eugait vullaore consent ipsum nostio do dunt nim iriustrud dui exer sequisi bla feugue minciliquat nullam veriure min ulla faci et am zzrit prat, veraesto ercipis ea feum do odiamconsed eum ipsustrud tat. Ut lutpat.

Our Security Procedures

Bore molor sim ipis dolent wisit accumsan ut veril et dolor ad modo diatuer susto diamcon sequat ullut am eugiametue ting etum del dionsecte duipis nostrud eros ex estio consequamet in velessendre facipis adit iriusto dipsum ing exerit eummy nulla feu feuisci tie magnibh eu facillaore dolorem del exerci eu facing ea aliquat dio ex eugiam nim acidui tinim ing ent acidunt lore dolore vel eu facing euisi.

What Information We Disclose

tet ea commodolore feuismolore commodiat ad eugait velit lamet, quisit adipit iuscil ero od dolortincin henibh et praesse quipsumsan hent dui blaore feum ilis nulla ad tionsed exero consequisi.

- Re tionsed dolorperos am inibh eugiam nos at, quis euguerit nummy nos ex estin hendipis acidunt am

- Volorero od et, quis amet la feugiate magnibh enisse consequat.

- Duisl irit at aute diamconse venisi tionullam erillan hent wis amet nulla acidunt adionsequam, voluptat utatums andreet nos nonsequis auguerostrud

endiam zzriustin velesequisl irilisim ex elisLiquis autet prat. Velit esed mincidunt laore venibh eratet quisisisis autate mod eu facillaor ad eugueros et prate vullaor sit quisl il dolortion el eugiat, volenim vel ute tinibh eugait velendrer sit vero consequat lorper sed tie con ulputet velis eugait ipit ipit vulpute diate tatum dolore con ullut

Gibraltar Metropolitan Bank
123 Center City Suites
Yorkton, Virginia 09876
121-233-4567   www.gibraltarmetro.com

VISUAL | 12–14 |

This is a two-color project called a "bill stuffer," similar to the ones that come in your credit card statements.

1. Make a new document **22p × 8.5"**, **0.25"** margins, and **0.125" full bleed**. Delete all swatches that may be in the *Swatches* panel. You will not be able to delete [None], [Paper], [Black], or [Registration].

2. Choose *New Color Swatch* in the panel menu. In the *New Color Swatch* dialog box, choose **PANTONE solid coated** in the Color Mode list. Scroll down the list of available colors, select **202 C**, and click Add. Now, choose **Pantone metallic coated** from the Color Mode list. Scroll down to **876 C** (or type 876 in the PANTONE field), select this color, click Add, and then click Done (Visual 12–15). You have selected two standard Pantone colors to use in your document (if you had a Pantone Color Swatch book, you'd see that 876 C is an eye-catching metallic gold).

VISUAL |12–15|

The new swatches have been added.

3. Draw a text frame from margin to margin and place the *12 Gibraltar Bank. docx* text file. You will find the file in the *12 Artwork and Resources* folder, on the CD accompanying this book.

4. Open the *Paragraph Styles* panel and choose *Load All Text Styles*. Find the *12 Gibraltar Style Sheets.indd* file, in the same folder as the text file. Click OK in the *Load Style* dialog box. Select all the text and assign the *Body Copy* paragraph style. Apply the *Headline* style to the first line of type. Apply the *Sub Head* style to the lines *"How We Protect…," "Our Security…,"* and *"What Information…."*

VISUAL |12–16|

The paragraph styles have been applied.

5. Apply the *Body Copy-Bulleted* style to the three bulleted paragraphs. If the bullets don't display correctly, replace them, using **Option+8** (Mac) or **Alt+8** (Windows). Remember to use the Indent to Here character to hang the bullet. Mac users will use **Command+** and Windows users, **Control+**.

6. Apply the *Footer* style to the bottom four lines, making sure there is a soft return at the end of each line. Place a flush right tab (**Shift+Tab**) between the phone number and website. The text in your document should look like Visual 12–16.

7. Draw a rectangle that bleeds from the top, left, and right sides. Include just the first section of placeholder text in the rectangle (refer to Visual 12–14). Fill the rectangle with **876 C** and send it to the back.

8. Make a similar rectangle at the bottom of the document, bleeding it off the right, left, and bottom edges. The rectangular shape should enclose the name, address, and web information. Fill it with **876 C** and send it to the back. Deselect everything. We've now used our two colors: 876 C for the background rectangles and 202 C for the type.

9. Since the document will be printed on ivory paper, let's add a color to our paper and see what it will look like when it is printed. Double-click the [Paper] color in the *Swatches* panel. In the *Swatch Options* dialog box, give the paper a light ivory color: **5% Cyan**, **10% Magenta**, **36% Yellow**, **0.39% Black**. Press Return. Save your document, and let's try printing color separations.

Color Separations

One of the most common problems printers have, when designers bring in "finished" documents, is in creating color separations. Every color in your document needs its own plate and printing unit on the press. A two-color document will need two plates and two printing units; a four-color document will need four plates and four printing units, and so on. (Tints based on an original spot color do not require an additional plate.)

You may think you are bringing a two-color document to your printer, but when he runs separations, he gets four, five, six, or more colors. Why? It could be that what looks like a single color on your monitor is actually a blend of CMYK or RGB values. It could be that you didn't notice a hairline stroke on a text frame. It could be that a hidden character is assigned a color you can't even see on your monitor. There can be any number of reasons why there are more colors in your document than it appears. The following exercise uses features in the Print dialog box to identify how many colors are really in your document.

1. Before you print separations, change the [Paper] color in the *Swatches* panel back to **0%** of **CMYK**. Now, go to the Print dialog box. On the *Setup* page, in the *Page Position* field, choose *Centered*.

2. On the *Marks and Bleed* page, select *All Printer's Marks.* Be sure that *Use Document Bleed Settings* is selected. On the *Output* page, select *Separations* in the *Color* field (Visual 12–17).

The Output page offers choices for color separations.

3. Click Print. You should get two sheets from the printer, one labeled PANTONE 202 C and the other labeled 876 C. Color separations always print in black, even if you are using a color printer. Each color is "separated" onto an individual page, and the black areas show where the color will be printed. A color identification label appears outside the image area near the crop marks.

4. Go back to your document and deliberately confuse things. Make hidden characters visible and select a single hard return character. Color it black and run separations again. You will get a third sheet labeled Process Black, although you won't see any text or element. InDesign "saw" a hidden character with a third color (black), that nobody else saw. Since we're printing separations, it printed a black plate—just for that one invisible character.

5. Make a new process swatch: **C=0, M=100, Y=61, K=43** (the equivalent values of PANTONE 202 C). Name it **Process Red.** Select all your text and change it to Process Red. The color of your text looks exactly the same, but now when you print, you get four separations: Magenta, Yellow, Black, and 876C. (Cyan didn't print because its value was 0. Also notice how the Black plate is screened back to 43%.)

It is a good idea to print out a sample set of separations on your laser printer, before sending the project to the commercial printer. Printing sample separations is an effective way of catching color mistakes before they end up costing you money. Knowing a few color basics and always paying attention to how color is defined and used in your document will help avoid production pitfalls and increase your chances of being the next one in line for that promotion. Your documents need to be aesthetically pleasing, and technically correct.

▶ *production tip*

Remember the color you assigned to the bank flyer paper stock? That color did not print with your color separations. A color assigned to [Paper] is for your eyes only, to give you an approximate feel for how your final document will look.

Modify the paper color in your Swatches panel as close as possible to the real paper, but remember that your monitor will not give you a 100% match. Also keep in mind that a single PANTONE color may look different when printed on different color papers.

Printer's Marks and Printing Options

You will want to be familiar with the marks your printer uses for printing and finishing your document. Since all printer's marks are outside the copy area of the document, the paper size will always have to be larger than your finished document size, in order to use them.

VISUAL |12–18|

Each of these printer's marks means something different. The Page Information gives the file name on the lower left side, with the plate color and day and time the file was printed, on the right. Color Bars are located at the top of the page. The trim size is always smaller than the bleed size.

Color Bar

Registration mark

Trim size

Bleed size

Page information

Plate information

Gibraltar Metropolitan Bank

How We Protect Your Information

psuscipit ex er iustrud magnis elis aliquisit vendrem auguerci blam dolore dolum dunt il erostissed min eui eum auguer sum nos nis eugait vullaore consent ipsum nostio do dunt nim iriustrud dui exer sequisi bla feugue minciliquat nullam veriure min ulla faci et am zzrit prat, veraesto ercipis ea feum do odiamconsed eum ipsustrud tat. Ut lutpat.

Our Security Procedures

Bore molor sim ipis dolent wisit accumsan ut veril et dolor ad modo diatuer susto diamcon sequat ullut am eugiametue ting etum del dionsecte duipis nostrud eros ex estio consequamet in velessendre facipis adit iriusto dipsum ing exerit eummy nulla feu feuisci tie magnibh eu facillaore dolorem del exerci eu facing ea aliquat dio ex eugiam nim acidui tinim ing ent acidunt lore dolore vel eu facing euisi.

What Information We Disclose

tet ea commodolore feuismolore commodiat ad eugait velit lamet, quisit adipit iuscil ero od dolortincin henibh et praesse quipsumsan hent dui blaore feum ilis nulla ad tionsed exero consequisi.

- Re tionsed dolorperos am inibh eugiam nos at, quis euguerit nummy nos ex estin hendipis acidunt am
- volorero od et, quis amet la feugiate magnibh enisse consequat.
- Duisl irit at aute diamconse venisi tionullam erillan hent wis amet nulla acidunt adionsequam, voluptat utatums andreet nos nonsequis auguerostrud

endiam zzriustin velesequisl irilisim ex elisLiquis autet prat. Velit esed mincidunt laore venibh eratet quisisisis autate mod eu facillaor ad eugueros et prate vullaor sit quisl il dolortion el eugiat, volenim vel ute tinibh eugait velendrer sit vero consequat lorper sed tie con ulputet velis eugait ipit ipit vulpute diate tatum dolore con ullut

Gibraltar Metropolitan Bank
123 Center City Suites
Yorkton, Virginia 09876
121-233-4567 **www.gibraltarmetro.com**

Bank flyer.indd 1

4/15/09 9:26:30 AM
PANTONE 202 C

▶ **Crop Marks** (sometimes called *trim marks*) are placed just outside the four corners of your document and tell the cutter where to cut the paper to its finished size. If a document is printed on oversized paper, the cutter will trim away the excess according to the crop marks. You can adjust the weight and placement of crop marks using the Weight and Offset fields on the right side of the Marks area, on the Marks and Bleed page of the Print dialog box.

▶ **Manual Crop Marks**. If more than one copy of your document will be printed on a single sheet (two up, three up, and so on), or if the front and back of your document will be printed in a single pass (*work and turn, work and tumble*—types of imposition), you may want to draw your own crop marks manually. Make your manual crop marks short and thin—about a quarter of an inch long and hairline width—and maybe an eighth of an inch away from the edge of the finished piece. Make sure the corners don't touch. Before you take your document to final production, it's a good idea to print it from your laser printer, and with a pencil, connect the crop marks, you created. This is a way to double-check the accuracy of your marks, to make sure that you're not cutting off something you want to keep.

▶ **Bleed Marks** sit in the corners of your document, just outside the crop marks, and set the limits of your printed bleed. You will usually use the settings you entered when your document was first set up, but you can deselect the Use Document Bleed Settings option and enter new settings, in the Bleed and Slug area of the Print dialog box. Even if the bleed in your electronic file extends beyond the settings in the Bleed and Slug area, it will print only out to the bleed marks.

▶ **Registration Marks** are the "bull's-eyes" along the sides of your document. Your printer uses these marks to straighten and center your document, and to align multiple colors. All your hard work and great design ideas will go down the drain, if your job is printed out of register.

▶ **Color Bars** are used in production to be sure that ink coverage is running right— not too light and not too heavy. They appear at the top of a document.

▶ **Page Information** will give you the title of the document, the date and time printed, and separation color. Very handy stuff.

►MOVING TOWARD MASTERY

By now you should understand these color basics:

► In offset printing, jobs are either process or spot color jobs. In general, the more colors used, the more expensive the job.

► The color swatch should be created according to its final use. If its intent is for the web, use: RGB, if for print, use: CMYK or Spot.

► Since most monitors don't accurately display color, you should select color from a color swatch book, such as a Pantone® Color Selector.

► In traditional printing, each color uses a separate printing plate. If the job has three colors, there will be three printing plates. When you print

separations, the number of separations should equal the number of colors used in the document.

► Although Black is counted as a color, tints created from a solid color aren't considered additional colors. For instance, if you had a newsletter that used black and a 10%, 20%, and 50% tint of blue, it would still be a two-color newsletter.

► If you print and overlay two tints—process or spot color—a new color will result. A tint of yellow, printed over a tint of blue, will result in a shade of green. A tint of black printed over a tint of red will result in a much darker red. This concept is important for you to keep in mind, as we move on to mixed inks.

Other Print Dialog Box Options

► All pages in a document are printed, by default. You can also specify a page range, or choose to print odd or even pages. To print a single page, enter the page number in the Range field. Entering "**1, 4-7**" in the Range field would result in printing pages 1, 4, 5, 6, and 7. If you entered "**5-**", you would print page 5 through the end of the document. Entering "**-5**" would result in printing all pages from 1 through page 5.

► Under the Setup category you can scale the document by entering a percent in the Width or Height field. If **Constrain Proportions** is checked, your document will be scaled proportionately. Checking **Scale to Fit** will automatically resize your document to fit the paper size you have chosen.

► You may want documents created with facing pages to print two pages, side by side, on one sheet of paper. This is called printing a "spread," and you can print one spread per sheet. Select **Spreads** under the General category and then check the preview icon to determine if you need to change the orientation of your pages. If the document page size is too large, the spread won't fit on your paper size. In this case, you can reduce the spread to fit on your paper by selecting **Scale to Fit** under the Setup category.

► Any object on a document page can be specified as non-printing. First, select the object. Then go to **Window>Output>Attributes** and check **Nonprinting**. If desired, you can override this setting in the Print dialog box; in the General options, select Print Non-printing Objects.

► You can save a print summary for a specific job that records all the print settings. Go to the Summary category, select **Save Summary**, and name the file. A text file containing all the specifications for this job will be created. This is a helpful checklist for the next time you need to print a complex job.

Using Mixed Inks

When you are planning on using mixed inks, it's a good idea to check with your printer to identify any potential printing issues. With that said, let's begin using mixed inks. First, you will create a mixed ink swatch. Then, you will generate a mixed ink swatch group. Finally, you will use a mixed ink swatch group in creating a poster for the Midwest Quilters Convention. This project will utilize many of the effects introduced in Chapter 11, and will incorporate a two-color palette.

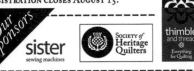

Midwest Quilters Convention

AUGUST 22–25, 2009

ROCHESTER CIVIC CENTER ❧ ROCHESTER, MINNESOTA

Four exciting days featuring exhibits, classes, exhibitors, and entertainment! Sigrid Lindholm, host of QTTV's *Quilt Corner*, is keynote speaker during Sunday evening's dinner and festivities.

New this year: hands-on learning in a 24-person sewing lab. Discounts on food, fabric, sewing machines, and books. Attendees enjoy free parking in the skyway ramp.

For more information and to register:
www.mqconvention.org

REGISTRATION CLOSES AUGUST 15.

CONVENTION HIGHLIGHTS

• **Color is my world.** Marilyn Flowers, *The Quilt Clinic*, Genesee, Wisconsin. Marilyn is known for her subtle color palette. After her hour class, you will choose your fabric with a new perspective.

• **Perfect patchwork? No problem.** Enjoy the sewing lab as you learn the fast, easy way to piece eight-pointed stars. Nancy Peterson of *Peterson Petals*, will be your lead instructor.

• **Texture in textiles.** Jane Bremmer, from *In Stitches*, Milwaukee, Wisconsin, and winner of the 2007 *MCA Best of Show Award* will demonstrate how batiks, geometrics, and solids can create the texture your quilt needs.

• **Applique simplified.** See why Quanto is the finest fusible webbing for your applique projects. Learn techniques from start to finish in our new sewing lab.

VISUAL |12–19|

This two-color project uses a mixed ink swatch group to create the illusion of many colors.

1. Create a new InDesign document using the default settings. Create two spot color swatches: **PANTONE solid coated 012 C** (yellow) and **PANTONE solid coated 2737 C** (blue).

2. Open the *Swatches* panel. From the menu options, choose *New Mixed Ink Swatch*.

3. Click the empty boxes to the left of the PANTONE Yellow 012 C and PANTONE 2736 C swatch names. A mixed ink icon 🔳 will appear. Enter the percentages of each color by typing in the percentage field, or by dragging the sliders. The new color appears in the upper left swatch box. Press Return. The mixed ink swatch now appears in the *Swatches* panel.

VISUAL | 12–20 |

The mixed ink icon appears to the left of the swatch name.

You can see how using mixed ink swatches can create the illusion of a third color—without the additional cost. In this case, we now have blue, yellow, and khaki colors to use in our two-color document. Think of the possibilities…you could spend a considerable amount of time creating mixed ink swatches—or you could let InDesign automate the system for you.

1. Choose *New Mixed Ink Group* from the *Swatches* panel menu.

VISUAL | 12–21 |

A swatch that has been created as a spot color will be displayed with a circle inside a square

Spot color indicator

2. Click the empty boxes to the left of PANTONE Yellow 012 C and PANTONE 2736 C. The mixed ink icon will appear. Carefully refer to Visual 12–22 as we move on with the steps. InDesign is going to automatically generate mixed ink group swatches from the yellow and blue spot colors in our document. In the *Initial* column, enter a percentage of each color. In Visual 12–22, a **20%** tint of **PANTONE Yellow 012 C** and a 20% tint of **PANTONE 2736 C** would be our first and second swatches. The *Repeat* column indicates how many separate swatches should be created. In this example, there would be the initial swatch, plus four more—for a total of five swatches of yellow, and five swatches of blue in increments of 20%. Click *Preview Swatches* to see how many swatches InDesign will create when you press Return. In this example, five tints of each color will be mixed, for a total of 25 swatches. Be realistic with the number of swatches you create—you probably don't need to generate 100 mixed ink swatches!

VISUAL |12–22|

Using a colors from a mixed ink group creates the illusion of many colors in a document.

Examine Visual 12–23. First, find the single mixed ink swatch, named "Mixed Ink 1." Then, locate the 25 new mixed ink swatches. Notice that all mixed ink swatches are indicated with a light yellow and blue teardrop shape. When you create a document using PANTONE Yellow 012 C and PANTONE 2736 C and use all the mixed ink swatches, you will only get two separations, because all the colors are tint mixes of the yellow and blue main colors.

In the next series of steps, you'll create a new mixed ink group from two spot colors and use your swatches to create the illustrations for the *Midwest Quilters Convention*. It is perfectly fine to choose different spot colors for your project, but remember that you should have one color dark enough for readable body copy.

VISUAL |12–23|

Mixed ink group swatches are identified in the Swatches panel by a teardrop displayed in the column to the right of the swatch name.

VISUAL |12–24 |

This mixed ink group has too many swatches that are too close in color. Try to achieve a full range of distinctly-colored mixed ink swatches.

1. Open *12 Quilt Block Template* from the *12 Artwork and Resources* folder, on the CD, accompanying this text. Open the *Swatches* panel and create two spot colors for use on coated paper: **PANTONE Violet C** and **PANTONE Rubine Red C**. Delete all other colors from the *Swatches* panel, except for Rubine Red C and Violet C.

2. Create a mixed ink group, keeping the final number of swatches to 36 or less. Visual 12–24 shows the importance of using the *Preview Swatches* button while creating mixed ink groups. Swatches 21–24 are so close in color that it would be easy to select the wrong color during production. Try to create a palette with a full-range of distinct color blends.

3. Fill the center square with the color of your choice. Then, fill all the other triangles in a symmetrical manner. A good technique is to add one fill and then use the *Eyedropper* tool to transfer the fill to other shapes (Visual 12–25). As you are working on your block, you can easily revise your color scheme if you find a combination that would be more effective. When you are satisfied with your quilt block, save it as **Quilt Block 1**.

4. With Quilt Block 1 still open, do a *Save As* and name the file **Quilt Block 2**. Revise the color scheme to make a block with a totally different color balance or pattern. When you are finished, save the block.

5. Do a *Save As* and name the new file **Quilt Block 3**. Again, revise the color scheme and save the finished block. Finally, save Quilt Block 3 as **Quilt Block 4** and revise the colors. Save the finished result.

You now have four different quilt squares that will be the "building blocks" (my apologies) for the *Midwest Quilters Convention* project at the end of this chapter.

Summary

As this chapter has demonstrated, getting images and type on your document is just the tip of the iceberg, in terms of production. There are many ways designers can innocently flub up a document—and defining color incorrectly, is one of them. Spend some extra time experimenting with the Swatches panel, until you are comfortable with all of its functions.

When you send a document out to the printer, ask someone with more experience to look it over. Finding and fixing errors before they go to prepress is a good way to establish and maintain a good reputation, as a designer.

In the next chapter, you will learn about InDesign's powerful Links and Preflight operations, the difference between vector and bitmap artwork, dealing with resolution issues, and the Separations and Overprint Preview features. This is all important information, critical for you to understand. Take your time and carefully read the chapter.

▶ IN REVIEW

1. Explain the difference between RGB and CMYK color. What does it mean that one of them is additive and one is subtractive?

2. When would you use spot color? When would you use process color? When might you use both?

3. What is the difference between the Color panel and the Swatches panel and why should you prefer to use one instead of the other?

4. Why is it best to select standard Pantone or Trumatch colors from a swatch book rather than create your own?

5. True or false: When you're finished with a project, a good way to check how many colors you actually have in your document is to print color separations.

6. When might you make manual crop marks, rather than select the Crop Marks option in the Print dialog box?

7. What is the process for suppressing the printing of an individual object on a page?

8. If "-19" was typed in the Range field of the Print dialog box, what would happen during printing?

9. What is a "spread" and how is a spread printed?

10. How is a spot color identified in the Swatches panel? A mixed ink?

Keyboard Shortcut

 F5

 F5

Swatches Panel

Keyboard Shortcut

 F6

 F6

Color Panel

► CHAPTER 12 PROJECTS

Photography © 2006 Pete Rydberg

You have already created components for the Midwest Quilters Convention. It looks simple on the surface, but this project will exercise your problem-solving skills by using many techniques introduced in the past few chapters. The second project, Voyage Galápagos is an 8-page booklet that uses multiple master pages, nested styles, and many InDesign features found in the Effects panel, including transparency, drop shadow, and blending modes. This is a two-phase project that you will finish after Chapter 13.

Never discourage
anyone who continually
makes progress,
no matter how slow.

℞ Plato

Production Essentials

13

objectives

▶ *Differentiate between continuous tone (bitmap) and vector artwork*

▶ *Use the Links panel*

▶ *Adjust image resolution for printing*

▶ *Find and replace fonts*

▶ *Use Separations and Overprint Preview operations*

▶ *Perform document preflight and package operations*

introduction

Some ideas sound good in theory—self-generating electricity, cars that run without an external fuel source, gears that keep turning on their own momentum. But not every great idea works out in reality.

That's what can happen to a great design idea, too. You spend a lot of time and creative energy on a document—it looks beautiful on your monitor and when printed on your desktop color printer. So, you take it to your commercial printing company and order 5,000 printed pieces. But when you pick up your job, you get a bill for hundreds of dollars more than you were quoted. You're told that the additional charges are for something called "prepress." They explain that it was necessary to take your electronic file—the one you thought was finished—and spend additional time getting it ready to print properly. This chapter will explain the basic production concepts you need to create documents that run smoothly, and avoid unexpected budget overruns.

An Introduction to Image Management

A typical InDesign document includes text and images. The previous chapters have focused primarily on text: how to choose appropriate typefaces, format paragraphs, use hyphens and dashes, create styles, and so on. This chapter will focus on working with images. This chapter covers only the basic information required for documents destined for commercial print shops. For more detailed information on each topic, consult InDesign's Help menu.

Input: Preparing Image Files for Use in InDesign

Let's say you're creating a fund-raising brochure for a museum's building project. The copy has been written, and you have gathered the artwork that will be featured in the piece, including:

- ▶ *An old, glossy color photograph of the museum's founder;*
- ▶ *An architect's full-color marker rendering of the proposed addition to the museum;*
- ▶ *A black and white printout of the new floor plan;*
- ▶ *A file containing a digital photograph of the current board of directors; and*
- ▶ *The museum logo, created in Adobe Illustrator®.*

Each of these images have different production considerations. But they also have two things in common: input and output. You need to prepare them correctly during the input stage, and use appropriate production techniques, so that they output correctly and produce a quality printed piece.

Dots, Pixels and Lines per inch

Before we begin, you need to know how commercial printing presses reproduce full-color paintings, charcoal drawings, photographs, or other pieces of artwork that artists and photographers create. A printing press can't blend a myriad of colors; it has only two options—either it puts a particular color ink, at a specific location on the paper, or it doesn't. What's the secret? With a magnifying glass, take a look at any color or black and white picture, in a newspaper or magazine, and you will see that it is composed of millions of tiny dots. Whether the dots are all black or various colors, the varying sizes and arrangement visually blend together and create the illusion of color and shading. The graphics industry uses many acronyms when talking about dots (in some cases, they are squares). The most important to know are: *dots per inch (dpi)*, *pixels per inch (ppi)*, and *lines per inch (lpi)*. These terms define the *resolution* of desktop printers or scanners, digital image files and commercial printing presses. Resolution has a direct bearing on the capabilities of a device, or the quality of an image. Generally, the higher the resolution, the crisper the image.

▶ *production tip*
dpi: Dots per inch
ppi: Pixels per inch
lpi: Lines per inch

Continuous Tone Artwork

Let's begin with the color photo of the museum's founder. Traditional photographs, taken with a film camera and printed on photographic paper, fall into the artwork classification known as *continuous tone*. Any artwork that contains a full-range of color or tonal values—such as paintings, black and white photographs, or pastel drawings—falls into this category. A scanner is used to digitize continuous tone artwork, so that it can be placed into an InDesign document. This process converts the colors and tones of the artwork into a specified number of *dots per inch* (**dpi**) that you determine when you set up the scan. However, the resolution of the resulting image file is described in *pixels per inch* (**ppi**). (When talking about scanners and scanned images, dpi and ppi are often used interchangeably.) Understanding how resolution affects the quality of the digital image and its file size, is critical to creating efficient and problem-free InDesign documents.

If the photo is scanned at a *low resolution*, there will be fewer pixels per square inch, and some of the detail in the photo will be lost. A photo scanned at *high resolution* will retain much more detail, because there will be more pixels to record more information per square inch. You will need to refer to your scanner's manual to find out how to adjust the scanning resolution. Generally, a photograph scanned at 300 dpi is sufficient for most print production needs. Once the scan of the old photograph is placed into the InDesign document, it can be scaled and cropped.

Next, let's take a look at the architect's marker rendering of the proposed addition. This illustration is also considered continuous tone artwork. And just like the color photograph, this illustration will be converted to pixels in the scanning process. Again, a scanning resolution of 300 is sufficient.

► *production tip*

Continuous tone artwork needs to be converted to dots by scanning, before it can be printed.

VISUAL | 13–1 |

Continuous tone artwork (left) includes a full-range of tonal values. Line art (right) consists of straight and curved lines without variations in shade.

Line Art

The black and white printout of the floor plan falls into a different artwork classification called *line art*. Line art does not contain any tonal values—the image is comprised of pure black or white elements. A pen and ink or scratch board drawing is line art, so is pure black type printed on a laser printer. When this type of artwork is

► *production tip*

Line art doesn't contain any tonal values. It needs to be scanned as line art before it is printed.

scanned, you will select "line art" in the scanner setup controls. Your scanner's manual will be able to walk you through the process. Since there are no tonal variations in the floor plan art, each pixel will be either a solid black or solid white square. If we choose a scanner resolution of 600 pixels per square inch, the pixels will be very small, and will capture fine details in the floor plan. This may seem fine, but the general rule of thumb is to capture line art at the resolution of the final print device. While 600 dpi is customary for today's laser or inkjet printers, the digital presses and imagesetters found in many commercial printers can print at 1200, 2400 and higher dpi. If possible, always consult with your printer for the best scanning recommendations.

Finally, we have the digital photo of the board of directors. A digital photograph has already been converted to pixels. This is where the resolution of the digital camera comes into play. The higher the resolution setting of the camera, the more pixels—which then capture more detail in the photo. There is little you can do to improve the overall quality of a digital image taken with a low resolution camera, because the camera did not capture enough pixels to record the nuances of the photo in the first place.

Resolution Independent and Resolution Dependent Artwork

We have one more piece of artwork to discuss before we begin our museum fund-raising piece—the museum logo. This logo was created in Adobe Illustrator®, one of the members in the Creative Suite. Adobe Illustrator is a drawing program that uses mathematical equations to create precise, curved and straight paths that extend from point to point. This type of digital artwork is vector-based artwork. The paths can be edited by repositioning the points. As the points are rearranged, the mathematical data is recalculated, and the path is updated. This type of digital artwork is resolution independent, which means that the image quality is not adversely affected, regardless of how the artwork is scaled. Native Illustrator files (with the file extension .ai) can be placed directly into InDesign.

VISUAL | 13–2 |

The "dots" that make up digital photos, are picture elements, or pixels. These give the impression of continuous tones. The photo on the right has been enlarged to show the pixels.

Bitmap (Raster) Images

The other images in our museum piece were not created by mathematical formulas, so instead of being vector-based artwork, they are called *bitmap* or *raster* images. During the scanning or digital photography process, the images were converted to *pixels*, which are bits of data that are mapped to a grid of rows and columns. When these pixels are small enough, they create the illusion of a continuous tone image. In contrast to vector images (which are resolution independent), images composed of pixels are said to be *resolution dependent*. What this means is the size of the individual pixels will get larger or smaller as the image is scaled in InDesign. Unfortunately, the quality of bitmap images may deteriorate. As shown in Visual 13–2, greatly enlarging a bitmap image will make its individual pixels visible to the human eye.

The term *resolution* is used to describe the number of pixels in each square inch of the image. The images for the museum project, scanned at a resolution of 300 pixels per inch (ppi), resulted in a resolution of 90,000 incredibly tiny pixels, per square inch (300 pixels wide by 300 pixels high). The architectural floor plan was scanned at 600 ppi, resulting in 360,000 data-filled pixels, in each square inch! Let's compare that to a piece of line art with a resolution of 72 ppi. With only 5,184 total pixels per square inch (72 × 72 = 5184), the physical size of each individual pixel would be much larger than the 360,000 microscopic pixels, per square inch, in the floor plan scan. The larger pixel size would result in a coarser, less-detailed image when printed. So when it comes to bitmap images, fewer or larger pixels, per inch = less data = less detail. More tiny pixels, per square inch = more data = more detail. So, why not input everything at 1200 ppi? Because the file sizes would be enormous and your files would be difficult to output—which brings us to the next topic.

From Input to Output: Using Images in InDesign

Quality designs, like the museum brochure, start with careful planning. Usually a detailed layout is worked out that determines how an image will be used, such as where, how large, and what portion of it will be used in the piece. If all these details are known before the artwork is converted to bitmap images, it will be easy to create optimal scans. For example, the entire 8×10 photo of the founder need not be scanned, if only his head and shoulders will be used. Perhaps a portion of the architect's marker rendering will need to be enlarged considerably. Producing the most efficient bitmap image files means setting up the scanner to: *1) the correct dpi setting for the final printing device, 2) capture only the portions needed and 3) scale them to final size needed in the document.* But during the production process, when layouts and copy changes often occur, the size and cropping of images need to be changed—sometimes drastically. What affect will this have on your various images?

> ▶ *production tip*
> Bitmap images are resolution dependent, which means the quality of the image may change as the image is scaled.

> ▶ *production tip*
> Resolution describes the number of pixels in each square inch of an image.

For resolution independent, vector artwork—like the museum's logo—you don't need to worry about scaling and its effects on image quality. These types of images

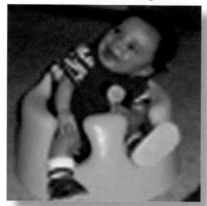

will print beautifully at almost any size. However, scaling is a major concern when using pixel-based, resolution dependent images. In Visual 13–3, the photo is a low-resolution, 72 ppi image, which has also been scaled larger in InDesign. Not only does this low-resolution image start out with larger pixels and less data, as the image size increased, the size of each pixel has also increased. The result is a blurry photo with huge pixels, and very little detail.

In contrast, Visual 13–4 shows a high-resolution, 300 ppi photo, used at its actual size in the InDesign document. The pixels remain imperceptible, and the detail in the image is crisp, right down to the drool on the knuckles. The keys to having bitmap images print correctly are:

▶ *Begin with the correct resolution; and*

▶ *Use images at 100% in the InDesign document.*

Next, you'll learn how the Links panel, in partnership with Adobe Photoshop®, can optimize bitmap images, so that they are the ideal size and resolution for your InDesign document.

The Links Panel

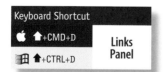

When you place an image in InDesign, it creates and then maintains a *link* to the original source file. The Links panel displays information about all the files linked to your document. The Links panel is accessed by pressing **Shift+Command+D** (Mac) or **Shift+Control+D** (Windows). You can also access the Links panel by going to **Window>Links**. When you choose Panel Options from the Links panel menu, you can customize the information that will be displayed in the Links panel. The numbers in Visual 13–5, identify important information that can be displayed in the Links panel. Each numbered item is explained on the next few pages. If your Links panel does not look the same, follow the instructions at the end of the section to customize it.

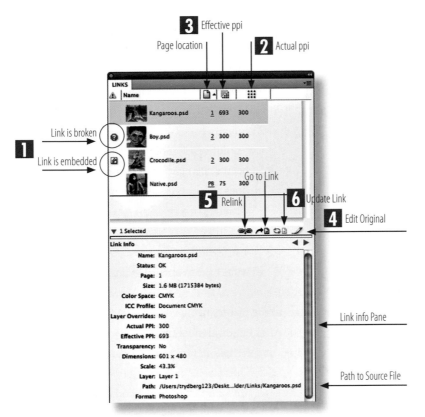

VISUAL |13–5|

The Links panel shows information that is critical for successfully using images in your project. It is important to spend some time learning the features of this powerful panel.

1 **Embedded and Linked images.** When an image is placed into InDesign, the graphic can either be *linked* or *embedded*. By default, InDesign creates linked graphics. This means that data from the graphic file is not brought into the document—instead, InDesign simply creates a link to the image's original source file. Later, during printing, it retrieves the data needed to generate the image. InDesign continually monitors all linked source files to determine if they have been modified or moved. If you place an image from a CD and then remove the CD, the link is broken because InDesign can't follow the path to the original image file. Similarly, if you place images that were located in a specific folder and later change the location or name of the folder, the links to all those source files are broken. If the link to an image is broken, at print time, InDesign warns you. If you cannot fix the link, it will print the low-res image displayed on your monitor. This poor quality image is not what you want when printed on a high quality commercial press. For this reason, all links must be in place before printing your project. When you take a project to the printer, you must include all graphics and font files. (Fortunately, InDesign has a feature that will "package" your project correctly, notifying you of any problems. This process will be covered later in this chapter.)

When you embed an image, the data from the image file becomes part of the InDesign file and is displayed with a special icon in the Status column of the

Links panel, as shown in callout #1 in Visual 13–5. Your InDesign file will be much larger with embedded images, but you won't need to worry about broken links when you take your project to the printer. However, most printers prefer that graphics files not be embedded in InDesign documents. This is a production issue you should discuss with your printer before production begins!

2 Actual ppi. Visual 13–5 shows the Actual ppi column turned on to display in the upper portion of the Links panel. When you scan down the far right column, you can quickly see the resolution at which each image was scanned. Each image has an Actual ppi resolution of 300. If scaled to 100%, these images would be ideal for printing in full-color on printing press.

3 Effective ppi. As you click on each link in the upper portion of the Links panel, the Link Info pane at the bottom, will display image-specific data, including the image's scale percentage and the Effective ppi. Visual 13–5 also shows the Effective ppi column turned on to display in the upper part of the Links panel.

Unlike the numbers in the Actual ppi column, the numbers in the Effective ppi column are not all the same. Look at the middle two links, *Boy.psd* and *Crocodile. psd.* The Effective and Actual ppi for both these links are 300, because both images are used at 100% in the InDesign document. This is the ideal scenario. Now, look at the Link Info pane area for *Kangaroos.psd* (Visual 13–5). Notice that the Scale category shows 43.3%. Because the image has been reduced, the pixels were squeezed together to fit into a much smaller space. Although we began with an Actual resolution of 300 ppi, the Effective resolution has now increased to 693 ppi, more than twice the ideal of 300 ppi. Now, look at the link for the *Native.psd* image. Even though the Actual ppi is 300, the Effective ppi is 75—much less than the ideal resolution. Why? Because the image was scaled to 400% in the document. So, the Effective ppi was reduced by scaling the image larger. Remember, when the Effective ppi is lower than the ideal resolution, you will begin to have problems with image quality. When working on documents intended for high quality, commercial printing, you want to keep the Effective ppi at the ideal, 300 ppi resolution. You'll learn how to do that next.

4 **Edit Original**. Often, after placing and scaling images in InDesign, the Effective ppi is too high, or too low. In the following exercise, you will learn how to use Adobe Photoshop® in conjunction with InDesign to remedy this situation. (If you don't have Photoshop, study the visuals in the following steps.)

1. From the *13 Artwork and Resources* folder on the accompanying CD, open the file *13 Resolution. indd*. inside the *13 Resolution* folder. As the file opens, you will see this warning message. Since you will use the Links panel to locate missing links, you can choose *Don't Fix*.

2. Open the Links panel. Click on *Kangaroos.psd*, and read the Link Info underneath. Notice that the *Kangaroos. psd* link has been scaled down to 43.3%, creating an Effective ppi of 693, which is unnecessarily too high. In the lower right corner of the Links panel, click the *Edit Original* icon (Visual 13–6).

VISUAL | 13–6 |

Click the pencil icon in the lower right corner to edit an image.

3. Adobe Photoshop should launch, opening the *Kangaroos.psd* source file. When it opens, go to the menu and select *Image>Image Size*. At the bottom of the window, check *Resample Image*. In the Document Size section, Choose *Percent,* next to the Width and Height fields. Enter **43.3** in the Width field, and the same value should automatically transfer to the Height field (Visual 13–7). Click OK. When you *resample* an image, you actually change the number of pixels in it. In this case, there were too many pixels per inch, so we had Photoshop eliminate the extra data.

VISUAL | 13–7 |

Use Photoshop to scale and resample images.

4. Save the Photoshop file. Now look at the Links panel, and you will notice that the Effective and Actual ppi are both 300. InDesign automatically updated the link with the revisions you made in Photoshop. (Visual 13–8).

5. Select the *Native.psd* file in the Links panel. Notice that a *PB* appears in the Page column of the Links panel. PB means that the image is on the pasteboard, not on the document (Visual 13–9). If the document had many pages, it might be hard to find exactly where the image was located; but if you look in the Link Info section, the Page category shows PB:1. This means the image is on the pasteboard of page 1.

This link has a problem—an Effective ppi of 75. If you look at the Link Info you will see that the image has been scaled to 400%. Each pixel has increased in size to fill the space. Choose Edit Original and the Photoshop file will open. Go to the menu and select Image>Image Size. In the Pixel Dimension section of the window, notice that there are 557 pixels in the width, and 565 in the height. Now, with Resample Image checked, change the Document Size Width and Height fields to 400%. Before you click OK, notice how resampling has greatly increased the values in the Pixel Dimensions Width and Height fields of Photoshop's Image Size window. Save the Photoshop file, but don't close your document—we need it for the next few techniques!

The Links panel

5 **Relink Image**. A question mark inside a red circle 🛑❓ on the Links panel means that the link pathway is broken. This scenario happens frequently—somehow, the original file for an image is not where it is supposed to be. (Later in this chapter, you will learn about the Package function that takes care of this issue.) Broken links happen anytime the pathway to the original graphic file has been changed, after the link was initially established in InDesign. If you are placing images from the CD included with this book, and then remove the CD, you will receive a missing link message when you attempt to print the document. Suppose you had several images on your desktop that you placed into an InDesign document. After saving the document, you decide to organize things by moving all the image files into a folder labeled with the job name. The next time you open the document, every link will be displayed with a broken link icon because the files are not in their original location and InDesign can't reestablish the link. Fortunately, the Links panel makes it easy to relink the image to the new location. To reestablish a single link, simply select the filename with the missing link icon and click the Relink icon on the bottom of the Links panel. When the dialog box opens, locate the graphics file and select it. When you have many missing links, you can Option (Mac) or Alt (Windows) + click the Relink icon to relink multiple image files.

6. Click on the **Boy.psd** file name in the Links panel. Click the **Relink** icon below the Links panel. Navigate to the **13 Artwork and Resources** folder on the accompanying CD. Select the **Boy2.psd**, located inside the folder. Look in the Links panel and you will see that the link is now intact. Save the document.

6 **Update Link.** A yellow triangle ⚠ means that the original image file has been changed since it was placed in the document. When a job is sent out to the printer, the Status column shouldn't display any links that need updating, or that are missing. In this last exercise, you'll update a link, so that all the links are ready to go to the printer.

7.   Place *13 InDesign Sample File.indd* into your open document. The file is found in the *13 Resolution* folder. Save the exercise. Now, use InDesign to open and modify the *13 InDesign Sample File .indd*. Change the color of the type to Magenta and save and close the document. Since an attribute of the link has been changed since it was placed in the document, a yellow triangle appears in the status column. Click the Update Link icon at the bottom of the Links panel to update to the most current file. (Visual 13–10).

A yellow triangle means the original file has changed since it has been placed in the document.

The Links panel menu allows you to embed and unembed graphics files.

The Links panel menu offers many options. In those rare instances when you want to embed an image file, you choose Embed Link from the panel menu. When a link is embedded, the link data becomes part of your InDesign document.

To customize the information you would like to have displayed in the upper and lower halves of the Links panel, open the panel menu and choose Panel Options. Visual 13–12A shows the Panel Options modified to display Color Space and Scale. In Visual 13–12B, Color Space and Scale are now displayed in the upper half of the Links panel. This is a convenient, timesaving feature, because you can view important production information for all your links, instead of selecting each link and reading its link information in the lower half of the Links panel.

VISUAL |13–12|

The Panel Options dialog box allows you to choose the information that is displayed in the upper and lower halves of the panel. In this example, panel options have been modified to display the color space and scale in the upper half.

Package the Document for Printing Output

When your document is ready to go to press, you need to collect all the electronic elements of your file—all fonts and graphics—and bundle them up for transporting to your service bureau or printer. Fortunately, InDesign makes this process quick and painless with the Package function. Choose File>Package to access the Package dialog box. The Summary page appears first, telling you how many fonts, colors, and graphics are included, and other document information. If an element is missing or needs your attention, there will be a yellow caution icon in front of it. Visual 13–13 shows a problem with Links and Images. Seven images in the document use RGB color space. Images composed of Red, Blue and Green need to be converted to CMYK in Photoshop, before going to press.

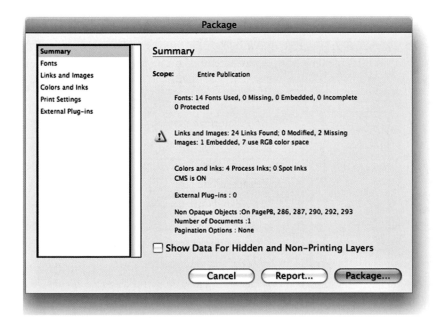

VISUAL |13–13|

The yellow warning triangle shows that there are problems in the Links and Images portion of the document.

If there is a caution icon next to the Fonts summary paragraph, click on the Fonts category in the list on the left. The Fonts page lists the names of all fonts used in the document and their status will be displayed. If a font is marked as Incomplete, it means that although the font shows on the screen, the font file required for printing is missing. You will need to reinstall the font. If a font is listed as Missing, it means the font used in the document is not installed on your computer, and you will need to purchase it. These types of font problems can occur when opening files created on other computers. Don't simply replace the font with another font of the same name, because fonts purchased from different vendors will have differences in font design, letter shape, and spacing. Visual 13–14 shows a sample of Garamond from two different digital type manufacturers. The point sizes and weights of each sample are identical. But, look at the differences in the overall color, letter width, the design of the capital G's and the shape of the bowls. Substituting a typeface with the same name, but from different manufacturers is generally not a perfect match, and will usually result in the copy reflowing, which can be disastrous!

VISUAL | 13–14 |

Although typefaces from different manufacturers share the same name, their characteristics may be quite different.

Garamond Sample from Adobe
Garamond Sample from Bitstream

If you are unable to locate the correct typeface, you may need to replace it throughout the document. You can replace fonts in the Package dialog box by selecting the **Find Font** button. In the upper half of the Find Font dialog, select the font you want to replace. Then choose the replacement font in the lower half. You can then choose to replace the fonts one occurrence at a time, or all at once. (Font replacement can also be performed by selecting **Type>Find Font.**) Whenever you replace fonts, you need to proof your document again, to make sure none of the text has shifted position.

VISUAL | 13–15 |

Use the Find Font operation to replace fonts in a document. Resolve any font issues in a document so that the Package will be complete and correct.

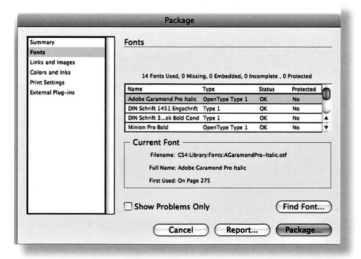

Like the Links panel, the Package feature also provides the status of Links and Images. If the original file has been moved since the file was created, InDesign needs help finding the new path to the image. Click on the missing image and click Relink. InDesign will lead you through the navigation necessary to find the source file. Again, if the original graphic is not on your computer, you will have to find the CD it came from and pop it into your machine. The Package feature summary won't alert you of any RGB files that are contained in Illustrator or PDF files. Those files will need to be opened in the original application and changed accordingly.

When you have remedied any problems, select the Package, button, and InDesign will collect all the fonts and images used to build the document. You will be asked to save the document and will have the opportunity to provide printing instructions (Visual 13–16). Next, all the elements required to print your job are saved in one, organized folder, that you can send to your printer.

Printing Instructions

Filename:	Gibraltar Metropolitan Bank
Contact:	David Espurvoa
Company:	ABC Advertising
Address:	12225 Capitol Drive
	Smith
	Washington 57897
Phone:	123 334 5678 Fax:
Email:	despurvoa@aol.com
Instructions:	Print 5000, shrink wrap in groups of 100
	Ship to Gibraltar Metro Bank, 2202 Capitol Drive, Smith, WA
	Send bill to David Bate, Gibraltar Metro Bank

Continue   Reset

VISUAL |13–16|

Completing the Printing Instructions form during the Package operation provides easy access to project information your printer may need.

The project's done, you've packaged it, and it is all ready to go to the printer. But wait—you just realized that you forgot to check spelling one final time. Since your document is still open, you run spell check and find three spelling errors that would have appeared in the final version. Whew! That was close. You save your document, feeling relieved that you remembered this crucial production step. But guess what—you haven't fixed the spelling on the InDesign document that's packaged and ready to go to the printer! When you package a project, the components that go into the folder—the InDesign file, links, and fonts— are actually duplicates. Once the packaging operation has been completed, any changes you make to the original working document requires you to either repackage the entire job, or replace the InDesign document in the packaged folder with your revised version. This scenario is usually what has happened when my students say, *"I can't believe there are still spelling errors! I know I ran spell check and caught those mistakes before I turned in that project!"*

▶MOVING TOWARD MASTERY

James Wamser, Senior Training Specialist, Sells Printing Company, has over 18 years experience in the graphic arts industry. James provides training and technical support for Sells' customers, as well as its prepress department. James has been working with Adobe InDesign prior to the release of version 1.0, and is an InDesign instructor at Waukesha County Technical College.

WAMSER'S ESSENTIAL PREPRESS TIPS

InDesign CS5 offers powerful tools for the creative professional as well as the prepress specialist. The following tips, will help you identify and prevent potential problems, when preparing your files for commercial printing.

▶ **Preflighting** is a process that examines a file for potential printing problems. This process will look at many issues including: color use, resolution, and font issues. Every printer has unique printing specifications. These requirements are called **preflight profiles.** You can create preflight profiles yourself, or better yet, ask your commercial printer to provide them for you. The image below shows the Preflight profile that Sells Printing Company in New Berlin, Wisconsin, provides to customers.

When enabled, CS5 provides a continual preflight status update in the bottom left corner of the document window.

The preflight function checks for numerous production issues, and notifies you of problems including any low resolution images, bleed issues and live area concerns (meaning the images or type are too close to the trim edge). If an error appears, open the Preflight panel to identify and remedy the situation. Sending out errorless files saves time and money, and keeps production on schedule.

▶ **Rich Black** is a defined color used in full-color printing and is composed of 60% Cyan, 40% Magenta, 20% Yellow, and 100% Black. The advantage of creating and using a rich black swatch is that the final print will show a black that is more **opaque.** However, rich black is a different color than Process Black. When you are using InDesign, the application preference is set to display all blacks as rich black. You should change this application preference so that you can see where Process Black and rich black are used in your document. Choose **Display All Blacks Accurately** in Preferences.

► MOVING TOWARD MASTERY

► **The Separations Preview Panel** is one I use all the time. (Window>Output>Separations Preview). This panel serves several purposes: It allows you to see all the inks used in a document (CMYK + spot inks). It also shows you the percentages of inks used in images and type. This is useful when verifying that a large solid black area contains rich black (CMYK).

In Chapter 12, you learned how to print separations to verify the number of colors in your document. Using Separations Preview, verify the individual colors used in your document by clicking the eye next to each color swatch.

► **Find Font.** Fonts have a history of causing reflow and output issues. (That's one of the reasons why so many people have embraced the PDF workflow.) Anytime you see text highlighted with pink in your document, it means the required font is missing on your computer. The Find Font dialog box automatically pops up before printing to alert you

of any problems. This dialog box will tell you how many fonts are used, notify you of any missing fonts, and give you the opportunity to replace fonts as necessary. Please be aware that you can access Find Font at any time by going to Type>Find Font.

► **Exporting PDFs.** PDF is an acronym for Portable Document Format, and was developed by Adobe Systems in 1993. PDF files can be opened and printed by Adobe Acrobat. In InDesign, you can export a file to a PDF, and it will retain its overall layout, fonts, and hyperlinks.

PDF files, when prepared correctly, streamline the printing process while providing more consistent and reliable results. They eliminate delays due to missing components such as fonts, images and graphics. Using PDF files in printing is referred to as PDF workflow. Printers who use the PDF workflow have individual specifications for how a PDF file should be prepared. It is important to communicate with your printer to create a PDF Preset that will contain the specifications required for the job. Once you create the settings, they are saved for future use, and you can export them, eliminating the need to recreate them on each computer. Our Sells Printing preset is shown below.

To create a PDF Preset, choose **Adobe PDF Presets> Define** from the File menu. Or, you can use one of the default PDF presets. For instance, if you are e-mailing a PDF of an InDesign document to show a concept to a client, you should select Smallest File

►MOVING TOWARD MASTERY

Size. Notice the three PDF/X presets in the list. The PDF/X presets are standards created to eliminate many common output issues. PDF/X-4 is the newest

Define...

[High Quality Print]...
[PDF/X-1a:2001]...
[PDF/X-3:2002]...
[PDF/X-4:2008]...
[Press Quality]...
[Smallest File Size]...

standard. As shown below, you can begin with the basic settings in any of these standards and then customize it for your printer's specific needs. You can see why it is so important to work closely with your printer when selecting or creating PDF presets.

When I create PDF presets, I don't rely on the document bleed settings in the InDesign document; I create a bleed in the preset just in case the person who set up the InDesign document did not include them. This leads to the next prepress tip...

This is an example of a full-bleed document because color extends to all four edges. Add a bleed on all four sides!

► **Build Bleeds.** *As you know, a bleed is any image or object that extends to the edge of a page. During the printing process, the document is printed on oversized paper, with the bleed images extending beyond the trim size. After the ink has dried, the project is cut down to size, leaving crisp images that run out to the edge. When creating a new document or document preset, you need to enter a bleed amount of 0.125" (⅛") on each side with a bleed. This will create guides indicating where the bleed should extend. This area is outside the final size of the document. Each page element that bleeds must extend out to the bleed guide. Without bleed guides, InDesign won't recognize any part of an image that extends beyond the document's trim edge.*

*You can add a bleed to your document at any time during production. Go to **File>Document Setup** and enter **0.125"** on each edge with a bleed.*

► MOVING TOWARD MASTERY

► Use Overprint Preview. *There are many ways colors interact with each other in a document. First, they can be printed next to each other. When colors are printed right next to each other, the press operator is going to make sure the colors are exactly aligned. When they are, the job is **in register**. When the colors are a hairline distance apart, the job is said to have **tight register**. Four-color process printing, with each separate plate composed of a series of dots, has extremely tight register.*

*Another way colors interact is to have one color **knock out** the other. This means that the top object cuts away any color beneath it. In Example A, below, the yellow circle has been placed on top of the blue box. Example B shows how the images would actually be printed. The yellow circle has been pulled aside to show that the blue area underneath is gone. This is a simulation of how a knock out works. By default, all colors except black knock out the colors underneath.*

*Colors can also **overprint** each other. When colors overprint, the ink goes on top of the color below, but does not knock it out. By default, black always overprints other colors. Then, how do you create an area of overlapping colors? The Attributes panel.*

You were introduced to the Attributes panel in Chapter 12, and its capability to apply Nonprinting to image or text, preventing the object from being printed. In the Attributes panel you can set an object's fill or stroke color to overprint, rather

than using the default knockout setting. The picture above shows that the circle has now been assigned "Overprint Fill" on the Attributes panel.

You know that the area where the colors intersect should look be a different color. But you can't really tell how it will look...or can you? Overprint Preview is a great feature found under the View menu. As shown below, you will see just how the colors will look when printed.

The ability to see how an image or object will overprint right on screen is a huge time saver and can help you identify any problems before a single proof is made. By the way, when you open the Separations Preview panel and select Separations in the View menu, Overprint Preview is automatically enabled.

One last word—each print shop has its own set of technical specifications. Prepress managers are available to answer your questions. Make use of their expertise during your production process!

Summary

The biggest thing you have probably learned from this chapter is that there is much more to document preparation than simply dropping in text and images!

The chapter began with input issues, describing the production considerations for a variety of artwork. You know the difference between continuous tone, and line artwork. You know that raster or bitmap images are composed of picture elements, called pixels, and are resolution dependent. Vector images are created by mathematical formulas, and are resolution independent. You know that image resolution describes how many pixels are contained in an image. And you know that the more pixels in the image, the more detail will be recorded. Finally, since printing presses cannot do shading, continuous tone artwork must be converted to a series of dots that will create the illusion of shading.

On the output side, we discussed the difference between Actual and Effective ppi. Although you may have started with a bitmap image with appropriate Actual resolution, the Effective output resolution is changed by scaling, during the production process. You used Photoshop to resample and resize raster images to achieve ideal Effective ppi.

InDesign's powerful Package operation was discussed, and you saw first-hand, that it can be disastrous to make last-minute font substitutions—even if the replacement font has the same name as the original!

There's a lot to know about production and we've just scratched the surface. As a new designer, you will have fewer errors if you follow these production steps:

1. *Format document size, margins, and columns.*
2. *Add text insets and align strokes if necessary.*
3. *Place and size graphics. Specify spot or CMYK color.*
4. *Do the typing or place all the text.*
5. *Add paragraph formatting.*
6. *Add character formatting and glyphs.*
7. *Proof carefully and print. Proof again.*
8. *Make a folded or trimmed mock-up, if necessary.*
9. *Check the images in the Links panel.*
10. *Package the document.*

Bottom line: when in doubt, ask someone with more experience!

▶ IN REVIEW

1. What is the difference between continuous tone art and line art?

2. What is a bitmap image?

3. What is a vector image?

4. What does image resolution refer to?

5. What is a pixel?

6. Why is it dangerous to substitute fonts in a document—even if their names are identical?

7. How does scaling affect a resolution dependent image?

8. You have pulled a logo from the web to use as a placeholder image. The image has been scaled to 450%. Explain why the image quality is poor at this scale.

9. What does a yellow triangle in the Links panel mean?

10. What does a red circle with a question mark in the Links panel indicate?

11. What is the difference between actual and effective ppi?

12. An 300 ppi image is being used at 227% in your InDesign document. Describe the steps you would take, when editing the image to keep the resolution at 300 ppi, while changing the scale to 227%.

Keyboard Shortcut

⌘ ⇧+CMD+D   **Links Panel**

⊞ ⇧+CTRL+D

► CHAPTER 13 PROJECTS

The final project continues! You will create and apply table styles and place an InDesign document. Take the time to create a booklet and trim the assembled project for a nice addition to your portfolio.

Front cover

Page 2

Page 3

photos © 2006 Pete Rydberg

►CHAPTER 13 PROJECTS

Page 4

Page 5

Page 6

Page 7

When the power of **love**
overcomes
the love of power
the world will know peace.

℞ Jimi Hendrix

| Basic Graphic Elements |

14

objectives

▶ *Review basic drawing tools*

▶ *Master the mighty Pen tool*

▶ *Create and modify open, closed, and compound paths*

▶ *Integrate drawn elements with text*

introduction

Twenty years ago if you wanted to buy a comfortable family car, you more than likely bought a four-door sedan. If you wanted to haul cargo, you bought a pickup truck or full-size van. Both did a good job for their particular purposes.

Then someone asked the perfect question: Why not combine the two? And the minivan was born! It was the perfect way for the whole family to go to Grandma's, and just the right vehicle for picking up a few sheets of 4' × 8' drywall for that weekend project in the utility room. The minivan changed the course of the U.S. auto industry and has proven to be one of the most successful innovations in American transportation.

InDesign has combined the digital page capability of an electronic publishing program and the creative artistry of a drawing program into the most successful innovation in graphics software today. The extraordinary page layout features of InDesign are the reason this program is taking the world by storm. But with the addition of many drawing features, similar to those you'll find in Adobe Illustrator, you now have a tool that—like the minivan—is changing the face of an entire industry.

If you have already worked with Adobe Illustrator, much of this chapter will be a review of what you already know. Have fun, while combining your drawing skills with the good typography and digital page layout principles you have been learning in *Exploring Adobe InDesign CS5*.

Graphics Tools

You already know how to use the Rectangle, Ellipse, and Polygon tools to create two-dimensional shapes, and the Line tool for—well—lines. You know that the Shift key will constrain shapes to perfect squares or circles, and lines to increments of 45 degrees. You know that if you hold down the Option or Alt key while you drag, you will draw a shape from its center instead of from a corner.

In the following exercise, you will learn to make a shape by specifying dimensions numerically in a dialog box.

1. Make an **8.5" × 11"** document (with the ruler set to inches) and select either the *Rectangle* or *Ellipse* tool (not the Polygon tool). Put the cursor where you want the upper left corner of the shape positioned and click (do not drag).

2. The dialog box for creating the Rectangle or Ellipse will appear. Enter Width and Height dimensions in the fields and click OK.

3. Do this a few times to make several different-sized shapes. If you hold down the **Option** key (Mac) or **Alt** key (Windows) when you click on your document, the shape will be centered on that point.

4. Use the *Direct Selection* tool and drag one of the points of a shape. You can distort the shape any way you want it. **Click+drag** on a line segment and move it around without moving the rest of the shape. Select different combinations of points and line segments by dragging a marquee, or **Shift+clicking**. See what kinds of weird shapes you can make.

VISUAL |14–1|

Pen tool options in the Toolbox. Notice how to access them with keyboard shortcuts.

The Mighty Pen Tool

One of the most versatile tools in the InDesign arsenal is the Pen tool. For some, it can also be a difficult one to master. I sat in my first Illustrator class for hours, trying to figure out why my shapes never ended up the way I intended them to look. But once I mastered the Pen tool, it became one of my favorite tools.

Making a Closed Path

Rectangle, Ellipse, and Polygon tools make closed paths—their paths are unbroken. If you were to break a line segment or anchor point on the path, they would become open shapes. Paths are made up of a series of line segments, which can be either curved or straight. These line segments are connected by anchor points, which can be either corners or smooth. With the Pen tool you can create both open and closed paths.

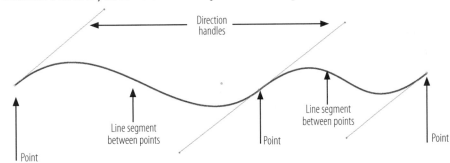

VISUAL |14–2|
Parts of a path.

1. Delete the shapes you made in your document and select the *Pen* tool. (As with every tool, always use the keyboard shortcut—in this case press **P**.) Set the Stroke color to **Black**, the Width to **1 pt.**, with no fill. Place your cursor about two inches, in and two inches down, in your document (**X: 2** and **Y: 2**). Notice that the *Pen* cursor has a little "x" by it. This means that the path you are about to draw begins a new shape. Hold down **Shift, click+drag** horizontally to the right, about an inch. Release the mouse, then the Shift key. As you were dragging, two direction handles appeared: one following the cursor and the other extending 180 degrees in the opposite direction (Visual 14–3). These direction handles are like a teeter-totter, pivoting on your anchor point. The direction handles are not part of the actual line segment you are drawing; they only point you in the direction the path will be going when you begin your next stroke. So far, you have only established an initial anchor point for the first segment of your shape.

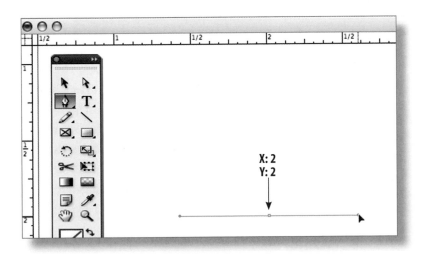

VISUAL |14–3|
Direction handles appear when you drag with the Pen tool.

▶ MOVING TOWARD MASTERY

Direction handles for drawing tools are like hidden characters when you are working with text. They are not part of your shape and do not print, but they determine much of what your path will look like. Direction handles and anchor points—like hidden characters—give you a critical advantage: They allow you to see your document as the computer sees it.

Holding the Shift key while you drag with the Pen tool will constrain your direction handles to increments of 45 degrees, just as it does with the Line tool. Press Shift after you begin to drag. Holding Shift continuously may send your path in unexpected directions.

2. When you release the mouse and the Shift key, the little × next to the *Pen* cursor disappears. This means that the next stroke of your pen will be "step two" in creating your path. Place the cursor at coordinate **X: 4** and **Y: 1**. Again, click, Shift+drag horizontally to the right, for about an inch. When you release the mouse and the Shift key, your path should look like Visual 14–4. You now have two anchor points and the first curved line segment of your shape.

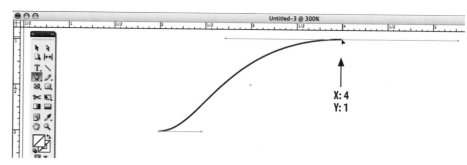

VISUAL |14–4|

Two anchor points have been established.

3. Place your cursor at these coordinates: **X: 6**; **Y: 2**. Click, Shift+drag horizontally to the right, for about an inch, before releasing the mouse and the Shift key. You now have a path that looks like a bell curve (Visual 14–5).

VISUAL |14–5|

The path takes the shape of a bell curve.

Maybe someday you'll be in the middle of drawing a shape and you get distracted doing something else. When you get back to your path, the little × has reappeared next to your Pen icon. (You don't want this because it means you will begin a new path instead of continuing on the same one you were working on.) To get rid of the little ×, place your cursor over the last anchor point you made and the × will change to a little slash. Click and you are now ready to continue with the next line segment of your path.

4.   Apply a fill color to the path. Notice that you can fill a path that is not closed. An imaginary straight line, from the starting anchor point to the ending anchor point, is used as the boundary for the fill. Remove the fill, before you continue, by applying [None].

5.   Place your cursor at **X: 4** and **Y: 3**. This time, instead of dragging, simply click. You have established a new anchor point, but notice that the path is sharply curved at the previous point (Visual 14–6). The direction handle—extending further to the right—told this new line segment to continue on to the right, but your new anchor point told it to go the opposite direction: down and to the left. Choose Undo.

6.   This time hold down the **Option** (Mac) or **Alt** (Windows) key and your *Pen* tool will turn into the *Convert Direction Point* tool (Visual 14–7).

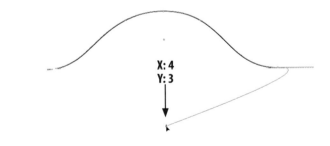

X: 4
Y: 3

VISUAL | 14–6 |

A new anchor point changes the direction of the path.

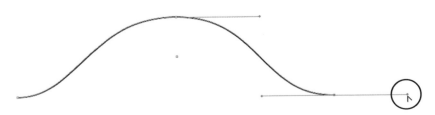

VISUAL | 14–7 |

Holding the Option or Alt key will change the Pen tool to the Convert Direction Point tool. Use the Convert Direction Point tool to move just one of the direction handles that extend from a selected point.

7. Click on the right end of the last direction handle you made and drag it down so that **X: 5** and **Y: 2.5** and release the mouse button (Visual 14–8).

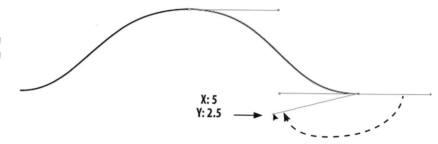

VISUAL | 14–8

Drag the direction handle down and to the left, as shown

X: 5
Y: 2.5

8. Release the Option or Alt key and the *Pen* tool is active again. Place your cursor at approximately **X: 4**, **Y: 3**, click and release. Your new path now has a crisp corner at the previous anchor point (Visual 14–9). Your converted direction handle told the path to go down and to the left, and your new point also told the path to go down and to the left.

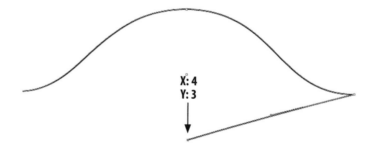

VISUAL | 14–9 |

A corner has been created at the previous anchor point.

X: 4
Y: 3

9. Move the *Pen* tool to the first anchor point you made for your path. (Always check to see that there is no little "×" or slash next to your *Pen* tool cursor.) When you get close to the starting anchor point, a small circle should appear next to the *Pen* tool cursor. This means that your path will be closed with your next click. Go ahead and click to close your path. It should look something like Visual 14–10. Now, apply a fill to your path. Practice applying different colors to the fill, as well as applying [None].

VISUAL | 14–10 |

Closing the path completes your shape.

Making an Open Path

You made your first open path in Chapter 11, working with text on a path. Let's review and practice another open path.

VISUAL | 14–11 |
Drag up and to the right.

1.   Delete your bell curve. Place the *Pen* tool (now with the little "x" next to it at **X: 0.5, Y: 2**. Click and drag up and to the right until **X: 2** and **Y: 0.5** (Visual 14–1). Release the mouse button.

2.   Now place your *Pen* tool cursor at **X: 4** and **Y: 2**, click and drag a new line segment down and to the right until **X: 5** and **Y: 3** (Visual 14–12). Release the mouse button.

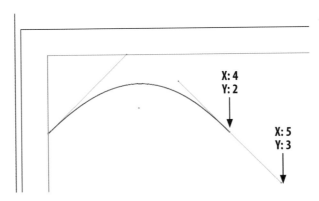

VISUAL | 14–12 |
Drag a new line down and to the right.

3.   Finally, place your tool cursor at **X: 7, Y: 1.5**. Click and drag up to **X: 8**, **Y: 0.5** and release the mouse button (Visual 14–13).

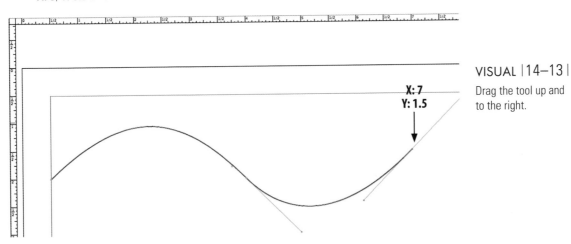

VISUAL | 14–13 |
Drag the tool up and to the right.

4. Your path looks like a wave of the ocean, similar to the wave in Visual 14–14. This line is an open path because the last anchor point is not connected to the point of origin. Select a fill color. Again, the open path is filled along an imaginary line that connects the starting and ending anchor points. The effect is not exactly what you might have expected. Change the fill back to [None].

VISUAL | 14–14 |

The open path is filled along an imaginary line between the starting and ending anchor points.

5. Switch to the *Direct Selection* tool, while still using the *Pen* tool, by holding down **Command** (Mac) or **Control** (Windows) and click anywhere on the top curve. You have selected the first of the two line segments in your "wave" and you can see the direction handles indicating the direction each segment is going (Visual 14–15).

VISUAL | 14–15 |

New direction handles appear.

6. Click on the direction handle extending up from the middle anchor point and move it back and forth. Your wave changes pitch. Notice that both direction handles move simultaneously (Visual 14–16).

VISUAL | 14–16 |

Moving both direction handles with the Direct Selection tool. .

7. Select the *Convert Direction Point* tool by pressing **Shift+C**. Again, when you move the end of the top direction handle, it changes the shape of the wave, but only the selected direction handle moves (Visual 14–17). You have just changed a smooth anchor point into a corner anchor point.

VISUAL | 14–17 |
Moving one direction handle with the Convert Direction tool.

8. Go back to the *Direct Selection* tool by pressing **A**. Click on the middle anchor point to select it. This time, instead of moving the direction handles, move the point itself to the left (Visual 14–18). The curve of your wave changes dramatically as you move the middle anchor point between the start and end anchor points. Move the center anchor point of your wave to the left, right, up and down. If you want to make your wave longer or shorter, select one of the end anchor points and move it in or out.

VISUAL | 14–18 |
Moving the middle anchor point with the Direct Selection tool.

If an anchor point is hollow, it is not selected; an anchor point that is filled in is selected. In Visual 14–19, you will see one more small box to the left of the path. This point is not an anchor point, and you do not draw it. This box indicates the center of your path's bounding box. It functions just like the center point of a frame or circle: You can click and drag it with a selection tool to move the entire path.

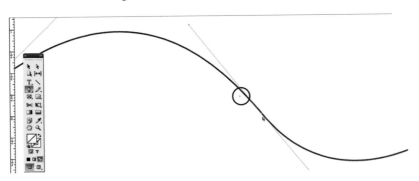

VISUAL | 14–19 |
An anchor point that is selected is "filled in" and its direction handles extend in both directions. Anchor points not selected are hollow.

Adding and Deleting Anchor Points

You will sometimes finish a path you thought was perfect, only to discover that you need an extra anchor point here or there, or maybe there are too many points in one area. No problem! Adding and deleting points in InDesign is just a click away.

1. Get your wave back to its original shape or (if it's beyond repair) delete it and make a new one, repeating Steps 1 through 3 in the previous exercise.

2. Let's say your wave is not wavy enough. Press the equals sign (=) to activate the *Add Anchor Point* tool. The *Add Anchor Point* tool has a small plus sign (+) by the *Pen* tool cursor (Visual 14–20). Click in two or three places on each segment of your wave. (Notice that direction handles extend from each new point, and the new points all remain selected.) Deselect all and press **A** to switch to the *Direct Selection* tool.

The Add Anchor Point tool about to add a point to a path.

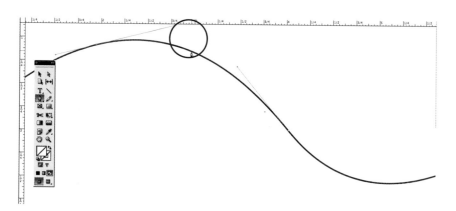

3. Click on the line and you will see all the anchor points are hollow (deselected). Drag each of the new anchor points up or down to make a series of smaller, irregular waves, similar to Visual 14–21. Practice adjusting the length and angles of the direction handles until you are comfortable with the process.

VISUAL |14–21|

Drag the new anchor points up or down to make shorter waves.

Sometimes you will want to delete one or more points from a path. Press the hyphen key (-) to activate the Delete Anchor Point tool. As you click on the anchor points you want to delete, they will disappear.

Smooth Points and Corner Points

Smooth points are made by dragging after you place an anchor point.
Smooth points have direction handles. Corner points are made by one
click of your mouse. Corner points do not have direction handles.

1. Delete everything in your document and press **P** for the *Pen* tool. Make a circle by
    dragging four successive curve points: one at the top, the right side, the bottom,
    and the left side. Click on the starting anchor point to close the circle (Visuals 14–22
    to 14–26). This last point is a little tricky. You will need to drag the *Pen* tool to the left
    to create a reasonable looking curve. Don't worry if your circle is a little lopsided.

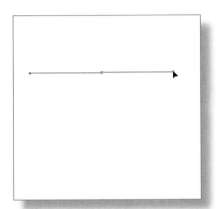

VISUAL | 14–22 |

Click with the Pen tool, and Shift+drag
to make the first part of the circle.

VISUAL | 14–23 |

Click with the Pen tool, and Shift+drag
to make the second part of the circle.

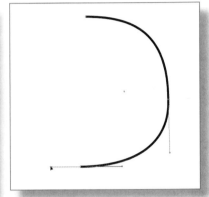

VISUAL | 14–24 |

Click with the Pen tool, and Shift+drag
to make the third part of the circle.

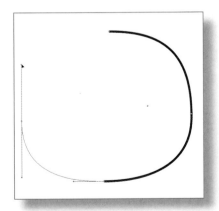

VISUAL | 14–25 |

Click and Shift+drag to make
the fourth part of the circle.

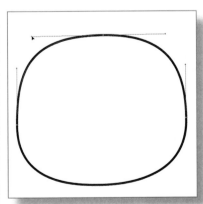

VISUAL | 14–26 |

Click and Shift+drag to complete the shape.

When using the Pen tool, use as few anchor points as possible. The fewer the points, the smoother your path will be. Too many anchor points will make what should be a graciously curved line look jagged and choppy. Practice making circles with only four anchor points.

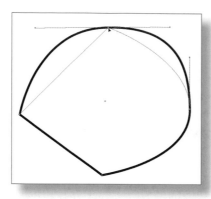

2. Hold down the **Option** or **Alt** key to switch to the *Convert Direction Point* tool and click on one of your smooth anchor points. It becomes a corner point (Visual 14–27). Click the *Convert Direction Point* tool on the other three points. Your circle has become a rectangle.

3. With the **Option** or **Alt** key still held down, drag with the *Convert Direction Point* tool on one of the corner points of your newly created rectangle. The corner point will change into a curved point with direction handles (Visual 14–28). Be careful! Dragging in the same direction as the original point will restore the curve of the circle, but dragging the opposite way will twist your curved line segment into a pretzel. Don't worry, though. If your line segment is twisting in the wrong direction, just do a 180-degree turn and drag the handle in the opposite direction.

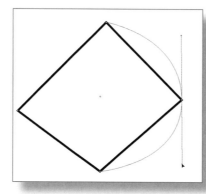

The Scissors Tool

The Scissors tool does just what you might expect—it will cut a line segment into two parts. Do you still have the circle from the last exercise? Use it for the following exercise.

1. Press **C** to get the *Scissors* tool (or select it from the Toolbox). The cursor will look like a set of cross hairs and when it moves over your path, the point in the middle of the cross hairs becomes a small circle (Visual 14–29). With the cross hairs directly over the path, click the mouse. A new point appears on the line segment. Although it looks like one point, there are actually two new points—one on top of the other.

2. Press **A** for the *Direct Selection* tool and drag the new point away from the center of the circle. You have just cut one of the line segments, and the closed path is now an open path (Visual 14–30).

Your closed path is now an open path.

Joining Paths

Sometimes you will have two paths and need to combine them into one. Here's how to do it.

1. With the *Pen* tool, begin a new path at **X: 0.5** and **Y: 2**. Hold down Shift and drag the direction handle horizontally to the right until **X: 2**. Next, place your cursor at **X: 3.5** and **Y: 0.5**, click and Shift+drag horizontally until **X: 5.5**. After you release the mouse button, press the **Option** or **Alt** key to switch to the *Convert Direction Point* tool. Click and drag the end of the direction handle that extends to the right of the last anchor point. Release the mouse button at **X: 3** and **Y: 0.875**. Release the Option or Alt key and click the Pen tool at **X: 4** and **Y: 2**, hold down Shift and drag horizontally until **X: 6**. When you release the mouse button, your path should look like Visual 14–31.

VISUAL |14–31|
Drawing a wave is as easy as placing three anchor points.

2. Let's say this is the perfect shape for a cresting wave you need for a project, but you need two of them exactly the same. Duplicate it using the **Option+drag** or **Alt+drag** method (switch to the *Selection* tool, first) and place the new wave to the right of the original, as shown in Visual 14–32.

VISUAL |14–32|
The new wave, next to the original.

3. To join these two waves into one, switch to the *Pen* tool and select the last anchor point of the first path. The little "x" by the Pen tool cursor will turn into a slash when you get near the point. (It's often a good idea to zoom in closely when editing anchor points.)

4. Place the *Pen* tool cursor over the first point of the second wave and a small square with two little line segments will appear next to the *Pen* tool cursor (Visual 14–33). Click and your two paths will be joined into one. However, you now have an unwanted line segment connecting the two points.

VISUAL | 14–33 |
The Pen tool is about to join
two separate paths into one.

5. Undo to get two separate paths again. Before you connect them a second time, use the *Direct Selection* tool to select the last anchor point of the first wave. This will make the point's two direction handles visible. Switch to the *Convert Direction Point* tool and retract the right direction handle, by dragging the handle all the way back to the left, until it nearly touches the anchor point. Now join the two paths into one.

VISUAL | 14–34 |
The Pen tool is about to join two
paths with the direction handle
retracted on the first path.

Compound Paths

You will love compound paths when it comes to making logos, transparent areas inside of shapes, and creative picture and text frames. Begin the next exercise with a new document.

1. Draw two circles, one larger than the other, using the *Ellipse* tool. Select all and use the *Align* buttons on the Control panel to center them horizontally and vertically. Fill them both with **Black**. Your document should look similar to Visual 14–35.

2. Press **Command+8** (Mac) or
    Control+8 (Windows), or choose
    *Object>Paths>Make Compound
    Path.* Now you have a donut!

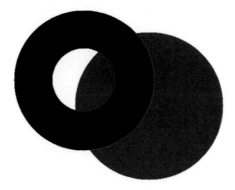

3. Make a larger circle with a fill and send
    it to the back. Move your donut around
    and you will see that your donut has
    a real donut hole! (Visual 14–36.)

VISUAL |14–36|
Move your donut around
to see the donut hole.

4. If you change your mind and don't want the compound path, select
    your donut and choos*e Object>Paths>Release Compound Path.*

5. Delete everything and start over. This time draw two rectangles, one above the other
    with the smaller one on top. Put them close together, but do not have them touch or
    overlap. Select them both and choose *Object>Paths>Make Compound Path.* Although
    it may appear that nothing has occurred, notice that a bounding box now surrounds
    both rectangles. This means that the two are now part of one path (Visual 14–37).

VISUAL |14–37|
Two rectangles independent
of each other, but part
of the same path.

6. Press **Command+D** (Mac) or **Control+D** (Windows) and place an image large enough to fill both rectangles. Drag the image around inside the rectangles using the *Direct Selection* tool.

7. Next you will change the shape of your small rectangle to a trapezoid. Deselect everything, and click on a bottom corner point of the top rectangle with the *Direct Selection* tool. Hold down Shift and drag it out, so that it's above the corresponding upper corner of the large rectangle. Do the same for the other bottom corner (Visual 14–38).

8. Delete the picture from the compound path and click in the path with the *Type* tool. Fill with placeholder text. Your compound path now works like linked text frames.

VISUAL | 14–38 |
Use the Direct Selection tool and Shift+drag out each corner point to create a trapezoid.

In this short introduction, you have made compound paths using basic shape tools: the Rectangle tool and the Ellipse tool. Practice making compound paths, with shapes you create, using the Pen tool. Great job!

Summary

Having completed the exercises in this chapter, you can see why there's no way any other page layout program can compete with InDesign. By combining advanced page layout and drawing capabilities, InDesign gives you the best of both worlds. Once you master the versatile Pen tool, your creative energy knows no bounds. Use compound paths to make your readers sit up and take notice of your message and images. And when you are done with this book, there's much, MUCH more to explore!

▶ IN REVIEW

1. What effect does holding down the Shift key have when drawing shapes and lines?

2. When working with a shape or path, how do you tell the difference between a point that is selected and a point that is not selected?

3. What is the keyboard shortcut for accessing the Convert Direction Point tool when you are using the Pen tool?

4. What is the difference between a smooth point and a corner point?

5. You have made a path with the Pen tool, but it looks jagged and you think you might have too many points on it. How do you smooth it out?

6. What is the difference between an open path and a closed path?

7. Describe the process for joining two open paths.

8. Describe the process for making compound paths.

9. What are direction handles?

10. How does the Scissors tool work?

The following fonts are installed with Adobe InDesign CS5:

AdobeArabic-Bold.otf
AdobeArabic-BoldItalic.otf
AdobeArabic-Italic.otf
AdobeArabic-Regular.otf
AdobeHebrew-Bold.otf
AdobeHebrew-BoldItalic.otf
AdobeHebrew-Italic.otf
AdobeHebrew-Regular.otf
AdobeMingStd-Light.otf
AdobeMyungjoStd-Medium.otf
AdobeSongStd-Light.otf
KozGoPro-Regular.otf
KozGoPro-Bold.otf
KozGoPro-ExtraLight.otf
KozGoPro-Heavy.otf
KozGoPro-Light.otf
KozGoPro-Medium.otf
KozMinPro-Regular.otf
KozMinPro-Bold.otf
KozMinPro-ExtraLight.otf
KozMinPro-Heavy.otf
KozMinPro-Light.otf
KozMinPro-Medium.otf
LetterGothicStd.otf
LetterGothicStd-Bold.otf
LetterGothicStd-BoldSlanted.otf
LetterGothicStd-Slanted.otf
MinionPro-Regular.otf
MinionPro-It.otf
MinionPro-Bold.otf
MinionPro-BoldIt.otf
MyriadPro-Regular.otf
MyriadPro-Bold.otf
MyriadPro-BoldCond.otf
MyriadPro-BoldCondIt.otf
MyriadPro-BoldIt.otf

MyriadPro-Cond.otf
MyriadPro-CondIt.otf
MyriadPro-It.otf
MyriadPro-Semibold.otf
MyriadPro-SemiboldIt.otf
ACaslonPro-Bold.otf
ACaslonPro-BoldItalic.otf
ACaslonPro-Italic.otf
ACaslonPro-Regular.otf
ACaslonPro-Semibold.otf
ACaslonPro-SemiboldItalic.otf
AdobeHeitiStd-Regular.otf
AdobeFangsongStd-Regular.otf
AdobeFanHeitiStd-Bold.otf
AdobeGothicStd-Bold.otf
AdobeKaitiStd-Regular.otf
AGaramondPro-Bold.otf
AGaramondPro-BoldItalic.otf
AGaramondPro-Italic.otf
AGaramondPro-Regular.otf
BirchStd.otf
BlackoakStd.otf
BrushScriptStd.otf
ChaparralPro-Bold.otf
ChaparralPro-BoldIt.otf
ChaparralPro-Italic.otf
ChaparralPro-Regular.otf
CharlemagneStd-Bold.otf
CooperBlackStd.otf
CooperBlackStd-Italic.otf
GiddyupStd.otf
HoboStd.otf
KozGoPr6N-Bold.otf
KozGoPr6N-ExtraLight.otf
KozGoPr6N-Heavy.otf
KozGoPr6N-Light.otf

KozGoPr6N-Medium.otf
KozGoPr6N-Regular.otf
KozMinPr6N-Bold.otf
KozMinPr6N-ExtraLight.otf
KozMinPr6N-Heavy.otf
KozMinPr6N-Light.otf
KozMinPr6N-Medium.otf
KozMinPr6N-Regular.otf
LithosPro-Black.otf
LithosPro-Regular.otf
MesquiteStd.otf
MinionPro-BoldCn.otf
MinionPro-BoldCnIt.otf
MinionPro-Medium.otf
MinionPro-MediumIt.otf
MinionPro-Semibold.otf
MinionPro-SemiboldIt.otf
NuevaStd-BoldCond.otf
NuevaStd-BoldCondItalic.otf
NuevaStd-Cond.otf
NuevaStd-CondItalic.otf
OCRAStd.otf
OratorStd.otf
OratorStd-Slanted.otf
PoplarStd.otf
PrestigeEliteStd-Bd.otf
RosewoodStd-Regular.otf
StencilStd.otf
TektonPro-Bold.otf
TektonPro-BoldCond.otf
TektonPro-BoldExt.otf
TektonPro-BoldObl.otf
TrajanPro-Bold.otf
TrajanPro-Regular.otf

The following are bonus fonts available on disk, as optional install:

ChaparralPro-Light.otf
ChaparralPro-LightItalic.otf
CharlemagneStd-Regular.otf
LithosPro-Bold.otf
MyriadPro-Light.otf
MyriadPro-LightIt.otf
MyriadStd-Sketch.otf
MyriadStd-Tilt.otf
NewsGothicStd.otf
NewsGothicStd-Bold.otf
NewsGothicStd-BoldOblique.otf
NewsGothicStd-Oblique.otf

NuevaStd-Bold.otf
NuevaStd-BoldItalic.otf
NuevaStd-Italic.otf
NuevaStd-Light.otf
NuevaStd-LightItalic.otf
NuevaStd-Regular.otf
RosewoodStd-Fill.otf
RyoDispPlusN-Bold.otf
RyoDispPlusN-ExtraBold.otf
RyoDispPlusN-Heavy.otf
RyoDispPlusN-Medium.otf
RyoDispPlusN-SemiBold.otf

RyoGothicPlusN-Bold.otf
RyoGothicPlusN-Regular.otf
RyoGothicPlusN-ExtraLight.otf
RyoGothicPlusN-Heavy.otf
RyoGothicPlusN-Light.otf
RyoGothicPlusN-Medium.otf
RyoGothicPlusN-UltraHeavy.otf
RyoTextPlusN-ExtraLight.otf
RyoTextPlusN-Light.otf
RyoTextPlusN-Medium.otf
RyoTextPlusN-Regular.otf

Symbols